Japan

Houghton Mifflin Company · **Boston**

Dallas

Geneva, Illinois

Palo Alto

Princeton, New Jersey

Japan

Tradition & Transformation   Revised Edition

(Edwin Oldfather)

Edwin O. Reischauer, *Professor Emeritus*

Albert M. Craig

Harvard University

Printed in the U.S.A.

Library of Congress Catalog Card Number: 88-83734

ISBN: 0-395-49696-9

ABCDEFGHIJ-VB-9543210-898

Contents

Maps and Charts

Preface

During the past decade, Japan has begun to adjust socially and politically to the actuality that it has caught up with the West. Its prowess in manufacturing has been matched by its advances in scientific technology, and it has begun to make its influence felt in world financial markets. In this volume, we have revised and updated the postwar chapter of the 1978 edition to take account of these and other changes. As in the earlier edition, the first five chapters of this book are by E. O. Reischauer, and the last three chapters are by A. M. Craig. The same chapters, along with chapters on China and on the Rim Nations of Korea, Taiwan, Vietnam, Hong Kong, and Singapore are also included in *East Asia: Tradition and Transformation* by the two authors of this volume together with John K. Fairbank.

Japan is a land of modest geographic size, but it is one of the larger countries of the world in population and today ranks in the top three in economic production, along with the two continental colossi, the United States and the Soviet Union. It is also one of the older nations of the world, being comparable in age to the lands of northern Europe. Though in culture it is a daughter of ancient China, just as the countries of northern Europe are offshoots of the Mediterranean civilizations of Greece and Rome, Japan has developed one of the most distinctive cultures in the world.

All this makes Japan a subject of much interest, but the unique course of Japanese history has made it of even greater significance. Despite its East Asian cultural origins, Japan evolved along a very different course from its neighbors; subsequently it became the only non-Western land to respond successfully to the challenge of superior Western technology in the nineteenth century; and today it has become a leading nation of the so-called First World—that group of industrialized and widely trading democracies which, but for Japan's membership, would be called "the West" or the "Atlantic Community."

As the only non-Western member of this otherwise purely Western grouping of nations, Japan stands in a very special relationship to the other industrialized lands. As the only non-Western nation that has made the transition to full industrialization and what for lack of a better term is commonly called institutional "modernization," it stands in a special relationship to the other still not fully industrialized or "modernized" non-Western cultures. Its success in negotiating this vast change and the great economic power this has produced are matters of importance to both groups of nations. Even more significant is the fact that Japan, in industrializing and in "modernizing" its institutions, has preserved a sharp self-identity and a considerable part of its traditional, pre-modern culture, despite the tidal wave of Western influences that has inundated it in modern times. These survivals from its past civilization give Japan an unusual cultural richness and seem to contribute special strengths as well as difficulties to its handling of the problems of modern urban society. These are qualities which have deep meaning for other peoples both East and West.

In writing a book of this broad scope, the authors have naturally relied on the work of a host of other scholars, both Japanese and Western. Some have given us personal help and advice; far more have aided us through their writings. We are deeply grateful to all of them, but it would be impractical to attempt to list even the more important of these colleagues in our effort. Nor is it feasible to offer here a bibliography on this vast subject; any bibliography small enough to be included in this volume would have to be absurdly sketchy and soon would be quite out of date. Here we limit ourselves to expressing our special gratitude to the late Serge Elisséeff, native of Russia, citizen of France, and pioneer in developing the field of Japanese studies at Harvard between 1932 and 1957.

The Romanization system for Japanese names and words used in this book is that of Hepburn, generally considered standard in the English-speaking world. The consonants are all pronounced roughly as they are in English. Japanese, however, has "long consonants," which are protracted considerably longer than ordinary short consonants and produce sharp differences of meaning, as in *kita,* meaning "north," and *kitta,* meaning "cut." This distinction does not occur in English, but is very important in Japanese.

Japanese vowels are pronounced as they would be in Italian, Spanish, or German. There are only five vowels, corresponding to the five vowels of the Latin alphabet, and two diphthongs, as follows:

a as in f*a*ther	*u* as in r*u*de
e as in *e*nd	*ai* as in t*ie*
i as in *e*qual	*ei* as in w*ay*
o as in *o*ld	

The vowels, particularly *o* and *u,* have long forms, Romanized *ō* and *ū,* which are held much longer than the sample vowels. This again is a phonemic distinction lacking in English, but crucial in Japanese, which produces words and names of entirely different meaning, as in *tsūchi,* meaning "notification," in contrast to *tsuchi,* which means "earth" or "soil."

E.O.R.
A.M.C.

Japan

1. Early Japan: The Absorption of Chinese Civilization

The Land and the People

Geographic Influence. Japan is part of the cultural area that we once called the Far East. This term was based on the now outmoded concept that Europe was the center of the world. But the region is certainly not "far" to the people who live there and who throughout history have probably outnumbered the peoples of Europe as well as those of the other major areas of high culture in the Middle East and the Indian subcontinent. For this reason, the neutral term "East Asia" for this cultural area seems more appropriate than Far East.

The culture of East Asia derived basically from the ancient civilization of North China. It grew to embrace all of modern China and the three peripheral lands of Korea, Vietnam, and Japan. Although the peoples of Central Asia were often involved with China through trade, war, and conquest and those of Southeast Asia beyond Vietnam have received waves of Chinese immigrants and have developed close economic relations with the East Asian countries, these two neighboring areas derived their underlying cultures from other sources.

Within East Asia, Japan throughout most of its history has followed a somewhat distinctive course. Probably the chief reason for this is its location as a relatively remote island country. The parallel with the British Isles, at the other end of the Eurasian land mass, is striking, but Japan's isolation from its neighbors is much greater. The Straits of Tsushima between Japan and Korea are approximately 115 miles wide, as compared to 21 miles for the Straits of Dover.

1

Unlike Korea and Vietnam, Japan was never invaded by Chinese armies. Chinese influences therefore penetrated Japan less steadily and strongly, and changes came relatively slowly and resulted more from the voluntary adoption of foreign ways or from internal evolution than from external pressure. As a result, more of the indigenous culture could be maintained. Old and outmoded habits and institutions could be lovingly preserved alongside the new. One spectacular example was the survival of the imperial family as the theoretical source of all political authority for a millennium after it had lost all real political power.

Relative isolation also made the Japanese more conscious of cultural borrowing than were other peoples. Foreign influences did not seep across land frontiers but came quite visibly by ship. Early in their history the Japanese developed the habit of cataloguing foreign influences and contrasting them with "native" characteristics. One result has been a frequent emphasis in Japanese history on primitive and therefore supposedly native Japanese traits. Another has been the myth that the Japanese have been merely a nation of cultural borrowers, although the truth seems to be that, because of their isolation, they have developed a larger proportion of their culture themselves than have most nations.

Japan is commonly described as a small country, which it is as compared with China or the United States. It is only the size of Montana, but a fairer comparison would be to the nations of Western Europe. Though smaller than France, Japan is larger than the British Isles, Italy, or the two Germanies combined. In population it is unquestionably a big country. For many centuries it has had a much larger population than any of the lands of Western Europe, and today with a population of more than 110 million it ranks sixth or seventh in the world.

This large population has been maintained even though the land is extremely mountainous, rising in central Honshū, the main island, to Fuji's 12,389-foot volcanic cone and the 10,000-foot peaks of the Japanese Alps. Less than one-fifth of the terrain is suitable for agriculture, though plentiful rainfall, hot summers, and intensive rice agriculture in irrigated fields have combined to make Japan one of the most productive lands per cultivated acre in the world. Most of agricultural Japan is made up of narrow river valleys and alluvial coastal plains separated from one another by stretches of rugged hills. Land communication therefore is not easy, but the surrounding seas have always provided links between the islands and along their coastlines as well as contact with the outside world. The seas also furnish the Japanese with abundant fish, which have traditionally provided the main source of protein in their diet.

The climate of Japan is salubrious, being generally similar to that of corresponding latitudes of the east coast of North America from Georgia to Maine, though Japan's more oceanic location makes summer temperatures

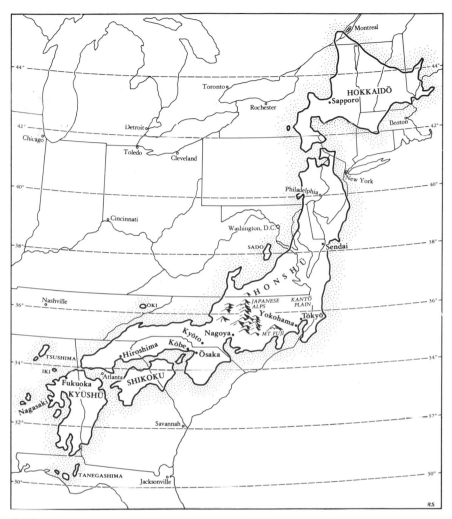

JAPAN SUPERIMPOSED ON THE UNITED STATES

less high and winter cold less severe. While extraordinarily deep winter snows—six feet on the level in some places—blanket the northern part of the Japan Sea coast, relatively mild and sunny winters along the southern Pacific coast permit double cropping as far north as the Tōkyō area.

Racial and Cultural Origins.   The Japanese as we know them today are a homogeneous Mongoloid people, much like their near neighbors in Korea and China. The Japanese language, however, is radically different from Chinese both grammatically and phonetically. Chinese has tones that determine the meanings of words, and it tends to be monosyllabic and is entirely lacking in inflections, depending on the position of words in the sentence for their grammatical relationship to one another. Japanese by contrast is not tonal but is polysyllabic and highly inflected, with a word order that differs radically from Chinese. It is, however, much like Korean and the other Altaic languages of North Asia, which include Mongolian and Turkish. It seems probable that the sharp differences of the Japanese language from Chinese helped the Japanese to preserve their cultural distinctiveness from China, despite the spate of Chinese influences in early times.

The Japanese achieved their present linguistic identity and physical makeup by the early centuries A.D. and perhaps even earlier. The dominant racial element, as well as the language, unquestionably came from the nearby continent—that is, Korea and the regions to the north of it. The archaeological record shows this conclusively, and the movement of peoples from Korea into Japan continued well into historic times.

Other groups, however, were probably absorbed into the mix. The Ainu, who were the chief inhabitants of the northern island of Hokkaidō until the past century and appear to have once occupied most of northern Japan, show certain traits of Caucasoid man, particularly in their hairiness of face and body, which are features notably lacking in most Mongoloids. The Ainu probably contributed appreciably to the Japanese genetic pool, perhaps accounting for the fact that many Japanese have more facial and body hair than their Mongoloid neighbors. Some early Japanese cultural traits and even elements of the language also suggest affinities with the Malay areas of Southeast Asia. This probably was not the result of direct movements of people from Southeast Asia to Japan but of cultural and possibly racial diffusion in early days from coastal South China southward to Southeast Asia and eastward to Korea and Japan.

At least two waves of Paleolithic culture reached the islands—the first some 100,000 or 200,000 years ago. Pottery dating back about 10,000 years—as old as any found anywhere in the world—has recently been discovered in Japan, but the first well known neolithic culture, named Jōmon for its characteristic "cord pattern" pottery, spread throughout Japan about 6000 years ago. The Jōmon people lived in sunken pit dwellings and subsisted by hunting, fishing, and gathering nuts, roots, and shellfish. They left behind extensive shell mounds and a wealth of pottery, unsurpassed in its richness and imaginativeness of design by any other stone-age culture in the world.

In the third century B.C. a new culture displaced Jōmon in western Japan and by the end of the first century B.C. had spread as far east as the Kantō Plain. Named Yayoi after a famous excavation site, it was characterized by a simple wheel-made pottery, by agriculture, including rice cultivation using techniques of irrigation still in practice, and by the presence of both bronze and iron. The bronze artifacts, which seem to have been used largely for symbolic purposes, included mirrors of Chinese type and weapons and bells too thin to have been functional. The agriculture as well as the bronze and iron of the Yayoi culture were no doubt derived ultimately from China, and the presence in Yayoi sites of Chinese coins and mirrors from the Earlier Han dynasty of the last two centuries B.C. are indisputable evidence of cultural contacts with China.

In the third century A.D. the Yayoi people of the Kinki, the historical capital region around the modern cities of Kyōto and Osaka, began to erect large earthen mounds over the tombs of their leaders, and this practice spread to Kyūshū in the west and later to the Kantō area in the east. The culture of the following centuries thus is known as the tomb culture. Some of the tumuli have a peculiar keyhole shape, square in front and round in the rear, and the largest, said to be the tomb of the Emperor Nintoku of the early fifth century, is about 120 feet high and 1500 feet long. On many of the mounds are found concentric circles made up of pottery cylinders, some of which are surmounted by simple but charming figures of men, animals, and houses. These are known as *haniwa.*

Many features associated with the tomb culture show strong new influences brought over from Korea either by new waves of invaders or through trade or military contacts. The tomb culture was obviously aristocratic, and its leaders were mounted warriors who carried long straight iron swords and wore helmets, padded garments, and armor made of iron slats, all of which had close parallels in contemporary Korea and Manchuria. The "curved jewels" (*magatama*), found in the tombs of this period, are identical to those found among southern Korean remains of this period.

The tomb culture, at the same time, was a clear outgrowth of the Yayoi culture and the direct ancestor of fully historical Japan. Its pottery was similar to that of Yayoi, though harder and more highly fired. Its agricultural techniques were the same, though iron was coming into common use for farm tools. Its houses were thatched structures raised off the ground, much like Japanese farm dwellings of more recent date. Gradually the tomb culture merged into the early historical Japan of the fifth and sixth centuries.

Ancient Japanese Society

Early Records. When pieced together, archaeological evidence, contemporary Chinese histories, and later Japanese accounts, which recorded the early myths and traditions, give a shadowy picture of the emergence of the Japanese state. The most important Chinese record (in the *Account of the Three Kingdoms,* compiled before 297 A.D.) details the route from Korea to Japan and describes the inhabitants of the islands. It portrays them as law-abiding people, fond of drink, concerned with divination and ritual purity, familiar with agriculture, expert at fishing and weaving, and living in a society of strict social differences indicated by tattooing or other bodily

Above: Pottery figure of the Jomon period. Below: Haniwa horse and warrior.

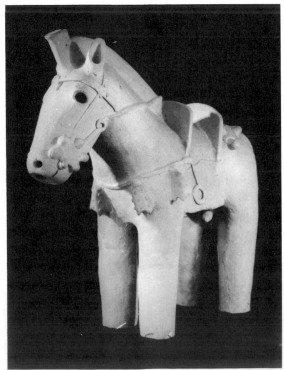

markings. The land is described as divided into one hundred "countries," varying in size from one thousand to seventy thousand households, some ruled by kings and others by queens—possibly a transition from matriarchy to patriarchy. The countries of the western part of the land were under the suzerainty of the unmarried queen Himiko of Yamatai, who was a sort of high priestess, and over whose grave a great mound was erected.

This and other Chinese histories record the coming of envoys from Japanese states to the Chinese court, the earliest in 57 A.D. A fifth-century Chinese history describes a Japanese ruler of the beginning of that century as having conquered fifty-five "countries" of hairy men (presumably Ainu) to the east, sixty-six "countries" to the west, and others across the sea to the north, meaning southern Korea.

The two most important Japanese accounts of early time are the *Record of Ancient Matters* (*Kojiki*), compiled in 712, and the *History of Japan* (*Nihon shoki* or *Nihongi*), compiled in 720. The authors of these works wove together often contradictory myths and traditions in an effort to enhance the prestige of the ruling family and create a picture of long-centralized rule and respectable antiquity comparable to that of China. While reasonably reliable on the later periods, their accounts give at best only vague hints about earlier happenings.

Both works start with creation myths centering around a divine brother and sister, who gave birth to the islands of Japan and a number of deities, including the Sun Goddess, Amaterasu. Her grandson, Ninigi, descended to earth and became the center of a cycle of myths localized in Kyūshū. He brought with him the Three Imperial Regalia, still the symbols of imperial authority in Japan. These are a bronze mirror (the symbol of the Sun Goddess and kept at Japan's greatest shrine at Ise), an iron sword, and a necklace of "curved jewels."

Ninigi's grandson (or great-grandson) moved up the Inland Sea, conquered the Kinki region, and established the Japanese state on the Yamato plain in that area. This was dated as happening in 660 B.C. Like later Japanese emperors, this first "emperor" became known by a posthumous title of Chinese type—in his case Jimmu, the "Divine Warrior." Subsequently, around 100 A.D., a martial prince conquered first the "barbarians" of Kyūshū and then those of the Kantō Plain, and about a century later an empress conquered Korea. Scribes from the Korean state of Paekche were installed at the court around 400 A.D. to keep records in Chinese.

Back of this largely mythological story lies some historical reality. Cultural waves did come from Korea to North Kyūshū and up the Inland Sea to the Kinki region. The latter did become the first and greatest center of tomb building, and the Yamato state of Japanese tradition may be the Yamatai of the Chinese texts under its priestess-queen, Himiko (meaning "Sun Princess"). The original Sun Goddess and occasional empresses fit in with the third-century Chinese picture of a transition from matriarchy to patriarchy. The conquests of Kyūshū and the Kantō by the Yamato state had taken place by the fifth century. There was a Japanese foothold in southern Korea. The reported introduction of Paekche scribes around 400 A.D. corresponds to a transition at that time from rulers with impossibly long reigns to emperors of normal life spans and believable activities. In fact, in the early fifth century the archaeological record, Chinese histories, and Japanese traditions merge into a single plausible story, which becomes convincing history by the late sixth century.

The Uji System.   The Japan that emerged slowly into the light of history was essentially a tribal society, like that of early Korea and perhaps somewhat comparable to the Germanic tribes of Roman times or to the later Scottish clans. It was divided into a great number of family or pseudofamily groups called *uji,* each under a hereditary chief and worshiping an *uji* god, commonly thought of as its ancestor. Subordinate to the aristocratic *uji* were occupational groupings known as *be,* organized as agricultural communities or performing other services, such as fishing, weaving, pottery making, and divining. Some *uji* had won supremacy over their less powerful neighbors, thus forming clusters of *uji.* It was probably groupings of this sort that constituted the hundred "countries" of the Chinese records of the third century. The many large tumuli scattered throughout much of Japan are good illustrations of the power and wealth held by such groupings.

The Yamato state was probably in origin such an *uji* cluster under its dominant sun-line *uji.* By the fifth century, however, it had won a vague supremacy over the other *uji* "countries." It classified these subordinate *uji* as either "country vassals" in charge of local areas or "attendant vassals" directly serving the sun line, and both types were bound to it by the establishment of real or fictive family ties. By the sixth century the sun line was treating these vassals as if they were appointive officials, and it also was expanding its own wealth and power at the expense of the local *uji* by creating directly subordinate agricultural *be* in their areas.

In an effort to put more order into the system, the Yamato court also organized the *uji* by ranks, reminiscent of the "bone ranks" of the contemporary South Korean kingdom of Silla. The two largest ranks, *Omi,* used for the lesser off-shoots of the sun line, and *Muraji,* used for the most important of the unrelated *uji,* were placed under a Great *Omi* and a Great *Muraji* respectively, and these two officers became in time the ruler's chief ministers.

Shintō.   Both the Chinese records and Japanese traditions make clear that there was no real line between religion and government in early Japan. No

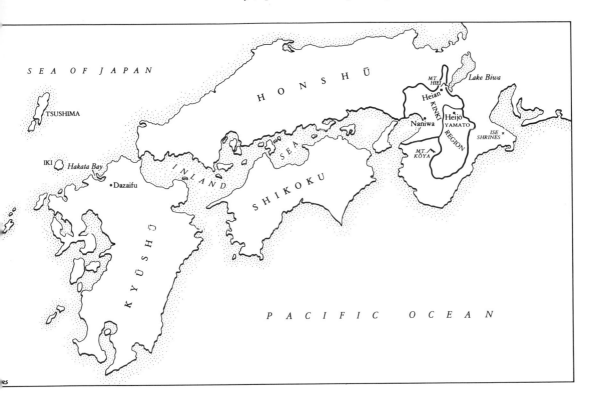

SEA OF JAPAN

TSUSHIMA

IKI Hakata Bay

• Dazaifu

KYŪSHŪ

H O N S H Ū

INLAND

SEA

SHIKOKU

MT. HIEI Lake Biwa
Heian
KINKI REGION
Naniwa Heijō
YAMATO
ISE SHRINES
MT. KŌYA

PACIFIC   OCEAN

WEST JAPAN IN ANCIENT TIMES

distinction was made between the *uji* chief's function as ruler over his people and his role as maintainer of the cult to the *uji* god. Even today the imperial family retains the sacerdotal functions of the early sun-line *uji* of Yamato. The political dominance of the sun line was expressed as the supremacy of its ancestral deity, the Sun Goddess, over other *uji* deities, and her worship grew from an *uji* cult into a national religion. The various other *uji* cults were integrated into an official mythology which made clear the supremacy of the Sun Goddess. By the eighth century there were more than three thousand officially recognized and ranked local shrines, about one-fourth of them supported by the government.

The *uji* cults were merely a manifestation of a broader current of animistic nature worship that underlay them. The early Japanese, awed by both the menacing and beneficent forces of nature, thought of the various natural phenomena as spirits or deities, which they worshiped under the name of *kami.* Thus they paid reverence to waterfalls, mountains, great trees, unusual rocks, even pestiferous vermin. The Sun Goddess and various *uji* gods seem in origin to have been such nature deities, put in anthropomorphic form and woven into a mythology. Emperors and other humans who inspired awe easily entered the category of *kami.* Thus the so-called divinity of the Japanese imperial line was a far cry from what divinity came to mean in the West. The fertility of nature particularly attracted worship, as is illustrated by phallic cults and the prevalence of shrines to the God of Rice. Both *uji* gods and nature deities were commonly symbolized by objects such as mirrors, swords, or "curved jewels."

Nature worship and its associated *uji* cults came in later times to be called Shintō, the "Way of the Gods," to distinguish it from Buddhism. It was not, however, an organized religion, but rather a loose conglomeration of cults and attitudes. It had no organized philosophy or even a clear moral code, except for a concept of ritual purity. Exorcism, cleansing ceremonies, or ritual abstention were thought to remove ritual impurity incurred by physical dirtiness, sexual intercourse, menstruation, childbirth, sickness, wounds, or death. A priestly class which performed these rites or served as mediums and diviners probably represented the Japanese variant of the shamans of Korea and Northeast Asia. The modern Japanese insistence on cleanliness and fondness for bathing in hot springs and deep tubs may hark back to these early concepts of ritual purity.

Japan still today is dotted with a myriad of Shintō shrines. Some are great cult spots like the Ise Shrines of the Sun Goddess, which, though periodically rebuilt, reflect in their clean simple lines Japanese architecture of about the sixth century. Others are sleepy village shrines, set among towering trees and dedicated to the original local *uji* god. Many are no more than miniature box-like structures on mountain tops or other places of natural beauty. All are marked by the *torii,* a simple gateway made of two uprights and one or two crossbeams.

Worship at Shintō shrines is uncomplicated, consisting largely of the clapping of one's hands to attract the god's attention and then bowing and possibly making offerings. Ritual purity is achieved by washing out the mouth with water or by the waving of a sacred branch by a priest. Shrine festivals are gay affairs. Food and amusement booths set up along the approaches to a shrine give a carnival atmosphere, and the young men of the community, sometimes in boisterous intoxication, may take the deity out in a portable shrine to visit and purify individual homes and shops. Shintō thus remains a simple, somewhat primitive religion compared to the great faiths of Asia and Europe, but its attitudes and practices have remained a major component of Japanese culture throughout history.

The Adoption of the Chinese Pattern

Korean and Chinese Influences. The growing strength and institutional complexity of the Yamato state were probably in part the results of continuing contacts with the continent, particularly Korea. There was a steady flow

Above: Main Building of the Inner Shrine (Naiku) at Ise. Although rebuilt every few years, the shrine buildings reflect an early architectural style. Below: A torii *in front of a small shrine.*

of people from Korea to Japan that lasted up until the early ninth century. Many immigrants came as well organized groups, whose leaders took a prominent place at the Yamato court because of the knowledge and skills they possessed. More than a third of the 1182 aristocratic Japanese families listed in a genealogical register compiled in 815 claimed Korean origin or Chinese ancestry through descent from families in the Han colonies in Korea.

This flow of people was probably facilitated by the Japanese foothold in Kaya (Mimana) in South Korea while it lasted. The Japanese myths describe this foothold as the product of conquest, but it is more probable that it resulted from alliances by the people of that area with closely related groups which had earlier crossed over to Japan. The Japanese hold over Kaya appears to have been at its height in the late fourth century, but it was eliminated in 562, and subsequent attempts up until 663 to revive it all failed.

Among the many elements of continental civilization which came to Japan by way of Korea was the Indian religion Buddhism, then at the height of its influence both in Korea and China. Buddhism probably drifted into the islands over a period of time, but its official introduction is dated in 552 (though probably more accurately in 538), when the Korean state of Paekche presented an image and scriptures to the Yamato court. The new religion was opposed by conservative groups but was supported by the Soga *uji,* which held the post of Great *Omi.* After emerging victorious over their rivals in a succession war in 587, the Soga firmly established Buddhism at the court, where it became a major vehicle for the transfer of much of Chinese culture to Japan, just as Christianity served as a vehicle for the transfer of Mediterranean civilization to North Europe.

Hitherto the cultural flow from the continent has been a slow and sporadic process, but with the adoption of Buddhism the Japanese began to make a conscious attempt to transplant elements of the continental civilization. As a result, the rate of cultural borrowing increased sharply, ushering in a new age in Japanese history.

There were probably several reasons for this rather abrupt change. For one thing, China was beginning to exert a greater cultural pull than before. In 589 the Sui dynasty reunited the country after more than three and a half centuries of division, and it was followed by the T'ang dynasty (618–907), one of the most glorious epochs of Chinese history. The Japanese too seem by this time to have attained a cultural level that permitted a more rapid rate of learning. Moreover the *uji* system, based as it was on familial and mythological ties, was proving inadequate to the needs of the time. It did not permit firm control over the local areas; the great court *uji* had come to overshadow the sun line itself, often disrupting the central government with their struggles for power; and succession wars were frequent because of the lack of a clear system of inheritance.

Prince Shōtoku. The victory of the Soga in 587 made them supreme at the Yamato court. Their chief put his niece on the throne and appointed as regent her nephew, Prince Shōtoku (574–622), who was also half of Soga blood. Shōtoku and the Soga proceeded to carry out a series of important innovations that signaled their determination to use Chinese patterns of society and government to strengthen the control of the central government in Japan.

In 604 Shōtoku adopted the Chinese calendar, and it was probably from about this time that interest in the Chinese calendar and history induced the Japanese to count back 1260 years—a major cosmological cycle according to Chinese ideas—to select the date 660 B.C. for the founding of the Japanese state. In 604 Shōtoku also issued a set of precepts, known as the "Seventeen Article Constitution,"* which advocated such revolutionary Chinese concepts as the complete supremacy of the ruler, the centralization of government, and a bureaucracy of merit. It also enjoined reverence for Buddhism and extolled the virtues associated with the Chinese philosophy of Confucianism.

In 603 Shōtoku adopted a major aspect of Chinese centralized bureaucratic rule—the system of personal court ranks for officials, assigned in accordance with the posts they held. These gradually replaced the hereditary *uji* ranks as the major designations of status. The court rank system, in the permanent form it achieved by the middle of the eighth century, had eight numbered ranks, each divided into "senior" and "junior" classes, and the classes from the fourth rank on down were further divided into "upper" and "lower" grades. Every government post carried with it one of the twenty-six specific ranks, from the "Senior First Rank" down to the "Junior Eighth Rank Lower Grade."

The Japanese had sent embassies to China in earlier centuries, but Shōtoku reinstituted embassies on a much larger scale, sending one in 607, another the next year, and a third in 614. The importance to the Japanese of these embassies can be judged from their size and the extreme perils they braved. By the eighth century it was customary to build four new ships for each mission, and some five hundred or six hundred men set sail on them. By this time Korean hostility had made the earlier route along the Korean coast unsafe, and the Japanese attempted to sail directly to China across the five hundred miles of open sea, without benefit of compass or much knowledge

---

*It is thought by some to be a later forgery, but in any case it probably represents Shotoku's ideas.

of the seasonal winds. Disasters were frequent, as can be seen in the vivid account of the clerical diarist Ennin, who accompanied the last embassy in 838.

The significance of the missions lay, not in their diplomatic achievements or incidental trade, but in what the Japanese participants learned in China. Students of all sorts accompanied the missions—Buddhist monks, scholars of Chinese history and literature, painters, musicians, and the like. Studying during the year the mission was in China or possibly for several years until the next mission brought them home, these men acquired knowledge and skills that were highly regarded at the Japanese court and contributed greatly to the cultural transformation of the country.

The Taika Reforms.   After Shōtoku's death, the Soga alienated the other court families by their despotic rule and were eventually crushed in 645 in a *coup d'état* engineered by a prince, the future Emperor Tenchi (reigned 668–671), and a supporter who was given as a reward a new family name, Fujiwara. As Fujiwara no Kamatari* (614–669), he became the progenitor of a line of nobles that was to dominate the Japanese court for many centuries. Tenchi and Kamatari embarked on a second great wave of reforms based on the Chinese model of centralized government. Students returned from earlier embassies played an important role, and five more embassies were sent between 653 and 669. One of the reforms introduced at this time was the adoption of the Chinese system of counting years by "year periods" of arbitrary length chosen for their magical potency or to change the luck. Not until 1868 did the Japanese put some order into this system by making "year periods" correspond with reigns. The "year period" adopted in 645 was Taika, meaning "Great Change," and all the reforms that were carried out over the next few decades have usually been lumped together as the Taika Reforms.

A capital with Chinese-style buildings was erected at Naniwa (in the present Osaka) at the eastern end of the Inland Sea; central government ministries were set up; efforts were made to establish uniform rule over the provinces and to institute the centralized Chinese system of taxation; a census was carried out in 670 to facilitate this effort; and law codes of Chinese type were drawn up. These reforms were made piecemeal, with pragmatic compromises with existing institutions and the power of the various *uji.* Many of the laws may have existed only on paper, but slowly the Japanese state began to be reshaped into the image of the T'ang government.

Tenchi's successors carried on his reforms, and the new centralized system

---

*As in other East Asian countries, the surname precedes the given name. The genitive *no,* making this name "Kamatari of Fujiwara," was dropped from names in later centuries.

of rule was eventually embodied in the Taihō law codes, which went into effect in 702, and was symbolized by the establishment for the first time in 710 of a supposedly permanent capital. This was Heijō, commonly known by its later name of Nara, located at the northern end of the small Nara (or Yamato) Plain. The period from 710 to 784 when Nara was the capital is known as the Nara Period and is usually considered the high point of the Japanese effort to adopt the Chinese political pattern.

The Nara Period

Government. Ch'ang-an, the T'ang capital, was both the symbol and the seat of China's centralized government. The Japanese did their best to create a comparable capital city. Nara was laid out in the same checkerboard fashion as a rectangle roughly three by two and two-thirds miles (Ch'ang-an was six by five miles), with the imperial palace at the northern end. Tile-roofed palace buildings and imposing Buddhist monasteries were erected. But even this reduced scale was far too grandiose for the needs of Japan in the eighth century. No city walls were built, since there were no enemies to ward off, and the western half of the city never materialized. After the center of government was moved, the whole city withered away, and modern Nara later grew up beside the Buddhist monasteries and Shintō shrines that had clustered around the capital.

A second effort at capital building proved more lasting. Kammu (781–806), who was the strongest emperor of the whole period, decided to leave Nara, perhaps because of the oppressive influence of its great monasteries. After an abortive effort in 784 to establish his capital a few miles to the north, he built in 794 a new city, called Heian, at the northern end of the small Kyōto Plain, just north of the Nara Plain. Laid out again in checkerboard fashion but on a slightly larger scale—three by three and one-third miles—Heian too lacked city walls or a western half. But it survived to become the modern city of Kyōto, which remained the official capital of Japan until 1868 and still maintains the original checkerboard layout of its main thoroughfares.

The new system of government was meticulously spelled out in the Taihō and later law codes, which were closely modeled on those of China. The basic concept in these was that the Yamato ruler was to be a Chinese-type emperor, concentrating in his hands all authority and power over a centralized state. Since Shōtoku's time he had been called *Tennō,* or "Heavenly Sovereign," a Chinese type of title. The change in the emperor's role, however, was much greater in theory than in actuality. The emperors continued to be dominated for the most part by the great court families around them, and their dual ritual functions as Shintō cult chiefs and Chinese-type rulers made their position so ceremonially onerous that

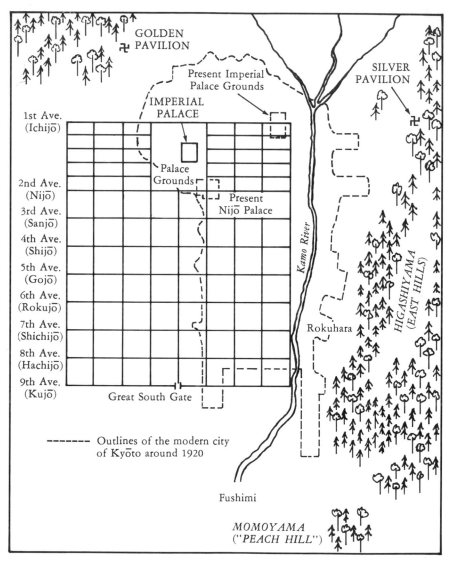

GOLDEN PAVILION

Present Imperial
Palace Grounds

SILVER
PAVILION

IMPERIAL
PALACE

1st Ave.
(Ichijō)

Palace
Grounds

Present
Nijō Palace

2nd Ave.
(Nijō)

3rd Ave.
(Sanjō)

4th Ave.
(Shijō)

5th Ave.
(Gojō)

6th Ave.
(Rokujō)

7th Ave.
(Shichijō)

8th Ave.
(Hachijō)

9th Ave.
(Kujō)

Great South Gate

Kamo River

Rokuhara

HIGASHIYAMA
(EAST HILLS)

------- Outlines of the modern city
of Kyōto around 1920

Fushimi

MOMOYAMA
("PEACH HILL")

THE HEIAN CAPITAL (KYOTO)

early abdication became a common practice already in the eighth century and remained the rule until the nineteenth. But feminine rule, which had been frequent in the past, was abandoned under Chinese influence. During this period a Buddhist monk, through his influence over the reigning empress, made a bid for the throne, and after she died in 770 and he was exiled, no woman ascended the throne again for the next nine centuries.

Under the emperor, the Japanese central government was a simpler and more logical organization than its T'ang prototype, since it was not the product of evolution but of conscious adaptation. It departed from the

Chinese pattern whenever the Japanese felt the need. At the top was a Grand Council of State headed by three Ministers. Below it were eight ministries, not the six of China, in order to include a Central Secretariat and a Ministry of the Imperial Household. Parallel to the secular Grand Council of State was an Office of Deities to supervise the emperor's cult functions and regulate the many Shintō shrines.

The court rituals and ceremonials were largely of Chinese origin. Orchestral music and stately dances borrowed from China were an important part of them. Including Central Asian and Indian influences, these T'ang dances and music (known as *gagaku* in Japan) are still maintained at the Japanese court, constituting the oldest fully authenticated musical and dance traditions in the world.

The whole country was reorganized into Chinese-type provinces, which were subdivided into districts and these into village units. By the ninth century there were sixty-six provinces, grouped into a capital region (later called Kinki) and circuits (*dō,* the Chinese *tao*), according to the routes by which they were reached. Of these the Tōkaidō, or "Eastern Sea Route," along the coast to the Kantō Plain, was to become the most famous. Dazaifu in North Kyūshū, which had developed earlier as an administrative sub-center, exercised some control over all of Kyūshū.

Governors and other officials dispatched from the capital controlled the provinces, but the officials in the districts and villages were local leaders. All rice lands were in theory government property and were supposed to be divided equally among the cultivators on the basis of detailed land and population records. Peasants paid equal taxes in the form of grain produce, textile produce, and *corvée* labor, which was the most onerous part of the tax burden. Military service was in theory included in the labor tax, but in actuality the Japanese, lacking powerful foreign enemies, never developed a Chinese type of draft army, and the palace guard groups remained the preserve of the aristocracy.

Society. According to the law codes, the Japanese seem to have taken over almost *in toto* the T'ang pattern of centralized bureaucratic government and its very complex system of landholding and taxation. The realities were probably much more of a compromise with the earlier *uji* society. But there was undoubtedly a great consolidation and extension of the power of the central government during the seventh and eighth centuries. The area of effective rule was expanded, as southern Kyūshū was fully incorporated into the state and a series of campaigns during the late eighth and early ninth centuries broke the power of the Ainu in North Honshū. A succession war in 672 and an uprising against the would-be monkish usurper in 764 were the last serious internal disturbances for almost two centuries. Eighth-century registers show a meticulous effort to carry out the system of equally divided rice fields, and there was a substantial flow of taxes from these fields to the capital, which continued, though at a slowly diminishing rate, for several centuries. The political forms and official titles established at this time survived until the nineteenth century, forming at least the theoretical framework and nomenclature for a millennium of political evolution.

Nara Japan, however, was in many ways vastly different from T'ang China. By comparison it was still economically backward. For example, the government issued copper cash in 708 and on some subsequent occasions, in imitation of the Chinese government, but barter remained the rule. The old court *uji* had been transformed into a broader court aristocracy (known as the *kuge*), but class lines remained sharp, and the great Chinese concept of a bureaucracy of educational merit was simply ignored. A central university of the Chinese type was created but was used largely to educate the sons of the court aristocrats, not as a channel for a wider recruitment of bureaucratic talent.

The court aristocracy fell into three distinct levels, with corresponding court ranks, while the descendants of the *uji* aristocracy in the provinces, who had been reduced to posts at the district level, were for the most part relegated to a separate series of "outer" ranks. Below them the peasantry probably achieved some rise in status and rights in their transformation from serf-like members of *be,* subservient to local *uji,* to citizens who paid taxes directly to the central government and had their rights to their lands guaranteed by this government.

The supposed nationalization of all agricultural lands and the taxation of all peasants was probably not carried through as sweepingly as the law codes imply. Much of the agricultural wealth of the old *uji* aristocracy probably remained undisturbed. In keeping with the T'ang system, the highest ranks of the aristocracy retained the income from their lands simply because of their ranks and the lesser aristocracy the income from smaller tracts because of their official positions. Thus some elements of the aristocratic *uji* system probably survived under the veneer of Chinese institutions of centralized government. But the reorganization of the Japanese state from the time of Prince Shōtoku through the Nara period did reduce drastically the wealth and the once autonomous power of the provincial *uji,* as both archaeology and the historical record clearly show.

Early Buddhism.   As we have seen, Buddhism was the first aspect of continental civilization consciously adopted by the Japanese. It originated in India, but, like Christianity or Islam, it is a universal religion in which all men are equal in the Buddhist "law," or teaching. Like Christianity and Islam, it spread widely, from India into the rest of South and Southeast Asia and northward around the Himalayan massif through Central Asia to China, Korea, and Japan. For a period centering around the sixth to eighth centuries it was embraced by most of the peoples of the eastern two-thirds of Asia, bringing to this vast area a sort of cultural unity it had never had before. This unity was subsequently lost as Buddhism largely died out in India, was stamped out in much of Central Asia and parts of Southeast Asia by Islam, and degenerated seriously in China and Korea.

Original Buddhism was based on certain premises common to Indian thought—that life was essentially painful and also unending, since one existence was tied to the next by *karma,* a term literally meaning "act" but implying a kind of moral causality. Birth leads to old age, death, and further rebirths in an endless chain of causality, which explains the difference in status and seeming injustices one sees in the world. The historic Buddha, known as Sakyamuni, who lived around 500 B.C., sought a way to escape the suffering inevitable in life and found it in a deep religious experience that made him the Buddha or "enlightened one."

The essence of the Buddha's ideas was expressed in the Four Noble Truths: life is painful; the origin of pain is desire; the cessation of pain is to be sought by ending desire; and the way to this goal is through his Noble Eightfold Path—that is, his rules for right living, which constituted an extremely ascetic way of life. The end objective was Nirvana, which was not described as the achievement of godhood or the salvation of the soul in the Western sense, but as the breaking of the chain of endless rebirths through the ending of all desires. Although literally meaning "emptiness," Nirvana was felt to be not simply extinction but something more, like the peaceful merging of a drop of water into the sea.

Buddhism early developed into a monastic church, and around the first century B.C. its oral teachings began to be written down in two closely related Indo-European languages. The Pali scriptures have been preserved in Ceylon, and the Sanskrit scriptures have been preserved largely through translations into Chinese and Tibetan. The Buddhist canon, known as the Tripitaka, or "three baskets," is traditionally divided into the *Vinayas* or "disciplines" for monastic life, the *Sutras* or "discourses," which constitute the major teachings, and the *Abhidharmas* or scholastic elaborations of the teachings. It is a huge collection of writings. The Chinese Tripitaka, for example, consists of more than sixteen hundred works in over five thousand sections.

Over time the doctrines of early Buddhism proliferated and eventually became divided into two major trends, which are known as Mahayana or the Greater Vehicle and Hinayana or the Lesser Vehicle, also called Theravada, "the doctrine of the Elders." Theravada, which remained closer to original Buddhism, is still the religion of Ceylon, Burma, Thailand, and Cambodia, while the Buddhism of China, Korea, and Japan stemmed largely from Mahayana.

The Greater Vehicle was "greater" in the sense of its all-inclusiveness.

Since it distinguished between absolute and relative truth, it could tolerate even contradictory ideas as representing various degrees of relative truth accommodated to the different levels of understanding of its believers. Mahayana developed a vast body of metaphysical speculation and a huge pantheon. In place of the godless religion of the historical Buddha, the Mahayanists have myriads of godlike Buddhas in eons of time. They also developed a new type of deity, the Bodhisattva or "Enlightened Existence," who, though he has achieved the enlightenment of a Buddha, stays back in this world to help others to salvation before passing on into Nirvana himself.

Because of the concept of Bodhisattvas dedicated to saving other weaker creatures, the emphasis in some sects of Mahayana Buddhism shifted from enlightenment through "one's own strength" to salvation through "the strength of another." Faith was all that was necessary. The *Lotus Sutra,* a popular Mahayanist scripture, predicts the eventual salvation of all sentient life. (Buddhism recognizes no division between humans and animals.) Naturally Bodhisattvas became the great popular gods of Mahayana Buddhism. For example, the Buddha Amitabha (Chinese: O-mi-t'o Fo; Japanese: Amida Butsu), who was a Bodhisattva in origin, became the great savior as the "Deity of the Western Paradise." Similarly Avalokitesvara (Chinese: Kuanyin; Japanese: Kannon), gradually changing in sex, emerged as the benign "Goddess of Mercy." Mahayana thus provided compassionate, comforting gods for every human need.

Nirvana also gradually changed its meaning, at least for the less sophisticated believers. Increasingly, it came to mean salvation in a very definite afterlife in paradise. Descriptions and portrayals of this paradise became quite specific and those of hell even more graphic and gruesomely convincing. The Bodhisattva ideal of aid to others led to a strong emphasis in Mahayana on charity—on good works to help others and to contribute to one's own salvation. Buddhism thus was turned somewhat from its original antisocial, contemplative bent. The concept of charity made social work important; the possibility of salvation through faith made monasticism, celibacy, and asceticism less necessary.

Buddhism in Japan.   At first neither the rich theological mix of Mahayana nor the austere concepts of early Indian Buddhism that lay behind it had much interest for most Japanese. Buddhism's appeal depended more on the reputation of the Buddha as a magical protector, more effective even than the Shintō gods, for both the state and individual families. In a way reminiscent of the *uji* cults of an earlier age, families established protective family temples. The Tōdaiji in Nara served that function for the central government and the imperial family. Emperors devoutly built and endowed monasteries, and around 770 the court printed a million Buddhist charms, many of which remain as the earliest examples of printing in the world.

The emperor Shōmu (reigned 724–749, died 756) was the most enthusiastic of all the imperial patrons of Buddhism. He set out to create a state cult of Buddhism which would parallel the centralized civil government. In 741 he ordered the establishment of an official branch monastery and nunnery in each province, and in 752 he dedicated at the Tōdaiji in the capital a gigantic fifty-three-foot, seated bronze image of Vairocana, the supreme and universal Buddha. Marred by later damages and repairs, it is no longer a great artistic work, but it is still one of the largest bronze figures in the world. The ritual objects used in the dedication ceremony together with Shōmu's personal belongings remain in a large storehouse nearby (called the Shōsōin), constituting a unique treasure of eighth-century musical instruments, painted screens, textiles, rugs, weapons, and the like, many of them imported from China or from even further afield in Asia.

The arts which surrounded Buddhism also constituted a major part of the religion's appeal to the early Japanese. It seems to have been easier for them to absorb and master these arts than the complex philosophic and political concepts, because no difficult language barrier stood in the way. In mastering these arts, the Japanese were actually making a great leap forward in technology. This was a time when they acquired new skills in architecture, bronze casting, bridge building, and a host of other technical fields. Some of the early Buddhist images in Japan were brought from Korea or were the products of Korean immigrants, but already in the seventh century the Japanese themselves were producing works of consummate beauty, and the full-bodied Buddhist images and realistic portrait statues of the Nara period are among the finest works of East Asian art of this epoch. Japanese sculptors, unlike Chinese and Koreans, made little use of stone but skillfully employed bronze, wood, clay, and lacquer.

The Buddhist temples built in Japan during the seventh and eighth centuries are the best remaining examples of classic T'ang architecture. The Golden Hall and pagoda of the Hōryūji, a monastery founded by Shōtoku on the western edge of the Nara Plain but apparently rebuilt a few decades later, are probably the oldest wooden buildings in the world. The Golden Hall is crowded with beautiful images from Shōtoku's time, and its walls are covered by frescoes (seriously damaged by a fire in 1949), which are reminiscent of the paintings in Buddhist cave temples in India. The Nara capital was graced by a number of great temples with stately tile-roofed halls and towering pagodas, some of which are still standing.

The Spread of Buddhism. Buddhism at first had been concentrated largely at the capital and had generally been limited to the ruling class. But in the eighth and ninth centuries it gradually spread to all parts of the country, and Buddhist ideas began to influence the whole of society. The new religion brought with it a new concept of the afterlife and new ethical values of

*Left: Late seventh-century Buddhist wooden image at a nunnery
attached to the Horyuji near Nara. Right: Eighth-century bronze
trinity in the Yakushiji ("Temple of the Buddha of Medicine")
near Nara.*

charity and service. The decline in tomb burials after the seventh century
and the adoption of cremation can be attributed to Buddhist influence.
Buddhist injunctions against the taking of life may also help account for the
decided decline in warlike ferocity among the Japanese at this time, the
substitution of banishment for execution, and a growing prejudice against
the eating of meat, though not of fish.

During the seventh and eighth centuries some of the major philosophical
schools of Buddhism, which had been transmitted from India to China, were
introduced to Japan. The Japanese, following the Chinese in their love of
classification, have labeled these the Six Nara Sects. The last of these was
brought by a Chinese monk, Chien-chen (Ganjin in Japanese), who after
five unsuccessful efforts finally reached Japan in 754, a blind old man.

Four of the Nara sects still exist as separate entities, but all were soon
overshadowed by two new sects introduced in the early ninth century. Their
success may have been in part due to the court's desire for religious counter-

Eighth-century Lecture Hall of the Toshodaiji ("Temple Brought from the T'ang") near Nara.

weights to the great monasteries of the older sects that had grown up around Nara, but probably owed more to the fact that the new sects represented trends in Buddhism that had greater appeal in Japan than did Indian philosophical niceties. Both new sects were introduced by student monks who accompanied the embassy to China in 804.

Kōbō Daishi returned to Japan in 806 with the Shingon ("True Word") sect. Its emphasis on incantations, magic formulas, ceremonials, and masses for the dead proved as popular in Japan as in China. The complicated iconography of its statues and paintings of Buddhist deities and its elaborate *mandara,* which are schematic representations of Shingon philosophical concepts, also had a great impact on the religious art of the time. Kōbō Daishi's monastic center on Mt. Kōya, south of the Nara Plain, is still one of Japan's most impressive Buddhist establishments, and he remains Japan's most popular religious hero, about whom a vast body of myth and tradition has formed.

Dengyō Daishi returned from China in 805 with the Tendai Sect (T'ien-t'ai in Chinese). Its eclecticism and classification of conflicting Buddhist doctrines as different levels of truth, each valid in its own way, were typical of Mahayana doctrines. The Tendai monastic headquarters was at the Enryakuji,

*Late seventh-century
wooden pagoda at the
Yakushiji near Nara.*

near the summit of Mt. Hiei a few miles northeast of Kyōto, where it came to be regarded as the spiritual protector of the capital. The third Enryakuji abbot, the traveler diarist Ennin, assured the later dominance of Tendai by combining its original teachings with the esoteric practices of the Shingon sect. Out of Tendai's diversity were to emerge most of the sectarian movements of later periods.

The question arises why Buddhism could spread so widely in Japan when a native religion was already well entrenched there. Buddhism of course had the advantage of being an element in the superior continental culture that was then sweeping Japan, but in addition it and Shintō operated at such different philosophical levels that they did not come into serious conflict, and Buddhism, as it had already demonstrated in its spread across Asia, had an extraordinary ability to adapt to and absorb the beliefs it encountered. Shintō gods and cults could be accommodated to Buddhism as subordinate local manifestations of Buddhist deities and universal Buddhist principles. Even the Sun Goddess came to be identified with Vairocana, whose alterna-

Eighth-century lacquer statue of the Chinese missionary priest Chien-chen (Ganjin).

tive name of Dainichi, or "Great Sun," aided this concept. The growing subordination of Shintō to Buddhism was elaborated and systematized under the name of Dual Shintō by monks of the Shingon ("True Word") sect in the twelfth century. Not until the nineteenth century was Shintō disentangled again from Buddhism.

Writing, Thought, and Literature.   The adoption of the Chinese pattern naturally included the borrowing of the Chinese writing system. But the pictographic and ideographic Chinese characters were ill-adapted to writing other languages, particularly the polysyllabic and highly inflected Japanese language. It was a major historical tragedy for the Japanese that they did not learn about phonetic systems of transcription until after the use of Chinese characters had become firmly established.

Chinese characters, each standing for a specific meaning and sound, could be borrowed as a whole. In fact, thousands of Chinese words were gradually incorporated in this way into Japanese. But for native Japanese words, the Chinese writing system was entirely inadequate. The early Japanese solved the problem simply by writing in the Chinese language, though on occasion they would laboriously spell out Japanese names and words syllable by syllable with Chinese characters used phonetically. It is a tribute to the diligence of the early Japanese that they were able to carry out such sweeping political and cultural changes in the seventh and eighth centuries through the medium of a radically different foreign language and an inappropriate and vastly difficult writing system.

With the writing system came the whole of Chinese literature and the thought associated with it, particularly Confucianism. Stemming from the ancient Chinese philosopher known in the West as Confucius (551–479 B.C.), Confucianism by this time had become a mixture of his teachings as developed by generations of disciples together with the accepted practices and attitudes of the centralized, bureaucratic Chinese state. Much of the classical literature of China had also become identified with Confucianism and came to be revered in Japan for this connection, as it was in China. Most prominent in this classic literature were the so-called Five Classics, which were mostly of non-Confucian origins, and the Four Books (a later designation), which included the two most important Confucian texts, the *Analects* (*Lun-yü* in Chinese; *Rongo* in Japanese), made up of the sayings of Confucius, and the *Mencius* (*Mōshi* in Japanese), the work of his most important disciple.

The Confucianism that was brought to Japan stressed above all else family solidarity, particularly filial piety, and loyalty to the ruler and all authority. It envisioned a hierarchical but harmonious society, in which the superior would be benevolent and the subordinate obedient. It assumed strong male dominance, which contrasted with the high status of women in early Japanese society but in time came to be the accepted Japanese attitude. It emphasized the inner virtues of a true gentleman, such as integrity, righteousness, and human heartedness, but also called for strict observation of external propriety and etiquette through careful attention to "rituals." By this time Confucianism was identified in China with most scholarship and learning and the stress on education through book learning. Although Confucianism never became an organized religion in Japan or even a major state cult, as it was in China, its attitudes and values from this time on became a major element in the thought and ethics of Japan.

The Japanese adopted many other Chinese ideas, such as notions of magic, divination, astrology, and geomancy. They also accepted the Chinese emphasis on the written record of the past as an aid in government, which resulted in the two great history works already mentioned, the *Record of Ancient Matters* of 712 and the *History of Japan* of 720. The latter was followed by five successive Chinese-type histories which take the record up to 887. Together with the *History of Japan,* these are known as the *Six National Histories.* Among other serious scholarly writings inspired by Chinese prototypes were local records (*fudoki*), started in 713, which were accounts of the geography, economy, legends, and political institutions of each province.

The Japanese also took on Chinese attitudes toward the literary arts, and a distinguished hand in Chinese calligraphy and a pleasing style in Chinese composition or native poetry became the essential marks of a person of breeding. An anthology of 120 Chinese poems by Japanese still remains from the Nara period, but it is overshadowed in size and quality by a great compendium of 4516 poems in Japanese, called the *Collection of Myriad Leaves* (*Man'yōshū*). The great majority of the poems in this collection are so-called "short poems" (*tanka*) of 31 syllables, divided into phrases of 5-7-5-7-7 syllables. Though a very restricted literary medium, the "short poem" has remained the favorite Japanese poetic form ever since. Normally a "short poem" suggests a natural scene and then by a deft turn uses this to evoke a surge of emotion. Commonly depending for interest on plays on words or literary allusions, "short poems" can only rarely be translated both artistically and accurately. The following, from the ninth century, however, is simple enough to lend itself to literal translation, though its very simplicity may make it atypical:

Haru tateba
kiyuru koori no
nokori naku
Kimi ga kokoro mo
ware ni tokenan

When spring comes
the melting ice
leaves no trace;
Would that your heart too
melted thus toward me.

The Modification of the Chinese Pattern

One can only marvel at the success of the Japanese in creating a fair facsimile of the Chinese political system and in moving from what was a relatively primitive society in the fifth century to a high degree of cultural sophistication by the eighth. The achievement is all the more surprising in that it was done without the stimulus of conquest from abroad and despite the wide expanse of open sea between Japan and China and the high barriers of language and writing. It stands in contrast to the much slower and less successful efforts of the North Europeans at this same time to master Mediterranean civilization. Part of the difference no doubt was because China, Japan's cultural model, was in full vigor, while the Roman model in the West was sinking into sad decay.

As we have seen, however, the Japanese copy of the Chinese political system was from the start far from exact. There had been no real effort to get away from a sharply divided class society or to create a bureaucracy. Even in China centralized bureaucratic rule tended to show signs of serious decline within a century of its inauguration and to break down completely within two or three. Without any real bureaucracy, there was even less to stop the erosion of the system in Japan. In fact, it evolved into something quite different from the original Chinese model. That this should have happened is less surprising than that the Chinese system operated successfully as long as it did and left a heavy residue of ideas and institutions that have influenced Japan ever since.

The Nara period is usually thought of as the time when the Chinese pattern prevailed and the Heian period which followed it, when the capital was at Heian, or Kyōto, as the time of a return to a more native pattern. Actually the periods do not coincide quite so neatly with the trends. The Heian period is usually dated from 794 to 1185 (although Kyōto remained the capital until 1868), and its early decades probably witnessed the high point of Chinese cultural influence in Japan. As we have seen, both the Tendai and Shingon sects were introduced in the early ninth century, and a great embassy went to China as late as 838.

In the course of the ninth century, however, there was a slow but major shift in the tide of Japanese history. Chinese institutions in Japan were becoming so modified that new borrowings from the continent seemed somewhat irrelevant. The Japanese aristocrats were now so at home in the continental culture that they felt free to depart from Chinese norms as they saw fit. Another factor was that by the ninth century T'ang was in serious dynastic decline. This was cited as a major reason for the decision not to send an embassy to China in 894. Trips were still made to China by monks and merchants traveling on Korean and Chinese ships, but the declining interest in learning from China reduced the cultural significance of these contacts for the next few centuries.

The Estate System.   Meanwhile profound changes were taking place within Japan. From the start, aristocratic families had claim to the income from extensive holdings on the basis of rank, office, or services, and these tended to become their permanent possessions. The same was true of lands assigned to Buddhist monasteries and great Shintō shrines. Such private holdings constantly grew, in part at the expense of public tax lands, but more as a result of the opening up of new rice paddies, for which the wealthy families and institutions were best able to undertake the substantial costs of drainage and irrigation. The court encouraged such reclamation of new land, permitting in 723 the retention of reclaimed fields for a generation or more, and making ownership permanent in 743.

The value of a private holding, of course, depended largely on its degree of tax exemption and independence from the central government. From the start these lands had enjoyed some exemptions from taxation, and these tended to expand. Owners hoped to win not just freedom from various sorts of taxes but protection from civil and criminal jurisdiction and eventually immunity from entry and inspection by government officials. One of the best ways to achieve these various degrees of independence was to commend holdings to powerful court families or religious institutions, whose prestige at court could ensure protection from government officials. Thus parcels of privately owned land tended to cluster together to form large private estates under the patronage and protection of powerful families and institutions. Such estates (called *shōen*) began to form in the eighth century, and they spread throughout Japan during the next four centuries until there were literally thousands of them. Unlike the manors of Europe, the estates were not unified pieces of land centering around a manor house and grazing land used in common (there were no dairy herds and few draft animals) but were made up of scattered tracts of agricultural land administered as a unit.

The central figure in the estate system was the proprietor, who was likely to be an aristocrat of influence either locally or at court. Above him might be a patron, who normally was one of the most prestigious of the court nobles or a great religious institution. Below the proprietor were the local estate managers, below these in turn the small holders who did the actual farming, and below them their dependent workers. All but the last category had their respective rights to parts of the income from the estate. These income rights, which were called *shiki,* meaning "function" or "office," were usually specified in documents and were both divisible and inheritable—by women as well as men. The resemblance of this system to the system of multiple rights attached to a single piece of land in feudal Europe is striking but perhaps not surprising. Both were survivals of elements of an earlier centralized administrative and legal system—the Roman in Europe—after centralized control itself had waned.

The public tax-paying domain did not disappear entirely into private estates. Much of the land, perhaps as much as half, was still outside them as late as the twelfth century. The administration of these public lands, however, gradually took on many of the features of the administration of the estates. There was no effort to redistribute land among the tax-paying peasants after the middle of the ninth century, and gradually the unit of taxation shifted from the individual male peasant to the land itself. Even at the height of the Chinese system, courtiers had gone with reluctance to provincial posts and even then largely for the income rather than the prestige or power. Increasingly in the ninth century it became the custom for governors to send deputies in their place and to regard a provincial appointment merely as a source of revenue. In fact, the right to select governors for certain provinces became itself in time a sort of possession, like the "patronage" over an estate. Minor court aristocrats, who went out to the provinces to make their fortunes as deputies or lesser officials, succeeded in making their posts hereditary and took on functions on the public lands comparable to those of the proprietors or managers of estates.

The whole economy and society of Japan thus was moving far from the Chinese pattern of centralized political control and back toward private and personalized relations reminiscent of the *uji* period. Each group, instead of being directly related to the central government, was more narrowly oriented toward the group immediately above it. On the estates, landless peasants worked for small holders, who were controlled by estate managers, who were answerable to proprietors, who in turn might be beholden to patrons. The names and theories were different on government lands, but the realities were becoming much the same. The local produce that flowed to the capital increasingly went into the hands of the great religious institutions and court families, members of which held posts as proprietors or patrons of estates or exercised the patronage of appointment to the provincial governments. Thus the chief ties, political as well as economic, between the provinces and the capital came to be through the great noble families and the powerful central religious institutions, rather than through the central government itself.

The great families and religious institutions of the capital area, though still associated with one another through the framework of the old centralized government, had in a sense become its multiple successors in the exercise of real power. This can be seen in their development of what amounted to small private family or institutional governments. The Fujiwara family, descended from Kamatari, the leader of the *coup d'état* of 645, is a good case in point. It resembled in a way the great *uji* of earlier times, having a family head, significantly called *uji* chief, and possessing a family temple and Shintō shrine at the old Nara capital. To administer its complex family affairs and the dozens of estates it owned throughout the country, it had a family government, headed by the family head and consisting of a series of bureaus, including an "administrative office" (*mandokoro*).

The Modification of Political Institutions.   The reshaping of society and the economy through the development of estates was a long slow process spreading over the eighth to the thirteenth centuries, but it was far enough advanced by the ninth to begin to have a visible effect on the outward forms of the central government. As the tax yield declined or was diverted into private hands and the area of effective control by the government shrank, the government was slowly starved both of economic sustenance and of functions to perform. But it did not wither away, as might have happened in a country more subject to foreign pressures. Maintained by the wealthy families around it, the central government became in large part an elaborate stage for their rivalries. It also continued to be regarded by the real holders of power as the ultimate source of all titles, ranks, and claims to legitimacy.

As the substance of administration ebbed from the offices of government, their rituals and ceremonies loomed all the more important and were maintained by the courtiers with meticulous attention to precedent. All the posts and titles of government were carefully preserved but increasingly became the inherited possessions of family lines. Eventually what had been actual governmental functions in the eighth century degenerated into purely honorary hereditary titles awarded regardless of the incumbent's age or ability, and subsequently some of these titles became little more than surnames or personal names.

In place of the now needlessly elaborate organs of state, simpler political institutions grew up in the ninth century to handle the remaining duties of the central government. Audit Officers, first appointed in 790 to audit the accounts of retiring local administrators, supplanted a variety of offices as the chief supervisors of the government's tax income and the most effective channel of control between the capital and the provincial governments. A Bureau of Archivists, established in 810, grew into the chief organ for drafting imperial decrees. Police Commissioners, first appointed around 820 in the capital, developed into the only effective organ of the central government for maintaining law and order and came in the process to administer a sort of customary law that was growing up around the old Chinese-type law codes. Together with some aristocratic provincial militia groups, they also became the only remnants of the Chinese concept of a centralized army.

The appointment of Audit Officers in 790 was the first of many efforts by the central government to stop the erosion of its income and powers. A century later two successive emperors tried hard to stem the tide but achieved little except to inspire the compilation in 927 of an elaboration of the old law codes.

The Fujiwara and the Retired Emperors.   The greatest change in the central government in the ninth century was the establishment of almost complete control over the imperial family by a branch of one of the great court families—the Fujiwara. It was able to do this in part through providing empresses and imperial concubines, in part because it was emerging as the family which owned the largest number of estates throughout Japan. Its head, Yoshifusa, put his seven-year-old imperial grandson on the throne in 858 and assumed for himself the post of regent. This was the first instance of a small child being made emperor and the first time the regent had not been a member of the imperial family. The next Fujiwara chief similarly served as regent for a child emperor and then continued in this capacity for an adult who came to the throne in 884, taking for this purpose the specially created title of *kampaku.*

After Yoshifusa had established the supremacy of the Fujiwara, members of the family continued to monopolize nearly all of the high government offices, to supply most of the imperial consorts, and to place sons of Fujiwara mothers on the throne. In fact, they so dominated the court that the period from 858 to 1160 is commonly called the Fujiwara period. The height of Fujiwara glory came under Michinaga (966–1027). The extent of his control over the imperial family can be seen from the fact that four emperors married his daughters, two were his nephews, and three his grandsons. His family "administrative office," rather than the organs of the central government, was the real center of power at the capital. Despite their great power, however, the Fujiwara never made the slightest move toward usurping the throne. The concept of hereditary authority and the special religious aura of the imperial line were too strong. It gradually became accepted, however, that the emperors reigned but did not rule.

Since the Fujiwara were content to derive their authority in theory from the imperial line, they could always be challenged by a vigorous emperor. For example, a retired emperor who did not happen to be born of a Fujiwara mother attempted to oppose Fujiwara domination by appointing Sugawara no Michizane, a lesser aristocrat but a renowned scholar, to a high post in 899, but two years later the Fujiwara chief managed to have this rival sent off into virtual exile in Kyūshū. Again in 1069 an emperor not born of a Fujiwara mother founded a Records Office in an attempt to confiscate all estates formed since 1045, but the effort was frustrated by the Fujiwara.

A more successful attempt to recapture power was carried out by the Emperor Shirakawa, who, after his abdication in 1086, successfully contested the supremacy of the Fujiwara by utilizing minor aristocrats who had made their reputations as scholars or in provincial administrations. This form of rule by retired emperors, which is known as *insei*, was continued by other retired emperors for a century after Shirakawa's death in 1129 and was sporadically revived for another century after that.

Meanwhile, however, the whole central government was declining rapidly and there was progressively less power for the Fujiwara and retired emperors to fight over. During the eleventh century, dwindling revenues resulted in the neglect of government buildings, which fell into serious decay. Lawlessness was becoming prevalent in the provinces, and acts of violence were occurring even in the capital. Deep rivalries divided and weakened the Fujiwara family, while the chief success the retired emperors had during their period of power was in further despoiling the public domain by turning much of it into estates owned by the imperial family.

The Culture of the Fujiwara Period

The gradual disintegration of the institutions of central government and the subsequent decline of law and order have given to the period from the tenth to the twelfth centuries an aura of decay and impending catastrophe. Such attitudes were commonly expressed in the writings of the time. But these centuries were in fact a period of great economic and cultural growth throughout the country. The estate system seems to have proved as conducive to economic and cultural development as had the more centralized but also more constrained system that had preceded it. The opening of new agricultural lands and the increase of the population in distant areas such as the Kantō and North Honshū were signs of economic growth as well as reasons for the decline of the centralized government. Communications actually improved, and the flow of goods throughout Japan was much greater by the twelfth century than it had been in the eighth. Many features of continental civilization that had been limited largely to the capital area in the eighth century had become widely diffused throughout Japan by the twelfth. A beautiful temple building, erected in 1124 at Hiraizumi in North Honshū by a locally powerful branch of the Fujiwara family, illustrates the high levels of provincial wealth and artistic achievement even in this remote area.

In the capital the court nobles, supported by their many estates, lived in luxury. Lacking real duties to perform in a government largely empty of meaningful functions, they led lives that were in many ways shallow, centering around symbols rather than realities. They occupied themselves in an endless round of ritual observances and dilettantish pastimes, such as judging the merits of flowers, roots, or shells or composing poems as a wine cup floated to each person in turn down a miniature winding waterway. The emphasis was strongly aesthetic: what counted was the proper costume, the right ceremonial act, the successful turn of phrase in a poem, and the appropriate expression of refined taste. Love-making was a major art in a society in which the institution of marriage was not sharply defined.

While full of Chinese elements, Fujiwara court culture was almost entirely free of any new efforts to imitate Chinese patterns. It was a complete and natural blend of now thoroughly assimilated Chinese elements and native tendencies. In this sense it was completely Japanese. In contrast to the stern asceticism and military virtues of later times, Fujiwara culture seems effete and effeminate. But its aesthetic sensitivity and creativity were to remain characteristic of all later Japanese civilization.

Buddhism.   During the Fujiwara period Buddhism in Japan, which up until the ninth century had depended heavily on successive waves of influence from the continent, developed into Japanese Buddhism. At court the emphasis on elaborate rituals in secular life was paralleled by a corresponding emphasis on Buddhist rituals, for which the esoteric cults of the Shingon and Tendai sects provided ample scope. At the same time, Buddhism, in spreading outward from the capital and downward in society and in amalgamating with the Shintō cults, lost some of its original emphasis as the magical protector of the state, becoming instead more of a vehicle of faith and hope for the common people.

This new and more popular Buddhism was based on Pure Land doctrines introduced from China in the ninth century, but now greatly developed by the Japanese themselves. The central concept was that the present was a degenerate age, known as "the latter period of the law," and that rebirth into the Pure Land Paradise of the Buddha Amida, who had vowed the salvation of all living creatures, could now be achieved only through faith. Salvation thus depended on the "strength of another," not on "one's own strength," and it could best be achieved through calling on the Buddha's name by chanting "Hail to the Buddha Amida" over and over. During the tenth century such ideas were popularized by priests who preached in the streets, but the most important figure in the new Buddhism was a more scholarly figure, Genshin (942–1017), whose *Essentials of Salvation* contained detailed descriptions of the horrors of hell and the bliss of paradise.

During this period Buddhism also became incorporated into the institutional life of Japan in a way it never had on the continent. In the course of the ninth century the government abandoned its effort to limit the size of the clergy by regulating ordinations, and the organized church grew without restrictions. The sectarian divisions of earlier times, which had been based primarily on philosophical differences, hardened into clear administrative hierarchies of mother and branch monasteries. Buddhist monasteries increasingly drew support from their own lands, and the great monastic establishments of the capital region vied with the powerful families as proprietors and patrons of estates throughout the country. Monasteries also began to form armed bands from among their younger priests and workers on their estates in order to protect their interests. The turbulence of the monks in the capital area and the armed rivalries between some of the great monasteries became legendary. Repeatedly after the late eleventh century priestly armies threatened the authorities in the capital, and the retired emperor Shirakawa quipped that the only things he could not control were the Kamo River (flowing through Kyōto), the fall of the dice, and the monastic armies. Thus the Buddhist church achieved a far greater economic and secular role in Japan than it ever had in China or Korea.

Art.   The Japanese during the Fujiwara period continued to use the basic Chinese artistic idiom but began to express through it typically Japanese tastes. The balanced, formal architecture of the T'ang was replaced in palace architecture by more airy pavilions connected by covered passageways and artfully placed in a natural setting of gardens and ponds. This style was to grow into the Japanese domestic architecture of more modern times.

In Buddhist sculpture and painting the emphasis was on the complex iconography of the ritualistic, esoteric sects and on representations of Amida and his Pure Land, but there also developed in painting a style of simple, flowing lines and flat colored surfaces quite unlike Chinese prototypes and fittingly called "Yamato pictures" (*Yamato-e*). Commonly such paintings were organized into picture scrolls, which in a continuous drawing or series of drawings told a story. The earliest remaining example illustrates the famous court novel, *The Tale of Genji* (*Genji monogatari*), but others portray monastic traditions or famous historical events.

The appearance at this time of hereditary families of artists, commonly maintained by adoption when heredity failed to produce talent, provides another example of how the continental civilization was fitted into a completely familial pattern. The same happened in the various other specialized fields of endeavor, such as scholarship, calendar making, music, calligraphy, and the like.

The Kana Writing System. During the ninth and tenth centuries it became customary for Japanese to read Chinese texts in native Japanese words and according to the Japanese word order. This, of course, was a sign of declining competence in the Chinese language, and by the tenth century much of the Chinese composed in Japan, which is known as *kambun* or "Han writing," had become so heavily Japanized that it can be understood today only by persons who know both Chinese and Japanese.

A more important development at this time was the appearance of purely phonetic scripts for writing Japanese. The poems of the *Collection of Myriad Leaves* had been spelled out syllable by syllable in Chinese characters used phonetically. In the course of the ninth century these characters were simplified to be nothing more than phonetic symbols, each representing a syllable. There were two systems, both called *kana*. Whole characters written cursively in abbreviated form became known as *hiragana* and selected parts of characters as *katakana*. The two systems were not fully standardized until the late nineteenth century, and variant forms are still sometimes used in handwriting.

The *kana* syllabaries were excellent ways to write the Japanese of the time, but because of the prestige of Chinese, well educated people continued to attempt to write in that language for most serious purposes, though with increasing admixtures of Japanese elements. Even those who wrote in Japanese were always tempted to insert Chinese words written in characters. The eventual outgrowth of both tendencies was the present mixed style of writing, in which Chinese characters are used for borrowed Chinese words and for those Japanese words (or at least their stems) which can be equated in meaning with specific Chinese characters, while *kana* is used for the inflections and other elements not easily represented by characters. Such a mixed style was evolving already in the eleventh century and thenceforth competed

Scene from a humorous scroll painting, attributed to Toba Sojo,
showing a frog as a Buddhist image, a monkey, fox, and rabbit
in clerical garb, a fox as an aristocratic court lady with attendants,
and a rabbit in a layman's black hat.

with the two other systems of writing—straight Chinese (or what the Japanese thought was Chinese) for documents and scholarly writing and pure Japanese in *kana* for poems and some prose texts.

The contemporary mixed style is probably the most difficult writing system in common use anywhere in the world. Each Chinese character may be read according to the Japanese approximation of its Chinese pronunciation (there is often more than one Japanese pronunciation, depending on the period and location in China from which the Chinese pronunciation was first learned). The same character could also have the pronunciation of one of several Japanese words that might be equated with it in meaning. A strictly phonetic system of writing would be preferable. But to return to writing in pure *kana* or, better still, to shift to the much simpler "Roman" alphabet (*rōmaji* in Japanese) would not be easy. This is because of the huge number of homophones in written Japanese, largely derived from Chinese words. Since Japanese is phonetically much simpler than Chinese, many words that are distinct in Chinese are pronounced alike in Japanese. For example, twenty different Chinese syllables, each differentiated further by four tones —a total of eighty separate sounds—all boil down to the single sound *kō* in Japanese. Though such homophones are easily confused in speech, they are quite distinct when written in characters. Thus a shift to purely phonetic writing in Japan would necessitate a massive alteration of the scholarly and technical vocabulary.

EXAMPLES OF THE DERIVATION OF KANA

Chinese character	安	以	加	多	奴	保
Original meaning	peace	take	add	many	slave	protect
Chinese pronunciation	*an*	*i*	*chia*	*to*	*nu*	*pao*
Katakana			カ	タ	ヌ	ホ
Hiragana	あ	い	か		ぬ	ほ
Phonetic value in Japanese	*a*	*i*	*ka*	*ta*	*nu*	*ho*

Literature. The *kana* syllabaries greatly facilitated writing in Japanese. The emphasis at court on the composition of poetry in Japanese continued, and a second anthology of about eleven hundred poems was compiled on imperial order in 905. Called the *Ancient and Modern Collection* (*Kokinshū*), it became the model for twenty more imperial anthologies compiled up to 1439. A preface to the *Ancient and Modern Collection* is one of the earliest examples of serious prose writing in pure Japanese, and the author of this preface also wrote a poetic travel diary, the *Tosa Diary,* in Japanese. Many other diaries were written at this time in either Japanese or Chinese, and the Japanese have ever since shown themselves to be inveterate diarists.

Around the year 1000, during the ascendancy of Fujiwara no Michinaga, there was a veritable outburst of literary activity in Japanese. This was largely the work of court ladies, whose lesser mastery of Chinese characters led them to write in Japanese—with great beauty—while most of their male counterparts continued to write proudly in Chinese—with artistically undistinguished results. Lady Sei Shōnagon's *Pillow Book,* compiled at this time, is a miscellany of witty and sometimes caustic comments on the court life about her. Other ladies wrote diaries or novels, all liberally sprinkled with poems. The greatest work was the massive *Tale of Genji* by Lady Murasaki, which recounts with great psychological subtlety and aesthetic sensitivity the life and loves of an imaginary Prince Genji, and in the process gives us a detailed picture of the court life of the time. *The Tale of Genji* has exerted immeasurable literary influence throughout Japanese history and the masterful translations of Arthur Waley and more recently Edward Seidensticker has become one of the great world classics.

In the late eleventh and twelfth centuries a new literary genre appeared. This was romanticized accounts of the period of Fujiwara dominance at court. The *Tale of Splendor* (*Eiga monogatari*) covers the period 889 to 1092 in chronological sequence and the *Great Mirror* (*Okagami*) the period from 850 to 1025 in biographic style. The shift from the official court histories written in Chinese, which came to an end in 887, to these more literary efforts at history writing in Japanese and centering on the Fujiwara, illustrates how far the Japanese had strayed from the Chinese patterns they had earlier adopted.

2. Feudal Japan: A Departure from the Chinese Pattern

The Rise of the Provincial Warrior Class

The Roots of Feudalism. For all its cultural brilliance, the Fujiwara court was not the direct ancestor of later Japanese society. It had grown too effete to continue its dominance. Instead it served as the transmitter of the now fully assimilated residue of Chinese civilization to another more vigorous group. This was the provincial warrior class, in whose hands the future of Japan was to lie.

The estate system gave the people in the provinces fiscal and legal protection against the officers of the central government, but it did not provide them local security. As the power of the central government and its provincial representatives waned, armed struggles between local groups over lands or offices increased in frequency, and piracy became endemic on the Inland Sea. To counter such conditions, provincial authorities during the ninth century acquired the right to maintain armed guards and in time were given military titles. Similarly managers or local proprietors of private estates developed armed bands to defend their interests. Thus military functions began to merge with political and economic roles. As such guard groups drew together for mutual security, they began to provide a lateral integration of local society to accompany the vertical integration of the provincial estates with the great families or religious institutions of the capital area.

Defense groupings of this sort grew up gradually between the ninth and twelfth centuries. They tended to be familial in organization, composed of head and branch families, but for geographic and other reasons nonrelated subordinates, known as "house men" (*kenin*), increasingly joined in. As these groups became more powerful and influential, they were able to provide not just physical security but also protection for the property rights of their members. In time they even became able to reward loyal members with new rights.

The mutual defense groups tended to form around lines of particular hereditary prestige. These were usually minor offshoots of the Fujiwara family or of the imperial line itself. On repeated occasions after 814, excess members of the imperial line were cut off from it and given the family names of Minamoto (also known as Genji) or Taira (also called Heike). Unable to achieve high office at court, these men would go out to the provinces in order to make their fortunes as provincial officials or estate proprietors and managers. Coming with the prestige of the court and imperial descent, they tended to form a top layer in the provincial aristocracy above the descendants of the old provincial *uji*.

The local armed bands thus were led by the most prestigious members of the local aristocracy, and they were in fact made up almost exclusively of the upper crust of provincial society. This was because the military technology of the day made fighting an expensive and therefore aristocratic profession. As in Europe at that time, the central figure was a mounted, armored knight with his supporting footmen. Unlike his European counterpart, however, the Japanese mounted warrior relied not on a lance but on bow and arrows and a curved sword—the finest blade in the world. His armor, made of thin strips of steel held together by brightly colored thongs, might look flimsy compared to European armor, but its lightness and flexibility probably made it more practical. As in Europe, warfare was conducted primarily as a series of individual encounters between knights, rather than through coordinated mass movements of troops.

The provincial warrior aristocracy that emerged during these centuries is known as the *bushi* ("warrior") or *samurai* ("retainer") class. It was made up in large part of the descendants of the old provincial *uji* aristocracy and clearly inherited the latter's military traditions, which perhaps had never been lost, despite the long-standing overlay of a Chinese-type of centralized civil government. As this provincial warrior class moved to the center of the historical stage during the twelfth century, it led Japan into a type of social and political organization more like that of feudal Europe than the Chinese centralized bureaucratic state. Military power absorbed into it political and economic authority, and all three became defined primarily in terms of rights to land, while personal lord-and-vassal relationships, often expressed in familial terms, became central to political integration.

Both Japanese and Western feudalism seem to have resulted from a mixture of two basic ingredients: administrative and legal institutions

A sixteenth-century suit of armor (little changed from the twelfth century).

surviving from a more centralized state and a system of personal bonds of loyalty. In Japan these two were derived respectively from the Chinese type of organization of the Nara period and the earlier familial pattern of *uji* society; in the West from Roman law and the German tribal war bands. The two basic ingredients have frequently been present together in human history, but apparently only rarely in the proper proportions to produce a fully feudal system. The Japanese is the only well documented case besides that of Europe.

The Rise of the Minamoto and Taira.   Two large-scale struggles between provincial warrior bands broke out almost simultaneously in the middle of the tenth century. In the Kantō region a Taira leader seized two provinces before being destroyed by his rivals in 940. The next year in the Inland Sea area a descendant of the Fujiwara was brought down after a decade of disorders. In the eleventh century a branch of the Minamoto won great power and prestige in East Japan, destroying in 1031 a rival Taira group in the Kantō area and then eliminating two powerful rival families in North Honshū in successive wars between 1051 and 1088. Warrior bands in East Japan seem to have been larger and stronger than elsewhere in the country, perhaps because of the remoteness of the area, the regional cohesiveness of the Kantō Plain as the largest agricultural area in Japan, and the stronger survival of military traditions there as a result of the long campaigns against the Ainu.

While the warrior bands in their struggles sought to have their rivals branded as "rebels" against the court, their clashes had little effect on Kyōto, except to stop temporarily the flow of income from the estates involved. However, provincial warriors were increasingly used in the capital as Police Commissioners and members of the palace guard groups, and as early as 889 the Bureau of Archivists organized its own defense unit out of such men. As we have seen, the great central monasteries developed armed forces made up in part of men drawn from their estates, and the great families did the same. Certain Minamoto warriors came to be known as the "claws and teeth" of the main Fujiwara family, while a Taira line, after eliminating a strong Minamoto leader in West Japan in 1108, became prominent at the capital as the military supporters of the retired emperors. Because of such military services at court, the leaders of these warrior bands were able to achieve court ranks and posts and by the twelfth century had sufficient influence to be able to serve as patrons of estates, to whom other local leaders might commend their holdings or from whom they might receive rights to lands in return for services.

In this way, provincial military leaders were assuming an increasing role in the old central government. This process was greatly accelerated when two successive small wars at the capital in the middle of the twelfth century suddenly revealed the dominant power these military men actually commanded. On the death of a retired emperor in 1156, a sharp struggle for control of the court broke out between two of his sons, supported respectively by rival claimants to the headship of the Fujiwara and the mixed groups of Minamoto and Taira warriors each side could muster. One group was headed by Taira no Kiyomori (1118–1181), whose main seat of power was in the Inland Sea area. The other group was headed by Minamoto no Tameyoshi, the leader of the Minamoto family that had won ascendancy in the Kantō area. Kiyomori's group emerged victorious and executed most of the remaining leaders of the other band. One of Tameyoshi's sons, Yoshitomo, had sided with the winning clique in 1156. He became dissatisfied with his share in the rewards and, supported by dissident elements among the Fujiwara, seized the capital in the winter of 1159–1160, but he and his supporters were soon destroyed by Kiyomori. These two brief military clashes, called the Hōgen and Heiji Wars from the names of the "year periods" in which they occurred, left Kiyomori and his warrior band in undisputed military control of Kyōto. A superb picture scroll of the Heiji War gives a nearly contemporary portrayal of some of its chief incidents.

Taira Rule. Kiyomori, who had long been prominent at court, settled down to the now time-honored practice of providing titular superiors with wives and dominating them without replacing them. Emperors, retired emperors, and Fujiwara regents and *kampaku* continued to maintain their respective pretenses to authority, but Kiyomori was the real source of power, ensconced in his palace at Rokuhara on the southeastern edge of the city. He gained title to many more estates in western Japan, promoted his relatives to high positions in the central government, rewarded his henchmen with governorships and posts on estates in the provinces, married his daughter to the emperor, and in 1180 had the satisfaction of placing his own infant grandson on the throne. Thus he dominated the court, despite determined opposition by the retired emperor. He had little control, however, over the great religious institutions of the capital region and still less over the remaining warrior bands in the provinces.

The role of Kiyomori and his immediate family as a new layer of court aristocrats may, in fact, have weakened the bonds of loyalty of their warrior associates in the provinces. In any case, when a disappointed imperial prince issued a call for military support in 1180, much of eastern Japan responded. Yoritomo (1147–1199), a surviving son of the former Minamoto leader, Yoshitomo, raised the standard of revolt in the mountainous Izu Peninsula, where he had lived in exile, and many of the warriors of the Kantō region rallied to him. Minamoto prestige was still strong in the area, and to these men a local military leader probably seemed more likely to respect and protect their interests and property rights as local officials and administrators of estates than a distant leader like Kiyomori, immersed in court life.

Yoritomo extended his control over the Kantō area, and his younger brother, Yoshitsune, then seized the capital area for him and pursued the Taira down the Inland Sea to its western end, where he finally annihilated them in 1185 at Dan-no-ura in a naval battle. Four years later Yoritomo destroyed the Fujiwara family of Hiraizumi in the north, bringing the whole of Japan under his military control.

The Kamakura Period

The Minamoto and Their Vassals. The Minamoto triumph over the Taira in 1185 signified a long step forward in the domination of Japan by the provincial warrior class and the development of a feudal society. Where Kiyomori's military control had not extended effectively to many parts of Japan, Yoritomo's military dominance was nationwide. Where Kiyomori had exercised his authority from Kyōto and largely through the old civil government, in the fashion of the Fujiwara before him, Yoritomo created a separate governmental structure, intertwined with the old civil administra-

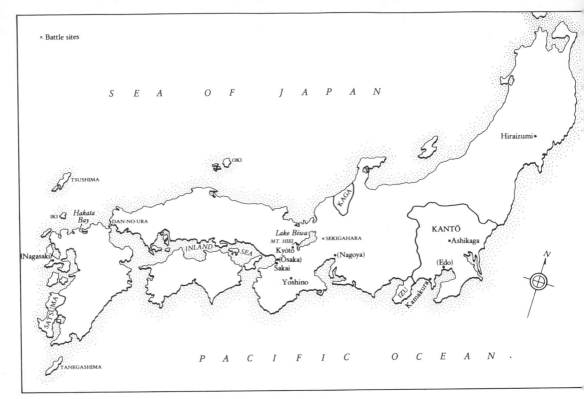

× Battle sites

SEA   OF   JAPAN

Hiraizumi•

TSUSHIMA

OKI

KAGA

IKI   Hakata Bay

DAN-NO-URA

KANTŌ
•Ashikaga

(Nagasaki)

Lake Biwa
MT. HIEI   × SEKIGAHARA

INLAND   SEA

Kyōto
•(Ōsaka)
Sakai

•(Nagoya)

(Edo)

IZU

Kamakura

N

SATSUMA

Yoshino

PACIFIC   OCEAN   •

TANEGASHIMA

MEDIEVAL JAPAN

tion but independent of it and separately based at Kamakura, a seaside
town in the Kantō, the seat of his military power.

After the Minamoto victory in 1185 the court bestowed on Yoritomo
high court posts and ranks and special titles to signify his military control
over the country. Eventually in 1192 he was given the title of *Seii-tai-
shōgun* ("Barbarian-Quelling Generalissimo"), once assigned leaders of
expeditions against the Ainu, but henceforth used in its shortened form of
shogun to denote supreme military command over all Japan. Since the post
of shogun was in theory purely military, Yoritomo's administration, or
shogunate, like that of later shoguns, was known as the *bakufu,* or "tent
government," in distinction to the Kyōto civil government.

Appointment to high office by the court was useful to Yoritomo in
providing him with legitimacy, but his real power rested on his personal
band of warrior vassals, called "honorable house men" (*gokenin*), which
he had built up in the Kantō. The confiscation of lands from the defeated
adherents of the Taira in 1185 gave Yoritomo ownership or control over
large numbers of estates throughout the country, and he also came to exercise powers of appointment to provincial posts in no less than sixteen
provinces. Thus he could reward his vassals with new appointments in the

estates and provincial governments. At the same time many warriors originally outside the Kantō band sought to protect their positions by commend-
ing their properties to Yoritomo and accepting vassalage as his "honorable
house men." Thus, although the ultimate right to posts in the provinces or
estates and income from them derived from the Kyōto court, Yoritomo
came to be directly responsible for the protection of many of these posts
and appointments to some of them.

In 1185 Yoritomo extended and systematized this old method of achieving power through patronage by appointing in each estate an additional
official called a steward (*jitō*) to assist in its administration and collect a
small military levy. In this way, he inserted his vassals into estates where
they had not been before and asserted his right to a share in taxation and
administration entirely outside the structure of the civil government. The
stewards, who often were incumbent managers given this additional title,
were assigned a part of the produce of their estates specifically as their
rights (*shiki*) for performing this new function in behalf of the Kamakura
shogunate. Like most other positions and incomes at this time, those of the
stewards were of course passed on through inheritance along with the duties
of vassalage to the Minamoto.

In 1185 Yoritomo also appointed leading vassals as protectors (*shugo*)
over one or more provinces, with responsibility for assigning local vassals
to guard duties and leading them in time of war. Thus through his vassals
scattered throughout the country as stewards and protectors, Yoritomo established direct administrative control over most parts of Japan and also
established small but effective provincial armies.

Because of the resistance of the retired emperors to these infringements
on the powers of the civil government, this new system was applied at first
only imperfectly in western Japan, but an opportunity to extend it more
fully came in 1221. In that year the retired emperor, supported by some of
the warriors and monasteries of the capital area, attempted an armed "rebellion" against Kamakura. This was easily crushed in what is known as the
Shōkyū War. The retired emperor was exiled from Kyōto, and most of the
other ringleaders were executed. The Kamakura shogunate confiscated more
than three thousand estates in central and western Japan owned by members
of the losing side, awarded ownership or posts in these to its own members,
and extended the steward system systematically to the whole nation. It placed
two deputies (*tandai*) in Kyōto, where they exercised respectful but firm control over the court from the old Taira headquarters at Rokuhara.

The Organs of Government.   To oversee the system he had created, Yoritomo set up at his headquarters in Kamakura a simple set of offices reminiscent of the family governments of the Fujiwara period. Already in 1180 he

had established a Retainers Office to supervise the military duties, rewards, and punishments of his vassals. An Administrative Office (so named in 1191) was a central administrative and policy-making organ, headed by a minor Kyōto aristocrat versed in law. An Office of Inquiry served as a final court of appeal, kept land and judicial records, and enforced legal decisions. All these offices operated as committees, issuing only unanimous decisions This prevented any one member from becoming an independent source of authority and gave all the protection of collective responsibility. Ever since this time the Japanese, whenever possible, have shown a strong preference for collective leadership and great skill in its operation.

Since the old Taihō Code had little applicability to the actual social conditions and land-owning system of the time, the law the Office of Inquiry administered was essentially customary law that had grown up among the warriors in the provinces. In 1232 the Kamakura government drew up the Jōei Code as a set of general legal and administrative principles to guide its members. This was the first codification of "feudal law" in Japan. Since the civil government had little power to carry out legal decisions, the court nobles as well as the warriors looked to Kamakura for justice, and its law became for all practical purposes the basic law of the land.

The system of government created by Yoritomo was a curious hybrid. It had a feudal core of a single large lord-vassal group, spread thinly throughout Japan, in control if not in possession of most of the estates, combining military, political, and economic functions of leadership, and possessing unchallengeable military power. But this band lived, as it were, in the shell of the old civil administration. The whole panoply of the imperial civil government remained, and the shogunate was in theory merely its military arm. Yoritomo and his vassals continued to sport titles and posts derived from the civil government. The imperial family and court aristocracy, as well as religious institutions, still owned great numbers of estates and drew revenue from them. Some land even remained in the public domain, paying taxes to the Kyōto government as well as supporting the warriors who held posts in the provincial administrations. Because of this combination of feudal and prefeudal elements in the Kamakura system, it is usually regarded as having been only protofeudal.

Yoritomo's system of rule, however, fitted the needs of the time very well. It lasted with relatively little change from 1185 to 1333—a period of history appropriately known as the Kamakura period. After the establishment of effective control by Kamakura throughout the country following the Shōkyū War of 1221, Japan enjoyed a century of internal peace and order perhaps unparalleled in its earlier history. Certainly the Kamakura system provided the most effective centralized control over all parts of the country that Japan had as yet known.

The Hōjō Regents. The Kamakura system survived despite two great challenges, the one internal and the other external. In theory it depended entirely on the personal loyalty of some two thousand scattered families of vassals to their lord, the head of the Minamoto family. The latter, however, disappeared quite early in the period. Yoritomo eliminated his brother Yoshitsune and other close relatives out of jealousy and suspicion. At the time of his death in 1199 he left only two sons, neither of any great ability, and they were soon pushed aside by the Hōjō family of Yoritomo's widow Masako.

The Hōjō, ironically of Taira descent, had served as Yoritomo's keepers in his Izu exile but had joined his cause. Masako and her father, Tokimasa, forced Yoritomo's incompetent eldest son to abdicate in 1203 in favor of his brother, who was assassinated in 1219, bringing the main line of the Minamoto family to an end. By this time Masako's brother, Yoshitoki (1163–1224), was dominant at Kamakura, but neither he nor his successors made any effort to usurp the post of shogun. Instead they exercised their power through puppet leaders, as the Fujiwara had in Kyōto. A Fujiwara infant, descended through his mother from Yoritomo, was brought to Kamakura and made titular shogun in 1226. In 1252 an imperial prince was chosen to fill the position. It is a tribute to the solidity of the system Yoritomo had constructed that although in theory it depended entirely on the personal loyalty of the vassals to him and his heirs, it survived the extinction of his line and operated successfully with a purely symbolic object of loyalty.

The Kamakura period was thus a period of rule more by the Hōjō family than by the Minamoto. Tokimasa had taken the post of chief of the Administrative Office, and the title of this post, *shikken*, held by successive Hōjō, came to signify "shogunal regent." Yoshitoki's son, Yasutoki (1183–1242), was the great consolidator of the Kamakura shogunate and of Hōjō power. He created a Council of State in 1225 to broaden participation in the government and made an uncle a "co-signer" of government decrees to share responsibility with him. Thereafter until the fall of Kamakura in 1333, two senior Hōjō occupied the paired posts of "shogunal regent" and "co-signer," while two slightly junior members of the family occupied the paired posts of deputies in Kyōto. Thus, the Hōjō as a family demonstrated great success at collective leadership.

The Mongol Invasions. The external threat to the Kamakura system came from the Mongols, who had overrun much of Asia and part of Europe, had fully incorporated Korea into their empire by 1258, and were to complete their conquest of China in 1279. Khubilai, who ruled from Peking over the main eastern domains of the Mongols, demanded Japan's submission in 1266. The Kyōto court was terrified, but the Hōjō leader haughtily refused.

Section of a picture scroll painted around 1293 depicting the Mongol invasion of 1274. It shows Mongol bowmen, a Japanese knight, and a bomb bursting in the air.

Finally in 1274 Khubilai dispatched a mixed Mongol and Korean force of about thirty thousand men from Korean ports to Hakata Bay in North Kyūshū. The local knights Kamakura mustered against these invaders were individually well armored and formidable fighting men, but the Mongols had much larger numbers, excelled at massed cavalry tactics, which had proved irresistible everywhere they had gone, and had superior weapons, such as catapults that flung gunpowder missiles. Before battle could be decisively joined, however, the Mongols sailed back to Korea in the face of unfavorable weather.

Khubilai renewed the attack in 1281, this time with a force of some 140,000 Mongols, Chinese, and Koreans, dispatched from ports in both China and Korea—probably the greatest overseas expedition the world had yet seen. Kamakura meanwhile had kept its retainers in western Japan on the alert and busy erecting a wall around Hakata Bay. With the aid of this wall, the defenders managed to keep the invaders contained on a narrow beachhead for almost two months, while smaller, more mobile Japanese boats played havoc with the Mongol junks. Then a typhoon struck, destroying much of the Mongol fleet and forcing the remainder of the Mongol force—perhaps less than half—to withdraw in defeat. The *kamikaze*, or "divine wind," of this typhoon has loomed large in the historical memory of the Japanese, confirming them in their belief that Japan was indeed a unique and "divine" country.

Early Feudal Culture

The Feudal Ethic.   The feudal period in Japan is sometimes viewed, as it is in Europe, as a dark cultural trough between an ordered antiquity and brilliant modern age, but this concept is quite incorrect. Not only did the Kamakura system provide a more efficient central control over all Japan than had existed before, but the whole economy stood high above earlier levels. Centers of paper making, iron casting, pottery making, and the like, spread more widely throughout the country, and there was a marked increase in trade with the continent. While the life of the court aristocrats became economically more constrained and culturally less creative, the culture they had helped develop spread much more widely throughout Japan. At the same time, the provincial warriors emerged as leaders in a vigorous new culture, quite different in some ways from what had preceded it and even further removed from Chinese norms than Fujiwara life had been.

This was particularly true in the field of ethics, as the warrior ethos contrasted sharply with the gentle but ostentatious aestheticism of the Fujiwara courtiers and the civilian, bureaucratic spirit of Sung China. The Kamakura warriors lived a life close to the land and to warfare. They were by profession leaders of the farming community and also soldiers. Life for them was simple and frugality a major virtue. Martial arts were all important—horsemanship, archery, and above all swordsmanship. They were proud of their armor and made a veritable cult of their swords. Bravery and the stoical acceptance of physical hardship were fundamental to their life style. All this required self-discipline and character building—concepts that became central to the whole warrior ethic. Death was preferred to surrender. The practice of suicide in defeat may have started to avoid torture, but it became institutionalized by the twelfth century as a matter of honor in the form of *seppuku,* or "disembowelment" (commonly known in the West as *harakiri,* "belly slitting"), which because of the lingering, painful death it produced demonstrated a warrior's disdain for suffering.

Loyalty was central to the whole system, because the feudal structure depended entirely on the personal loyalty of the vassal to his lord or to the group, when the lord was himself merely a symbol of group solidarity. In a society in which all status was inherited, living up to the honor and obligations of one's ancestry loomed particularly large. Strong emphasis was placed on fidelity to one's word and the concept of honor. A vassal owed his lord complete, unquestioning loyalty, even to death. He was to sacrifice his own family, if need be, for his lord, and sometimes did so. The contrast was marked with China, where the first loyalty usually remained to one's own family. But loyalty, of course, remained the weakest as well as the most critical link in the feudal system. Treachery was all too common at times of crisis.

The Japanese feudal ethic differed in some important ways from that of Europe. The bond of loyalty, for example, was seen not so much in legal or contractual terms, as it was in Europe, as in ethical absolutes. The difference may have been the result of the Roman emphasis on law in the West and the Chinese concept that good government is essentially a matter of ethical conduct—of moral example and absolute obedience. The Japanese also had nothing comparable to the Western cult of chivalry, in which women were regarded as weak, romantic figures to be courted and protected. In Japanese feudal society, women not only could inherit both property and positions in the system but were expected to demonstrate the same bravery, stoicism, and loyalty as their men. Another difference from feudal Europe was that the warriors, while often illiterate themselves, showed deep respect for scholarship and the arts. Probably because of the strong Chinese emphasis on writing and learning, warriors even in this age of the sword took pride in literary accomplishments or at least respected them.

This stronger emphasis on learning and cultural achievements together with the greater wealth and more effective organization of twelfth-century Japan, as compared with early feudal Europe of the ninth and tenth centuries, may account for the much greater transfer of the higher culture of earlier periods to feudal Japan. Many artistic and literary trends continued unchanged. But there was, at the same time, a sharp break in basic spirit between Kamakura Japan and earlier periods. Certain of the new elements in Japanese culture which first became clear in the twelfth and thirteenth centuries were to remain characteristic of Japan until the present day. The ethical code of the warriors has been an active force in Japanese society until recent times. The agrarian bias and the emphasis on loyalty, bravery, stoicism, frugality, and the martial arts of early feudalism all survived until modern times. So also did the cult of the sword and the concept that suicide was an honorable and admirable way out. While the world of the Fujiwara diaries and novels is so remote from modern Japanese as to be hardly comprehensible, the tales of the twelfth-century wars and the attitudes of Kamakura warriors are perfectly understandable and still strike responsive chords.

The Popular Faith Sects.   The early feudal period in Japan, as in Europe, was a time of religious fervor. There was a great resurgence of vigor in Buddhism, which led to the founding of a number of new sects, largely in revolt against the older, established sects. This religious awakening has commonly been interpreted as a pessimistic reaction to the decline of the old central government and the resulting military disturbances, which made people feel that the degenerate period of the "latter end of the law" had arrived and that only faith in the Buddha could bring salvation. But the ferment in Buddhism was probably more a sign of its spread to new classes and its further assimilation into Japanese life. The Pure Land doctrines of salvation through faith in the Buddha Amida had started to spread in the Fujiwara period but now achieved great popularity among the common people, who found this an understandable and attractive concept. At the same time, the rising warrior class found solace and support in the meditative aspects of Buddhism, known as Zen. It is significant that the new sects, unlike the older ones, which had been centered on the court aristocracy, were oriented toward either the lower classes or the warriors.

Feudalism is often viewed in retrospect as an extremely repressive system, but in twelfth- and thirteenth-century Japan it seems actually to have given the lower classes a more important and secure position than they had enjoyed before. In any case, the common man, who is almost nonexistent in Fujiwara literature, appears prominently in the picture scrolls and even in the literature of the Kamakura period, and in the faith sects of Buddhism he found a medium of self-expression. Commoners were among the religious leaders of these sects, and their message was directed primarily to the man in the street and paddy field. The leaders of these sects wrote in simple Japanese, rather than classical Chinese, the earlier language of Japanese Buddhism; they encouraged the translation of the scriptures into the vernacular; and they showed strong egalitarian tendencies in contrast to the aristocratic nature of the earlier Buddhist sects. Since salvation through faith was open to everyone—even women—all people were in a sense equal.

The first of the new sects was named the Pure Land (*Jōdo*) Sect for Amida's Pure Land Paradise. It was founded in 1175 by Hōnen (1133–1212). His emphasis on salvation through calling on the Buddha's name obviated the need for temples, priests, and rituals. The traditional sects were outraged and in 1207 managed to have Hōnen temporarily banished from Kyōto.

One of Hōnen's followers, Shinran (1173–1262), further popularized his ideas and carried them to their logical conclusion. He insisted that a single sincere utterance of the Buddha's name sufficed for salvation, condemned self-conscious virtue as undermining simple faith, verged toward monotheism in his concentration on the single Buddha Amida, discarded most of the scriptures, repudiated the monastic church, and encouraged priests to marry and lead normal lives among their congregations. His branch of the movement, in typical reformist style, grew into the separate True Pure Land Sect, or as it is usually known the True Sect (*Shinshū*). Its practice of marriage of the clergy spread in time to most sects, and it became the largest branch of Japanese Buddhism, followed by the Pure Land Sect. The Eastern and Western Honganji ("Temples of the Original Vow") in Kyōto are the impressive headquarters of the two main branches of the True Sect.

*A segment of a picture scroll of the late Kamakura period, depicting
the life of a popular Buddhist religious leader, Ippen Shōnin
(1239–1289).*

Another major sect of the popular faith movement was founded in 1253
by Nichiren (1222–1282), a man of humble origin from the Kantō. He
stressed the Lotus Sutra, rather than Amida, as the object of faith and
taught his followers to chant "Hail to the Lotus Sutra of the Wonderful
Law." His movement was fittingly named the Lotus Sect, but it came to be
known by his name as the Nichiren Sect. He was a passionate, street-
preaching revivalist, who harshly condemned all other types of Buddhism.
He predicted dire consequences unless the Japanese embraced his views,
and the Mongol invasions were seen as fulfilling his prophecies. He
showed a strong nationalistic bent, and his name, which means "Sun Lotus,"
can also be taken to mean "Japanese Buddhism."

It is worth noting that the popular faith sects developed striking parallels to Christianity, just when Japanese feudal institutions were producing
political and social parallels with Europe. One cannot but wonder if there
are some causal links between these respective institutions and beliefs. In
any case, the emphasis in the new sects on salvation through faith in a
single object of worship (either Amida or the Lotus Sutra) and an after-

life in a very definite paradise was much more similar to basic Christian concepts than to original Buddhism. The organization of the church around congregations rather than monasteries, the marriage of the clergy, the translation of scriptures, and the nationalistic tinge of Nicheren, all remind one also of Christian developments during the Reformation.

Zen.   Elements of Zen, the meditative type of Buddhism, had been present in Japanese Buddhism for centuries, but it was introduced as a sectarian movement at this time by monks returning from studies in China, where it had become the dominant form of the religion. Eisai (1141–1215) brought back from China the Rinzai Sect of Zen in 1191 and Dōgen (1200–1253) the Sōtō Sect in 1227. Eisai incidentally is also known as the introducer of tea to Japan.

Zen stemmed from one of the earliest and most fundamental aspects of Indian Buddhism, but in China it had also drawn on the native philosophy of Taoism, incorporating its emphasis on individual character and a closeness to nature, together with its anti-intellectual and antitextual bias. Zen stressed the transmission of truth from master to disciple (rather than through scholastic study), rigorous methods of meditation, strict discipline of character, individualistic independence of authority, and salvation in the more traditional Buddhist sense of enlightenment (*satori*) through self-understanding and self-discipline. In the Sōtō Sect the emphasis was on *zazen,* or "sitting in meditation," as a means of attaining *satori,* while in Rinzai a special emphasis was put on the *kōan,* an insoluble or even nonsense problem designed to jar the meditator into sudden intuitive enlightenment. While Zen's meditative practices made it seem quietistic, its discipline produced rugged individualists who could easily be men of action.

All this had a special appeal to the relatively untutored Kamakura warriors with their great need for stoicism and self-discipline. When Eisai, like Hōnen, was expelled from Kyōto, he won the patronage of the shogunate at Kamakura. In time five official Zen temples were established at Kamakura and at Kyōto, and these and other Zen temples became increasingly important as centers of art, literature, and learning at this time of declining cultural activity at the Kyōto court. Warrior leaders came to draw on the Zen priesthood for both scribes and high advisers, and they themselves sometimes retired to Zen monasteries when they wished to escape the pressures of secular life. In fact, the warriors as a whole seem to have drawn special spiritual and psychological strength from Zen, which contributed to the strength of character, firmness of will, and imperviousness to suffering on which they prided themselves.

Literature and Art.   The literature and art of the Kamakura period reflect the duality between a continuing but gradually waning court aristocracy

*Wooden guardian deity dating
from around 1200, at the
Kōfukuji,a monastery near Nara.*

and the rising warrior class. Some of the literary activity of the early feudal period was simply a continuation of Fujiwara literary trends. There was, in fact, a fresh revival of the overworked "short poem." The wandering monk Saigyō (1118–1190) proved to be one of Japan's greatest poets in this medium, while *The New Ancient and Modern Collection,* completed in 1205, was the greatest of the later imperial anthologies. Novels and diaries continued to be written, but the most famous prose work to emerge from Kyōto society was the *Record of a Ten-Foot-Square Hut*, attributed to Kamo no Chōmei (1151–1213) and describing his life as a recluse after he retired in disappointment from the court.

In contrast to the refined and gently melancholy works of the Kyōto courtiers, the tales of the exploits of the warrior class, which began to appear at this time, overflow with vigor and vitality. Even their language is different and much more modern, showing a heavy admixture of Chinese words and influences of the Kantō dialect. These stirring war tales, though historically accurate in broad outline, are full of imaginative detail. They had a great vogue at this time, often being chanted to the accompaniment of the lute, and they have remained immensely popular ever since and a major inspiration in later literature and drama.

The greatest of the war tales, dating probably from the early Kamakura period, is the *Tale of the House of Taira,* telling of the wars between the Taira and the Minamoto. Two shorter works of about the same time, the

Scene from the "Scroll of the Hungry Spirits," dating from the Kamakura period. It depicts souls damned to perpetual hunger, scavenging in the streets. Around them are ordinary citizens, including two ladies on the left and a monk in the center holding a rosary.

Tale of the Hōgen War and the *Tale of the Heiji War* treat these limited parts of the story, while the whole saga was reworked again in the middle of the thirteenth century as the *Record of the Rise and Fall of the Minamoto and Taira.* The *Mirror of the Eastland,* based largely on the official records of the Kamakura shogunate, is the major historical source for the period from 1180 to 1266.

The revived vigor of Buddhism was reflected in a second great flourishing of Buddhist sculpture, which drew heavily on the traditions of the Nara period. Unkei and other great sculptors produced marvelous life-like statues, while the religious fervor of the age is illustrated by the one thousand identical, many-armed images in the "Hall of Thirty-Three Bays" in Kyōto and the beautiful fifty-two-foot bronze Great Buddha erected in Kamakura in the middle of the thirteenth century.

The styles of painting of the Fujiwara period were continued, but the subject matter of the picture scrolls shows the influence of Kamakura society. War scenes are common, as in the scroll depicting the Mongol invasion and the three scrolls illustrating the *Tale of the Heiji War.* Many other scrolls illustrated the histories of monasteries, portrayed the lives of Buddhist saints, such as Hōnen, or revealed the terrors of damnation.

The Ashikaga Period

The Collapse of the Kamakura Shogunate.   A century after the victory of
the Kamakura military band, it was still sufficiently intact to rise magnifi-
cently to the Mongol challenge, but the strenuous defense efforts these
onslaughts necessitated put a serious strain on both the economic position
and the loyalty of Kamakura's retainers and thus accentuated internal weak-
nesses already appearing in the system. This was particularly true because,
unlike earlier wars, the Mongol invasions left no spoils to be divided
among the victors to renew their loyalty to the system.

As with most ruling classes, the Kamakura warriors over the years became more luxurious in their habits, despite repeated sumptuary regulations
issued by the shogunate. At the same time, their economic position tended
to decline. This was because the full status and duties of a vassal might be
inherited by all his sons, but his landholdings and income, which did not
increase, had to be divided among them. As the class grew in numbers, its
per capita income inevitably shrank, making it increasingly difficult for
some warriors to maintain the necessary equipment of a knight. Some
became so impoverished that in 1297 the shogunate issued an order can-
celling the debts and mortgages of its retainers. Such acts came to be
known as *tokusei*, or "virtuous government," but they had no lasting effect,
because they merely worsened the terms of borrowing for the retainers.

The passage of time also proved corrosive to the cohesiveness and the
personal loyalty on which the whole Kamakura system depended. It was
gradually undercut first by geographic spread and then, with each successive
generation, by the dimming of memories of the twelfth-century campaigns
in which the bonds of loyalty had been forged. Shared interests with other
local warriors began to loom larger than ties to distant Kamakura and its
purely symbolic shogun. Loyalty might be felt more strongly to personally
known local leaders, sometimes particularly prominent stewards, but more
commonly provincial protectors. Such local strong men gradually came to
form a new class of feudal leaders, occupying an intermediary position
between the shogunate and its retainers. The old nation-wide warrior band
was gradually being replaced by a large number of local leader-follower
groupings.

In 1333 the weakening Kamakura shogunate finally fell victim to these
divisive tendencies. The incident that destroyed the system grew out of the
ambition of the Emperor Go-Daigo (1318–1339) to keep the succession
in his branch of the imperial family (two rival lines had developed in the
second half of the thirteenth century) and to restore actual political power
to the emperors. When Kamakura attempted to force Go-Daigo to abdicate
in 1331, he launched a revolt, supported by the great monasteries of the

capital region and some local military leaders, such as Kusunoki Masashige, who by turning traitor to Kamakura and espousing Go-Daigo's cause won for himself the undying reputation of being the greatest of all Japanese "loyalists." The Kamakura forces captured Go-Daigo and sent him into exile, but various military groups, motivated probably by local rivalries and ambitions, joined the revolt. Go-Daigo escaped, and the Kamakura general sent to recapture him in 1333 suddenly switched sides, seizing Kyōto in the emperor's name. This man, Ashikaga Takauji (1305–1358), a prominent provincial protector of the Kantō, apparently wished to replace the Hōjō in power, but East Japan now erupted in revolt, and another prominent Kantō vassal captured Kamakura, destroying the Hōjō and their government.

During the next three years Go-Daigo sought to restore imperial control over Japan, recreating some of the old civil organs of government and assigning the leading generals to governorships. This brave attempt (known from the "year period" as the Kemmu Restoration) proved to be only an anachronistic interlude in Japanese feudal history. The clock could not be turned back to the age of Yoritomo, much less to the Nara period. No one, least of all a nonmilitary man, could control the many lord-and-retainer groupings into which the military class of Japan was dividing. When Go-Daigo sided with Ashikaga Takauji's rivals, the latter turned against the emperor, seized Kyōto in 1336, and set up a new emperor from the other line. Go-Daigo escaped and established a second imperial court at Yoshino in the mountains south of Nara. The more than half-century (1336–1392) that this rival court survived is known as either the Yoshino period or the period of the Northern and Southern Courts (*Nambokuchō*).

The Ashikaga Shogunate. Takauji took the title of shogun in 1338 and attempted to recreate a unified political system centered on Kyōto, but although his descendants did manage to retain the title until 1573, their shogunate was a far cry from that of Kamakura. In fact, it represented a distinctly different stage in the development of Japanese feudalism.

Unlike Yoritomo, Takauji had become shogun, not as the unchallenged leader of a triumphant, unified warrior band, but merely as the most successful among a number of ambitious military leaders. He and his successors never laid claim to the direct loyalty of the bulk of the warrior class, as Yoritomo had, but recognized that the warriors were in fact divided into many separate lord-and-retainer groupings. All they attempted to do was to extend their control over these lords. Actually they did not succeed even in this restricted effort. Their shogunate never achieved full military control over all Japan, and warfare remained endemic throughout most of the period.

The Ashikaga shogunate was at best an uncertain coalition of major

military families, which recognized only grudgingly the overlordship of the
Ashikaga. In theory these other families derived from the shogunate their
positions as protectors over one or more provinces, but in actuality their
power rested on the estates they themselves controlled and on the personal
loyalty of the lesser warrior families in their regions. They so fully appropriated local political as well as military authority that the practice of appointing civil governors was dropped. While these regional military leaders
were not full territorial lords like the *daimyō* of later times, they were
clearly their forerunners and have often been called "protector daimyo"
(*shugo-daimyō*).

The Ashikaga established a façade of centralized government, consisting
of various administrative and judicial boards, some of them the same at
least in name that Kamakura had used, but these and other administrative
organs were little more than an outward expression of the loose coalition
between the Ashikaga and some of the chief protector families, particularly
those of the central region around Kyōto. Some of these families were descended from the Ashikaga or related to them by marriage or by old bonds
of loyalty. Residing usually in the capital, rather than in their respective
provinces, these central protector families formed the inner core of the
Ashikaga shogunate, while more distant provincial protectors remained
peripheral and to a large extent independent of it.

An Administrator, traditionally drawn from one of three protector families, shared power with the shogun in Kyōto. Next to this post ranked the
head of the Retainers Office, drawn from one of four other families. At
Kamakura there was a Kantō Administrator, a post held by a branch of the
Ashikaga family, and in Kyūshū and the far north there were deputies
(*tandai*). Behind this formal structure of a centralized government, however, the realities remained very different. The Ashikaga depended for their
income on their own landholdings and such trade taxes as they were able
to impose around Kyōto, while their power rested on the balance of forces
they were able to achieve with their leading vassals.

The existence between 1336 and 1392 of the rival southern court of
Go-Daigo and his descendants at Yoshino opened the way for countless
local wars and vendettas between claimants to estates and local power,
fought in the name of one or the other imperial line. However, in 1392
the third Ashikaga shogun, Yoshimitsu (1358–1408), finally managed to
force Go-Daigo's line to return to Kyōto, with the promise that it would
alternate on the throne with the northern line—a promise that was never
fulfilled. Yoshimitsu had meanwhile been eliminating his most serious military rivals, and, with the defeat of the powerful Ōuchi family of west
Japan in 1399, his power was for the moment unchallenged. The next three
decades were the only period of real peace and stability during the whole
Ashikaga shogunate. The Ashikaga had in 1378 established their head-

quarters in the Muromachi district of Kyōto, and the period after the reunification of the two courts in 1392 is often called the Muromachi period.

The temporary order created by Yoshimitsu began to disintegrate after the death of his grandson in 1428. In 1439 the shogun joined with the Uesugi family of the Kantō in eliminating the Kantō branch of the Ashikaga and transferring the post of Kantō Administrator to the Uesugi. A succession dispute in the Ashikaga family led to the outbreak of open warfare in 1467 between two major groupings of the great families, led respectively by the Hosokawa and the Yamana. Known as the Ōnin War, this military free-for-all lasted until 1477, laying waste Kyōto and leaving the shogun and his government powerless vestiges of what had been at best only a partial restoration of central political authority.

The Kamakura shogunate had been a feudal, military government living within the shell of the old imperial government and landholding system, but Go-Daigo's bid for power had brought the warriors in force into Kyōto, where they contended for power and in the process all but destroyed the shell of civil government, while in the provinces they stifled central authority. Whatever central authority emanated from Kyōto was that of the shogunate rather than the imperial government. Already before the collapse of Kamakura, the stewards had so expanded their rights to the income from their estates that in many cases this income had become divided into halves which gave support respectively to the original Kyōto owners and to the local stewards. Under Takauji it became generally accepted that the provincial protectors had the right to half of the total income for military purposes, thus further cutting into the revenues received by the court and its aristocracy. This income continued to dwindle as the incessant wars of the Ashikaga period gave ample opportunity to local strong men to reduce the remaining property rights of the Kyōto aristocracy. Starved of sustenance, many of the old court families withered away, and the great main line of the Fujiwara family, split since 1252 into five branches named after the streets in Kyōto on which they lived or for their hereditary government posts, sank into political impotence, although it continued to occupy the chief civil positions around the throne until the nineteenth century. Even the imperial family, deprived of many of its estates as the result of Go-Daigo's unrealistic attempt to regain power, relapsed into political passivity.

Meanwhile the warriors had been consolidating family power. The constant warfare of the period necessitated a gradual shift from the Kamakura practice of dividing patrimonies to a system of inheritance of all or most of a family's holdings and authority by a single heir. Unlike primogeniture in European feudalism, in Japan the father retained the right to choose any of his sons as heir and, if lacking one, to adopt a son, who commonly was a son-in-law or a member of a collateral branch of the family.

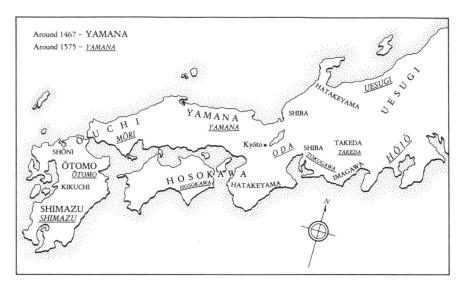

MAJOR DAIMYO OF THE 15TH AND 16TH CENTURIES

The Emergence of the Daimyo System. The Ōnin War of 1467–1477 proved to be merely the opener of a century of constant warfare unparalleled in Japanese history, but much like conditions in feudal Europe. Local wars raged all over Japan between rival claimants to land and local leadership. The Ashikaga shoguns lost all control over the provincial lords and became so enfeebled that the virtual deposition of the last of them in 1573 passed almost unnoticed. The period between 1467 and 1568 is appropriately called the age of the Warring States (*Sengoku*), and in its crucible of constant warfare was forged a new form of Japanese feudalism, most closely parallel to that of Europe.

The drastic decline of shogunal power merely reflected the rising power of local military leaders, who began to develop into true territorial lords in complete control of well defined geographic areas and populations. From this time on these local lords can properly be termed daimyo, though those of this century are often called the "warring states daimyo" (*sengoku-daimyō*), in contrast to those of a later and more peaceful age. Some of the daimyo families, such as the Shimazu of Satsuma in southern Kyūshū and the restored Ōuchi of west Japan, were the descendants of prominent old families, but many more were from newly risen warrior lines which had overthrown the local protectors in a process the Japanese have called "the inferior overcoming the superior." The provincial protectors proved to be very vulnerable during this time of constant warfare, because their authority commonly did not coincide in geographic extent with the lands and vassals that actually supported them, and these were often interspersed with lands and warrior groups not under their control. The emerging daimyo by contrast carved out clearly defined areas of complete control, and thus were less vulnerable to attack and better able to mobilize their forces.

In the process of consolidating their domains, the daimyo wiped out the last vestiges of the old estates and the remaining income these had paid to the court aristocracy. This plunged the imperial court and its aristocratic families into serious economic want. At times in the first half of the six-teenth century the court was so poor that it could not carry out even the most basic court ceremonies, such as enthronements. What income it had was largely derived from the largess of affluent military men or fees from Kyōto merchant groups seeking the supposed protection of the court's con-tinuing prestige.

As the estates disappeared, the peasant population became organized for the most part into semiautonomous, tax-paying villages. These were more natural and unified areas than the old estates had been, centering frequently on sources of water used in common for irrigation or on the ancient local shrines, some dating back to the *uji* period. These villages continued to serve as the chief administrative units of rural Japan up until recent decades.

The daimyo commonly drew up "house codes," which combined moral maxims with an outline of the basic laws and administrative system of their domains. All the military families in a domain had to be completely subservient vassals of the daimyo. The more important might receive from him their original lands or new ones as subfiefs, in which they could have their own "rear vassals." They held these subfiefs at their lord's sufferance, however, and, unlike the vassals of European feudalism, they did not hold allegiance also to another lord for other lands. The lesser warrior families became little more than a salaried officer class, administering the daimyo's domain and leading his armies. In part this change reflected a shift in military technology. Large bodies of foot soldiers (*ashigaru* or "light foot"), armed with pikes, had replaced the mounted knight as the backbone of military power. Warfare was no longer a matter of multiple individual combat but of massed soldiery.

A daimyo's prestige was measured by the size of the area he controlled and his wealth in terms of the rice production and tax yield of its villages. The daimyo also controlled and taxed the artisans and merchants in his domain and utilized the latter as the transport corps of his army. All re-sources were devoted to maximizing military power, and those domains that were most efficiently organized were able not only to flout central authority but to bite off pieces from their weaker neighbors or swallow them whole.

While the authority of the central government all but vanished during the period of the Warring States, it had been replaced by a much more complete and efficient administrative control at the local level than had ever existed before. To the Europeans, who first arrived in Japan in the middle of the sixteenth century, the daimyo appeared to be little "kings." Thus the daimyo domains were developing into firm building blocks out of which a much more solid centralized political structure could in time be constructed.

The daimyo domains that emerged during this century of warfare were of varying sizes, and some areas remained fragmented among a number of smaller warrior families. The great monasteries retained their extensive estates, protected by their own military men, and, with the growing importance of the common foot soldier in warfare, commoners, supported by petty local warriors, were also sometimes able to challenge feudal power. Rioting villagers and townsmen had begun to be a serious problem as early as 1428, sometimes forcing the cancellation of their debts under the name of "virtuous government" (*tokusei*). The town of Sakai, today a part of the great metropolis of Ōsaka at the eastern end of the Inland Sea, managed to develop a limited degree of autonomy. The adherents of the True Sect won military control over the province of Kaga on the west coast in 1488 and retained it for almost a century, while other members of this sect, commonly called the "Single Minded" (Ikkō) sect because of its religious fanaticism, were able to exercise military control over other smaller areas from time to time.

The protracted fighting and endless intrigues of the Warring States period has made it a romantic age, which has often drawn the attention of later authors and modern film makers. In the course of all this fighting, most of the great families of the middle years of the Ashikaga period, such as the Yamana, Uesugi, and the Ashikaga themselves, were eliminated by newly risen rivals or drastically reduced in power and wealth. The Ōuchi of western Japan were replaced in 1557 by their former vassals, the Mōri. The Hosokawa survived only through a distantly related line in Kyūshū. Of all the great military families of the early Ashikaga period, only the Shimazu in their remote fastness in southern Kyūshū survived to play an important role in later times.

High Feudal Society

Economic Growth. One might assume that the constant warfare of the Ashikaga period might have slowed or even reversed economic development, but this was not the case. In fact, political decentralization seems to have stimulated the economy. This was because the provincial warrior families and emerging territorial lords were naturally concerned with increasing local production and thus their own income or tax yield. Under this sort of locally-oriented political leadership, new lands were opened to cultivation, irrigation was extended, agricultural techniques were improved, and specialized local cash crops were increased. As a consequence there appears to have been a doubling or tripling of production per acre in parts of the country during this period. Specialization in economic functions also became more common, as the basic economic unit grew from the relatively small estate to the much larger local domain, and there was a great increase in handicraft production and of trade both locally and between regions. These stirrings of economic growth were already noticeable in the late thirteenth century but became much more marked in the fourteenth and fifteenth.

One clear sign of economic development was the proliferation of local markets, held once in each ten-day "week," under the patronage of influential shrines or temples or some local feudal leader. Another sign was the gradual appearance of trade towns at ports or around great religious institutions. The clearest sign of economic growth was the gradual shift between the twelfth and fifteenth centuries from barter to the use of money in trade. In the eighth and ninth centuries the Chinese-type civil government had, in imitation of China, issued copper coins, but the people had not become accustomed to their use. Now there was a genuine demand for money, and, in the lack of an effective central government to mint coins, these were supplied for the most part by importing copper cash from China, supplemented in time by paper money orders for the transfer of large sums. A money economy led to the develoment of pawnshops and other types of moneylenders, including Buddhist institutions. As we have seen, the indebtedness of the steward class had become so serious by late Kamakura times that the government ordered the cancellation of their debts, and similar debt cancellations were frequent in the Ashikaga period.

The many political authorities of feudal Japan were all eager to erect barriers to tax the trade that passed through their areas. To protect themselves against such multiple taxation and the other economic hazards of an unsettled time, the producers or transporters of certain goods, such as paper, salt, and the rice beer called *sake,* and the members of certain trades, such as carpenters or actors, grouped together into guilds (*za*), analogous to the medieval guilds of Europe. Under the patronage of a prestigious religious institution, the Kyōto court, or a local feudal authority, to which they paid fees, the guilds succeeded in establishing protection from extortion by other authorities and some degree of local monopoly under which their trade or profession could flourish. The center of industrial and commercial activity was Kyōto, which, despite the wars that ravaged it, remained a city of a few hundred thousand. As the feudal lords developed complete territorial mastery, however, the merchant groupings fell increasingly under their control, and the guild organization was gradually replaced by "official merchants" closely supervised by the daimyo and serving the needs of his government, thus setting the pattern of political control over economic activities that has remained characteristic of Japan ever since.

Overseas Trade. Unlike the countries of late feudal Europe, Japan lacked the economic stimulation of close neighbors, but, despite its relative isolation, international trade increased greatly during this period. Japanese traders had been venturing abroad since the eleventh century, and the casting of the Great Buddha of Kamakura in the thirteenth century seems to have been financed in part from foreign trade. Japanese merchant adventurers, whose activities often shaded off into piracy, were a scourge to the Koreans already in the early fourteenth century and a few decades later became a serious nuisance to the Chinese as well. Known simply as "Japanese pirates" (*Wakō*), these warrior-merchant adventurers from the coastal communities of western Japan often seized what they wanted when the restrictive trade policies of the Koreans and Chinese denied them the trade they sought.

The Koreans managed to lessen the pressures of Japanese piracy by making an agreement in 1443 for a generous flow of official trade—some fifty ships a year. The number was subsequently increased, and the Japanese were given the right to maintain permanent trading settlements in three port towns in southern Korea. The Ming dynasty in China after 1368 also tried to control Japanese piracy through official agreements. Yoshimitsu, after consolidating his control over the country, responded to Chinese requests by agreeing in 1404 to the sending of one official trade mission every ten years. To regulate this trade, the Chinese government issued booklets of tallies, which the missions were to carry with them. To fit into Chinese concepts of the world order, the Japanese traders were regarded as bearers of tribute to China, and the Ming issued to Yoshimitsu a patent as the "King of Japan" and "subject" of the Ming. Yoshimitsu's acceptance of this investiture has brought down on his head the uniform condemnation of Japanese historians.

The official tally trade never lived up to the expectations of either the Chinese, who saw in it a way to control Japanese piracy, or the Japanese, who were only seeking trade profits. The Japanese, instead of sending a mission once every ten years, seem to have sent six between 1404 and 1410 before breaking off the agreement. It was revived in 1432, and while only eleven missions went between then and 1549, many more ships went in each mission than were authorized, and these were in fact not under the control of the Ashikaga but were dispatched by Buddhist monasteries, Shintō shrines, and local lords. The Ōuchi family of west Japan actually captured the tallies in 1469 and thereafter controlled the official trade.

Meanwhile illegal trade and piracy expanded greatly, undoubtedly accounting for the greater part of the flow of goods between China and Japan. The records of the tally trade, however, give a good picture of the nature of this flow. Japanese exports were not merely raw materials, such as sulphur and copper, but also fine manufactured goods, such as painted folding fans, apparently a Japanese invention, picture scrolls, and especially the highly prized swords of Japan. No less than 37,000 swords are said to have been exported to China by the embassy of 1483 alone. In return Japan imported silks, porcelains, books, paintings, and, above all else, copper cash. The mission of 1453 alone is recorded as having brought back 50 million coins. Clearly international trade was becoming important in the economy of Japan, and the country, once so far behind the continent in technology, was drawing abreast of China.

Zen Culture. The great economic growth of Japan during the political confusion of the Ashikaga period was paralleled by a remarkable cultural flowering. This was the product of several factors: the fusion of the vigor of the warrior class with the refinement of the old Kyōto aristocracy, the merging of these traditional Japanese cultural flows with the philosophy and aesthetic attitudes of Zen, and strong new cultural influences introduced from China by Zen monks. Thus several hitherto distinct cultural streams flowed together, forming a strong new current which was to dominate Japan culturally until modern times.

The shogun's court in Kyōto was the center of this cultural activity, and the later shoguns are more renowned as cultural leaders than as statesmen or warriors. Even Yoshimitsu is best known for the coterie of artists, scholars, and literary men he presided over at his monastic retreat, the Golden Pavilion (Kinkakuji), which he built in 1397 in the Northern Hills (Kitayama) of Kyōto. The eighth shogun, Yoshimasa (1443–1473; died 1490), living after the Ashikaga had lost most of their power, was at least able to parallel Yoshimitsu's cultural achievements. In 1483 he built in the Eastern Hills (Higashiyama) of Kyōto his own monastic head-quarters, known as the Silver Pavilion (Ginkakuji). These two shogunal retreats have given the names Kitayama to the middle period of Ashikaga culture (1392–1467) and Higashiyama to the later phase (1467–1568).

Zen monks played a prominent role at the court of the shoguns, and official patronage was given to the five great Zen temples of Kyōto and Kamakura. The Enryakuji, the Tendai center on Mt. Hiei, and other great old monasteries remained rich and powerful, but they had become intellectually moribund and morally lax. Homosexuality, for example, was common, as it was among the whole warrior class of Japan. Meanwhile intellectual and cultural leadership had passed to the newer Zen monasteries. The Zen master Musō Kokushi (1275–1351) set the pattern by exercising great influence over Takauji and persuading him to erect a network of Zen monasteries throughout the country and to send a trading ship to China to raise funds for the building of a great monastery in Kyōto, the Tenryūji. Other Zen monks continued to serve as shogunal advisers, as chief intermediaries in the official relationship with China, and as drafters

The Silver Pavilion and garden built by Yoshimasa in 1483.

of the shoguns' messages to the Ming emperors. They also were the leading artists, scholars, and literary men of the day and often the arbiters of aesthetic taste.

The cultural dominance of Zen monks was so great that the whole culture of the Ashikaga period may appropriately be called Zen culture. Zen culture, however, is no more easy to define than is Zen philosophy. Words such as *yūgen,* "mystery," which the Japanese have commonly used to describe it, leave the subject still mysterious. Drawing on Zen philosophy and the associated arts that had been developed in Sung China, Zen culture blended these with the delicate sensitivity, impressionism, and love of form and ritual of the Kyōto court and the rugged strength of personality of the warrior tradition. The originally Taoist sense of man's identity with nature and the Zen desire for an intuitive understanding of the basic principles of the universe merged with the native Japanese sensitivity to the beauty and wonder of nature; the intuitive indirection of Zen fused with the Japanese tendency toward allusion and suggestion; and Zen and warrior discipline and restraint combined with the older Japanese love of form and ritual. The result was a disciplined tranquillity and sophisticated simplicity that bordered at times on self-conscious aestheticism. Universal truth and beauty were to be perceived through some small but carefully created symbol. The little was preferred to the big, the intimate to the impressive, the simple to the complex, the natural to the artificial, the old and misshapen to the new and perfect. The emphasis on the small and simple could degenerate into a snobbish pose of mock simplicity, but it admirably fitted the relative poverty of feudal Japan and significantly has a revived appeal today in Japan and also in the West in this more affluent and complex age.

Zen culture is perhaps best presented not by verbal description but in Zen fashion by example. The tea ceremony is one of the most characteristic expressions of Ashikaga taste. It is a gathering of a few lovers of art in a simple, bare room close to the beauties of nature. The tea is prepared in slow, graceful motions and drunk in similar fashion from a bowl—by preference a simple, seemingly coarse type of pottery. The bowl and other articles used are then admired and discussed. Spiritual calm is the effect produced as much as aesthetic appreciation. Developed in the course of the fifteenth century, the tea ceremony reached final shape under Sen no Rikyū (1521–1591). In modern times it has become embalmed as one of the social graces every well-bred bride should master. Flower arrangement, which emphasizes not the artificial, massed bunching of flowers, which is the Western tradition, but a naturalistic arrangement of a few flowers or sprigs, is a similar Zen art, which in modern times has undergone the same fate at the hands of mass society.

Art.   The greatest of the Zen arts was the Sung style of landscape painting, in which the artist seeks to portray the essence of nature by eliminating minor detail and accenting with bold brush strokes what he sees to be essential. Or, again, he may select some small aspect of nature to serve as a microcosm epitomizing the whole. In these paintings, man and his handiwork—temples, bridges, boats—usually appear as minor details, blending into the great pattern of nature. The Japanese Zen painters produced works hardly distinguishable from those of China, and yet, instead of being merely imitative, they are often great masterpieces themselves. The greatest of the Zen artists was probably Sesshū (1420–1506). (See page 68.) The hereditary Kano school of artists painting in this tradition stemmed from the

Autumn landscape
ink on paper by Sesshū
(1420–1506).

late fifteenth century and remained the dominant "official" school until the
nineteenth century.

Stately, heavy-roofed Zen temples were a common architectural expression of the Ashikaga period, but the smaller, lighter Silver and Golden Pavilions better typify the spirit of the time. These were closer to domestic
architecture, in which modern Japanese tastes were beginning to make their
appearance. These tastes showed a preference for natural wood finishes instead of painted interiors, and twisted tree trunks rather than artificially
shaped lumber. Thick rush floor mats called *tatami* were sometimes spread
over the whole floor area of each room, and the *tokonoma* was developing
into a standard feature of domestic architecture. This is a recessed alcove for
the display of one or at the most a few choice art objects, instead of the masses
of *objets d'art* which traditionally crowd Western rooms.

The fifteenth-century "rock garden" of the Ryōanji in Kyōto.

Most important was the emphasis on the setting of a building—that is, the surrounding garden. Landscape architecture, deriving originally from China, was developed in the Ashikaga period into one of Japan's most distinctive and today most influential art forms. The Golden and Silver Pavilions were really gardens graced by a single unpretentious building. The Zen temples all looked out on carefully planned and executed gardens. The effort was not to shape nature to fit man's propensity for geometric regularity, but to reproduce in small the untamed magnificence of nature. Musō Kokushi was one of the first great masters of landscape architecture in Japan and is credited with the beautiful Tenryūji gardens. The essence of the Zen spirit is perhaps to be found in the "rock garden" of the Ryōanji in Kyōto, in which nothing but a few rocks and well-raked white sand suggest the grandeur of a vast seascape.

Literature. Zen monks were less dominant in the literature of the Ashikaga period than in the art. This may have been because their writings,

A temple garden near Kyōto (the Sambōin of the Daigoji).

known as "the literature of the Five Monasteries," were largely in classical Chinese and therefore outside the mainstream of Japanese literature.

The Ashikaga period witnessed a reviving interest in ancient customs, early Japanese literature, and the history of Japan. The first critical and analytic Japanese history, the *Jottings of a Fool,* by the monk Jien, had appeared in 1220, and at the beginning of the Ashikaga period, Kitabatake Chikafusa, a warrior supporter of Go-Daigo, continued this tradition in the *Record of the Legitimate Succession of the Divine Emperors,* which championed Go-Daigo's cause and helped establish the nationalistic doctrine that Japan's unique superiority derived from its unbroken line of emperors. There were also stirrings in Shintō. The great old shrines, such as that at Ise, which had lost their financial support from the now destitute court, developed popular organizations of supporters who made pilgrimages to these shrines. A priestly family in Kyōto named Yoshida also developed in the fifteenth century a new syncretic Shintō philosophy, called Yoshida Shintō, which was based on forged texts claiming that Buddhism and Confucianism were derivatives from fundamental Shintō truths.

*Photograph of masked Nō actor performing a dance, with musicians
in back and the traditional pine tree painted on the back wall.*

Many of the literary trends of Ashikaga times were simply the continuation of earlier currents. *Grasses of Idleness* (*Tsurezuregusa*) by a courtier
named Yoshida Kenkō (1283–1350) was reminiscent of the *Record of a
Ten-Foot-Square Hut* of the Kamakura period. Similarly the *Record of the
Great Peace,* which tells of the endless warfare between 1318 and 1367,
was written in the manner of the earlier war tales. The *Otogi-zōshi* ("Com-
panion Booklets") were comic, romantic, or wondrous popular stories,
which had evolved from the Buddhist cautionary tales, historical romances,
and novels of the Fujiwara period. In poetry, the "chain poem" (*renga*),
in which two or more poets took turns composing alternate three- and two-
line units, were an outgrowth of the earlier "short poem." "Chain poems"
represented a further development of the Japanese tendency toward a subtle
and complex associative technique, and at the hands of masters they could
be sustained poetic efforts of much greater scope than the "short poems,"
but they could also degenerate into little more than word games.

The most significant and original literary development of the Ashikaga
period was the *Nō* drama. Earlier symbolic court dances and mimetic per-

formances among the people had evolved by the fourteenth century into simple plays, and these developed at Yoshimitsu's court into the Nō drama, chiefly at the hands of Kan'ami (1333–1384) and his son Seami (1363–1443). Nō is not unlike the drama of ancient Greece. It is performed on an almost bare stage by a chief actor and assistant, both elaborately costumed and masked, and perhaps a few subsidiary characters. There is always a chorus which fills in the narrative, and both actors and chorus chant their lines to the accompaniment of rhythmic, orchestral music. The librettos are largely in poetry or highly poetic prose. Action is restrained and very stylized, and the climax of the play is always a symbolic dance performed by the chief actor.

In presentations, Nō dramas were usually interspersed with comic interludes, called *Kyōgen,* or "Crazy Words," which were burlesques of contemporary feudal society. The Nō dramas themselves normally dealt with Shintō gods or famous figures in Buddhist or secular history. They often centered on the concept of salvation through faith of the popular faith sects, and the usual possession of the chief actor by the spirit of a deity or deceased person is reminiscent of the shamanistic mediums of ancient Japanese folk religion. Thus Nō is not specifically Zen in inspiration, but it offers a good example of the refined and disciplined spirit of Zen aesthetics and of the cultural creativity of the Ashikaga period.

3. Tokugawa Japan:
A Centralized Feudal State

Political Reunification

By the middle of the sixteenth century, certain changes were occurring in the Japanese economy and society that were similar to developments which are normally associated with the breakdown of feudalism in Europe. Domestic commerce and international trade were expanding rapidly; in fact, Japanese merchant-pirates not only ranged widely along the coasts of China but had become active throughout the waters and coastal communities of Southeast Asia. The functional line between warriors and peasants was being lost as a result of the development of massed foot-soldier armies. As a consequence, religious groups of commoners were able to challenge feudal rule in parts of Japan, while the old warrior class was becoming transformed into a professional military and administrative bureaucracy. The close ties of the aristocratic warriors to the land, which had characterized feudalism in both Europe and Japan, were disappearing, since the samurai, as the warriors were generally coming to be known, were being gathered by the various daimyo around their castle headquarters, while the peasantry was being organized into semiautonomous tax-paying villages, ruled directly by the lords. The multiple overlapping jurisdictions which had been common in earlier feudalism were also being eliminated as the political authority of the individual daimyo became more direct and absolute throughout his realm.

In Western Europe such conditions were accompanied by political centralization under the leadership of national kings at the expense of feudal institutions. In Japan a much more rapid and in some ways more thorough centralization of political power occurred in the late sixteenth century, but through the use of a basically feudal pattern. The daimyo domains, which had become quite efficient units of local control, were used to build a surprisingly uniform and solid national political structure. This use of long familiar institutions is perhaps one reason for the great speed with which the Japanese were able to create effective national unity after so many centuries of disruption. Other factors may have been the cultural and ethnic uniformity within Japan resulting from its isolated location, the strong tradition of national unity inherited from earlier times, and the whole East Asian assumption that a unified state was the natural setting for society.

Japan's centralized feudalism, while seeming almost a contradiction in terms from the point of view of the European feudal experience, proved to be an extraordinarily stable political system, which served well for almost three centuries. This long success was perhaps made possible because the relative remoteness of the islands permitted Japan to isolate itself from external pressures for most of the period. In any case, this apparently anomalous use of feudal institutions to create centralized political power constituted the third major stage in Japanese feudalism, contrasting with the single lord-vassal band of the Kamakura system and the constantly warring, multiple lord-vassal groupings of the Ashikaga period. Although the corresponding phase in European history was represented by the essentially postfeudal early modern monarchies, the Japanese did not necessarily fall behind in institutional development, despite their more old-fashioned feudal framework. Japan in the seventeenth century was perhaps more effectively united than any European state, and Japanese levels of efficiency in political administration and economic integration were probably not exceeded anywhere in Europe before the nineteenth century.

The Coming of the Portuguese.   While isolation helped make possible the long perpetuation of the centralized feudal system, international influences seem to have contributed initially to the reunification of Japan. Less than a half-century after the Portuguese had found their way around Africa to India in 1498, some of them reached Tanegashima, an island off the southern tip of Kyūshū, apparently in 1543. Two years later Portuguese traders started visiting west Japanese ports regularly, and in 1549 the famous Jesuit, Francis Xavier, initiated the Christian missionary movement in Japan.

The Portuguese, with their own feudal background, found the martial skills and sense of feudal honor of the Japanese more admirable than the traits of other Asian peoples they had encountered. The Japanese at first were not much attracted by Christianity, which seemed to them merely a variation of the popular faith sects of Buddhism. Nevertheless, they were eager for the profits of trade, and some Kyūshū daimyo, noting the respect of the Portuguese merchants for the Jesuits, showered favors on the missionaries in an effort to attract trade to their domains. A few, motivated perhaps by a desire as much for economic as for spiritual gain, embraced Christianity and forced the people in their domains to follow suit. The small Ōmura daimyo, who was converted as early as 1562, founded the port of Nagasaki on the west coast of Kyūshū and in 1571 made it the center of the Portuguese trade. In 1579 he actually assigned control of the town to the Jesuits. The much greater Ōtomo daimyo of northern Kyūshū was converted in 1578.

The religious intolerance of the missionaries soon stirred up opposition among the Buddhist clergy, and this in turn led to sporadic persecutions of Christians by the political authorities, but the religion spread rapidly in Kyūshū and also in the Kyōto area. In fact, the Japanese, with their consciousness of having learned much from abroad—that is, from China— proved more open to Western ideas as well as goods than were other Asian societies. Japan became the Jesuits' most promising missionary field in Asia, and it is estimated that there were 150,000 Japanese converts around 1582, some 300,000 by the end of the century, and perhaps as many as 500,000 in 1615, thus constituting a greater percentage of the population than Christians do today.

Eventually the bond between Japanese Christians and their loyalty to a distant, alien pope led Japanese leaders to view Christianity as a potentially subversive force. In a sense foreign trade too was disruptive to agrarian-based feudalism. Other aspects of the contact with the West, however, were probably more enriching and stimulating than disruptive. The trade brought new plants, such as tobacco from the Americas, and fascinating new goods, such as clocks and spectacles. There was a veritable craze for European things; modish Japanese sometimes even adopted European dress; and certain Portuguese words, such as *pan* for "bread," entered the Japanese vocabulary. Many of the painted folding screens popular in this period portray the strange foreigners and their ships. Since the Portuguese arrived in Japan from the south and seemed to the Japanese to be swarthy southerners, these paintings are called "Screens of the Southern Barbarians" (*Namban-byōbu*).

The greatest and most lasting European influence in Japan at this time proved to be on military technology, and through it on political organization. The arquebuses of the Portuguese were the first firearms the Japanese had encountered, but they immediately saw their value. Cannon were first used in warfare in Japan about 1558, and within two decades the firepower of musketeer corps had become the decisive factor in battles in the field. The richer daimyo who could afford the new weapons became still more dominant over their weaker and less modernized rivals and thus moved swiftly toward a consolidation of political power.

*Outer walls and gate (lower left) and inner walls and central tower
(upper right) of Himeji castle, west of Ōsaka, dating from the late
sixteenth century.*

Another result of European military technology was the appearance of
great castles. Stockades and little castles, which hitherto had been scattered
on strategic high points, were replaced by a single large central castle in a
daimyo's domain. Many castles of this type were built all over Japan in
the last quarter of the sixteenth century. They were more like sixteenth-
century fortresses in the West than like medieval European castles, consisting of concentric circles of broad moats and great earth-backed walls,
quite impervious to the cannonfire of the day. The castle buildings themselves were relatively flimsy, decorative wooden structures with white-
washed mud walls. Around the central castle were clustered the residences
of the daimyo's retainers and a commercial town, which was the economic
heart of the domain. Such sixteenth-century castle towns were the origin
of most of the great and middle-sized cities of modern Japan.

The Conquests of Oda Nobunaga and Hideyoshi.   Three successive military
leaders—Oda Nobunaga (1534–1582), Hideyoshi (1536–1598), and

Tokugawa Ieyasu (1542–1616)—building on each other's work, unified Japan and created the lasting pattern of centralized feudalism. Their technique was to develop a strong coalition of daimyo under their own hegemony, win control over the central capital area, with its imperial court symbolizing political legitimacy, and then extend their authority over the other coalitions of daimyo.

Oda Nobunaga was the heir of a newly risen minor daimyo in the area east of Kyōto around the modern city of Nagoya. In 1568 he seized Kyōto, ostensibly in support of a claimant to the position of shogun, but he drove this last shogun out of Kyōto in 1573, thus ending the Ashikaga shogunate. Protected on the east by an alliance with another fast-rising daimyo, Tokugawa Ieyasu, Nobunaga set about consolidating his power in the capital region, destroying in 1571 the Enryakuji, the great Tendai center on Mt. Hiei; forcing other centers of monastic power into submission; crushing various local daimyo; subduing the True Sect adherents of Kaga on the west coast; and finally in 1580, after a ten-year war, capturing the great castle headquarters of the sect in the modern Osaka. Nobunaga's long battle against Buddhist secular power led him to take a friendy attitude toward the Christians, thus permitting the phenomenal success at this time of the missionaries in the capital area.

Nobunaga confiscated the lands of those he conquered and either absorbed these into his own domain or assigned them to his vassal daimyo. He also centralized power more thoroughly. In 1571 he started a survey of the agricultural lands he controlled; in 1576 he began to confiscate the weapons of the peasantry; and he also standardized weights and measures. In 1576 he commenced construction of a great castle headquarters at Azuchi on the east shore of Lake Biwa east of Kyōto. Nobunaga did not succeed in asserting his authority over all of Japan, however. His armies were still locked in struggle with the Mōri of the extreme western end of Honshū when in 1582 he was killed in Kyōto by a treacherous vassal.

The leader of Nobunaga's armies against the Mōri was his ablest general, Hideyoshi. This man exemplified the rise of the nonaristocratic foot soldier, for he was of such humble origin that he had no family name by birth, though he later adopted the surname of Toyotomi. He had been appointed to be one of the four guardians of Nobunaga's heir, an infant grandson, but he soon managed to establish his own hegemony over Nobunaga's coalition of daimyo in central Japan and then set about eliminating the remaining daimyo groupings in the peripheral areas. In 1585 he subdued the island of Shikoku, and after an inconclusive battle in 1584, Tokugawa Ieyasu in the east accepted vassalage under him in 1586. The same year Hideyoshi invaded Kyūshū with an army of 280,000 men, forcing even the powerful Shimazu of the extreme south to accept his suzerainty. Then in 1590 he destroyed the Hōjō of the Kantō (a newly risen family not descended from the Hōjō of the Kamakura period). Meanwhile the Date of the Sendai area and the other great daimyo of the north had been overawed into submission. Thus by 1590 Japan had once again been reunited politically.

Like many successful generals before him, Hideyoshi dreamed of more worlds to conquer, which in East Asia meant, of course, China. He may also have been motivated by the practical objective of giving outlet abroad to the excess military spirit and power that centuries of incessant warfare had built up in Japan. When Korea refused his armies free passage, he dispatched to the peninsula in 1592 an invading force of 160,000 men— an army considerably smaller than those he had used against either the Shimazu or the Hōjō. The Japanese, with their firearms, quickly overran Korea but then withdrew southward in the face of massive Chinese armies. After long but unsuccessful negotiations, Hideyoshi renewed the war in 1597, but upon his death the next year, the Japanese armies withdrew precipitously. He himself never went to Korea but left the campaigns to his chief vassals. While the invasion had a devastating effect on Korea, it had little lasting influence on Japan, except for the technological and artistic stimulus of Korean porcelain makers and printers brought back to Japan by the retreating Japanese army.

Hideyoshi's Government.   Hideyoshi extended and systematized the methods of rule he had inherited from Nobunaga. Like Nobunaga, he did not take the title of shogun—he was considered ineligible since he was not of Minamoto descent—but again like Nobunaga he drew on the prestige and legitimacy of the imperial court and in return gave it far more generous economic treatment than it had received for some centuries. He managed to claim descent from the Fujiwara family and on this basis assumed in 1585 the old title of *kampaku*, used for a Fujiwara regent of an adult emperor.

Hideyoshi's actual authority, however, rested on his military might and the lord-vassal relationship with the daimyo. As the power center of his regime, he built a great castle on the site of the castle headquarters that Nobunaga had captured from the True Sect. Around this castle developed the port city of Ōsaka. He also built in 1594 a great palace for himself at Momoyama, a little south of Kyōto. His own extensive domains centered on these two headquarters and in the rich rice lands the Oda had controlled to the east in the Nagoya area. Around this central region were grouped the domains of his most trustworthy vassals, while beyond them in more peripheral areas extended the relatively large domains of the other daimyo who had more recently accepted his suzerainty. To assure his control over the daimyo, he kept their wives and heirs as hostages at his headquarters, and he moved some of the daimyo to new domains, where the common people would feel less loyalty to them. For example, Tokugawa Ieyasu was moved to the small village of Edo (the modern Tōkyō) in the Kantō, where he was given a huge domain confiscated from the Hōjō and their allies. Ieyasu's domain, in fact, was even larger in tax yield than that of Hideyoshi himself.

The organs of Hideyoshi's central government were at best rudimentary. Some of his vassal daimyo were assigned administrative titles and functions, but not until 1598, the year of his death, did he create a more elaborate system of three five-man boards made up of leading vassals. Hideyoshi's rule was basically personal and maintained by a heavy-handed threat of overwhelming military power. The daimyo domains constituted the autonomous units of local government and the supporting components of his armies. He did not tax them directly but forced them to bear heavy military burdens and the costs of his ambitious construction projects. Despite this seemingly decentralized system of local autonomy, he actually conducted himself as the *de facto* ruler of the country, demanding strict obedience from his vassal daimyo, controlling the major cities directly, regulating foreign trade by requiring his vermilion seal for overseas expeditions, and minting copper, silver, and gold coinage.

In 1585 Hideyoshi started a new cadastral survey of agricultural areas to ascertain and regularize tax yields. All lands were registered uniformly according to their productivity by *koku* (4.96 bushels) of rice. A daimyo by definition had to have a domain of at least 10,000 *koku* (49,600 bushels) yield.

As a man who himself had risen from the bottom of society to supreme political control, Hideyoshi was probably quite aware of how unstable this sort of social mobility could make a feudal system. He therefore drew a new and largely artificial class line between the samurai class and commoners. Families that remained active in agriculture in the villages, however aristocratic their origins, were classified as peasants and thus clearly separated from the professional military retainers who served Hideyoshi or his vassal daimyo. This distinction was reinforced by a nationwide "sword hunt," started in 1588, to deny the peasantry all arms. Hideyoshi also issued a series of laws designed to freeze the social classes, preventing military retainers from leaving their lords' service to become merchants or farmers and prohibiting farmers from deserting their fields to become merchants or laborers.

Hideyoshi was eager to maintain trade with the Europeans, but his desire for stability made him view Christianity with disfavor. He was suspicious that it might serve as the basis for subversive cooperation among the Kyūshū daimyo. In 1587 he suddenly ordered all the missionaries banished from Japan, although the order was not rigorously enforced, and he also commanded his vassals to secure his permission before embracing Christianity. The arrival of Spanish Franciscans in 1592 and their subsequent bickering with the Portuguese Jesuits further deepened his suspicions. So also did the close association of Christian missionaries and European soldiers in establishing colonial outposts, as in Manila in the Philippines. In 1597 he abruptly enforced his ban by crucifying nine missionaries and seventeen of their Japanese followers.

Nobunaga and Hideyoshi presided over one of the most exuberant periods in all Japanese history in terms of artistic expression and life style. In sharp contrast to Zen concepts of aesthetics, their tastes ran to the imposing and even gaudy. They built monumental and sumptuous castles and palaces adorned with elaborate carved or lacquered woodwork and sliding panels and screens decorated lavishly with gold leaf and bold paintings by the leading artists of the day. Even the "tea ceremony" Hideyoshi held in Kyōto in 1587 was a veritable public art festival, attended by thousands over a ten-day period and featuring art exhibits and dramatic and dancing performances.

The Tokugawa Shogunate

Ieyasu Founds the Shogunate.   Hideyoshi, like Nobunaga, left only an infant heir, Hideyori, whom he had placed under the joint regency of Tokugawa Ieyasu and four other of his leading vassals. Since Ieyasu was by far the most powerful, with a domain of 2,557,000 *koku* and no less than thirty-eight rear vassals of daimyo rank (more than 10,000 *koku*), many of the other daimyo began to look to him as their *de facto* lord, but a coalition of western daimyo resisted his domination. Ieyasu crushed his opponents in 1600 at Sekigahara in the low pass between the capital area and the plain around Nagoya, confiscated the domains of some eighty-seven daimyo, reduced the lands of others, and exacted written oaths of fealty from all who remained. Then in 1603 he legitimized his hegemony by having the court assign him the old title of shogun, thus founding the Tokugawa shogunate that was to last more than two and a half centuries until 1868.

Ieyasu permitted Hideyori to retain Ōsaka castle and a relatively large domain of 650,000 *koku*. He realized, however, that the heir of Hideyoshi constituted a possible rallying point for resistance. He therefore trumped up an excuse for laying siege to Ōsaka castle in 1614, renewed the attack in 1615, and seizing this stronghold, destroyed Hideyori and his supporters.

Warned by the inability of Nobunaga and Hideyoshi to pass on their power to their heirs, Ieyasu took steps to insure that his death would not lead to a quick transfer of hegemony to some rival family. In 1605, two years after assuming the title of shogun, he resigned in favor of one of his adult sons, Hidetada, chosen more for his steadiness than for his brilliance. Leaving the Edo castle to Hidetada, Ieyasu ruled Japan from then until his death in 1616 from the modern Shizuoka in the area where the Tokugawa had first arisen. Hidetada followed Ieyasu's lead by resigning the post of shogun in 1623 in favor of his adult son Iemitsu, who ruled as shogun until his death in 1651. Under these first three shoguns, the Tokugawa system of government took full shape.

Ieyasu and his descendants built on the achievements of Nobunaga and Hideyoshi, utilizing their basic method of ruling the nation through a tightly controlled coalition of ostensibly autonomous daimyo. They did not proceed to a more complete political unification of Japan, which their over-whelming military power might have made possible, probably because there seemed no need for this. Japan's geographic isolation secured it against serious foreign pressures, and Tokugawa power and prestige faced no chal-lenge at home. In fact, Ieyasu had gained by far the most complete and efficient control over all parts of the country that Japan had ever seen. In one sense, however, the Tokugawa system was regressive. It rested almost exclusively on agricultural taxes, whereas in the preceding centuries the ruling classes had increasingly drawn support also from commerce and even international trade. But the peace created by the Tokugawa made agricultural income adequate to the needs of government, at least initially.

The Daimyo System. The daimyo domains, which were known as *han*, fluctuated in number from 245 to 295 but tended to average around 265. They varied greatly in size from the minimal ones of 10,000 *koku* to 22 great domains of over 200,000 koku. During the seventeenth century in particular, *han* were sometimes confiscated, when a daimyo lacked an heir or was judged to have misruled, and many of the smaller daimyo were moved, together with their retainers, from one domain to another, thus receiving "promotions" or "demotions" in the size of their domains.

Tokugawa power centered in the shogun's own lands which constituted in a sense a super-daimyo domain. It grew to a whopping 6,480,000 *koku,* embracing about a quarter of the agricultural production of the whole country and somewhat more of its population. It was located largely in the Kantō, around Kyōto, and along the south coastal region in between. In addition the shogun directly ruled the major cities, such as Edo, Kyōto, Ōsaka, and Nagasaki, and owned the most important mines. His direct retainers, or samurai, were divided into two main categories. Some five thousand "bannermen" were senior retainers, the more important of whom held fiefs, although of less than daimyo size. The remainder together with some seventeen thousand lesser retainers, called *gokenin* or "honorable house men" as in the Kamakura period, received hereditary salaries. The government was based at Edo, where Ieyasu completed in 1606 the greatest of all the castles. Its outer moats made a rough circle two miles in diameter, and its inner portions still constitute the spacious and beautiful moats, walls, and grounds of the present imperial palace in the heart of Tōkyō.

The shogunal domain was buttressed by those of some twenty-three collateral Tokugawa families, known as "related *han*" (*shimpan*). Some of these were relatively large *han* which formed an outer line of defense. The three major ones, founded by three of Ieyasu's sons, were strategically situated east of Edo at Mito (350,000 *koku*), between Edo and Kyōto at Nagoya (619,500 *koku*), and southwest of Kyōto at Wakayama (555,000 *koku*). These three major collateral lines, known as the "Three Houses," were designated to supply an heir to the shogunal post if the main line ran out. Many of the other collateral daimyo were given the earlier family name of Matsudaira. Together the collateral lines controlled some 3,370,000 *koku* of rice produce.

Interspersed with the shogun's domain and the *han* of the collateral daimyo, but also scattered further afield at strategic spots, were the domains of the *fudai* daimyo ("house daimyo"), who were families first raised to daimyo status by Ieyasu or his successors and were for the most part descendants of men who had already been Ieyasu's vassals before his victory in 1600. Although the *fudai* grew to number 145, their domains were relatively small, and only one, the Ii, enfeoffed east of Kyōto, ranked as a great daimyo (originally 350,000 *koku*). The aggregate holdings of the *fudai* were about 6,700,000 *koku*.

A third category of daimyo was the *tozama*, or "outer" daimyo, the descendants of already established lords who became vassals of Ieyasu only after 1600. Some, such as Shimazu (770,800 *koku*), centered in the province of Satsuma in southern Kyūshū, and Mōri (369,000), centered in the province of Chōshū in western Honshū, had been his enemies at that time and continued a well-concealed tradition of hostility toward the Tokugawa throughout the period. Others, like Maeda at Kanazawa in Kaga on the west coast, the largest of all the daimyo (1,022,700 *koku*), had been his allies. The "outer" daimyo declined gradually to ninety-seven in number, but their domains were mostly large, totaling around 9,800,000 *koku*. Almost all were located in the peripheral parts of Japan in the north or in the west, where they would be less of a menace to the great central power block of the Tokugawa.

The bulk of the retainers of the daimyo, like those of the shogun, were salaried, but the more important ones were enfeoffed. In some peripheral domains, there was a class of petty "village samurai," who were self-supporting farmers. Most samurai, however, were gathered at the daimyo's headquarters.

The daimyo were in theory autonomous within their domains and free of taxation by the shogun's government. In actuality, however, they bore heavy financial burdens, and their freedom of action was severely constrained. As in Hideyoshi's system, they had all the responsibility for local

A two-page woodblock print of a daimyo (in a palanquin) and his entourage passing the gate of a daimyo mansion on the way to the shogun's castle on New Year's Day. In the foreground is the head of another procession. The traditional pine and bamboo decorations in front of the gate are still displayed at New Year's. The text at the top is a poem in good classical Chinese describing the scene. From Illustrations of Famous Places in Edo *(Edo meisho zue), printed in 1834 and 1836.*

government, were required to provide component parts for the shogun's army, and were repeatedly called upon for expensive construction services, such as the building of the Edo castle. They might be punished by the diminution or confiscation of their domains if they were judged guilty of disloyalty or serious misgovernment. Edo's laws were considered the supreme law of the land. In 1615 Ieyasu issued a code, revised in 1635, called *Laws for the Military Houses,* which regulated the lives of the military class, limited the military establishments and fortifications of the daimyo, prevented them from entering into alliances with one another, and set up many other restrictions on their activities.

The Tokugawa sought to bind the major daimyo families to them through marriage, but their chief methods for insuring the loyalty of their vassals were two old feudal institutions: the holding of hostages and periodic attendance and service of the vassal at the lord's court. From the start the daimyo had voluntarily sent their wives and heirs to Edo as hostages, and this system was made mandatory in 1633. Barriers on the roads

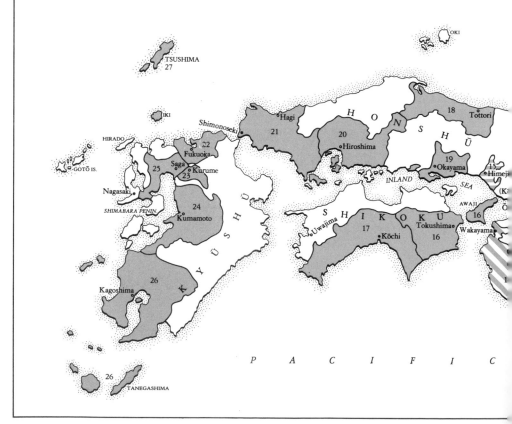

1 TSUGARU	15 SAKAKIBARA
2 SATAKE	16 HACHISUKA
3 NAMBU	17 YAMANOUCHI (TOSA)
4 SAKAI	18 IKEDA
5 DATE	19 IKEDA
6 UESUGI	20 ASANO
7 HOSHINA (MATSUDAIRA)	21 MŌRI (CHŌSHŪ)
8 TOKUGAWA (MITO)	22 KURODA
9 MAEDA (KAGA)	23 ARIMA
10 TOKUGAWA (OWARI)	24 HOSOKAWA
11 MATSUDAIRA (ECHIZEN)	25 NABESHIMA (HIZEN)
12 II (HIKONE)	26 SHIMAZU (SATSUMA)
13 TŌDŌ	27 SŌ
14 TOKUGAWA (KII)	

MAJOR DAIMYO DOMAINS

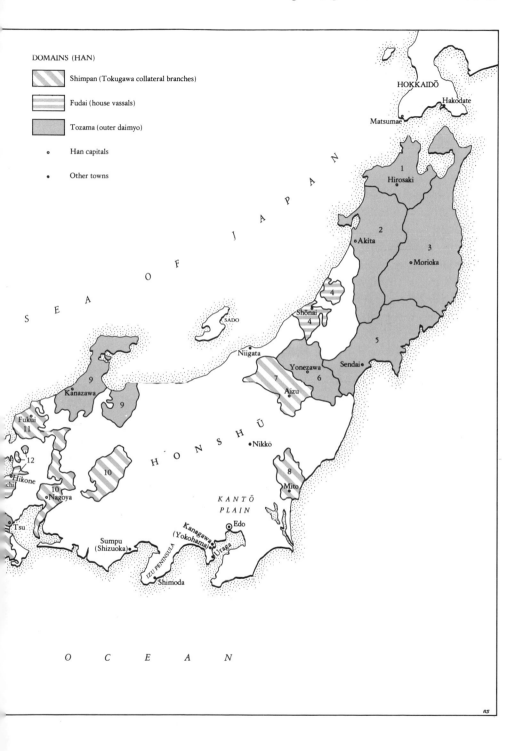

DOMAINS (HAN)

Shimpan (Tokugawa collateral branches)

Fudai (house vassals)

Tozama (outer daimyo)

o Han capitals

• Other towns

HOKKAIDŌ

Hakodate

Matsumae

S E A   O F   J A P A N

1
Hirosaki

2
Akita

3
Morioka

SADO

4

Shōnai
4

5

Niigata

Yonezawa

6

Sendai

7
Aizu

9
Kanazawa

9

Fukui
11

12

Hikone
chi

10

10
Nagoya

H O N S H Ū

Nikkō

8
Mito

Tsu

KANTŌ
PLAIN

Sumpu
(Shizuoka)

Kanagawa
(Yokohama)

Edo

Uraga

IZU PENINSULA

Shimoda

O   C   E   A   N

RS

leading into Edo kept a watch for women leaving the city or guns entering, for either might signify a plot against the regime. Attendance by the daimyo at the shogun's court also started on a voluntary basis but was made into a rigid compulsory system after 1635. Called "alternate attendance" (*sankin kōtai*), this system required most daimyo to spend alternate years in Edo.

Both the hostage and the "alternate attendance" systems required each daimyo to maintain one or more costly residences in Edo. Daimyo processions going to or from Edo, sometimes consisting of several thousand people, became a colorful feature of the time, especially along the Tōkaidō, the great coastal road between Kyōto and Edo. The large expenditures for these expeditions and for the Edo residences of the daimyo, often amounting to more than half of a daimyo's income, seriously weakened the daimyo financially, making revolt all the less probable. Long residence in Edo also transformed the daimyo families over time from local warriors into courtiers, further lessening their threat to the regime. And the constant flow of a large proportion of the ruling class between Edo and the provinces created a greater degree of cultural, intellectual, and ideological conformity in Japan than any other country in the world could boast before the nineteenth century.

The Shogun's Government.   The shogunal government, or *bakufu,* had a double function: it administered the shogun's super-domain, and it also controlled the daimyo and set national policy, ostensibly in behalf of the emperor's civil government in Kyōto. The Tokugawa treated the emperor generously and with respect, as the ultimate source of their own legitimacy, but maintained a firm control over his court. The palace was rebuilt, and the emperor and his nobles were assigned 187,000 *koku* in support. In 1615 Ieyasua promulgated a code of laws for the court and its nobility which made clear their purely symbolic and cultural role and gave the shogunate control over all court appointments. A Kyōto Deputy and garrison were established at the Nijō castle in Kyōto to assure Edo's mastery over the situation there and in west Japan.

The shogun's own government was staffed by the *fudai,* or "house," daimyo and his personal retainers. Positions were assigned in accordance with family status, but within these bounds men were selected for their talent, and exceptionally able or favored administrators were occasionally promoted in both post and feudal status. At the top were two councils. The senior one, called the "elders," which was usually made up of from four to six larger "house" daimyo, had authority over national affairs, including the control of the daimyo and the court. The "elders" took monthly turns as officer in charge, and one of the group in time came to be recognized as the head of the council, but the post of Great Elder, a sort of prime minister, was usually filled only in time of crisis. The junior council, called the "young elders," also consisting usually of from four to six smaller "house" daimyo, had charge of the shogun's "bannermen" and lesser retainers, the shogun's own military forces, and his household staff.

Beneath these councils was a great proliferation of offices, usually headed in typical Japanese fashion by paired officials or a group who shared responsibility and power. Chamberlains exercised considerable influence at the shogunal court, especially in the middle years of the Tokugawa. Four Commissioners of Finance supervised the income of the shogunate and oversaw the work of the forty-odd intendants who administered and collected taxes from the shogun's domain. Four Commissioners of Temples and Shrines supervised the Buddhist monasteries and Shintō shrines of the land, whose total holdings had been reduced to a mere 600,000 *koku*. Paired Town Commissioners controlled each of the major cities, and those at Nagasaki supervised foreign trade as well. Four inspector generals and lesser inspectors checked on the activities of the daimyo and served as police officers. Some slight degree of order was given to the jumble of laws and edicts issued over the years by occasional codifications, which had become necessary by the middle of the eighteenth century.

The daimyo domains tended to mirror the shogunate both in administrative organization and in laws. A daimyo's chief retainers, usually called "house elders," constituted a top council, and lesser samurai occupied the middle and lower posts in the system, first in accordance with their specific family status and only secondarily in accordance with their abilities.

Social Classes. The Tokugawa followed Hideyoshi's lead in seeking to insure political stability by limiting social mobility. The Chinese concept of a natural social order consisting of a clear hierarchy of classes proved useful in imposing artificial limitations on social change. The Tokugawa, in fact, adopted the ancient Chinese theory that there were four natural classes, which in descending order were: 1) the warrior-bureaucrats, in place of the scholar-bureaucrats of China; 2) the peasants or primary producers; 3) the artisans or secondary producers; and 4) the merchants, whose contribution to society was least valued.

The highest of the four recognized classes consisted of the shogun, daimyo, and their retainers. The daimyo fell into categories by origin and wealth, and the retainers into a great number of levels running from richly enfeoffed "house elders" and "bannermen" down to common foot soldiers with only subsistence salaries. All had specific hereditary status and incomes which were changed only under unusual circumstances, and they occupied posts in the shogunal or *han* governments commensurate with their hereditary status, from high councilors down to gate guards. Together they constituted around 6 per cent of the total population—a far higher percentage than that of the feudal aristocracy of Europe. Many samurai were in income and function hardly aristocrats, but they all felt great pride in their status, symbolized by the wearing of two swords, one long and the other shorter. Any samurai was considered to be far above any commoner and at least in theory had the right to kill a disrespectful commoner on the spot.

The line between the samurai and commoners was strictly maintained, but below it class lines were largely theoretical. Artisans and merchants were not really differentiated and tended to form a single "townsmen" (*chōnin*) category. The concept that the merchants were the lowest class of society was patently absurd, because many were men of great wealth, and increasingly this group took the lead in cultural life. Peasants were by function distinct from townsmen but commonly migrated to the city or engaged in artisan or merchant activities in the countryside. Village society was divided between leading, land-owning families, often the descendants of former warrior lines, which were usually in control of the autonomous village governments, and humbler peasants who had little or no land of their own. Agricultural taxes were high—up to 40 to 50 per cent of the yield—but, since these supported not just the shogun and daimyo and their administrations but the whole broad samurai class, they are not to be compared to taxes in other societies where the upper classes derived their income from resources other than taxes.

Outside of the theoretical four-class system existed the tiny group of court aristocrats, a much larger category of Buddhist monks and Shintō priests, and a group of "outcasts" (known as *eta*) at the bottom of society, who are best compared to the "base people" of Korean history. Living largely in the Kyōto area and west Japan, these "outcasts" constituted around 2 per cent of the population. They seem to have originated in pre-Tokugawa times from persons defeated in warfare, criminals, and groups whose professions, such as butchery or leatherwork, were considered demeaning, since they violated Buddhist dictates against the taking of animal life.

At all levels of society the family (or "house," *ie*), rather than the individual, was considered the basic unit, carrying with it not just property rights but specific social status, which the individual family head simply fulfilled. Most families were grouped into administrative units. Among the lower samurai these were functional groups, and among peasants and sometimes townsmen they were groups of mutual responsibility for taxes and legal liability.

Forcing all people into the rigid Tokugawa social mold was not easy after the social fluidity and confusion of the sixteenth century, and frictions developed, especially at the points of contact between classes. Particularly troublesome was the problem of members of the samurai class who had lost their specific niches in the system, perhaps through the elimination of their lord, or through a failure to fit in, because of personality or inclination. As late as 1651 such masterless samurai, known as *rōnin* ("wave men"), were the center of a plot against the shogunate.

Isolation. The Tokugawa might not have been able to maintain so stable a system of rule or such great social rigidity if they had not also isolated Japan from the upsetting foreign influences that had poured in during the sixteenth century. Actually Ieyasu, like his predecessors, was eager for commerce with the outside world. He tried to persuade China to agree to official trade through licensed ships and, when frustrated in this effort, created instead in 1604 a government-supervised monopoly in Chinese silk. Desirous of attracting European trade to his home region, he allowed the Spanish Franciscans to establish a mission at Edo. He also permitted the Dutch in 1609 and the English four years later to set up trading posts at Hirado, an island off the northwest coast of Kyūshū. He learned from these nonproselytizing Protestants and also from his foreign trade adviser, Will Adams, an English pilot of a Dutch vessel stranded in Japan in 1600, that there were Europeans who were perfectly ready to trade without conducting missionary activities.

Like Hideyoshi, Ieyasu viewed Christianity as essentially subversive, and as early as 1606 he started issuing anti-Christian decrees. His successor, Hidetada, banned all missionary activity in 1612 and commanded the "house" daimyo and all people in the shogun's domain to renounce the religion. In 1614 a minor Christian daimyo was exiled to Manila and more than two-thirds of the 156 European missionaries then in the country were expelled, although more continued to slip in. Four missionaries were executed in 1617 and 120 missionaries and converts in 1622. The daimyo were forced to join in the persecution, including even the great Date of the North, who had sent a large mission to the papacy by way of Mexico in 1613. By 1629 it had become customary to force suspected Christians to step on some Christian symbol, such as a bronze plaque portraying Christ or Mary, and to execute or force into apostasy through torture those who refused to step on this "treading picture" (*fumi-e*). The Catholic church recognizes 3125 martyrdoms in Japan between 1597 and 1660.

The persecution of Christianity came to a climax in 1637–1638 when some twenty thousand Christian peasants, supported by "masterless samurai," rose in revolt in western Kyūshū because of oppressive taxation. They fended off a much larger shogunal army from an old castle on the Shimabara Peninsula but were finally crushed and slaughtered. Except for the survival of a few isolated communities of crypto-Christians, the Shimabara revolt marked the virtual end of Christianity in Japan. Starting in 1640, all Japanese were forced to register at local Buddhist temples as a means of keeping check on their religious affiliations.

The fury of the anti-Christian persecution, together with the Tokugawa policy of closely regulating foreign trade as part of their control system, eventually carried the shogunate into almost complete national isolation. In 1616 European ships were limited to the two ports of Nagasaki and Hirado, and in 1623 the English gave up their trading contacts with Japan as unprofitable. The next year the Spanish were expelled because of complicity in missionary activities. In 1635 all Japanese were prohibited on pain of death from going abroad or from returning home if already overseas, for fear that they might bring back Christian doctrines. To help enforce this ban, a prohibition was placed on the building of ships of more than 500 *koku* capacity, thus limiting Japan to smaller vessels suitable only for coastal transport. These measures brought to a sudden halt more than a century of tremendous overseas activity and left large groups of Japanese traders and fighting men stranded throughout Southeast Asia, to be absorbed into the native populations. A single Japanese community in the Philippines is said to have numbered three thousand in the early seventeenth century.

As an aftermath of the Shimabara revolt, the Portuguese were expelled in 1639, and their envoys were executed when they returned the next year. This left only the Dutch among the Europeans still trading with Japan, and their representatives were moved in 1641 from Hirado to the tiny island of Deshima in Nagasaki harbor, where they were kept as virtual prisoners. Chinese merchants were also allowed to trade at Nagasaki, but under strict controls. Two other foreign trade contacts were also permitted—one with Korea through the Sō daimyo of Tsushima, the islands in the straits between the two countries, and the other by way of "tributary" missions to China from the king of Ryūkyū (Liu-ch'iu in Chinese, and now known as Okinawa), the island chain stretching south of Kyūshū, which the Shimazu daimyo of Satsuma had subjugated in 1609 and made a closely controlled vassal domain.

Substantial amounts of silver and copper and later dried marine products were exported through Nagasaki in return largely for Chinese goods, but this trade had relatively little effect on the Japanese economy as a whole. While Chinese intellectual influences through imported books remained strong, all other foreign influences were virtually eliminated. Political and social pressures from abroad were reduced to zero, and a strict ban was maintained on all Western books and on Chinese books mentioning Christianity. The isolation of the country, although artificially created and maintained, was perhaps more complete than it had been in any period since primitive times. Through the Dutch and Chinese at Nagasaki, the authorities kept watch on developments in the outside world, but for most practical purposes Japan developed over the next century and a half almost as if the rest of the world did not exist.

In this cocoon-like isolation, the hitherto rapid rate of technological, political, and social change that had marked the sixteenth century slowed down precisely at the time when change was accelerating in the West. The Japanese, who had been technologically and institutionally abreast of the Europeans in many respects and ahead in some at the start of the seventeenth century, fell drastically behind. This might be viewed as a national tragedy for which the Japanese paid bitterly in their frenetic efforts to catch up in the nineteenth and twentieth centuries. At the same time, the Tokugawa period was a time of great cultural creativity. By turning inward on their own resources, the Japanese had a chance to develop fully their own identity and culture, producing in the process distinctive personality traits, social skills, and artistic achievements that constituted an invaluable national heritage.

Social and Economic Development

The Transformation of the Samurai Class.   The pattern of social organization and political rule that had been established in the first half of the seventeenth century hardened into well-accepted practice by the end of the century and continued with only minor modifications until the middle of the nineteenth century. For exactly two and a quarter centuries after the suppression of the Shimabara revolt in 1638, there was no significant political change or any warfare in Japan—only occasional riots by villagers or townsmen or perhaps a political assassination. This was probably the longest period of complete peace and political stability that any sizable body of people has ever enjoyed. And yet it was a time not of stagnation but of very dynamic economic and cultural growth. After centuries of warfare and disunity, peace alone proved a strong stimulus to change, as did also the thorough centralization of controls that the Tokugawa had instituted.

The impact of peace and political unity was felt perhaps most strongly by the samurai class itself. To rule a land at peace, the Tokugawa needed educated administrators more than rough soldiers. The writing brush replaced the sword as the chief implement of the samurai, as they rapidly evolved from a body of fighting men into an urbanized class of well educated bureaucrats and petty government functionaries. Numerous enough to have furnished the mass armies of a country in constant civil war, they provided in time of peace a superabundance of would-be administrators, which proved a needlessly heavy burden on government finances.

The samurai remained organized for the most part into military units and made a fetish of their two swords, but warfare had become a matter of theory, not practice. Schools were founded in the various domains to teach the military arts, but gunnery and the use of firearms, which had proved the decisive military techniques, were largely ignored in favor of the medieval military disciplines of swordsmanship and archery, which were favored for their character-building qualities as much as for their military value. From this grew the emphasis on other character-building martial arts, such as the wrestling-fighting technique of *jūdō* and its modern variant *karate*.

The samurai value system, which had been a natural outgrowth of a feudal warrior society, gradually became transformed into a self-conscious philosophy. The feudal ethical principles of unquestioning loyalty to one's lord, fierce defense of one's own status and honor, and strict fulfillment of all obligations became codified as *Bushidō*, the "Way of the Warrior." Social realities, however, were moving away from the feudal conditions that had created this value system, as is illustrated by the prohibition in 1663 of suicide by retainers in order to "follow their lord in death." The famous incident of the "Forty-Seven *Rōnin*" of 1702 illustrates the same point. A minor daimyo, humiliated by a shogunate official, drew his sword within the Edo castle, for which offense he was forced to commit suicide and his domain was confiscated. His retainers, now made "masterless samurai," disarmed official suspicion by two years of dissolute living but then fulfilled the medieval code of ethics by assassinating the Edo official in vengeance for their lord. The public was thrilled, and the event became Japan's favorite dramatic theme, but the authorities coldly forced the forty-seven to commit suicide. Law and order triumphed over loyalty.

Confucianism. As the samurai turned increasingly into a hereditary civil bureaucracy, Confucianism, which in China had developed into the philosophy of a bureaucratic ruling class, began to take on a new meaning and an increased appeal. In a country at peace, the Confucian concept of political leadership as dependent not so much on brute military force as on ethical example and moral suasion became important. It was largely through Confucian learning that the rude warrior class of the beginning of the seventeenth century was transformed by the end of the century into a literate officialdom, deeply steeped in ethical precepts.

Confucianism had been considerably reworked and amplified in China by a series of philosophers during the Sung dynasty (960–1126), and this Neo-Confucianism had been introduced to Japan by Zen monks. Fujiwara Seika (1561–1619), however, forsook Buddhist orders to become Japan's first lay Confucian philosopher, and his disciple, Hayashi Razan (1583–1657), served as an adviser to Ieyasu on legal and historical matters. In 1630 the Hayashi family founded a school at Edo which grew into the official Confucian University under its hereditary leadership. Similar Confucian schools were also founded in many of the domains. Together they helped spread the Chinese concept of an essentially secular society, based on a natural, moral order, and epitomized by a centralized state, administered by an educated, ethically upright bureaucracy.

The Confucian emphasis on filial piety and loyalty and its concepts of a hierarchy of classes fitted early seventeenth-century Japan, but there was nonetheless a basic clash between the military, hereditary origins of the samurai class and the civil, bureaucratic ideal of government imbedded in Confucianism. This heightened the tensions already developing between the feudal value system the samurai had inherited and the social and political realities in which they operated. Confucianism emphasized centralized, imperial, civil rule, rather than a feudal, military hegemony, which was the origin of the Tokugawa system. It stressed uniform bureaucratic relationships in government, rather than the personal bonds of loyalty on which feudalism was based. It maintained that individual learning and moral excellence were the qualifications for political leadership, not hereditary status.

The resulting tensions were perhaps in part disruptive but in more ways creative. Confucian concepts provided an alternate pattern of political organization to the shogunate, which contributed to the transformation of Japan during the nineteenth century. They helped Tokugawa society move slowly toward the recognition of personal merit as well as family status. Most official posts came to carry specific salaries in addition to the incumbent's hereditary stipend, and in time a system of supplementary stipends was developed to permit particularly able administrators to qualify in status and income for higher posts. Despite these relaxations of the hereditary system, however, demands for recognition of merit over birth grew toward the end of the period.

The conflict between Chinese political and philosophic principles and Japanese social realities may help explain the development in Tokugawa society of greater pressures on the individual for conformity and stricter and more artificial rules of conduct than existed in China. These in turn may account for the tenseness that seems to characterize Japanese personality and the great Japanese emphasis on self-discipline and will power. In any case, whatever the causes, the Japanese of the Tokugawa period seem to have developed an extremely strong sense of honor, duty, and obligation and a dogged determination to live up to all that society expected of them. These qualities gradually spread from the samurai to other classes. The mixed feudal and Confucian values of the Tokugawa period thus left Japan a legacy of extraordinary formalism and rigidity on the one hand but also of strong inner discipline and personal drive on the other.

The contradictions between Confucian ideas and the inherited Japanese tradition may also have helped keep Japanese thought from becoming as limited by an official orthodoxy as happened in China and Korea. The multiplicity of locally autonomous regimes, of course, was another important reason for intellectual diversity. The Chu Hsi (Shushi in Japanese) school of Neo-Confucianism was established as orthodoxy by the shogunate, but heterodox Confucian schools also flourished, as well as much pragmatic economic and scientific thought.

Shintō too continued its role in the life of the people through the great historic shrines and the many small local ones with their periodic festivals. The Tokugawa even added a major cult of their own. Ieyasu's spirit was enshrined by his grandson Iemitsu in a great complex of shrines and temples set in a magnificent setting of giant cryptomeria trees at Nikkō on the northern edge of the Kantō Plain.

Buddhism also had its place. The anti-Christian edict of 1640 forced all Japanese to register as parishioners of some local Buddhist temple, which also performed for them such rites as marriages and funerals and maintained the family graves. The shogun and daimyo also built and patronized new Buddhist temples in their respective capitals. Today's parks at Ueno and Shiba are the vestigial remains of the chief shogunal temples of Edo. The unifiers of Japan, however, had drastically reduced the wealth and political power of the Buddhist church, and the shift of interest of the samurai class to Confucianism now robbed Buddhism of much of its intellectual and cultural vigor. Thus during the Tokugawa period, the Japanese, like the Chinese and Koreans before them, became an essentially secular society, dominated by the philosophy of Neo-Confucianism.

The Growth of Commerce.   Despite Japan's relative isolation from world trade, the prolonged Tokugawa peace produced an almost explosive expansion of commerce. This was furthered by the centralization of political controls and ironically by the agrarian orientation of the ruling class and its disdain for trade, which Confucian concepts had further strengthened. Relying basically on agricultural taxes, the shogunate and domains taxed commerce less heavily, thus permitting it to grow more easily.

The system of "alternate attendance" at Edo also contributed greatly to the commercialization of the economy and the development of a single broad national market. The "alternate attendance" system forced the daimyo to expend much of their income to maintain residences with large staffs at Edo and to pay for the annual movement of themselves and great numbers of their retainers between their domains and Edo. This required large money resources that could be provided only by the sale of local products outside of their domains. For this purpose some domains developed monopolies over local agricultural, marine, forest, or handicraft specialities. Sugar cane in the southernmost islands of the Shimazu domain of Satsuma is a good example. Most domains, however, had to rely on the sale of surplus rice to the central cities.

There was a rapid growth of cities and towns throughout Japan. The roughly 6 per cent of the population that constituted the samurai class was largely concentrated at Edo and in the various daimyo castle towns. Merchants and providers of other services were required in comparable numbers in the cities and towns to supply the needs of this large upper class. As a consequence, although in the past Kyōto had been the only city of significance, as both the capital and the center of commerce, Japan now became a land of many large and small cities. Edo in the eighteenth century approached a million in population and was possibly the largest city in the world at that time, as it is again today under the name of Tōkyō. Ōsaka, which because of its location at the head of the Inland Sea became a major center of commerce, paralleled Kyōto in size at about 400,000. The castle towns of the daimyo ran from a few thousand inhabitants for a small daimyo to close to 100,000 for such large domain capitals as Kanazawa (Maeda) and Nagoya (Tokugawa).

Barter all but disappeared in this commercial urban economy, and an adequate supply of currency, of course, became essential. The shogunate from the start minted gold coins and copper cash and later silver coins too. A great deal of commercial paper also developed. The individual daimyo used rice and silver certificates as paper money within their domains—some 1600 different issues have been identified—and commercial notes and money orders of private merchants and bankers were widely used for large transactions, thus greatly expanding the monetary resources of the country. The great variety of currency and repeated debasement of the coinage by the shogunate, however, always kept the monetary situation complex.

Most of the domains of western Japan maintained commercial offices and warehouses in Ōsaka to dispose of their excess produce and acquire needed commodities. At first these were run by their own retainers, but in time they were entrusted largely to men of merchant origin. Rice markets grew up in both Ōsaka and Edo and by the eighteenth century were dealing in futures, much like the contemporary wheat markets of London and Amsterdam. A widespread system of coastal shipping developed in order to supply the two great centers of commerce and consumption at Edo and Ōsaka. This, together with the many roads and post stations needed for the large-scale movement of men in the "alternate attendance" system, gave Japan a complex and well-developed communications network, though land transport was still quite backward, since a shogunate ban on wheeled vehicles necessitated the use of pack horses and human porters.

The Townsmen. The shogunate and domains controlled the merchants in their respective areas as they saw fit. Some were designated as "honorable service merchants" (*goyō shōnin*), who helped supply the shogunal or daimyo households. Arbitrary monetary contributions might be exacted from merchants in time of need, and unbecoming acts or displays of wealth by members of this theoretically lowest class might result in complete confiscation of their property. Frequently the authorities recognized various monopoly guilds of local merchants, from which they collected fees, and by the end of the seventeenth century a variety of great wholesale guilds in

Wholesale sake *firms located along a canal, from* Illustrations of Famous Places in Edo *of 1834 and 1836.*

Ōsaka and Edo had developed with official sanction. In 1721 the shogunate even started licensing merchant associations (*kabu nakama*, which literally means "stock companies"), and the practice increased later in the century as the shogunate's finances deteriorated. Similarly the daimyo domains, in increasing financial desperation, turned to *han* commercial monopolies in an effort to bolster their finances.

Thus the ruling classes held the merchants down socially and sometimes controlled their economic activities in order to extract fees from them, but by and large, with feudal and Confucian contempt for commerce, they turned their backs on trade, leaving it largely in the hands of the urban merchants. Except for relatively light taxes for urban services, there was no direct taxation, and government fees were not very heavy. Since the three largest cities and the major centers of trade were all within the shogun's great central domain, the bulk of the more important merchants were under shogunal jurisdiction. This was a great advantage for them, because the shogunate, controlling as it did the whole economic heartland of Japan and possessing large agricultural resources as compared to its samurai population, was a relatively lenient master, and it also afforded the merchants of its area considerable protection in their dealings with the daimyo domains. While Tokugawa merchants did not have the freedom or prestige of their counterparts in Europe at this time, they were much more protected from arbitrary confiscation or ruinous taxation and controls than were merchants in most parts of Asia. Thus they could afford to make longer-range investments of capital.

A number of great merchant houses developed during the Tokugawa period. The house of Mitsui started in the province of Ise in *sake* brewing, added pawnbrokerage and moneylending, opened a dry goods store in Edo in 1673, established branches in Kyōto and Ōsaka, became official banker to the shogunate in 1691 and the banking agent of several daimyo, and survived to become in modern times one of the largest private economic enterprises in the world. The Kōnoike house, also starting in *sake* brewing, entered into moneylending and shipping at Ōsaka after 1616 and became the financial agent for many *han*. Sumitomo, starting in iron goods and drugs in Kyōto, became a major trader and refiner of copper and still is an important component of Japanese industry.

The great spurt in urban and commercial growth produced by peace and centralization had largely run its course by the early eighteenth century. Thereafter the pace slackened, but the social effects of the commercial explosion continued and actually grew stronger. Tied as the samurai class was to income from agriculture, which grew less rapidly than commerce and handicrafts, its share of national wealth declined, although its members increased somewhat and its standards of consumption greatly. Most daimyo and many samurai came to live well beyond their means. As a consequence they fell heavily in debt to urban merchants and moneylenders. This situation was already severe by the end of the seventeenth century, and it grew steadily worse during the remainder of the period.

The indebtedness of the top social class to the lowest class obviously undermined the whole theory and spirit of the Tokugawa system. So also did the urban milieu in which the samurai lived. Already transformed from warriors into civil bureaucrats, they now found themselves living in an environment in which the economic patterns and cultural tone were increasingly set by the despised merchant class. One philosopher likened the samurai, with their constant comings and goings to and from Edo, to transients residing in an inn owned and operated by the townsmen. The domains could attempt to extricate themselves from debt by commercial operations and the reduction of their retainers' stipends in the guise of loans. This last measure, of course, only worsened the plight of the samurai. The poorer ones, who in any case received only minimal stipends in rice, were frequently forced to eke out their inadequate income by cottage industries, such as the making of straw sandals.

The Peasantry.   Change came more slowly to the rural villages where the bulk of the population lived. Nevertheless peace and unity, together with specialization of crops, expanded acreage, improved irrigation, better seeds and tools, increased use of fertilizers, and more double cropping, resulted in a considerable expansion of agricultural production. The Japanese peasant was becoming the most technologically advanced farmer in Asia. There was a great increase in commercial crops, such at cotton, tobacco, and mulberry leaves for silkworms, and cereal production seems to have doubled between 1600 and 1720. Thereafter agriculture expanded less rapidly as it approached the narrow limits set by geography.

The Japanese population grew with the economy but not as rapidly. It stood at about 30 million at the time of the first census in 1721, which is thought to have been a 50 per cent increase over the estimated 20 million for 1600 and was well above the population of any European country at that time. In the second half of the Tokugawa period the population grew hardly at all, despite a continued, even if slower, growth of the economy. As a consequence, there was a clear rise in living standards throughout the Tokugawa period, even for the peasantry. What had once been luxurious city ways became commonplace in the countryside too. Thus during these centuries, the Japanese economy outpaced the population.

Why this happened in Japan, as it was happening at much the same time in Western Europe, is not clear, although it may be connected with the feudal social pattern, in which there is room in each family for only one heir and therefore, unlike other traditional societies, a large family is a burden rather than an asset. One rural response was the practice of infanticide, known by the agricultural term of "thinning" (*mabiki*). In any case, the rise of the Japanese economy above mere subsistence levels permitted the development of relatively high standards of literacy, economic institutions, and government services, and these high standards helped make possible Japan's successful modernization in the nineteenth century.

Despite generally improving economic conditions, however, the economic position of large parts of the peasantry seems to have deteriorated during the second half of the Tokugawa period. This was reflected in the rising number of famines and also of "peasant uprisings," which usually were peaceful demonstrations against increased taxes or misgovernment and turned to violence only late in the period.

The root cause of this situation seems to have been a growing imbalance in the distribution of rural wealth. Farming units had once been made up typically of several collateral and servitor families grouped around a central family, providing it with labor and depending on it for security in a largely subsistence agriculture. As a result of the commercialization of the whole economy, the geographic specialization of crops, and the development of village industries in *sake* brewing, cotton spinning, weaving, dyeing, and the like, this pattern began to dissolve. Subsistence farming was replaced by specialized cash crops, which made all peasants more vulnerable to outside economic vagaries. At the same time, the large farm units began to break up into smaller family-size units, as the richer families found it more advantageous to concentrate their own efforts on their best piece of agricultural land, rent out the remainder to tenants, and then invest their profits in village industries, which brought in a larger return than agriculture. Meanwhile the former dependent families, now cut free as tenants, farmed the less fertile fields but commonly bore a disproportionately heavy portion of the taxes, assigned by the richer families which dominated the autonomous village governments. Thus the richer peasants became richer, and the poorer ones lost their former security of association with them.

This whole transition was slow and uneven, coming much earlier in the central and economically more advanced areas, especially the regions around Kyōto and Ōsaka, than in more peripheral areas. Its effects were not limited to the increase of rural unrest. By the early nineteenth century poor peasants were becoming accustomed to working for wages on the farms of richer peasants or in village industries. Thus they were forming a reservoir for urban factory labor when Japan subsequently industrialized. Many richer peasants had turned into aggressive rural entrepreneurs. Often well-educated, such peasant entrepreneurs led a second great wave of commercial expansion in the late eighteenth and early nineteenth centuries, invading even the urban strongholds of the great merchant houses. A harbinger of the future was the silk-weaving town of Kiryū on the northern edge of the Kantō Plain, which had dormitories for workers already in the eighteenth century and five thousand looms by the middle of the nineteenth.

Tokugawa Culture

Confucian Scholarship.   Cultural and intellectual developments during the Tokugawa period tended to separate into two fairly distinct streams, the one dominated by the samurai class and the other by the townsmen. The samurai, proud of their feudal heritage and immersed in Chinese Confucianism, did not prove to be very innovative in the fields of literature and art, but the needs of bureaucratic rule and the stimulus of Chinese learning produced an outburst of scholarly and philosophical activity among them. Classical Chinese became once again the language of most serious writing and the prime subject of samurai education in the many *han* and private academies that were founded, especially after 1700. Many samurai mastered a grammatically correct and even elegant Chinese written style, although then as now almost no Japanese knew the spoken language or even the real Chinese pronunciations for the characters, which were read according to the greatly modified Japanese pronunciations for them.

History writing—the vital core of Chinese scholarship—naturally attracted major attention. The Hayashi family of official shogunal Confucian scholars completed in 1670 the *Comprehensive Mirror of Our Country*, a chronological history based on Chinese models. The *Veritable Records of the Tokugawa*, a massive chronological compendium of shogunal activities based on Chinese prototypes, was compiled between 1809 and 1849. Meanwhile Tokugawa Mitsukuni (1628–1700), the daimyo of Mito and a grandson of Ieyasu, had started a large project known as the *History of Great Japan*, which was partially completed in 1720 but did not reach final form until 1906. Many individual scholars, such as Arai Hakuseki (1657–1725), who was a leading shogunate official, also produced important historical works.

In addition to the Hayashi family in Edo, there was a great number of samurai scholars at Edo and in the various domains who propagated the orthodox Chu Hsi school of philosophy. Among them, Kaibara Ekken (1630–1714) of northern Kyūshū helped spread these ideas to the lower classes by writing in Japanese. Some samurai scholars, however, protected by their respective daimyo from Edo's periodic insistence on orthodoxy, followed other lines of Chinese Confucianism.

Nakae Tōju (1606–1648) was inclined to the Idealist School of the Ming Confucianist, Wang Yang-ming (Ōyōmei in Japanese). His disciple, Kumazawa Banzan (1619–1691), a "masterless samurai" who rose to become the chief official of the important "outer" domain of Okayama in western Honshū, advocated the return of the samurai to the soil and a more austere form of life. Wang Yang-ming's emphasis on the individual's intuitive moral sense, on personal discipline, and on action rather than words appealed to the samurai, since these concepts, which were probably at least in part of Zen inspiration even in China, had become part of the samurai heritage through Zen influence during the Ashikaga period. It is significant that some of the men most active in transforming Japan in the second half of the nineteenth century were influenced by the Wang Yang-ming school of thought.

Another heterodox school, called "Ancient Learning" (*Kogaku*), followed the lead of contemporary Ch'ing scholars in attempting to get back of the Sung philosophers to earlier Confucianism. Yamaga Sokō (1622–1685), a "masterless samurai," contributed to the development of the "Way of the Warrior" as a comprehensive philosophy. Itō Jinsai (1627–1705), who actually came from a merchant family in Kyōto, stressed the virtues taught in the early Confucian works, especially the *Analects* and *Mencius*, and Ogyū Sorai (1666–1728), the son of a doctor in the shogun's service, went back to the still earlier Five Classics, but at the same time was an advocate of utilitarian policies, greater shogunal absolutism, and more recognition for men of individual talent.

Perhaps because Confucian theory and Japanese political and social realities did not fit together very well, Tokugawa thinkers on the whole seem to have remained somewhat more pragmatic than their counterparts at this time in China and Korea. Good examples of this are to be found in the work of the great mathematician, Seki Takakazu (1642–1708), and the cartographer, Inō Tadataka (1745–1818). Many Confucian thinkers paid attention to the practical economic problems that were bothering the shogunate and domains. While most intellectuals remained tied to the agrarian biases of feudalism and Confucianism, some developed iconoclastic ideas. Kaiho Seiryō (1755–1817), for example, ridiculed the samurai disdain for the profit motive and advocated that government frankly exploit commerce.

In time, scholarly activities also spread to the merchant class and even to the peasantry, as is illustrated by the many technical books on agriculture that appeared from 1697 on. Rural society even produced a peasant sage, Ninomiya Sontoku (1787–1856), a very successful farmer from near Edo, who helped institute practical agricultural reforms in the area and taught mutual cooperation and long-term planning for the peasant community.

"Dutch Learning."   By the eighteenth century the fear of Christianity had so receded that it became permissible again to show interest in Europe and its technology. For example, the great Edo statesman and scholar, Arai Hakuseki, manifested frank admiration for Western science in his book *A Report on the Occident*, which was based on his interviews with an Italian priest who had smuggled himself into Japan in 1708 and had, of course, been promptly imprisoned. In 1720 the shogunate relaxed its ban on Western books, except for those treating Christianity, and scholars began to go to Nagasaki to learn Dutch from the official interpreters who dealt with the Dutch merchants there. As a consequence, the whole study of Europe and its science came to be known as "Dutch Learning" (*Rangaku*). The presence between 1769 and 1786 at the Dutch trading post in Nagasaki of two scholarly Europeans, the Swedish physician Thunberg and the Dutchman Titsingh, proved a great stimulus. Western medicine had an especial appeal as being clearly more scientific and effective than Chinese medical theory and practice. The Shimazu domain in southern Kyūshū established a medical school as early as 1774, and in the same year Sugita Gempaku (1733–1817), after prodigious efforts, produced a translation of a Dutch medical work. In 1783 another physician, Ōtsuki Gentaku (1757–1827), published *An Introduction to Dutch Learning*, which was a great help to other scholars in their study of the Dutch language and Western science.

"Dutch Learning" opened doors to many new and admittedly useful fields besides medicine, such as cartography, botany, and more modern gunnery. Some scholars, such as Hiraga Gennai (1728?–1779), showed a wide range of scientific interest, and some even wandered into what were felt to be subversive areas of thought. Hayashi Shihei (1738–1793), who in 1786 wrote *A Discussion of the Military Problems of a Maritime Country,* was im-

Woodblock print by Hayashi Shihei, based on a sketch he made while being entertained by the Dutch at Nagasaki. The empty chair is the one he vacated to make the sketch.

prisoned for criticizing the shogunate for the weakness of its defenses against the Russians in the North. Honda Toshiaki (1744–1821) attacked the whole isolation policy, and Satō Nobuhiro (1769–1850) advocated a more centralized form of government. Actually such men had little influence on political developements in Japan, but the existence by the nineteenth century of a considerable body of scholarly men able to read Dutch and knowledgeable about the Occident and its science was a tremendous advantage to the Japanese when they decided in the middle of the century to attempt to catch up technologically with the West.

"National Learning" and Shintō.   The emphasis on history in Confucian scholarship drew attention to Japan's pre-Tokugawa and pre-Confucian traditions. Tokugawa Mitsukuni's *History of Great Japan* followed the lead of Kitabatake Chikafusa of the fourteenth century in ascribing Japan's greatness to its divinely descended, unbroken line of emperors. Yamazaki Ansai (1618–1682), an orthodox Confucianist, equated the Shintō foundation myths with Chinese cosmology and nationalistically asserted that, if Confucius or Mencius were to lead invading armies, it was the duty of Japanese to repel even these founding sages of Confucianism. Many other Confucian

scholars, despite their strong orientation toward Chinese civilization, also looked to Japan's antiquity for "unique" national virtues.

These trends were strengthened by a largely literary movement called "National Learning" *(Kokugaku)*. Two Shintō priests, Kada Azumamaro (1668–1736) and Kamo Mabuchi (1697–1769), drew attention once again to ancient Japanese poetry, and Kamo's disciple, Motoori Norinaga (1730–1801), a merchant's son and himself a physician, devoted more than thirty years to writing a great *Commentary on the Record of Ancient Matters (Kojiki den)*, Japan's earliest historical work. Inspired by men of this type, many scholars as well as dilettantes took up the study of the ancient language and early literature. While the main thrust of "National Learning" was literary and philological, Motoori and his predecessors had imbued it also with a strong nationalistic content. They rejected the secular rationalism of Confucianism and sought the true, unsullied Japanese spirit in early mythology, ancient poetry, and purely Japanese prose works such as *The Tale of Genji*. Hirata Atsutane (1776–1843), a physician of samurai origin, while unconsciously eclectic in his inclusion of Confucian, Taoist, Buddhist, and even Western ideas in his brand of "National Learning," aggressively asserted Japan's national superiority as the land of the gods.

The emphasis on ancient Japanese virtues and the imperial line easily led to doctrines subversive to the Tokugawa system. A teacher at the imperial court and his noble pupils were punished in 1758 for subversive tendencies, and two other teachers were executed in Edo in 1767. At the same time, these attitudes, when combined with the deep awareness of national identity fostered by the self-conscious policy of isolation, produced by the nineteenth century a strong national consciousness not unlike the nationalism that had developed in the West.

Revived interest in Japan's early history and literature may also have contributed to the appearance among the peasants in the early nineteenth century of several popular religious movements that were eclectic in content but basically Shintō in emphasis. Usually called Shintō sects, these actually independent religions commonly promised immediate worldly benefits for the believers and sometimes stressed faith healing. Some of these "sects" are still strong. Tenrikyō, the "Teaching of Heavenly Truth," founded by a peasant woman in 1838, has today a great center in a town (renamed Tenri) a little south of Nara, complete with a university, museums, and a large religious headquarters.

Urban Culture. While commoners contributed to the intellectual life of the Tokugawa period, townsmen fully dominated many other aspects of the culture. The rapidly increasing wealth of the cities offered possibilities for social innovation and aesthetic creativity. The commercial port of Ōsaka and the townsmen quarters of Kyōto and Edo permitted social and cultural opportunities undreamed of in samurai or village society. A distinctive townsmen's style of life developed and with it new emphases in culture.

Most townsmen of any standing were literate, as were the richer peasants. In some domains commoners were permitted to attend the official domain schools, but there was in addition a great network of small private schools for commoners—more than ten thousand are known to have existed—usually called "temple schools," not for their religious affiliations but because of their usual location in Buddhist temples. Since virtually all samurai were educated, this made for a quite literate society. It has been estimated that by the middle of the nineteenth century roughly 45 per cent of the male population could read and write and perhaps 15 per cent of the women—figures not far behind the most advanced countries of the West at that time.

The urban merchants were basically sober, hard working, and disciplined, much like the samurai and peasants. The great merchant houses developed family codes similar to those of the samurai houses and a keen sense of honor, discipline, and obligation, derived largely from samurai ethics. There were also merchant philosophers. Ishida Baigan (1685–1744), a peasant by origin who worked his way up in a Kyōto merchant house, developed a philosophy he called "Learning of the Mind" (*Shingaku*), in which he taught that honest and diligent merchants, as stewards of the country's wealth, performed a national function comparable to that of the samurai. This concept, like that of "the calling" in Protestant thought in the West, gave moral legitimacy to merchants, who in a closed, class society, were denied an equal social status. It also provided a rationale for moneymaking and for dynamic achievement within one's status, which proved extremely important in Japan's modernization in the nineteenth century. It seems likely that there is a causal relationship between the parallel feudal backgrounds of Japan and Europe and their modern goal- rather than status-oriented ethics.

For all the sobriety of Tokugawa merchants, their urban culture showed great vigor and panache. The city man tended to be quick-witted and cocky, contemptuous of the stolid peasant and disdainful of the haughty but poor samurai. Since profits were the measure of success, he was extremely money-conscious and fond of luxuries. Ceremonies became ever more elaborate; novelty was highly esteemed; fashion was important—the latest feminine fashions in hair styles or sleeve lengths, or masculine styles set by leading actors or recognized dandies.

The urban merchant reserved his home for his serious moneymaking activities and his family. The long, warrior-dominated feudal age had left women entirely subordinate to men throughout Japanese society. Marriages were arranged for the interests of the family, not for romantic love, and women were kept at home to bear children and perform the household duties. The townsmen went elsewhere for their diversions. Amusement quarters in the cities, provided with restaurants, theaters, and houses of prostitution, served as the centers of social life and aesthetic activity. Here the merchant could relax from his serious role as businessman and family head to enjoy the company of gay companions and women not constrained by the prevailing social codes.

The women of the amusement quarters were usually indentured servants, sold by impoverished parents, but the more beautiful and gifted were trained in singing, dancing, and conversational skills to become talented courtesans, known in more modern times as *geisha,* or "accomplished persons." They were divided into many categories, and those in the higher grades were considered the setters of feminine styles. They were also assiduously courted by wealthy patrons, who not infrequently purchased their freedom and set them up as their recognized mistresses or even legal wives.

The social and cultural activity centering around the amusement quarters provided an exuberant release from the rigidities of the Tokugawa system. Even samurai, themselves confirmed urban dwellers by this time, were attracted by it, participating in increasing numbers, though always in theory incognito. Borderline groups, such as "masterless samurai," who were free of shogunal or domain discipline, entered in more wholeheartedly. Thus there developed a compartmentalization of urban life between family and business or government service on the one hand and leisure and amusements on the other. Modern city life in Japan still shows the residue of this division. But there were inevitable clashes between the two, as was shown by efforts of the authorities to curb activities in the amusement quarters and still more by the conflicts that went on in the hearts of those who participated in this double life. A favorite theme of the literature and drama of the period was the clash between duty (*giri*) and emotion, or "human feelings" (*ninjō*). In a typical case, a young man's love for a courtesan, running counter to his duty to family and society, could be resolved only by the double suicide of the ill-fated lovers.

It took several decades after the founding of the Tokugawa shogunate for these urban social phenomena to develop, but the second half of the seventeenth century saw a sudden flowering of townsmen culture. The period is usually known as Genroku from the name of a "year period" (1688–1704). The center of townsmen culture at this time was Ōsaka, for Kyōto was now losing its cultural lead and Edo was still a raw, new city, dominated by its heavy samurai population. By the latter part of the eighteenth century, however, Edo had become the cultural as well as the political center of the nation.

The urban culture of the Tokugawa period tended at times toward flamboyance, but it was saved from ostentatious display and garish vulgarity by two factors—the watchful eyes of a repressive government, which was quick to issue sumptuary laws, and the simple, almost austere aesthetic canons inherited from the Ashikaga period. The result was an extraordinarily sophisticated blend of verve and daring with an underlying sense of restraint and discipline. The aesthetic tastes produced by this blend still persist in Japan and have recently proved to have a wide appeal in many other countries.

Literature.   Numerous publishing houses flourished throughout the Tokugawa period, issuing a flood of printed books from inspirational essays to pornography. Printing had been known in Japan since the eighth century but had been used only sparingly and usually for weighty works of scholarship. Korean printers brought back by Hideyoshi's armies as well as a mission press founded by the Jesuits may have helped revive interest in printing in the late sixteenth century, but the basic reason for the great increase in printing was the development of a large literate public. Most popular books were printed in the *kana* syllabary or with *kana* readings beside Chinese characters. At first there was some use of movable type, but this technique was soon abandoned in favor of woodblock printing—that is, the use of a single carved block of wood for each printed page—which permitted the inclusion of illustrations that helped attract readers.

Early Tokugawa popular writings were largely uplifting tracts, known as "*kana* booklets," on religion, morality, or history, but these in time became enlivened by amusing anecdotes and other realistic touches. Practical but interesting guidebooks to amusement quarters, with descriptions of the more prominent courtesans and actors, also appeared. Such more popular works were called "fleeting-world booklets" (*ukiyo-zōshi*), for the term "fleeting world" (*ukiyo,* literally "floating world"), which reflected the Buddhist emphasis on the transience and vanity of life, had acquired the connotations of "up-to-date" and "stylish."

From such beginnings, Ihara (or Ibara) Saikaku (1642–1693), an Ōsaka townsman, developed character portrayals of amusing townsmen types. His first important work, *An Amorous Man,* published in 1682, created an entirely new literary genre. He followed this with comparable books, such as *An Amorous Woman, The Everlasting Storehouses of Japan,* and *Twenty Examples of Unfilial Conduct in this Land.* Saikaku was a master of allusive and poetic diction and of the plays on words that Japanese love, but he was also extremely realistic. His chief interest was the moneygrubbing, self-made businessman and his less disciplined, spendthrift heirs. Saikaku's cynicism came as a refreshing departure from the heavy moralizing of earlier writers. "Money," he wrote, "is the townsman's pedigree."

Ejima Kiseki (1667–1736) wrote critiques of actors and courtesans and, after breaking with his Kyōto publishers, the Hachimonjiya ("Figure of Eight Store"), turned to sketches of merchant families, as in his *Characters of Modern Sons*. His basic theme was that "parents toil, their children idle, and the grandchildren beg." Among later Tokugawa authors, Takizawa Bakin (1767–1848), the son of a masterless samurai, was a prolific writer of long, didactic novels much influenced by Chinese models and samurai morality. A more interesting figure was Jippensha Ikku (1766–1831), a samurai by origin, whose immensely popular *Shank's Mare Travels* (*Hiza-kurige*), which appeared serially, was a picaresque novel about two wandering rogues whose misadventures are a parody of samurai pretensions.

Even in poetry, the Tokugawa period produced a distinctive new form. The initial three 5-7-5 syllable lines of a certain type of "chain poem" developed into an independent seventeen-syllable form called *haiku*. Unlike the classic "short poem," the *haiku* was up-to-date in both vocabulary and concepts, and its brevity fitted the wit that was so appreciated by the townsmen. The following example, chosen for ease of literal translation, illustrates some of the technique and spirit of *haiku:*

> *Tsuki ni e o*   *To the moon, a handle*
> *sashitaraba yoki*   *add—a good*
> *uchiwa kana*   *fan indeed!*

Haiku composition became a craze among all classes. One of the earliest and probably the greatest *haiku* master was Matsuo Bashō (1644–1694), a former samurai who became an aesthetic wanderer. His most famous work, *The Narrow Road of Oku,* is a poetic account of a trip to northern Honshū.

The Theater.   In the field of drama the samurai class patronized and kept alive the *Nō* of the Ashikaga period, but the townsmen developed new forms. One was the puppet theater, which was called *Jōruri* from a popular form of recitation to a three-stringed banjo-like instrument. The puppets at first were small and operated by men out of sight but grew to be about two-thirds life size, each operated by three men, with further assistants, all in plain view of the audience but supposedly rendered invisible by black shrouds. At the side of the stage, a chanter, with musical accompaniments recited the story, taking the parts of all stage characters. This form of theater, called Bunraku, can still be seen today.

The *Jōruri* dramatic form was developed in the late seventeenth century chiefly by two men, Takemoto Gidayū (1651–1714), who founded a very successful puppet theater in Ōsaka, and Chikamatsu Monzaemon (1653–1724), a man of samurai origin who was the chief writer for this theater. Other theaters and authors soon appeared, and the competition between them became keen. Chikamatsu, living a century after Shakespeare, was in a

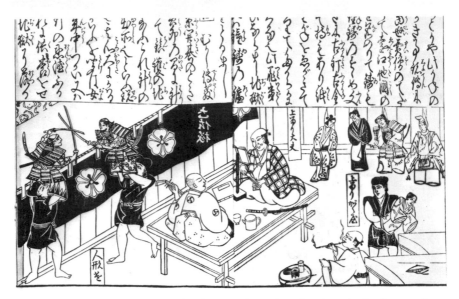

Illustration from a book printed in 1690 showing the backstage of an early puppet theater. On the left are the puppets and their manipulators, in the center the reciter and his accompanist, and at the right puppets hung up for future use. The text above is of an encyclopedic nature.

sense the creator of the modern Japanese theater. He never departed from a conventional poetic meter and a highly ornate style for narrative passages, but he developed a fine dramatic structure and turned his attention to the portrayal of character and psychological analysis. Many of his plays were loose, episodic, thrill-packed reworkings of earlier historical and literary themes, although in time he took up recent political events, only thinly disguised by being placed in earlier periods. His most popular work was *The Battles of Koxinga* about the famous Chinese-Japanese pirate known in Chinese as *Kuo-hsing-yeh* (1624—1662). This play ran for seventeen consecutive months when it was first produced. Chikamatsu's more interesting works are his twenty-four contemporary domestic plays, which dealt in a highly realistic fashion with life problems the townsmen knew from intimate experience, such as the clash of duty and emotion that might lead to double suicide. Several of his plays were based on well-known contemporary scandals in Osaka society.

A popular theater with live actors had developed early in the seventeenth century but had been so sex-oriented and mixed with prostitution that the authorities had permanently banned women from the stage. Male impersonators of female roles developed to take their place, but this form of theater, known as *Kabuki,* was at first eclipsed by the puppet stage and only began to win out in popularity in the eighteenth century. *Kabuki* borrowed the

Woodblock print of 1740 by Okamura Masanobu showing a Kabuki theater in Edo. Note on the left the runway through the audience to the stage.

violence and exaggerated gestures of *Jōruri* and also its repertoire, adapting the plays of Chikamatsu and other *Jōruri* dramatists to its use and developing new plays from *Nō* dramas or recent events, placed for safety from the authorities in an earlier historical setting. The most popular of all *Kabuki* plays was *The Treasury of Loyal Retainers* (*Chūshin-gura*), based on the 1702 incident of the Forty-Seven *Rōnin. Kabuki,* like *Nō,* utilized instrumental accompaniments and an on-stage chorus to chant narrative sections. It also showed the influence of *Nō* in the dances that highlighted many plays. But it was at the same time far more realistic. Stage settings became extraordinarily close to reality, the revolving stage was developed for rapid shifts of scene, and a runway down through the audience permitted "roadway" scenes and a sense of intimacy between the audience and actors. *Kabuki* is still very much alive in Japan today.

Art. The grandiose, ornate type of architecture developed in the late sixteenth century was continued in the Tokugawa period and is well represented by the baroque grandeur of the shrines and temples dedicated to Ieyasu at Nikkō and the decor of the rooms of the Nijō castle, the Tokugawa headquarters in Kyōto. The more sophisticated, restrained trends of the Ashikaga period were also continued in the Katsura detached palace in Kyōto, with its extensive but very beautiful garden, and at a more modest level provided the prevailing spirit of most domestic architecture and land-scape gardening.

With the decline of Buddhist intellectual and religious vigor, most religious sculpture became uninspired and imitative, as had happened earlier in China and Korea, and what vigor remained in the sculptor's tra-dition was devoted largely to ornamental architectural details and small ivory carvings (*netsuke*) used for the fastenings of tobacco pouches and the like. The industrial arts, however, all developed greatly. The Korean potters brought back by Hideyoshi's armies helped start Japan on a glori-ous period of porcelain making, and there was great activity in lacquer wares and in silk brocade work, centering at Kyōto.

Painting remained probably the most vigorous field of artistic expression. Under the Kano school of painters, the Ashikaga traditions of painting in the Chinese style were maintained, and new Chinese influences gave rise in the eighteenth century to the so-called Southern (*Nanga*) or Literati (*Bunjinga*) school of painting, which followed in name as well as in style Chinese prototypes of the Ming and Ch'ing periods.

At the same time strong new native artistic traditions arose, which were increasingly to dominate the artistic expression of the age. For example, some artists strayed far from Chinese canons by freely manipulating the traditional elements of landscape painting to form bold, almost abstract design effects. Their favorite mediums were lacquer ware and large folding screens. The greatest artist in this style was Ogata Kōrin (1658–1716). Other artists, possibly influenced by the down-to-earth tastes of the towns-men, moved toward greater realism. Hanabusa Itchō (1652–1724), also a *haiku* poet, based his realism on the "Yamato pictures" style of the late classic period, while Maruyama Ōkyo (1733–1795) adopted Western prin-ciples of perspective. Shiba Kōkan (1738–1818) went further in the Euro-pean style, experimenting with copper plate etchings, oil paints, and even Occidental subject matter.

The most significant artistic developments of the Tokugawa period grew directly out of the interests and way of life of the townsmen. These were the realistic paintings, called "pictures of the fleeting world" (*ukiyo-e*), of courtesans and city life, and the colored woodblock prints developed from this style. Simple monochrome woodblock prints had been used for centuries in China for religious pictures and book illustrations and came into common use in publications in Japan in the seventeenth century, but they were now developed into extremely complex, multicolored repro-ductions of paintings. With meticulous accuracy a wood carver would make from the artist's original painting a large number of different blocks— sometimes several dozen for a single picture—to reproduce each color and shading to be superimposed on one another in the final print. Woodblock pictures of this type thus represented a triumph of technical skill and at the

Kitchen scene, a polychrome woodblock print by Utamaro.

same time the first effort in the world to produce in full color great works of art at a reasonable price for sale to a broad public.

Hishikawa Moronobu (died 1694) was one of the greatest *ukiyo-e* painters and the first of the great woodblock artists. Suzuki Harunobu (1724–1774) was the first master of the multicolor techniques. Sharaku, who was active briefly around 1794–1795, produced an amazing series of caricatures of actors. Kitagawa Utamaro (1753–1806) was famous for his beautiful women. The last great woodblock artists turned more to famous scenes and landscapes. Katsushika Hokusai (1760–1849), who showed the influence of Western concepts of perspective, is famous for his "Thirty-Six Views of Mount Fuji," while Andō Hiroshige (1797–1858) is best known for his "Fifty-Three Post Stations on the Tōkaidō." Considered vulgar and plebeian during the Tokugawa period, woodblock prints were the first form of Japanese art to attract wide attention and admiration in the West.

The Erosion of the Tokugawa System

The "Dynastic Cycle" in Tokugawa Japan.   After the Tokugawa system had been well established by the middle of the seventeenth century, the chief historical developments in Japan were in the fields of economic growth, social evolution, and cultural innovation. Political incidents and change were by comparison minor and seemed more a matter of decline than progress, as political institutions derived from the experience of the six-teenth century proved less and less adequate to the conditions and problems of the eighteenth and nineteenth. In a country that was undergoing a tre-mendous commercial development and dynamic, even if partially concealed, social change, government remained entirely in the hands of a feudal aristocracy, devoted to the warrior traditions of the past and desperately attempting to maintain its agrarian basis of support. The consequence was a long but losing battle for the political authorities.

A strong sense of frustration permeated the ruling class in the second half of the Tokugawa period. Although the country as a whole was growing steadily more prosperous and the new urban culture was vibrantly vigorous, the two classes of most concern to the government were declining in relative economic position and in some cases even in absolute terms. The shogunate and domain governments were becoming heavily indebted to the merchant class, and the resulting cuts in the stipends of their retainers reduced many samurai to poverty. The growing division between the rich and poor peas-ants was leading to economic insecurity and serious want for many in the countryside.

Thus the history of the Tokugawa period, from the perspective of the government, showed some of the characteristics of the "dynastic cycle" of China. There was a strong beginning, but after about a century of relatively untroubled rule, government finances were badly undermined, the morale of the ruling class was eroding, and the whole theory of society and govern-ment appeared to be challenged. But the comparison with the Chinese dynastic cycle should not be pressed. Political control remained firm and relatively effective throughout the Tokugawa period, and the unprecedented peace and order of the period were broken only by minor incidents of no national significance or by natural calamities beyond man's control. In 1657 much of Edo was destroyed by the first of many fires that ravaged the city. In 1703 Fuji erupted disastrously, though for the last time, and in 1783 occurred an even more destructive eruption of Asama, a still very active volcano in central Honshū. Crop failures periodically produced famine conditions in parts of the country. But all this did not affect the basic system itself. Political administration remained stable and largely routine, high-lighted only by periodic but increasingly unrealistic efforts to return to the ethical values and economic and social conditions of the early seventeenth century.

Alternating Decline and Reform.   The first three shoguns were strong, able rulers, but, as was typical of Chinese dynasties, most of the later leaders were weaker or more inept men. The fifth shogun, Tsunayoshi (1680–1709), left a particularly unfavorable reputation. After the Great Elder was assassinated by a "younger elder" in 1684, Tsunayoshi ruled largely through his Grand Chamberlain, Yanagizawa Yoshiyasu (1658–1714), a favorite whom he raised from relative obscurity to be a 150,000-*koku* daimyo. He was naturally criticized for this and also for resorting to currency debasement in the face of mounting financial problems and for his many capriciously disruptive policies, such as his Buddhist-inspired protection and patronage of animals, particularly dogs, for which he won the sobriquet of the "Dog Shogun."

Following Tsunayoshi's death, the great scholar Arai Hakuseki was the chief shaper of government policy from 1709 to 1716. He attempted to cut shogunal expenses, recreate a sound currency, and restore among the samurai the high morale and discipline of the early Tokugawa period. This effort was continued on a more significant scale by the eighth shogun, Yoshimune (1716–1745; died 1751), who had been brought in to fill the post from the collateral Tokugawa line at Wakayama. His efforts, which are considered the first of the major rallies aimed at restoring the original vigor of the system, have been called the Kyōhō Reforms from the name of the "year period." Yoshimune set an example of simplicity and uprightness, issued a plethora of moral and sumptuary laws, and strove to revive the old martial spirit and at the same time to further learning and a sense of responsible leadership. He initiated administrative reforms, inaugurating a census in 1721 and codifying the Tokugawa laws. But the results proved for the most part disappointing even to him. His policies basically worked against the needed adjustments to the economic and social realities of the time. With his agrarian bias, he managed to increase agricultural production while depressing the rest of the economy. The resultant fall in rice prices hurt the very groups he was most concerned about, the samurai and peasants, because their incomes were largely in rice. In terms of Tokugawa ethics, Yoshimune was a great hero, but, in terms of Japan's economic and social evolution, he was a wrong-way leader.

Under the tenth shogun, Ieharu (1760–1786), the chief determiner of government policy was Tanuma Okitsugu (1719–1788), another favorite of modest origin, who was raised to be a 57,000-*koku* daimyo. Tanuma has been roundly condemned as a corrupt traitor to the Tokugawa ethical system, but he was at the same time an able pragmatist, more in tune with the basic economic currents of the time. He further expanded agricultural production, but he also encouraged foreign trade at Nagasaki, which Yoshimune had reduced. He tightened up the traditional shogunal monopolies in gold, silver, and copper and added new ones. More significantly, he expanded the practice of licensing merchant associations and began to develop taxes on commerce, though in a haphazard fashion. To bolster shogunal finances, he again resorted to the debasement of the currency, but he added a useful set of silver coins to the existing coinage. His period of leadership may have been characterized by decline in the traditional morality, but it was also a time of great economic growth and development.

The death of Ieharu in 1786 led to Tanuma's immediate downfall and a vigorous attempt to "return to Yoshimune." The new dominant official at Edo was Matsudaira Sadanobu, a grandson of Yoshimune and the daimyo of one of the major Tokugawa collateral lines. Sadanobu's efforts, known as the Kansei Reforms, centered on strict financial retrenchment, strong sumptuary laws, limitations on commerce, and the restoration of the morale and prestige of the samurai class. He canceled the debts incurred by the direct shogunal retainers after 1785 and like Yoshimune cut back again on foreign trade. Sadanobu's reform efforts, running as they did against the vigorously expanding commercial economy, collapsed even more rapidly than those of Yoshimune.

The young shogun, Ienari (1787–1831; died 1841), on coming of age in 1793, dropped Sadanobu and thereafter let shogunal finances and the national economy drift. The shogunate itself remained financially afloat through repeated currency debasements, which yielded quick profits for Edo but of course led to economic confusion and a rapid rise in prices. Most domains fell badly into debt, sometimes coming to owe ten to twenty times as much as their annual incomes, and poorer samurai were increasingly forced to supplement their incomes by handicraft or commercial activities. Such conditions were aggravated by serious crop failures and famines between 1822 and 1836, and a pervading sense of crisis developed.

When the already retired shogun Ienari died in 1841, another determined effort to turn the clock back was launched under the leadership of one of the "elders," Mizuno Tadakuni (1793–1851). Mizuno's policies, usually called the Tempō Reforms, were the same old nostrums of financial retrenchment, sumptuary laws, currency reform, and moral exhortation. He also attempted to force all peasants who had migrated to the cities without proper papers of authorization to return to their villages, exacted huge forced loans from some seven hundred urban merchant houses, suddenly abolished in 1841 all the government-licensed merchant associations, and decreed a 20 per cent cut in all prices and wages. The result was economic chaos, and most of the reforms soon had to be dropped, as was Mizuno himself in 1843. Meanwhile many of the domains were carrying out their own Tempō Reforms. Started in some cases in the 1830's, these *han* reforms, implemented as they were in smaller, more manageable, and less commercialized areas, sometimes proved more successful in restoring a domain's finances than the shogunate efforts had been.

Japan in the Mid-Nineteenth Century.   Many historians, influenced by the pattern of the Chinese "dynastic cycle" and still more by modern Western history, have argued that Japan by the middle of the nineteenth century stood on the brink of "dynastic" collapse and even a bourgeois revolution. Growing disequilibriums in income, decreased morale, if not efficiency, among the ruling groups, and heightened economic expectations had produced a steady upcreep in popular disturbances among the peasantry and even among city dwellers. City rioting first appeared in Edo in 1732, became more serious in Tanuma's time, and took a somewhat revolutionary turn in 1837, when Ōshio, a former official in the city government of Ōsaka, led an attack on Ōsaka castle in an effort to win relief for the city poor. Natural disasters, as in the crop failures of the 1820's and 1830's, may also have become more politically disruptive toward the end of the period.

There were also many new trends that could prove subversive to the Tokugawa system. The military effectiveness of the samurai had declined seriously, and their sense of personal loyalty to the shogun or daimyo had become more a loyalty to the system, in which individual men were little more than symbols. There was a rising awareness of the supreme national symbol of the emperor and a growing demand for the recognition of individual talent in addition to hereditary status. The commercial economy and urban society and culture had expanded far beyond the narrow feudal confines of the early seventeenth century. The aggressive entrepreneurial spirit of urban merchants and rich peasants, with its strong overtones of an achievement- rather than status-oriented ethic, was not at all in line with the emphasis of the ruling class on an unchanging agrarian economy and society. There was a growing diversity of intellectual trends among all classes, including a rising interest in Western science. By the 1840's there was also a mounting apprehension over the now greatly increased military power of the Western nations and their aggressive actions in neighboring countries.

Thus the Tokugawa system was under many pressures that had not existed in the seventeenth century, but one should not assume from this that it was about to collapse of its own weight, like an undermined Chinese dynasty, or that Japan was about to be swept in the European fashion by a bourgeois revolution. Japan in 1850 was still free of any serious external pressures. While social tensions had indeed developed, perhaps most severely among impoverished samurai and peasants, and many imperfections and illogicalities strained the social and political system, the samurai Confucian ethic still pervaded the nation, and the whole Tokugawa political structure still stood firm. If Japan had continued free of foreign encroachment, the Tokugawa system might well have continued for quite some time longer without major change. At the same time, severe strains between the theories and realities of government and society and a pervasive ferment beneath the surface calm made Japan more prepared for rapid change than were either China or Korea.

4. Japan's Response to the West

The Impact of the West

Early Pressures. The Japanese by 1639 had so successfully closed their doors to the outside world that subsequently Japan all but dropped out of the consciousness of Europeans. Even the Catholic missionaries eventually gave up their attempts to re-enter the country, and few Western ships came near Japan. The only important exception was the annual Dutch vessel from the East Indies to the Dutch trading post on the island of Deshima in Nagasaki harbor. Occidentals simply accepted the inaccessibility of the islands as a fact of political geography, and, absorbed in their expansion into other, much larger areas in Asia, came to regard Japan as a remote, poor country of little interest. But increased Western activity in the Chinese area in the late eighteenth and early nineteenth centuries drew attention once again to Japan. Western ships started to frequent Japanese waters, and demands began to grow in the West that Japan follow China's lead in opening its doors to commercial and diplomatic contact.

The Russians were the first to exert pressure on Japan. During the eighteenth century Russian and Japanese explorers and traders sometimes encountered one another in the Kuril Islands and Sakhalin, north of Japan's northern island of Hokkaidō. In 1809 the Japanese explorer Mamiya Rinzō (1780–1845) had even ventured up the Amur River. Russian representatives attempted to open official relations in Hokkaidō in 1792 and at Nagasaki in 1804, but both times they were firmly, though courteously, refused. The Russians in pique raided Japanese outposts in the islands north of

Hokkaidō in 1806 and 1807, and the Japanese retaliated by capturing some Russians in 1811 and holding them imprisoned for two years.

Meanwhile the British too were beginning to return to Japanese waters. English vessels visited Hokkaidō in 1797, Nagasaki in 1808 in search of Dutch ships under Napoleonic control, and Edo Bay in 1818. An armed clash occurred in 1824 between British sailors and Japanese on a small island south of Kyūshū.

By the middle of the nineteenth century, the United States had replaced both England and Russia as the nation most interested in opening Japan. Large numbers of whaling vessels from New England frequented the North Pacific, and the great circle route across the Pacific brought American clipper ships close to the shores of Japan on their way to and from Canton. The American crews were naturally interested in obtaining supplies in Japanese ports and in reducing the dangers of capture and mistreatment by the hostile Japanese. As steam came into use, moreover, coaling stations in Japan appeared an attractive possibility. For these various reasons, opening the ports of Japan became increasingly important to Americans, just at the time when westward expansion overland was bringing them to the Pacific and "manifest destiny" seemed to beckon them on across the seas.

As early as 1791 two American ships had entered Japanese waters, and in 1797 another visited Nagasaki, chartered by the Dutch authorities in the East Indies to replace their own ships, cut off from them by the Napoleonic wars. An American businessman in Canton dispatched a small vessel, the *Morrison,* to Japan in 1837 to repatriate seven Japanese castaways and, through this act of good will, to open up relations with Japan, but the unarmed ship was fired on by the Japanese and driven off. In 1846 Commodore Biddle entered Edo Bay and tolerated various indignities from the Japanese in a vain effort to open negotiations. In 1849 Commander Glynn took a stiffer attitude at Nagasaki but proved no more successful, though he was able to pick up fifteen stranded American seamen.

Japanese Reactions.   The Japanese reacted sharply to these invasions of their cherished seclusion. Following the Russian raids in the north, the shogunate for a while took over the Hokkaidō domain of Matsumae in order to strengthen defenses in that area. In 1806 it also issued instructions to local authorities to drive off all foreign ships and in 1825 strengthened this stand by ordering that they destroy foreign intruders with "no second thought," although in 1842 it realistically relaxed these orders to permit the local authorities to provide foreign ships with supplies when this was deemed necessary to avoid violence.

The Japanese leaders thus remained firmly determined to maintain the traditional policy of isolation and opposed to any capitulation to what seemed to them to be Western affronts to Japan's national dignity. Men from the collateral Tokugawa domain of Mito, which had long been a center of strong nationalist sentiment with pro-emperor overtones, led in advocating a hard line. In 1825 Aizawa Seishisai (1782–1863), in a document called *New Proposals,* urged the shogunate to "smash the barbarians whenever they come in sight." He argued that foreign trade was economically injurious to Japan, that foreign contacts would undermine Japanese morale, and that the only sound defense was to build national strength through greater unity and the judicious use of Western techniques, while excluding Westerners themselves. This general position was subsequently developed further by Fujita Tōko (1806–1855), another influential Mito intellectual. In 1830 Tokugawa Nariaki (1800–1860), the daimyo of Mito, called for political reform, emphasizing these Mito views. He argued for continued isolation to be backed up by greater national unity and military renovation. Specifically he urged the shogunate to relax the controls which had kept the daimyo militarily weak and financially impotent. He started vigorous reforms within his own domain, borrowing Western military techniques to strengthen the domain army.

It was clear to some Japanese, however, that foreign naval power was too strong for Japan to resist. Scholars of "Dutch Learning" in particular could see that blind resistance was dangerous. Their voices were not as inconsequential as they had been in the past, since the increasing menace of the West had drawn attention to Western science and military technology. In 1811 the shogunate itself had established an office for the translation of Occidental books, which in 1857, under the name of Institute for the Investigation of Barbarian Books, became a school of Western science and languages. Similar schools were established by several of the larger domains, notably Mito, Satsuma, Chōshū, Tosa in Shikoku, and Hizen (Saga) in Kyūshū, all of which were to play significant roles in the following years. (See map, pages 84—85.) Some scholars of "Dutch Learning" spoke out boldly. In 1838 Takano Chōei (1804–1850) issued a pamphlet urging the opening of Japan to foreign contact, but was imprisoned for his audacity and eventually was forced to commit suicide. Sakuma Shōzan (1811–1864), an expert on Western-style gunnery, in an effort to justify the technological changes that he realized were necessary, coined the slogan "Eastern ethics and Western science," a concept which, like its counterpart developed in China, was to prove comforting to a whole generation of modernizers.

The Opening of Japan.   The United States eventually determined to take decisive action to open Japan's ports. It chose for the purpose Commodore Matthew C. Perry and assigned him three steam frigates and five other ships—a quarter of the American navy. Perry, proceeding by way of the Indian Ocean, reached Japan in July 1853. After several days of diplomatic sparring at Uraga near the mouth of Edo Bay, he forced the Japanese to accept a letter from the president of the United States to the emperor of Japan and then departed, promising to return the next spring for the answer. Perry never discovered what had been well known in the Occident two centuries earlier—that the "emperor" he was attempting to deal with was actually only the shogun.

The Japanese realized that their small vessels and antiquated shore batteries were no match for the fleet at Perry's command or the still larger British naval forces in Asian waters. Edo lay exposed to the superior guns of the West, and the water-borne food supply of this city of over a million was completely vulnerable to blockade. The shogunate authorities were also aware that the British had recently defeated China in the so-called Opium War of 1839–1842, and the Dutch had repeatedly warned them through Nagasaki that they would have to accede to foreign demands.

One might imagine that, since the exclusion policy had been created by the Tokugawa shoguns in the seventeenth century, they could abandon it with impunity in the nineteenth. But the policy meanwhile had become sacrosanct and the shogunate flabby and irresolute, pulled in a variety of directions by the "house" daimyo who staffed its higher posts, the collateral domains which controlled much of its military power, and the "public opinion" of its own retainers. Being divided itself on this intensely controversial problem, the shogunate could present no united front to the rest of the nation or to the West.

Since 1845 the chief figure among the shogunate "elders" had been Abe Masahiro, an able, young "house" daimyo. Abe realized that general understanding would be necessary for the extremely unpopular but unavoidable policy of opening the country to more foreign contact. He therefore referred the problem posed by Perry to all of the daimyo. This was a momentous step, unprecedented in two and a half centuries of shogunate rule. It opened the door to discussion and criticism of all shogunate policies, thus starting a rapid erosion of Tokugawa prestige and authority. The last years of Tokugawa rule, from 1853 until the ultimate collapse in 1868, are fittingly known as the *bakumatsu,* or "end of the shogunate."

Abe's appeal to the daimyo produced no national consensus. The replies were overwhelmingly antiforeign but often ambiguous. About a third of the leading domains realized that Japan must make some concessions on trade, the profits of which could then be used to strengthen defenses. Some opposed trade but advised making enough concessions to give time for further military preparations. The rest demanded that no concessions be made and the Americans be driven off. The shogunate's Confucian scholars, who had also been consulted, took the same line, and the imperial court, insulated from foreign pressures in its inland capital of Kyōto, was also known to be strongly isolationist.

*An 1854 woodblock print giving a "true image" of Commodore
Perry of the "North American Republican State" and a picture of
Adams, his second-in-command, from a (1854) scroll depicting
the American expedition.*

Perry returned in February 1854 and insisted on conducting negotiations
further up Edo Bay at Kanagawa, now part of the great port city of Yokohama. The Japanese finally accepted what they felt were the minimum
American demands. In the Treaty of Kanagawa, signed on March 31, they
agreed to open two quite unimportant and isolated ports. These were
Shimoda at the end of the mountainous Izu Peninsula and Hakodate in
Hokkaidō. They also agreed to an American consul at Shimoda and promised
to give good treatment to shipwrecked sailors. One element included from
the unequal treaty system the British had imposed on China was the most-
favored-nation clause—additional privileges granted to other nations would
automatically come to the United States as well. The shogunate concluded
similar treaties with the British on October 14, with the Russians at Shimoda
on February 7, 1855, and then with the Dutch. The Russian treaty added
Nagasaki as an open port and another aspect of the Chinese treaty system—
extraterritoriality, which permitted foreigners in Japan to be tried by their
own courts and laws.

These treaties were hardly the full commercial agreements the Western
powers desired, and so they kept up their pressures for increased trade
relations. The outbreak of the Anglo-French War in China in 1856 and
the announcement by the British that they intended to negotiate a com-

mercial treaty with Japan made the shogunate realize that the Perry treaty had given only a brief respite. To forestall greater demands, it signed agreements with the Dutch and Russians in October 1857 for carefully regulated trade at Nagasaki and Hakodate, but it was left to the American consul, Townsend Harris, to force Japan fully open to trade.

Harris, who had arrived in Shimoda in 1856, gradually convinced the shogunate authorities that it would be better to conclude a full commercial treaty with a relatively peaceful and friendly United States before a less favorable treaty was wrung from them by the stronger and more demanding European powers. The resulting treaty, signed on July 29, 1858, called for an exchange of ministers; the immediate opening to trade of Kanagawa and Nagasaki in addition to Shimoda and Hakodate; the opening between 1860 and 1863 of Niigata on the west coast and Hyōgo (the modern Kōbe) to trade and Edo and Ōsaka to foreign residence; moderate limitations on import and export duties; and extraterritorial privileges for Americans. Within the next several weeks the Dutch, Russians, British, and French made similar treaties, but heightened the inequities of the treaty relationship by fixing Japanese import duties at relatively low levels.

Even before the Harris treaty went into effect in the summer of 1859, foreign traders began to settle in large numbers at the harbor of Yokohama, close to Kanagawa, and this unimportant fishing village soon grew into the chief port for foreign trade. Since the gold-silver ratio in Japan was 5 to 1, in contrast to the worldwide 15 to 1 ratio, and also because the value of Japanese coinage was fixed by the shogunate and was not dependent on the metallic content of the coins, the injection of foreign currency thoroughly disrupted the Japanese monetary system. This together with the heavy foreign demand for certain export commodities, particularly silk and tea, the inflow of cheaper foreign manufactures, particularly cotton textiles, frantic efforts to increase armaments, and growing political disruption resulting from the foreign threat, set off a severe inflationary spiral. The shogunate did its best to limit foreign trade by every possible tactic but was frustrated by the determination of the Westerners and the eagerness of commercial groups in Japan for quick profits.

The most serious consequence of the treaties was the presence in Japan of considerable numbers of Westerners, whom most Japanese regarded with great distrust and hostility. Troubles inevitably resulted between fervid samurai activists and Western diplomats and traders. There were several assassinations in 1859, and in 1861 Harris' Dutch interpreter, Heusken, was cut down. The British legation in Edo was attacked that same year and burned down in 1863. In 1862 four Britishers riding in the hills back of Yokohama were attacked by samurai in the procession of the daimyo of Satsuma, and one of them, Richardson, was killed. Such incidents resulted in heavy indemnities, which strained the shogunate's finances, and they further eroded Edo's authority, ground as it was between the arrogant, demanding Western powers and intransigent native isolationists.

Political Ferment in Japan

Japanese Responsiveness.   To observers at the time, Japan's position seemed even more precarious than that of China. Divided among more than 260 autonomous feudal regimes and united only under a shogun whose authority and power were fast disintegrating, Japan seemed politically more backward and less capable of effective action than the centralized and thoroughly bureaucratic Chinese government. Its feudal class society seemed ill prepared to respond to the challenge of more modernized Western nations. Its pre-industrial economy was no match for European machine production. It lacked the great continental solidity of the vast Chinese Empire, and its small islands were pathetically exposed to Western sea power.

And yet, Japan responded to the challenge of the West with much greater speed and far more success than China. No wars were fought, no smuggling trade developed, no territory was lost. There was turmoil, but out of it soon emerged a radically changed political system under which the Japanese moved rapidly toward becoming a modern power. Obviously Japan in the mid-nineteenth century, even though it had derived a large part of its higher culture from China, was a very different country, capable of very different responses to the Western challenge.

One clear and crucial difference lay in the respective attitudes toward the outside world. The Chinese, long accustomed to the idea that China was the unique land of civilization, could not accept the multi-state international concepts of Europe, did not believe that there was much of value to be learned from "barbarians," and, although outraged by Western presumptions, could not really see the seriousness of the challenge, assuming that these new "barbarians," like others before them, would come to comprehend the superiority of China and accept it. The Japanese, on the other hand, were linguistically, culturally, and geographically distinct enough from the Chinese to have developed a strong feeling of separate identity and, because of their acute awareness of China, also had a clear sense of the plurality of nations. The European system of equal and independent states was easy for them to accept. Well aware of all that they had learned over the ages from China and even from Korea and India, they could readily see that there was much of great importance to be learned from the West too. Accustomed to thinking of China as far larger, much older, and more advanced than Japan, they had no sublime sense of cultural superiority but rather a nagging fear of inferiority. Thus, when menaced by the West, they did not react with disdain but rather with that combination of fear, resentment, and narrow pride that one associates with nationalism. In fact, their reaction proved extremely nationalistic. Despite the intensity of rivalries among the various domains, most Japanese leaders in the face of the foreign menace seem to have placed national interests ahead of old feudal loyalties.

The very decentralization and diversity of the Japanese political and social system also permitted a greater variety of responses than appeared in China, and out of this diversity, through a rough process of trial and error, some responses emerged that proved successful. For example, while most of the domains were too small or too politically divided to react effectively, enough could to provide a variety of responses. Sharp class divisions had the same effect. While the samurai, with their feudal military background, showed a much keener appreciation of the superior military power of the West than did the Chinese civil bureaucracy, Japanese peasant entrepreneurs and city merchants, with their emphasis on personal economic goals, responded quickly to the new opportunities for foreign trade. The broad and functionally stratified samurai class, constituting around 6 per cent of the total population and including many men close to the grubby minor details of the economy and administration, also produced a much wider spectrum of responses than did the relatively narrow higher bureaucracy and elite of gentry degree-holders in China.

Another Japanese advantage was its extraordinary cultural homogeneity and economic and intellectual centralization. This was in part the result of Japan's geographic isolation and much smaller size in terrain and population than China. But homogeneity and centralization were even more the product of the whole Tokugawa system of control, particularly the institution of "alternate residence" of the lords at Edo. Unlike China, where inland areas were often quite unaware of the foreign threat, all parts of Japan responded immediately, even if in diverse ways. This situation, together with the relatively large size of the Japanese ruling class and the high levels of political administration and economic integration, which rising standards of living and high literacy rates had made possible, meant that Japan was far more capable than China of carrying out a unified, effective response to the West, once one had been decided upon.

Ironically, the very erosion of the foundations of the Tokugawa system also proved advantageous for the Japanese. In China, dynasties had come and gone, but the basic political, social, intellectual, and even economic system had remained extraordinarily stable for a millennium. It was hard to imagine, much less adopt, any other system. But in Japan the feudal social and political structure of the early seventeenth century was clearly outmoded by the nineteenth. The economy, society, and culture had evolved beyond it. Both the Confucian concept of the right of the man of personal merit to political leadership and the ancient Japanese tradition of imperial rule were fundamentally subversive to the Tokugawa polity. Thus other systems of political organization were not only imaginable but were secretly desired by some. There was a certain restiveness in society, particularly among the lower samurai. The rigid political structure was seriously undermined, and, beneath the surface calm, pressures were building up along dangerous fault lines within the society. A relatively light external blow thus could set Japan in motion in a way that much heavier blows could not move a basically far more stable China. As a consequence, Japan got off to a more speedy start in adjusting to the new world conditions, and this in turn gave it a decisive advantage during the following century.

The Emergence of the Imperial Court.   Abe had placed the shogunate in an anomalous position when he was forced to conclude the treaty with Perry against the expressed opinions of most of the daimyo and the known disapproval of the imperial court. To strengthen his position he took the novel step of having the court give formal sanction to the treaty. He also brought powerful collateral and "outside" daimyo into the inner councils of government, putting Nariaki of Mito in charge of coastal defenses.

The "house" daimyo, who traditionally dominated the Edo government, resented the role of these outsiders. Under Hotta Masayoshi, who replaced Abe late in 1855, they reduced Nariaki's influence and attempted to regain full control over the government. They also moved toward further concessions to the Western powers because, being more fully involved in the situation at Edo, they were more aware of Japan's serious plight than were the great lords from less exposed areas.

Before concluding the commercial treaty with Harris in 1858, Hotta again asked the daimyo for their opinions. Again the response was largely negative, even if somewhat more realistic than in 1853. Hotta also took the unprecedented step of going to Kyōto to obtain the emperor's approval in advance. But the imperial court was awakening from its long political slumber. The revived interest during the Tokugawa period in Japan's ancient history and the growing emphasis on the unbroken imperial line as the chief source of Japan's assumed superiority over other countries, had gradually called attention to the emperors and built up their prestige. Now both the shogunate and many of the domains were turning to Kyōto at this moment of crisis in the nation and uncertainty in Edo. Bolstered by the opposition of some of the largest domains to Hotta's policies, the court gave an ambiguous reply, which amounted to a refusal.

At this juncture, on May 30, 1858, Ii Naosuke, the lord of Hikone, the largest domain among the "house" daimyo, assumed the post of "great elder," the shogunal premiership which was filled only in times of crisis, usually by the head of the Ii family. Ii adopted a strong stance in an effort to regain control over the country. He signed the treaty, refused to go to

The first Tokugawa embassy sent abroad, in Washington in 1860.

Kyōto when summoned by the court, forced it to give its approval to the treaty, and decided a dispute over the shogun's heir in favor of the immature daimyo of the collateral domain of Wakayama over Nariaki's adult and able son, Keiki, who was the candidate of a faction that looked toward reform of the shogunate. When these acts were greeted by violent criticism and an upsurge of subversive, pro-emperor agitation, he responded by placing Nariaki, Keiki, and a few other major daimyo in domiciliary confinement, punished several court nobles and shogunal officials, and carried out a purge of pro-emperor intellectuals in Mito.

Ii's effort to restore Edo's authority seemed for a while to be succeeding, but it collapsed when a group of extremist Mito samurai assassinated him on March 24, 1860. It has been argued that, had Ii lived, the shogunate might have survived under his strong leadership to play a major role in Japan's subsequent modernization, but this seems improbable, because the shogunate, heavily burdened by tradition, was less capable of revolutionary change than were other groups. And Ii's reassertion of Tokugawa absolutism was more apparent than real. Actually, Edo's prestige and authority had both been greatly reduced. All over the country samurai activists were expressing their opinions freely on all matters of national policy. Despite long-standing prohibitions, daimyo and their agents, and even samurai acting on their own initiative, now felt free to approach the court in Kyōto to win it over to their views. Imperial sanction was becoming necessary for any major policy decision.

The imperial court thus emerged as the focus not only for opposition to Edo's foreign policies but for efforts to reform the government and society in the face of the foreign menace. The slogans of "honor the emperor" (*sonnō*) and "expel the barbarians" (*jōi*) became the twin rallying cries of the opposition. Both had strongly anti-shogunate overtones and were therefore taken up with particular enthusiasm by the samurai of some of the "outer" domains that had always nurtured resentment of Tokugawa rule. So strong was the appeal of these slogans that even Ii had been forced to give to the court vague promises that the "barbarians" would be expelled as soon as Japan was strong enough.

There was also a definite breakdown of feudal discipline as the domains began to assert their independence of Edo and restless samurai acted independently of their domain governments. Many samurai became "masterless samurai" in order to be free to agitate in Kyōto or elsewhere in behalf of the policies they supported. Known as *shishi,* or "men of determination," it was activists of this sort who killed Ii and went on to leave a wide trail of political assassination throughout Japan.

The shogunate was clearly in a hopeless position. Edo could not withstand foreign pressures for trade, yet was forced by public opinion to make promises to "expel the barbarians." Its authority over the domains and control over the individual samurai was fast ebbing. The shogunate had been forced to recognize the ultimate political authority of the imperial court. Both the political order and the economic system on which it stood were giving way under the Western impact. Ii had sought to shore up the tottering structure, and his death removed its last firm support.

The Rise of Satsuma and Chōshū.   No new "great elder" was appointed, and the shogunate floundered around indecisively. The initiative was lost to the imperial court and some of the "outer" domains. In particular Satsuma in southern Kyūshū and Chōshū at the western tip of Honshū came to the fore. They were among the largest domains, being ranked officially as the second and ninth in income. Their samurai forces were proportionately even larger, since both domains had been drastically reduced in geographic area but not in retainers as a result of the wars at the end of the sixteenth century.

Chōshū and Satsuma—particularly the latter—were relatively backward areas economically and socially, being located on the periphery of the nation, but this was an advantage rather than a handicap. It meant that the morale and cohesiveness of their samurai were less eroded than in the more advanced central parts of the country, where the bulk of Tokugawa power lay. They also had the advantage of strong anti-Tokugawa traditions dating back to their defeats more than two and a half centuries earlier. Mito, in contrast, being part of the Tokugawa power structure, faded from the political scene after the death of Nariaki in 1860, when the anti-Edo movement started to become truly revolutionary. Some other great domains were also inhibited from taking a strong stand because of traditional loyalty to the Tokugawa.

Another reason for the emergence of Satsuma and Chōshū was their financial strength at a time when most domains were seriously in debt and their samurai under heavy financial pressures. Satsuma and Chōshū had the money not only to bolster samurai morale but to buy Western arms and finance decisive action. Although in the early nineteenth century Satsuma had been burdened by a crushing debt, it had started vigorous reforms in 1830, at the very beginning of the so-called Tempō Reforms. It had canceled the domain's debts and strengthened its commercial monopolies, particularly of cane sugar, of which Satsuma, for climatic reasons, had a virtual monopoly in Japan. Both efforts had succeeded in large part because of the relative backwardness of the area.

Chōshū's Tempō Reforms had started in 1838 and had featured the reduction of samurai debts and the slashing of domain expenditures, in part through the reduction of monopolies, which was more typical of the Tempō Reforms than Satsuma's strengthening of monopolies. But the chief reason for Chōshū's financial solvency seems to have been an unusual institution known as the "nurturing office." Founded in 1762 as an emergency fund to help the domain's government and samurai in times of need, it had become an investment organ, particularly successful as a merchandiser of the surplus rice of the domain and as a storer of goods and provider of funds to other domains engaged in transport activities on the Inland Sea. By regularly investing part of the domain's revenues through this office, instead of devoting all its financial energies to repaying its debts, Chōshū stumbled into a system of deficit financing. Thus, during this period of creeping inflation, it profited from the gradual diminution of the value of its debt and the enhancement of the value of its investments.

Politics in Chōshū, as in many other domains, had become a matter of rivalries between samurai factions, which alternated in power by winning the support of the daimyo and his major retainers, the so-called house elders. In 1857 a moderate reform faction replaced the conservative faction in power and decided that Chōshū should take part in national politics. But it was not until 1861 that it took a specific step, proposing to the Kyōto court that the emperor should order the shogun to embark on a policy of "expansion across the seas," thus achieving a "union of court and shogunate" (*kōbu gattai*). Both Kyōto and Edo were agreeable, the one because the proposal was an open recognition of the emperor's political primacy, the other because it won the court's support for the shogunate's foreign policy.

Nothing, however, came of Chōshū's effort to mediate between Kyōto and Edo, and it was soon eclipsed by a more specific set of proposals for a "union of court and shogunate" put forward by Satsuma in May 1862. As a result, Satsuma was authorized by the court to bring order to Kyōto by suppressing the many extremist "masterless samurai" who were active there. It also persuaded Edo to make Keiki the guardian of the young shogun and appoint the collateral lord of Echizen, Matsudaira Keiei, as a sort of acting prime minister. Matsudaira, in an effort to win a broader national consensus, relaxed the last shogunate controls over the domains, abandoning the old hostage system and reducing the presence of daimyo at Edo under the "alternate attendance" system to a meaningless one hundred days every three years.

Meanwhile Chōshū had become more radically pro-emperor in its stance. This was largely because of the influence of a young teacher of military tactics, Yoshida Shōin (1830–1859). Yoshida had studied "Dutch Learning" in both Nagasaki and Edo and had been deeply influenced by the pro-emperor Mito thinkers. He had also attempted to smuggle himself out of the country on one of Perry's ships in 1854 but was imprisoned instead. Back in Chōshū, he opened a school and implanted his radically pro-emperor thoughts in a number of young men who were to play an important role in building the new Japan. Although he himself was executed in 1859 for having planned to assassinate the Edo representative in Kyōto, one of his disciples, a high-born samurai named Kido Kōin (1833–1877), became an important figure in the domain government and helped swing it toward an openly "honor the emperor" and "expel the barbarian" policy.

Because of Chōshū's new radicalism, the court shifted its support away from Satsuma to Chōshū, which started to organize a rudimentary government in Kyōto as well as small bodies of "imperial troops." Chōshū was supported for a while in its strong pro-emperor stand by Tosa, a major "outer" domain in Shikoku, but a more moderate Tosa faction regained control of the domain early in 1863 and adopted a more cautious policy. Swarms of activist "masterless samurai" in Kyōto, however, gave strength to the imperial cause by assassinating moderates, and meanwhile a body of some two thousand peasants, the so-called Heavenly Chastising Force, aroused by samurai radicals, attacked the shogunate authorities in the Nara area south of Kyōto.

The Resort to Military Force

Trials of Strength. The Chōshū-dominated court induced the shogun in the spring of 1863 to come to Kyōto, where he was forced to set June 25, 1863, as the date when the "barbarians" would be expelled. This placed the shogunate in a humiliating position, because it was obviously unable to carry out this promise, but it also put Chōshū out on a limb. When the appointed day arrived, the shogunate did nothing, but the Chōshū forts along the Strait of Shimonoseki, at the western end of the Inland Sea, started to fire on foreign ships. In response, an American warship shelled the forts on July 16 and sank two Chōshū gunboats recently bought at Nagasaki, while four days later French warships sent ashore landing parties which destroyed the forts and their ammunition.

Chōshū's impractical foreign policy had undermined its prestige and alarmed other Japanese. On September 30, 1863, troops from Satsuma and Aizu, a collateral domain in northern Honshū, whose lord had been appointed by Edo to be the military governor of Kyōto, carried out a *coup d'état* at the court, driving the Chōshū forces out of the city. The long Tokugawa peace had at last been broken. A group of moderate nobles was put in control of the court, and its incipient government organs and "imperial troops" were disbanded. Early in 1864 six "outer" and collateral lords were made a body of "participating daimyo" to aid the court, but, lacking any unity of policies or effective administrative organs, they soon broke up in futility.

Since Chōshū had reconstructed its forts and continued to fire on Western vessels, a combined fleet of seventeen British, French, Dutch, and American ships demolished the forts again in September 1864. The Western powers then made Chōshū agree not to refortify the straits and extorted a promise of an indemnity of $3 million from the shogunate. Subsequently, in June 1866, the powers agreed to a postponement of the payment in return for various new trade concessions, including a drastic lowering of import duties from around 20 per cent to a mere 5 per cent.

Chōshū's repeated military defeats at the hands of the foreign powers forced its leaders to recognize the impracticality of their foreign policy. They also came to see the inadequacy of their military strength in the domestic contest. Chōshū troops had marched on Kyōto in the summer of 1864 but had been defeated on August 20 at one of the gates of the imperial palace by the forces of Satsuma and Aizu. It was clear that Chōshū would have to redouble its efforts to build up and modernize its military strength.

Chōshū had started to form rifle units in 1857, and in 1860 it had embarked on a program of purchasing Western ships and guns. In 1863 it began to form a peasant militia and to organize rifle units composed of both samurai and commoners, such as the famous Kiheitai ("Irregular Troops Unit"), and these programs were now expanded. The use of peasant soldiers was a revolutionary departure from the whole Tokugawa system— socially and politically as well as militarily. The new units were officered in large part by young extremists, including former disciples of Yoshida Shōin, and thus gave added strength in domain politics to the extremist faction and new routes to power for its humbler members. For example, two young samurai, Inoue Kaoru (1835–1915) and Itō Hirobumi (1841–1909), who two years after participating in the attack on the British legation in

Edo in 1861 had gone to England to study, rose to influence as commanders of two of the new mixed units and went on to become major figures in the modernization of Japan. In fact, Itō, who was a peasant by birth but the adopted heir of a family of the lowest samurai status, was to become perhaps the most important architect of the new government, illustrating by his career the large role of lowly but ambitious samurai in the revolutionary transformation of Japan.

Satsuma too had learned much the same lesson as Chōshū about the inadequacy of traditional Japanese military power. Following the assassination of the Englishman, Richardson, by Satsuma samurai in 1862, the British exacted an indemnity of £100,000 from the shogunate and subsequently sent a fleet to Kagoshima, the Satsuma capital, to force punishment of the culprits and the payment of an indemnity by the domain. The Satsuma forts fired on the British ships on August 15, 1863, and the latter responded by leveling much of the city. Satsuma ended up with an indemnity payment of £25,000, largely borrowed from the shogunate, and a profound respect for and interest in the British navy. It immediately set about procuring Western ships with British aid, thus laying the foundations for what was to grow into the Imperial Japanese Navy.

The Chōshū Wars.   The Chōshū attack on Kyōto in August 1864 induced the shogunate at last to take firm action, and it dispatched against Chōshū an army of 150,000 men made up of levies from a large number of domains. The series of disasters that befell Chōshū in 1864 discredited the reformist clique, and its conservative opponents, who had consistently opposed the policy of involving Chōshū in national politics, came back into power in November of that year. Faced with the overwhelming might of the shogunate, the conservatives capitulated on January 24, 1865, accepting the mild demands for an apology, the execution of three "house elders" held responsible for Chōshū's policies, and promises to return seven extremist court nobles who had fled to Chōshū and to disband the new mixed units that had attacked Kyōto. The leniency of the shogunate's terms were a reflection of its own weakness. The domains that made up its army were not willing to bear the costs of a long campaign, and some of them, like Satsuma, were not ready to see the shogunate's power enhanced through the complete elimination of Chōshū.

Although the Chōshū government bowed to the shogunate, the extremist leaders of the mixed rifle units were unwilling to see their base of power destroyed. They refused to disband their units, and even before Chōshū capitulated to the shogunate they started armed resistance against the domain government. Winning skirmish after skirmish, they finally seized the Chōshū capital on March 12 and set up with the reformist faction a coalition regime in which Kido proved to be the dominant figure. The victory of the mixed units in the Chōshū civil war was a turning point in Japanese social and military history. Samurai of humble birth had defied with impunity their domain government, and mixed peasant and samurai forces had proved superior to its aristocratic, class army.

The outcome of the civil war in Chōshū also nullified the results of the shogunate expedition against Chōshū. Edo, buoyed by its assumed success in the campaign, had ordered the restoration of the "alternate attendance" system, but the daimyo simply ignored its orders. Now the shogunate saw that it would have to start all over again to bring a rebellious Chōshū into line. When a year of maneuvering to build up support for its policies and overawe Chōshū into accepting its terms failed to produce results, it finally dispatched a second army against Chōshū in August 1866. But this time the shogunate lacked the military superiority it had enjoyed before. Its army was less well organized and less united in purpose. Satsuma and some other powerful domains refused to participate. And Chōshū was now more unified, led by more determined men, and militarily stronger, having in the meantime improved and standardized its weapons and reorganized the whole of its forces into modernized military units. Though outnumbered, the Chōshū soldiers outfought the shogunate army; some of the participating domains withdrew their support; and by October the shogunate was compelled to sue for peace.

The Collapse of the Shogunate.   A single domain had defied and defeated Edo. The end of the shogunate seemed only a matter of time, and its downfall was now hastened by the decision of Satsuma and Chōshū to cooperate with each other. The whole Tokugawa system depended on mutual antagonisms among the domains. Satsuma and Chōshū by tradition were as unfriendly toward each other as toward the shogunate, an attitude sharpened by their rivalry for leadership in Kyōto after 1861 and by Chōshū's more intransigent stand on foreign policy. But these differences gradually lessened, as Chōshū was forced toward Satsuma's more realistic approach to the "barbarian" problem and both came to feel greater fear of restored shogunate power than jealousy of each other. They began to see that a league of major domains under the emperor would be a more effective and safer political system for themselves and for Japan than any patched up union between the court, the domains, and the shogunate.

The Satsuma leaders, Ōkubo Toshimichi (1830–1878) and Saigō Takamori (1827–1877), a man of dominating personality though of lowly samurai birth, were becoming increasingly suspicious of the shogunate's intentions. Some Edo officials were advocating a policy of reform and military modernization to be followed by the complete crushing of Chōshū and the subsequent suppression of other domains, such as Satsuma. They were strongly backed by the French Minister, Léon Roches, who hoped for increased French influence through a restored shogunate. Through his efforts, a French school was opened at Yokohama, a naval dockyard was built at Yokosuka nearby, and large quantities of weapons were imported. Not to be outdone, the British Minister, Sir Harry Parkes, who had played a large role in opening China, supported Satsuma with information and arms, while Satsuma itself moved toward a rapprochement with Chōshū. Two pro-imperialist "masterless samurai" from Tosa, who had taken refuge in Satsuma and Chōshū from the moderates in their own domain, acted as intermediaries in bringing these two mutually suspicious and hostile domains together. Finally on March 7, 1866, Saigō and Ōkubo concluded with Kido in Kyōto a secret alliance.

Keiki, who had been the unsuccessful candidate for shogun a decade earlier, succeeded the young, childless shogun in January 1867 and immediately set about modernizing the shogunate's forces and reorganizing its administration. Late in 1866 he had tried to organize a council of leading daimyo, through which the shogunate would retain its primacy while surrendering its monopoly of power, but the effort failed when only five of the twenty-four invited daimyo came. Tosa now proposed that the shogun return his political power to the emperor and head a council of daimyo under the latter. This solution would have relieved the shogun of the burden of full responsibility for national and foreign affairs while leaving him his source of income and power—his personal domain which was at least seven times the size of the largest daimyo domain. Keiki accepted the proposal on November 8, 1867, but this "imperial restoration" came to naught when the other daimyo again ignored his invitation to join the council.

Meanwhile Satsuma and Chōshū had decided on more radical action. Through Iwakura Tomomi (1825–1883), a court noble with close associations with Ōkubo, they obtained an entirely irregular "imperial rescript," calling for the destruction of the shogunate. Then on January 3, 1868 (the ninth day of the twelfth month of 1867 according to the Japanese calendar), the Satsuma and Chōshū forces, aided by those of the collateral domains of Echizen and Nagoya and the "outer" domains of Tosa and of Hiroshima in West Honshū, seized the palace and announced another "imperial restoration."

Keiki was inclined to accept the results of this *coup d'état* and retreated with his troops from Kyōto to Ōsaka to avoid clashes with the "imperial forces." But some of the collateral and "house" daimyo and many of the officials in the shogunate were not prepared to acquiesce meekly to this power grab by their old rivals. The shogunate forces marched from Ōsaka on Kyōto but were defeated south of the capital on January 27. They outnumbered the "imperial forces," but once again victory went to the side with technological superiority.

Satsuma soldiers fresh from victory in the war against the shogunate. All wear Western-style uniforms and two have Western-style haircuts, but they carry samurai swords. (Their rifles are not shown in the picture.)

The "imperial forces" then moved on Edo. Keiki, who himself came originally from pro-imperialist Mito, decided to capitulate, but die-hard shogunate supporters put up a fight in Edo, principally on July 4 at what is now Ueno Park. Aizu in northern Honshū desperately resisted the "imperial forces" but was crushed by November. The Tokugawa navy, which slipped out of Edo Bay, continued the fight in Hokkaidō. When it finally surrendered in May 1869, the whole of Japan came under the control of the revolutionaries.

The Creation of the New Government

The New Leadership.   The overthrow of the Tokugawa had proved relatively easy. While the shogunate was immobilized by its own inner divisions and most of the rest of Japan, divided into units too small or too indecisive to take effective action, stood by and watched, a handful of able young samurai from Chōshū and Satsuma had gained control over their own domains and then, through a bold use of the power of these two domains, had seized control over the whole nation with great speed and relatively little bloodshed. But to transform this military victory into lasting political power was another matter.

In theory an "imperial restoration" had taken place on January 3, 1868, but this was largely a matter of symbolism. The Japanese were much too accustomed to figurehead emperors, shogun, and daimyo to return easily to personal imperial rule. Nor were the emperor and his court prepared for actual political leadership. The Emperor Kōmei, who had been a foe of the extreme pro-imperial faction, had died early in 1867, to be succeeded by his son Mutsuhito, then only fourteen. Mutsuhito, who reigned until 1912, was in time to grow into an impressive and possibly influential figure. Known as the Meiji emperor for the new "year period" of Meiji ("Enlightened Rule") adopted in 1868, he became the personal symbol of the modernization of Japan, and the great political change became known as the Meiji Restoration. But in 1868 he was obviously too young to rule, and he seems never to have been more than one among many determiners of policy. Nor were the courtiers around him, the descendants of the ancient Fujiwara aristocracy, able to guide the nation. Iwakura and a few others, controlling as they did the imperial source of legitimacy, did become powerful figures in the new government. But most of the courtiers continued in merely symbolic roles as before.

Since the extremists of southwest Japan had acted in the name of their respective daimyo, it was natural for these daimyo to figure in the new government, but their role too was largely symbolic, as it had usually been in their own domains, and in time they were dropped even from titular posts. The real leadership was largely in the hands of the samurai who had engineered the revolution, although it had to be exercised tactfully by them through layers of daimyo, court nobles, and the emperor. Such a cumbersome structure led to anonymity and vagueness in leadership, but it was a system long familiar to the Japanese.

The new leaders were a remarkably young group of men. Iwakura, the oldest, was forty-three in 1868. The three most powerful men of samurai origin, Kido, Ōkubo, and Saigō, ranged between thirty-five and forty-one while Itō was a mere twenty-seven. For the most part they were of relatively humble birth. Kido was among the few who might have attained local, but scarcely national, political leadership under the old system. Iwakura, though a court noble, could never have hoped for real political power, and most of the others could have been nothing more than petty functionaries or possibly scholars. Clearly they had few emotional commitments to the *ancien régime*. They also were obviously men of exceptional talent, resilience, and daring to have risen so rapidly to the top.

The New Policies.   The new leaders had two decided advantages over their predecessors. They were freer of the yoke of tradition and thus more capable

*The Meiji emperor as a young man and Ōkubo Toshimichi as a
leader in the Meiji government.*

of drastic innovation. More important, the turbulent fifteen years since the coming of Perry had helped clarify what course Japan would have to take to retain its independence. It was obviously impossible to "expel the barbarians." Instead Japan would have to try to match Occidental military power and industrial skills. Only then could it hope to be secure against the West, regain control over its tariffs, and eliminate the other unequal features of the treaties. It was also becoming clear that, before Japan could match Occidental military and economic power, it would first have to create a much more centralized and modern government and would have to carry out major economic and social reforms.

Already on April 8, 1868, the revolutionaries had the emperor issue a "Five Articles Oath" (or "Charter Oath"), which indicated the course they hoped to follow. One article stated that "deliberative assemblies shall be widely established and all matters decided by public discussion." This was probably not so much a promise to create democratic institutions, of which the new leaders knew little, as an assurance that other samurai groups not yet represented in the new government would not be frozen out. Two of the articles promised a revolutionary break with the feudal class restrictions of the past: "The common people, no less than the civil and military officials, shall each be allowed to pursue his own calling so that there may be no discontent"; "Evil customs of the past shall be broken off and everything based on the just laws of Nature."

The last article propounded what was to prove the basic philosophy of the whole effort: "Knowledge shall be sought throughout the world so as to strengthen the foundations of imperial rule." Japan was to be modernized and strengthened through the use of Western knowledge, because the only defense against the West lay in the creation in modern form of the ancient Chinese ideal of "a rich country and strong military" (*fukoku kyōhei*), which could best be achieved through Western technology.

This was a surprisingly frank disavowal of the crude "expel the barbarian" concept with which most of the revolutionaries had started and which had helped them so much in their overthrow of the Tokugawa. But now that they were in power, this sort of simplistic xenophobia was an embarrassment, and they severely suppressed its continuing advocates. Would-be assassins of the British minister were treated as common criminals, and the leaders of friendly forces which clashed with French marines and sailors in Ōsaka early in 1868 were forced to commit suicide. The whole change in attitude was symbolized by an audience with the emperor arranged in March 1868 in Kyōto for the representatives of the foreign powers.

The Organs of Government.   It was easier to establish general policies than to carry them out. The new government had fallen heir to the position of the shogunate, which faced insoluble foreign problems, was financially bankrupt, had never exercised direct rule over most of Japan, and had lost much of the control it had once possessed. What organs of centralized government there were had been largely destroyed by the revolution. The new regime, like the old, was virtually powerless before Western military might, and the 5 per cent tariff rates imposed by the 1866 agreement left the country without economic defenses against the cheap manufactured goods of the West.

None of the new leaders had had any experience in operating a national regime, but by trial and error they evolved a system of government that worked, however makeshift its elements. On January 3, 1868, the day they assumed power in Kyōto, they created "three offices" to constitute the new government. On June 11, they reorganized the government under a Council of State, named after the ancient Grand Council of State and divided into legislative and executive branches, in apparent imitation of the division of powers in the American government. On August 15, 1869, the Council of State was reorganized with six ministries under it. Because of the archaic relationship between Shintō and the imperial family, however, it was outranked by an Office of Shintō Worship (actually the same name as the ancient Office of Deities). The old system of court ranks for government officials was also revived. Finally on September 13, 1871, the Council of State was divided into three chambers for legislative, administrative, and judicial functions, and the Office of Shintō Worship was realistically downgraded to the level of an ordinary ministry.

Such rapidly changing government bodies were less important than were the men who staffed them. The top posts, normally held by court nobles or daimyo, were largely symbolic. Attempts to draw into the administration the representatives of the various domains through representative assemblies, as promised in the "Five Articles Oath," proved unworkable, because the whole concept was not clearly understood, and the effort was abandoned after 1870. The important members of the government had proved throughout to be the samurai activists themselves, who usually filled the posts of Councilors and subordinate positions in the ministries. Gradually they moved up to positions of titular responsibility. This first happened in 1871 when Ōkubo became minister of finance, and by 1873 it had become the rule for the heads of ministries to be the young samurai who actually ran them.

Meanwhile the imperial capital had been moved to Edo, which had been the real political capital of Japan for two and a half centuries. On September 3, 1868, it was renamed Tōkyō ("Eastern Capital'"), and the next May the emperor was moved into the old shogunal castle, which thenceforth became the imperial palace.

The Centralization of Power. Central organs of government did not themselves create centralized rule. To do this, the new government had to establish its authority over the more than 260 separate domains, which in theory were autonomous and some of which had become all but independent during the final years of the shogunate. The daimyo and the great bulk of the samurai in all the domains, including those who had engineered the "imperial restoration," were scarcely prepared to see their domains swallowed up into a new and more centralized form of government, but this is precisely what the new leaders achieved in an amazingly short time, and with great enhancement of their own power. This surprising turn of events was possible only because of three factors: the leaders saw clearly the need for a fully centralized government if Japan were successfully to resist the West; they were themselves already in control of the domains whose military power underlay the imperial government; and the other domains had no basis for unified action and, although unclear as to what was happening, were eager not to be left out in the great reshuffle of political power that was obviously underway.

The new government divided the shogun's territory into prefectures for administrative purposes, and from the start it asserted rights of taxation and control over the domains, making the administration of the domains approximate that of the prefectures and in 1869 abolishing the barriers on highways and custom duties some of the domains had maintained. The key move, however, came when Kido and Ōkubo persuaded their respective daimyo in Chōshū and Satsuma and also the lords of Tosa and Hizen (in Kyūshū) to return their domains to the emperor on March 5, 1869. Many other daimyo followed suit, not wishing to be discriminated against by the new government, and the remainder were ordered to do likewise in July. This "return of the *han* registers" was accomplished so easily because it was a largely symbolic act, and the daimyo, as expected, were reappointed as governors. The stage, however, was now set for the complete abolition of the domains on August 29, 1871. Most of the daimyo and samurai were thunderstruck, but all complied meekly. Confused, bankrupt, and divided by mutual suspicions, the domains could put up no effective resistance against the new government, which was able to command support from all over Japan by championing the now popular concepts of "imperial rule" and "national unity" in the face of the foreign menace. Thus the domains, some of which had existed as effective political units for three or more centuries, were wiped out at one bold stroke, and all of Japan was divided into three urban prefectures (*fu*) and seventy-two other prefectures (*ken*). The number was reduced to a total of forty-five in 1889—exclusive of Hokkaidō and the Ryūkyū Islands—and has remained unchanged since.

The leaders in Tōkyō saw clearly that military strength was a crucial factor not only for the central government's control over the nation but in the effort to defend Japan from the West. At the time of its victory over the shogunate, the new government had only a few small volunteer units under its direct control and had been forced to rely on the support of domain armies, principally those of Chōshū and Satsuma. A much larger and more centrally controlled military was an obvious necessity. In 1871 the government formed an Imperial Force of ten thousand men drawn from the domain armies of Satsuma, Chōshū, and Tosa and trained along French lines. Then in 1872 it divided the ministry of military affairs into army and navy ministries.

The new navy was made up of ships from the shogunate fleet and from the various domains but was largely officered by men from Satsuma, who were to dominate it for the next several decades. Meanwhile the new army came under the leadership of men from Chōshū, particularly Yamagata Aritomo (1838–1922). Born into a family of the lowest samurai rank in Chōshū, Yamagata had studied under Yoshida Shōin, had commanded the Kiheitai in the Chōshū civil war, and after a year of study in Europe had returned to Japan in 1870.

The most important military innovation came with the issuance on January 10, 1873, of a conscription law, carefully prepared by Yamagata, who soon thereafter became army minister. All men, regardless of social background, were made liable for three years of active military service followed by four in the reserves. Universal conscription which had been prefigured by the use of commoner volunteers in the mixed units in Chōshū a decade earlier, was probably the most revolutionary step in the modernization of Japan. For almost three centuries commoners had been denied the right even to possess swords. The whole class system had depended on the clear functional division between them and the samurai. Now the weaponless masses suddenly became the foundation of a greatly expanded and entirely centralized and modernized military system. Naturally it took several years to put universal conscription fully into effect, but as it gradually became a reality the new government established unchallengable control over the country.

Consolidating the New Regime

Finances. The ease with which the central government had pushed the domains into oblivion in 1871 is to be explained in part by the generous financial settlement it provided the feudal classes. The daimyo were particularly well treated. When they had been made governors over their old domains in 1869, they had been given one-tenth of the former domain taxes as their private income, and this they retained in 1871. Since the central government took over the costs of local government and the old domain debts, the daimyo were better off financially than before. The samurai were treated less well. Their stipends were continued, but reduced between 1869 and 1871 to about two-thirds of what they had been before.

It has been argued that the new government needlessly complicated its financial problems by paying off the daimyo and samurai so generously, but this is doubtful. The samurai class constituted around 6 per cent of the total population, or about ten times the percentage of the privileged classes in France at the time of the French Revolution, and it would have been difficult and dangerous to attempt to dispossess so large a group that had long monopolized the martial arts and political leadership. Moreover, loyalty to the daimyo remained strong, and the new leaders were themselves mostly men of samurai origin with close ties to their own daimyo and domains. A less generous settlement might not have been possible in the early 1870's. As we shall see, the new government, as it grew stronger, did reduce the terms of its settlement to the point where serious revolts resulted. Actually, the government seems to have steered a successful course between the twin perils of financial bankruptcy and the danger of pushing the daimyo and samurai to unified rebellion or creating, as in France, a permanent resistance by supporters of the *ancien régime.*

There is no denying, however, the serious financial plight of the new government. It had no sources of revenue beyond those that had proved inadequate for the shogunate and domains, but it was burdened with the costs of the campaigns it had fought to come to power, the accumulated debts and indemnities of the shogunate and domains, and many new costs involved in trying to modernize the country, as well as the normal expenses of government and the payments to the daimyo and samurai. Little help could be expected from custom duties because of their limitation to 5 per cent in the agreement of 1866, which had also saddled Japan with an expensive program of building lighthouses and setting out buoys and lightships.

Today technologically backward regimes can often count on financial aid from abroad in the form of loans on easy terms or outright grants, but this was unthinkable in the nineteenth century. The Japanese, in their fear of Western encroachments, were reluctant to place themselves under the financial wing of any foreign nation, and the Western nations and bankers, looking upon Japan as a poor risk, required especially high interest rates and firm guarantees. Except for loans floated in London in 1869 to finance railroad construction and in 1872 to help cover the costs of the liquidation of the domains, borrowing abroad was not important in financing the new government.

The seriousness of the government's financial situation can be seen from the fact that receipts in 1868 were hardly more than a third of expenditures, and more than a third of these were in the form of forced loans, which, in the fashion of the shogunate, the new government exacted from the great merchant houses. The situation was only a little better in 1869, and the government had to resort to issuing large quantities of paper notes, which naturally fell in value and contributed to an already chaotic currency situation left over by the previous regime. But in the early 1870's the government's financial position improved. As it got full control over the country, its tax income rose to 60 per cent of expenditures by 1872, and, more important, confidence in its future increased so greatly within Japan that the government had little difficulty in borrowing what it needed domestically.

Meanwhile Tōkyō was carrying out a series of monetary, banking, and tax reforms, which helped stabilize its financial position. The prime movers in these reforms were Ōkuma Shigenobu (1838–1922), a Hizen samurai of iconoclastic temperament who became vice-minister of finance in 1869, and Itō, who had been sent to the United States to study currency systems and served as his assistant. The two set up a modern mint, adopted the American system of national banking, which never worked well in Japan and was subsequently abandoned, and established a uniform decimal currency in 1871 with the *yen* as its unit.

In July 1873, a few months before Ōkuma became minister of finance, a thorough revision of the agricultural tax system was begun. The land tax was the chief source of government income, constituting as late as 1880 four-fifths of all tax revenue. Before the tax reforms of 1873, agricultural taxes had been figured as percentages of agricultural yields, as they had been in feudal times, but, since the amount paid varied with the harvest, government budgeting had been difficult. Hence in 1873 these percentages were changed to a fixed tax in money based on land values. With the intention of taking half of the productivity of the land as taxes, the government at first set the tax at 3 per cent of assessed land values, but when this proved unrealistically high, it reduced the tax in 1876 to 2.5 per cent.

To carry out the new tax system, the ownership of all land had to be clearly established. This was done in 1872. Hitherto cultivators, feudal lords, and in many cases an in-between group of nonfeudal landlords had all had rights to the land, but now it was established that the man who paid the taxes, usually a cultivator or landlord, was the owner. Thus in modern Japan, unlike most of postfeudal Europe, there were no remaining feudal estates, but there was considerable tenancy from the start. The fixed money taxes contributed to an increase in tenancy, because in years of bad harvest poorer peasants could not meet these fixed payments and had to mortgage their land. About a quarter of the land was farmed by tenants even before the change in the tax system, and this figure shot up to 40 per cent in the next two decades and to 45 per cent by 1908.

The Abolition of Feudal Privileges.   The young samurai leaders, who had themselves risen to power in defiance of feudal restrictions, had promised in the "Five Articles Oath" to remove feudal social limitations, and they lived up to this promise with remarkable speed. They abolished class restrictions on professional fields of activity in 1869 and the next year permitted commoners to assume family names. In 1871 even the *eta* and other outcast groups, who at the time constituted between 1 and 2 per cent of the population, were given full legal equality, although social discrimination against them remains strong even today.

The samurai were still distinguished from commoners, but their separate classification carried no legal privileges and in time became a matter of only historical interest. Some of the abler samurai became officials in the new government, but most lost their functional positions in society when the domains were abolished and the military was turned from a closed class profession into a mass conscript system. Their pride was further hurt when they lost their distinctive badge of prestige. In 1871 they were permitted to discard the long and short swords they traditionally wore, and in 1876 they were ordered to do so.

Another serious blow was their loss of economic privilege. Even before 1868 most had eked out only an impoverished existence on their small stipends, and these had been reduced considerably since then. In 1873 the government offered the poorer samurai the option of a final lump-sum payment, and in 1876 it commuted into government bonds all samurai stipends on a sliding scale that gave proportionately more to the poorer samurai. On average the samurai received only 264 *yen* apiece, roughly half the value of their already reduced stipends. Most of them, unable to adjust to the new conditions, sank into poverty and disappeared as a class. The financial settlement with the daimyo at this time was again much more generous. The government bonds they received in 1876 in lieu of further annual payments made them relatively wealthy capitalists and the source of a large proportion of the banking capital of the period.

These swift social and economic changes naturally were not accomplished without considerable turmoil. More capable and enterprising persons were able to find enticing new opportunities, but most people found it difficult to adjust. A large proportion of the big urban merchant firms, accustomed to privileged patronage from the shogunate and domains, went bankrupt. Many peasants were bitterly opposed to the fixed monetary tax and to conscription, which was defined as a "blood tax." Peasant uprisings, which had doubled in number during the troubled last years of the shogunate, became even more frequent after 1868, rising to a crescendo in 1873 following the conscription law. But disaffection among former samurai was, of course, a much more serious threat and a matter of far greater concern to the new leaders than urban unrest or peasant disturbances. They made special efforts to settle indigent samurai on new lands as farmers or to absorb them into the government, the military, and the new industries.

Foreign Policy.   To some of the more traditional new leaders, foreign wars seemed a solution to the problem of samurai unemployment and a means of restoring feudal military virtues. Korea had insultingly rebuffed Japanese efforts to modernize relations between the two countries and modify the treaty of 1606 under which trade had been conducted at Pusan on the south coast of Korea by the Sō, the daimyo of Tsushima. Taking advantage of this situation, the group in charge of the government in the summer of 1873 decided on a military expedition to chastise Korea.

This decision had been made possible by the absence from Japan of many of the stronger and more enlightened members of the government. In November 1871 Iwakura had led abroad a mission of forty-eight members to see the West at first hand and persuade the foreign powers to modify the unequal treaties inherited from the shogunate. Two other leading figures in the administration, Kido and Ōkubo, and a number of rising stars such as Itō had gone with Iwakura. The Iwakura Mission went first to the United States and then to various countries in Europe. Although it proved of great educational benefit to its members, it failed completely to induce the Western powers to modify the treaties.

While Iwakura and the others were abroad, the government had been left largely in the hands of Ōkuma, Saigō, who had been the chief general in the campaigns of 1868, and Itagaki Taisuke (1837–1919), a Tosa soldier-samurai who had become disgruntled by the predominance of men from Satsuma and Chōshū in the new government. These three made the decision for a Korean campaign, but Iwakura and his colleagues, who re-

Saigō Takamori.

turned to Japan in September 1873 fully conscious of Japan's weakness as compared with the West, were appalled at the plan and managed to have it overruled. This split the ruling group, and Saigō and Itagaki resigned in disgust.

To mollify the defeated party, a less hazardous expedition was agreed upon. The Ryūkyū Islands, inhabited by a people who in language and culture are a variant of the Japanese, had their own line of kings, who for centuries had been tributary to China but since 1609 had been tightly controlled vassals of the daimyo of Satsuma. In 1872 the Tōkyō government had extended its control over the islands, and now it decided to send a punitive expedition of thirty-six hundred men against the aborigines of the east coast of Taiwan for having killed fifty-four shipwrecked Ryukyuans in 1871. The expedition was successfully accomplished in 1874 but raised a diplomatic crisis with China. Peking, unaware of the niceties of Western international law, settled the dispute by paying Japan an indemnity for the costs of the expedition and for the murdered Ryukyuans, thus recognizing in Western eyes Japan's claims to the islands, which in 1879 were made Okinawa Prefecture, named for the largest island.

Relations with Korea were settled by borrowing a page from Perry's book. The Japanese made a show of naval power in 1875 and, after a brief military encounter, forced the Koreans to sign the Treaty of Kanghwa on February 27, 1876. Two ports were opened to Japanese trade in addition to

Pusan, where Japanese already resided, and Korea's independence was asserted, though China continued to claim suzerainty.

The Suppression of Samurai Opposition.   The Taiwan expedition and other measures did little to relieve the financial plight of most samurai, some of whom began to resist the new policies by force of arms. The outbreaks occurred principally in the domains in western Japan from which the new leadership had largely been drawn, perhaps because the samurai there were not much awed by these new upstart leaders who had once been their own comrades. A mutiny occurred among the mixed units of Chōshū as early as 1870. When Saigō resigned from the government in 1873, a large proportion of the Satsuma soldiers in the new imperial forces returned with him to Satsuma, leaving the central army all the more in the hands of Chōshū men. In February 1874, two thousand former samurai of Hizen, under the leadership of Etō Shimpei, a disillusioned member of the new government, rose in revolt and seized the domain capital of Saga. Smaller revolts followed in various parts of Kyūshū and in Chōshū in 1876.

The most serious samurai uprising, however, occurred in Satsuma. There discontented samurai had clustered around Saigō, and hotheads among them forced him in January 1877 into the position of leading an armed revolution against the government he had done so much to create. Saigō's forces at their height numbered around forty thousand, but Tōkyō sent against them all its military power—the new conscript army, the navy, and the national police force, which had been built up mainly of former samurai as a major bulwark of the central government. In bloody fighting the Satsuma forces were finally crushed, and in September Saigō and his chief lieutenants met their end. The peasant army, backed by better weapons and superior transport facilities, had won the day. Once again modernized organization and technological superiority had proved decisive. Saigō himself became in retrospect the most popular and romantic hero of the Meiji Restoration, but his defeat spelled the end of the old order. The new government had met its last great domestic challenge. Henceforth it could push ahead to modernize Japan and build up its power against the outside world, free of any fear that reactionary forces would overthrow it at home.

5. Modernization in Meiji Japan

Economic Development

The Roles of the Government and the People. The new leaders, even when struggling with the problems of creating a centralized administration and staving off attacks by outraged samurai, never lost sight of the need to develop a "rich country" if Japan were to have the "strong military" that could win it equality with the West. They approached the problem of modernizing Japan's economy and society with remarkable breadth of understanding and openness of mind. They could expect no foreign aid, but they were at least free of foreign ideologies of modernization. In contrast to the often unrealistic assumptions of the twentieth century, no one in Japan or abroad thought that the Japanese should or could suddenly convert their feudal society into a full-fledged democracy or their backward agricultural economy into a fully industrialized one. The lower level of expectations permitted a much more pragmatic, step-by-step approach to the problem than is common in developing countries today.

Perhaps in part because of this sounder approach, the results were more spectacular and came more quickly than anyone could have foreseen. Within a mere half-century, the Meiji leaders achieved their goals, creating a relatively sound and modernized economy, on the basis of which Japan was able to win the national security and equality they longed for. In terms of their own objectives, their achievements constitute the national Cinderella story of modern times, even though, as in Bismarckian Germany, their emphasis on military power and national, as opposed to individual, prosperity bequeathed serious problems to later generations.

The question of the respective roles of the government and people in the economic development of Meiji Japan is of special interest today, when the proper balance between the two is an issue in many developing countries. In Japan, the government provided a favorable environment for economic growth by removing feudal restrictions on trade within the country and on individual activities, by assuring internal stability, and by providing sound currency, adequate banking facilities, a reasonable tax system, and efficient government services. It also took a direct role in industrial development. It pioneered many industrial fields and sponsored the development of others, attempting to cajole businessmen into new and risky kinds of endeavor, helping assemble the necessary capital, forcing weak companies to merge into stronger units, and providing private entrepreneurs with aid and privileges of a sort that would be considered corrupt favoritism today. All this was in keeping with Tokugawa traditions that business operated under the tolerance and patronage of government. Some of the political leaders even played a dual role in politics and business. Inoue of Chōshū, for example, became a sort of arbiter of the affairs of the great house of Mitsui.

Still, all these efforts would have meant little if there had not been an eager response by thousands of private Japanese to the new economic opportunities. In the long run, it was private initiative that produced the bulk of Japan's economic modernization and growth. A host of petty entrepreneurs appeared and also exceptional men who dared to experiment on a large scale with modern Western techniques of economic organization.

Although private individuals at first showed reluctance to enter the hazardous and little understood field of machine production, which grew in any case only very slowly, they responded vigorously to the opportunities created by foreign trade and the new government policies in the more traditional areas of the economy. As a consequence, during the first two decades of the Meiji period, growth in agriculture, commerce, and traditional forms of manufacturing quite overshadowed the development of new industries. In the decade of the 1880's alone agricultural acreage increased by 7 per cent and average yields per acre by 21 per cent. Total agricultural production doubled in the next twenty-five years. The economy as a whole thus developed a sound foundation for the modern industries which the government sought to foster at the top of the economic pyramid. This was probably one of the chief reasons for the difference between Japan's subsequent rapid industrialization and the less successful efforts in China and other Asian countries, where modern industry initiated from the top often sank into the quagmire of a stagnant local economy.

Early Industrialization.   Regardless of the growth of the traditional economy, however, modern industry was still essential to Japan if it was to

*Train on the Tōkyō-Yokohama railway, a favorite subject for early
Meiji woodblock artists.*

withstand the Western menace. The government leaders were particularly
interested in developing the strategic industries on which modern military
power depended. The shogunate and some of the stronger domains, such
as Hizen, Mito, and Satsuma, had led the way in borrowing Western technology to smelt iron and cast cannon. They had also started to build
Western-style ships, and by the time of the Restoration the shogunate and
domains together possessed 138 such vessels, either built in Japan or bought
abroad. They had also started to master Western navigational techniques.
In 1860 the shogunate had been able to send an entirely Japanese-manned
steamer, the *Kanrin-maru,* across the Pacific to accompany a shogunate
embassy to the United States.

The new government inherited from the shogunate two modern ship-
yards, at Yokosuka and Nagasaki, and added another at Hyōgo (the
modern Kōbe). It also operated large factories in Tōkyō and Ōsaka for
making cannon, rifles, and ammunition, and three small gunpowder plants.
Though Western models were used, foreigners themselves were not employed in these five arsenals for security reasons.

The government also took the lead in developing modern communications, because of the public nature of this undertaking and its great cost.
Internal transportation within Japan was extremely backward and expensive
since there were few navigable rivers or good roads. It was said to cost as
much to move goods fifty miles inside Japan as all the way from Europe.
Consequently, railways, once constructed, proved immensely profitable.

A nineteen-mile line was laid between Yokohama and Tōkyō in 1872, and a similar line from Kōbe to Ōsaka, completed in 1874, was extended to Kyōto in 1877. Telegraph lines, which were cheaper to construct and important for administrative control over the nation, linked all the major cities by 1880.

The nonstrategic industries had to be developed too if Japan was to compete successfully with the West and eliminate the dangerous imbalance that had developed in its foreign trade. Actually a silk blight in Europe in the 1860's had produced such a strong demand for Japanese silk and silkworm eggs that Japan enjoyed a favorable balance of trade for a decade, but the recovery of the European silk industry and the lowering of tariffs in 1866 combined to produce large deficits after 1869. The imbalance was heightened by charges for shipping, insurance, and other services the Japanese were still too inexperienced to provide. The inflow of foreign manufactured goods disrupted many handicraft industries on which peasants depended for much of their livelihood, and the outflow of specie undermined the value of paper money and credits, thus contributing to the economic plight of the samurai. New industries were desperately needed to stem the inflow of foreign goods and give employment to peasants and samurai.

The government established a ministry of industry in December 1870. The next year Itō took charge of it as vice-minister and in 1873 became minister, remaining in this key post until 1878. The ministry encouraged the private development of manufacturing and industries through technical assistance, easy credit, and subsidies, but the results were meager, and many of the new ventures went bankrupt. Capital was scarce and interest rates as a result high, usually above 10 per cent. Moreover, the Japanese themselves had had little experience with machinery, and foreign technicians were inordinately expensive.

The government, therefore, became increasingly involved in industrial and mining ventures. By 1873 its bureau of mines employed thirty-four foreigners. In 1874 it bought out a coal mine started in 1869 by Hizen with English technical and financial aid, and it went on to develop eight other modern coal mines and invested heavily in a modern iron mine in 1881. It also built a machine tool factory in 1871, a cement plant in 1875, a glass factory in 1876, and a brick factory in 1878, all in Tōkyō. Most Japanese coal, iron, and copper mines, however, remained unmodernized and in private hands, although private capital did introduce modern methods into such relatively simple processes as match and paper making.

The Textile Industry.   The most important industrial field was textiles, since these made up half of Japan's imports between 1868 and 1882.

Woolens had become significant for the first time in Japan because soldiers and government functionaries now wore Western-style woolen uniforms and many other men were adopting Western dress. Since this was an entirely new industry for Japan, the government was forced to develop it itself, building a mill in 1877–1878, which remained the chief producer until after 1900.

Cotton yarn and goods constituted a much bigger industry. In attempting to compete with foreign production, however, domestic manufacturers found themselves handicapped by a more costly and inferior local cotton fiber, and eventually the Japanese were forced to give up growing cotton. The industry also lacked mechanical experience and adequate capital for the large scale of production needed to make costs competitive with those of the West. As a result, the government was forced to play a large role initially. An Edo merchant had ordered American spinning machinery as early as 1864, and Satsuma set up a textile factory with British spindles and looms in 1868 and built another in Osaka in 1870. The latter was taken over in 1872 by the government, which also built two other mills in 1880 and 1881. A more important step was the creation in 1878 of a fund of 10 million yen to provide loans on easy terms to private entrepreneurs. As a result, private interests began to move cautiously into the cotton textile field.

Silk reeling, on the other hand, was mechanized with relative ease, and the government's role was limited to providing technical advice and operating a few pilot plants. Turning the silk reel by steam or water power, which produced much finer silk than reeling by hand, was a simple process requiring only modest capital, while all the other steps in silk filature remained hand processes at which the Japanese were already expert.

The first mechanical silk-reeling plant was established in 1870 by a collateral daimyo in the silk-producing area of central Honshū, and the government established three pilot plants between 1872 and 1877. Government plants, however, accounted for only a tiny fraction of mechanical silk reeling in Japan. The rest was developed by private entrepreneurs. The house of Ono built a silk-reeling plant in Tōkyō late in 1870 and seven more in 1872–1873. Local businessmen in the silk-producing areas of central Honshū followed suit. By 1880 some 30 per cent of Japanese silk exports were machine-reeled products which outclassed the hand-reeled silk of the rest of Asia and competed well with European silk. Silk accounted for some 43 per cent of Japanese exports, and, chiefly because of the brisk demand for it abroad, Japan's foreign trade began to show a favorable balance in the mid-1880's. Thus the industry that contributed most to the balancing of foreign trade was developed almost completely by private capital and enterprise.

The Development of Hokkaidō.   Japan's only unexploited frontier was in Hokkaidō, and its development seemed important to the Meiji leaders for both economic and strategic reasons. The Japanese had exercised some control over this cold, inhospitable island since about the eleventh century, but in the early nineteenth century the Japanese population was still limited chiefly to the coast and the extreme south, while the rest of the island and the small ones to the north were inhabited for the most part by Ainu aborigines. The Japanese, however, had surveyed and mapped the islands and waters north of Hokkaidō and were exploiting their fisheries.

Because of the opening of Hakodate to foreign ships through the Treaty of Kanagawa in 1854, the shogunate took over direct control of Hokkaidō from the Matsumae daimyo, as it had on certain previous occasions. It also agreed in 1855 to Russian demands for a rough delimitation of the northern boundary, with Kunashiri and Etorofu, the two large southern islands in the Kurils, assigned to Japan and the two countries continuing their joint occupation of Sakhalin. A clearer settlement of the northern boundary was reached in 1875 when Japan ceded its interests in Sakhalin in return for Russia's relinquishment of its claims to the central and northern Kurils.

The new government embarked on an ambitious program of colonizing Hokkaidō. In 1869 it gave the island its present name, meaning "Northern Sea Circuit" (previously it had been known as Ezo, meaning "barbarian"), and it created a Colonization Office under a Satsuma samurai, Kuroda Kiyotaka (1840–1900). Kuroda in 1870 went to the United States, where, on President Grant's advice, he hired the United States Commissioner of Agriculture, Horace Capron, at the princely salary of $10,000 plus expenses, and a staff of American experts to advise on the development of Hokkaidō. Remaining in Japan until 1875, these men left an unmistakably American cast—dairy herds and silos—to the rural landscape of Hokkaidō.

Between 1869 and 1881 the population of Hokkaidō more than quadrupled, reaching 240,391, agricultural acreage increased more than tenfold, and the fishing industry more than doubled. In 1883 the island was given a normal prefectural system of local government, though it continued to be called a "circuit" (*dō*), rather than a prefecture (*ken*). By 1918 a further tenfold increase in population had taken place, and Hokkaidō had become securely Japanese and an important part of the economy.

Financial Retrenchment.   The development of Hokkaidō, though valuable in the long run, added to the financial drain on the central government during the 1870's. Meanwhile the government's many industrial enterprises were for the most part losing money. These costs on top of the heavy expenses for liquidating the old regime, especially the bond payments of 1876 and the Satsuma Rebellion the next year, severely strained the government's financial credit. By 1880 its paper currency had fallen to hardly more than half its face value, and a serious inflation had set in. Rice prices more than doubled between 1877 and 1880, and inflation drastically cut the real value of the fixed land tax on which government finances depended.

In the face of this financial crisis, the government decided on a policy of economic retrenchment and deflation. The first major step, announced on November 5, 1880, was the sale of all nonstrategic government industries. A prime advocate and the chief executor of this retrenchment policy was Matsukata Masayoshi (1835–1924), a Satsuma man of humble samurai origin, who was appointed minister of finance in 1881 and remained in that key post until 1892.

Because of the weakness of private capital and the unprofitability of most government industries, Tōkyō had difficulty in finding buyers for its industrial ventures and eventually had to dispose of most of them at very reduced rates, ranging between 11 and 90 per cent of the original investments. Most were sold, sometimes without competitive bids, to insiders, that is, to businessmen or government officials already closely associated with the leaders. As Japan's industrialization began to overcome its initial handicaps in the next few years and return handsome profits, particularly on the basis of the reduced prices at which the government industries had been bought, the few who had been in a position to purchase these enterprises grew wealthy and came to control a large share of Japan's modernized economy. All this contributed to the eventual concentration of much of Japanese industry in the hands of a few giant corporations—the zaibatsu, or "financial cliques," as they were later called pejoratively.

This outcome of the retrenchment policy has given rise to Marxist interpretations that the chief motive for the sale of government industries was the commitment of the government leaders to large-scale capitalism. There is no real evidence for this theory, however, and it assumes an understanding by the Japanese leaders of the long-range effects of their actions and a preference for capitalism over government ownership that seem altogether improbable. All the contemporary documents show that the political leaders were desperately trying to cut government expenditures, and the sale of the industries was but one aspect of a drastic reduction in the budget. Their favoring of insiders is also understandable. They were interested primarily in the nation's economic growth. Selling the industries at reasonable prices to men they felt were competent seemed the best way to ensure their continued development. This was far more important to the national interest than the payment the government received. As it turned out, most of the industries sold did not for a decade or more make profits comparable to the return in other economic fields. The purchasers' faith in the future of industry in Japan is, in fact, more surprising than the low prices they paid.

Matsukata's retrenchment policies were successful, and by 1886 he had the government back on an even financial keel. New taxes were instituted, and a centralized, European-style banking system, under the newly founded Bank of Japan, was substituted in 1882 for the earlier American system. The whole economy, too, although temporarily depressed by the deflationary policies, soon recovered and surged ahead even more rapidly than before. Deflation had weeded out the unsound speculative ventures that had flourished under the inflationary conditions of the late 1870's, leaving only the sounder enterprises. These profited from the return to hard money and the drop in interest rates from around 15 per cent to around 10. Private management of the former government industries, being free from cumbersome bureaucratic control, seems also to have been more efficient. The Japanese were in the meantime beginning to overcome initial handicaps, such as the high cost of internal transport and inexperience with machinery. In short, Japan was ready for an industrial "breakthrough"—at least in certain fields.

The Business Community.   The men who led the rapid development of the Japanese economy in the next few decades were as remarkable a group as the Meiji political leaders themselves and in many ways much like them. They too were obviously men of exceptional talent, flexibility, and daring to have emerged so successfully from the economic confusion of the preceding years. Like the political leaders, they were often motivated as much by patriotism as by personal ambition. They realized that they too were strengthening the country and establishing its security. The government leaders concurred, and society accorded them a surprising degree of respect and prestige, considering the traditional Japanese contempt for economic activities.

One might suppose that the urban merchants, who had so dominated the culture as well as the economy of the late Tokugawa period, would have comprised the bulk of the new business leadership, but their role actually was relatively small. Their past experience of subservience to the shogunate and domains seems to have inhibited them from developing new entrepreneurial skills. They stuck for the most part to traditional merchandising and banking activities. Those who attempted to branch out into new fields often went bankrupt, as happened to the houses of Shimada and Ono. The once great house of Kōnoike survived but gradually lost ground.

Among the bigger concerns, only the house of Mitsui made the transition with complete success. This it did under the leadership of Minomura Rizaemon (1821–1877), an orphan of obscure origin, whose appointment as general manager was unprecedented in Mitsui history. He established a close relationship with Inoue, moved the firm from Kyōto to Edo, sent five members of the Mitsui family and two employees to the United States to study modern business methods, and separated the rest of the firm from its merchandising branch, which in time was modernized into Mitsukoshi, one of Tōkyō's great department stores. Mitsui eventually developed into the largest of the zaibatsu firms. The third largest zaibatsu company, Sumitomo, also grew out of an old merchant firm, which like Mitsui dated back to the seventeenth century but had specialized in copper mining.

Men of samurai background played a much larger role in developing the new economy than did the urban merchants. This may seem strange in view of the traditional samurai contempt for business and the profit motive, but it can be explained by samurai traditions of leadership, their high standards of education, the tremendous interest in economic problems among samurai intellectuals during the second half of the Tokugawa period, the managerial skills some samurai had developed as domain or shogunate officials, and the severe financial difficulties in which most samurai found themselves in the 1870's.

In the large samurai class, however, it was only a few rather untypical figures who distinguished themselves as successful businessmen. The more affluent samurai, together with the daimyo, provided much of the new banking capital out of their government bond payments, but the banks were closely supervised by the government and did not represent significant samurai entrepreneurial activity. Actually most of the many companies founded by samurai failed because of their business inexperience.

The most outstanding example of a successful samurai entrepreneur was Iwasaki Yatarō (1834–1885). He had been the supervisor of Tosa's mercantile operations in Nagasaki and, after the dissolution of the domain, managed to make its commercial and shipping interests his private firm, subsequently named Mitsubishi. He was much favored by the government, which saw in him a person who could develop a Japanese shipping line that would eliminate dependence on foreign ships. During the Taiwan expedition of 1874 the government had him operate the thirteen ships it had bought and subsequently gave them to him. He was again put in charge of marine transportation during the Satsuma Rebellion and was given nine more ships. His line began to operate abroad in 1879, and eventually Mitsubishi grew to be the second largest of the zaibatsu.

Even men of peasant origin became important business leaders. The lowering of the land tax in 1876, together with the continuing inflation, brought the tax burden in rural Japan below what had been normal levels. This resulted in considerable rural prosperity and a chance for the wealthier peasants to invest in agricultural improvements and in expansion of their traditional industrial and commercial enterprises. The mechanization of silk reeling, for example, was largely the work of enterprising peasants. Others ventured further afield. Yasuda Zenjirō (1838–1921) ran away from his peasant home to Edo, where he became a successful banker and the founder of the fourth largest zaibatsu firm. Another man of rural origin, Asano Sōichirō (1848–1930), acquired control and then ownership of the cement factory that the government had built and turned this hitherto financially disastrous undertaking into a great success.

The most outstanding businessman of peasant origin was Shibusawa Eiichi (1840–1931). Born near Edo into a rich peasant family engaged in the indigo-dyeing business, Shibusawa was given a good education and developed great ambitions. He left home in 1863, determined to achieve samurai status, became enrolled as a samurai under Keiki, and accompanied Keiki's younger brother to Europe on an official mission in 1867. After Keiki's abdication, Shibusawa started a banking and trading company for his former lord but was soon drafted to serve in the new central government. Under the patronage of Ōkuma and Inoue he rose rapidly, becoming one of the major figures in the finance ministry. However, he resigned from the government in 1873 and became president of the First National Bank, which he had helped found by forcing Mitsui and Ono banking interests into a merger. In 1880 he organized the Ōsaka Spinning Mill, which soon became Japan's first major industrial success. From this beginning he went on to become one of the nation's greatest entrepreneurs, having a hand in the creation and management of more than a hundred companies.

Industrial Success.   Under the leadership of men of this sort, Japanese industry began to overcome its initial handicaps and to grow at an accelerating pace. Shibusawa's Ōsaka Spinning Mill spearheaded the new industrial advance. It was much larger than earlier mills, thus cutting overhead costs, and Shibusawa had trained a young man in England to run it with the most up-to-date techniques. The mill had already proved a great financial success by 1884, in the midst of the deflationary depression. In the next few years there was a rush of entrepreneurs into the spinning industry, particularly in Ōsaka, the old center of the cotton trade.

The boom in spinning was followed by a more general boom. New firms prospered in such diverse fields as mining, weaving, cement, beer, chinaware, gas, and electricity, but the greatest growth came in cotton spinning and railway transportation. Between 1883 and 1890, government railways expanded from 181 to 551 miles and private railways from 63 to 898 miles. Cotton spindleage almost tripled between 1882 and 1887 and production grew tenfold in the next five years. By 1894 the Japanese spinning industry had become so efficient that its products began to venture into the world market on a significant scale, and in 1897 Japan became a net exporter of cotton yarn. By the end of the century cotton spinning and weaving employed 247,117 persons, or 63 per cent of all factory workers.

The 1880's also saw the emergence of a trend toward mergers and cartel-like organization among Japanese business concerns, in place of sharp competition. Such trends have been common in mature industrial economies but perhaps appeared so early in Japan because of the government's eagerness for economic efficiency and the long tradition among Tokugawa businessmen of forming monopolistic associations under official sponsorship. In 1885 the competing steamship lines of the Mitsubishi and Mitsui interests were merged into the Japan Mail Line (Nippon Yūsen Kaisha, or N.Y.K.), under Mitsubishi domination. Under Shibusawa's leadership a tight cotton-spinners cartel was also organized to allocate the inadequate supply of skilled labor, to arrange for noncompetitive purchase of raw cotton and the sale of cotton yarn abroad, to assign quotas in times of overproduction, and to arrange mutually advantageous compacts with shipping lines and merchandising firms. Thus by the 1890's the pattern had been set for the development of industry-wide cartels and of "combines" of interlocking business interests in finance, commerce, and manufacturing.

Industrial growth in Japan, as in other countries, was not a straight-line development. The boom years of the 1880's were followed by a period of slower expansion, but Japan's victory in the Sino-Japanese War in 1895 set off another upsurge in all the established industrial fields and in certain new ones such as chemical fertilizers. Another slowdown followed in which existing companies were amalgamated into larger and stronger units. Then the Russo-Japanese War of 1904–1905 brought a third and bigger boom. Cotton weaving began to catch up with cotton spinning; the electric industry grew as railways were electrified and cities installed street lighting and streetcars; shipping tonnage and services abroad expanded rapidly; the production of coal almost tripled in the decade after 1904; the Yawata Iron Works, founded by the government in 1901 at the northeastern tip of Kyūshū, helped Japan to meet a significant proportion of its iron and steel needs; and a few other heavy industries began to join the simpler light industries as important components of the economy. Thus, during the two and a half decades following Matsukata's financial reforms, one industry after another came of age, and Japan, with its industrial base now diversified and soundly established, entered on a period of sustained industrial growth.

The Transformation of Society

Westernization.   Industrialization as well as political and military modernization depended on new skills, new attitudes, and broader knowledge. The leaders had realized from the start that social and intellectual modernization was prerequisite to successful innovation in other fields. But in the social and intellectual areas, as in economics, the responsiveness of thousands of individuals from all classes was more important in the long run than the planning of the authorities.

Many innovations were not really necessary to modernization but were merely imitations of Western customs. At the time, however, the distinction between fundamental features of modern technology and mere Occidental pe-

*An 1877 woodblock print showing the Ginza in downtown Tōkyō,
with modern brick buildings, rickshaws, and a horse-drawn
streetcar.*

culiarities was by no means clear. If it was necessary to use Western weapons,
there might also be virtue in wearing Western clothes or shaking hands in the
Occidental manner. Moreover, the Meiji Japanese had good reason to adopt
even the more superficial aspects of Western culture. The international
world of the nineteenth century was completely dominated by the Occident,
and in view of the arrogant Western assumption of cultural superiority, the
Japanese were probably right in judging that they would not be regarded
even as quasi-equals until they too possessed not only modern technology
but also many of the superficial aspects of Western culture. The resulting
effort to borrow almost anything and everything Western may now seem
amusingly indiscriminate, but it is perfectly understandable.

Some innovations were inspired by mixed desires for technological progress and cultural conformity. For example, Western hygienic practices were
introduced, and Japanese in time became enthusiastic wielders of tooth-
brushes and consumers of patent medicines. The Gregorian calendar, together with the seven-day week and Sunday holiday, was adopted and the
sixth day of the twelfth month of 1872 (the fifth year of Meiji) was made
January 1, 1873 (Meiji six). Mail service was introduced the same year,
and in 1886 Japan joined the international metric agreement, adopting the
metric system for general use in 1924. A curious hybrid of East and West
was the rickshaw, invented in Japan in 1869. It was an ingenious combina-

tion of superior Western-style wheels with cheap Eastern labor and spread widely throughout Asia before giving way in Japan itself in the twentieth century to motorized transport.

Many innovations were only for psychological effect—on Westerners or on the Japanese themselves. Western-style haircuts, in place of the samurai shaved pate and long peripheral hair tied in a top knot, were a major symbol of Westernization. Soldiers and functionaries were put in Western-style uniforms, and men of prominence often adopted Western clothes and even the full beards then in style in the Occident. Western dress was prescribed for all court and official ceremonies in 1872. In the latter part of the Meiji period the cutaway (called *mōningu* for "morning coat") became so entrenched that it is still in general use for formal occasions, and *haikara* ("high collar") became a popular word for "fashionable." Meat eating was encouraged, although previously it had been considered immoral because of Buddhist attitudes, and the beef dish of *sukiyaki,* developed at this time, became a popular hallmark of Japanese culture. Western art and architecture were adopted, producing an ugly Victorian veneer in the cities and depressing "Western rooms" in the mansions of the wealthy.

The craze for Westernization reached its height in the 1880's. There were even efforts to make social relations between the sexes conform to Western practice. Women of good families were taught foreign languages and ballroom dancing. In 1883 the government erected in Tōkyō an elaborate social hall, called the Rokumeikan, where dances were held every Sunday night for the political elite and the diplomatic corps. A great fancy-dress ball was held there in 1887, with the chief government dignitaries in attendance.

This, however, proved to be the last straw for more conservative Japanese. There was a general revulsion against unnecessary imitation of the West, accompanied by a re-emphasis of native values and traditions. Many superficial aspects of Western culture, such as ballroom dancing, were dropped, permitting significant technological innovations to free themselves of the onus of association with useless and irritating peculiarities. The same cycle of enthusiastic and somewhat indiscriminate adoption of Western ways, followed by the rejection of certain less essential aspects of these innovations, was to repeat itself more than once in subsequent Japanese history and can also be discerned in other Asian countries.

Legal Reforms.   To win acceptance by the West, it was essential that the Japanese reform their legal institutions along Occidental lines. Extraterritoriality was among the most galling features of the unequal-treaty system, but there was no hope of eliminating it until the Western powers had full confidence in Japanese legal processes. Legal renovation was also fundamental to technological modernization and was necessitated by the abolition of the old class structure and the other great changes taking place.

Western concepts of individual rather than family ownership of property were adopted, although for purposes of formal registration of the population the law continued to recognize the old extended family, or "house," consisting of a patriarch and those of his descendants and collateral relatives who had not legally established a new "house." Concepts of legal rights, as opposed to the traditional emphasis on social obligation, came to permeate the new laws. The structure and procedures of the courts were made to conform to those of the West, and torture as an accepted legal practice was abolished in 1876. But some innovations, such as the prohibition of prostitution and mixed bathing, which were adopted simply to placate Western prejudices, proved ineffective and were subsequently abandoned.

Most of the legal reforms ware instituted piecemeal, and a thorough recodification of the laws proved a difficult and slow task. Drafts, drawn up largely under French influence, were submitted in 1881 and again in 1888. A complete code, revised largely on the basis of German legal precedent, finally went into effect in 1896.

Religion.   One feature of Western civilization which the new government made no move to adopt was Christianity, even though this would have created a more favorable impression on Westerners than any other step it could have taken. Prejudices against Christianity ran much too deep in Japan. In fact the new government re-established in 1868 the old Tokugawa bulletin boards proscribing the religion, and it aroused a storm of protest from the foreign diplomats by rooting out a clandestine community of some three thousand Christians which had remained in the Nagasaki area from the period of Catholic missions in the sixteenth and seventeenth centuries. Not until the members of the Iwakura Mission had seen how strongly Westerners felt about their religion did the government in 1873 drop the old ban on Christianity, and even then only indirectly by removing the public bulletin boards on the grounds that their content was already well known.

But Christianity had in the meantime re-entered Japan. As early as 1859, American Protestant missionaries had taken advantage of the Harris treaty to come to the open ports. One of them, Dr. J. C. Hepburn, a medical missionary of the American Presbyterian Church, compiled a Japanese-English dictionary, published in Shanghai in 1869, which established the standard system for romanizing Japanese that still bears his name. Catholic missionaries also started to regather their remaining flock in the Nagasaki area. A Russian Orthodox monk, Nikolai (1836–1912), came to Hakodate in 1861 and moved in 1872 to Tōkyō, where he became the bishop and later the archbishop of a flourishing missionary church.

Gradually hostility toward Christianity abated, and the government in the 1880's adopted a clear policy of religious toleration, tacitly accepting

Christianity, together with Buddhism and Shintō, as one of the three major religions of Japan. Aided by its association with Western civilization, which many Japanese felt to be the obvious "wave of the future," Christianity also attracted many inquiring Japanese intellectuals from the samurai class, who saw in it the key to Western progress and strength. They also saw in Protestant Christianity a new code of personal ethics and loyalty that would strengthen Japan at this time of confusion over the old codes of conduct.

Niishima Jō (1843–1890), a samurai from central Honshū who had gone to America in 1864, where he had graduated from Amherst College and become an ordained Congregational minister, founded a school in Kyōto in 1875 that grew into Dōshisha University. A group of young samurai from the Kyūshū domain of Kumamoto, who had been converted by an American teacher of English, transferred to this institution in 1876 and later became prominent Christian leaders. The influence of Dr. William S. Clark, the president of the Massachusetts Agricultural College, who had gone to Japan in 1876 to take charge of the newly founded Sapporo Agricultural College (later Hokkaidō University), led to the conversion of several able young samurai, including Nitobe Inazō (1862–1933), who became a leading scholar and educator, and Uchimura Kanzō (1861–1930), who reacted to the sectarian divisions and close national affiliations of the Protestant missionaries by founding a "No Church" (Mukyōkai) movement.

Christianity thus had a strong impact among Japanese intellectuals, but its popular appeal remained small. Although Christians had constituted close to 2 per cent of the Japanese population in the early seventeenth century, in 1889 they numbered less than a quarter of 1 per cent, divided among forty thousand Catholics, twenty-nine thousand Protestants, and eighteen thousand Orthodox, and the number of Christians in recent times has never reached as much as 1 per cent of the population.

The lack of popular interest in Christianity did not mean a return to native religions and philosophies. Despite the Confucian background of the leaders, Confucianism, as the orthodoxy of the Tokugawa system, stood discredited in their eyes. While Confucianists were the most effective critics of Christianity and in time won acceptance from the government leaders for some of their attitudes, many of the fundamental concepts of Confucianism were obviously not suited to the new situation.

Shintō was in better repute because a revived interest in it had been a key element in the intellectual trends that led to the "imperial restoration." The creation in 1869 of the Office of Shintō Worship above the organs of civil government was an effort to establish a Shintō-oriented government, modeled on the semi-theocratic state of more than a millennium earlier, but this proved impractical. Despite the official favor shown to Shintō, this simple nature worship did not have much to offer men of the new age, institutionally or intellectually. The attempted revival had little inner life and soon faded away. The government continued to control and support the more important Shintō shrines, but the Shintō cults themselves lapsed into their traditional passive state, forming no more than a quiet ground swell in the emotional life of the people. Only the so-called popular Shintō Sects, such as Tenrikyō, which were recently founded, eclectic religions, popular among the lower classes, continued to show much vigor.

The favored status of Shintō contributed to a violent disestablishment of Buddhism in the first years of the new regime. The Buddhist clergy had gained administrative control over a large proportion of the Shintō shrines almost a thousand years earlier, and under the Tokugawa most Japanese had been forced to register for census purposes as members of Buddhist parishes. Now this latter practice was discontinued, the administrative association of Buddhist and Shintō institutions was dissolved, and Shintō properties were restored to their own priests. These measures inspired a general anti-Buddhist outburst, in which church property and many artistic treasures were destroyed.

Buddhism thus was hard hit, but the persecution together with the challenge of Christianity actually helped it shake off some of its lethargy of recent centuries. There was a gradual revival of Buddhist scholarship. The large True Sect (Shinshū) showed particular vitality, and adopted in time some of the organizational techniques of the Christian churches, including foreign missions to the nearby continent, Hawaii, and the West Coast of the United States.

Secular Thought.   The failure of the Japanese to accept Christianity and the superficiality of much that they did borrow has given rise to the assumption that only the externals of Western civilization were accepted and that native traditions were impervious to the ideals and values of the West. Thus some observers have felt that Sakuma was right in his slogan of "Eastern ethics and Western science," which many of the Meiji leaders endorsed. In practice, however, no clear line could be drawn between the external aspects of Western civilization and its internal value system. The legal forms of the West, for example, inevitably brought with them the concepts and value judgments on which they were based. Moreover, the Japanese of the early Meiji period, although naturally influenced by the feudal and Confucian elements in their past, remained nonetheless open to the ideas and institutions of the West. Scientific techniques and external fashions were easier to understand and adopt than were Western ideas and values, but these too seeped in and profoundly influenced society.

The Meiji leaders were themselves thorough-going utilitarians and pragmatists. They were neither doctrinaire traditionalists nor blind followers of the West. All of them were ready to champion Western ideas when these seemed useful or an inevitable trend or to defend traditional points of view when these seemed of continuing value. They took advantage of any idea or technique that gave promise of helping to build "a rich country and strong military."

These attitudes were perhaps a natural outgrowth of the pragmatism of Tokugawa thought and the secular and agnostic tendencies of Confucian philosophy, but they were also influenced by Western ideas. The Meiji leaders, while ignoring Christianity, found encouragement for their points of view in the growing secularism, nationalism, and materialism of the nineteenth-century West. They easily adopted the Occident's confidence in science as the panacea for all problems. They found the utilitarianism of Jeremy Bentham and John Stuart Mill very appealing, and Herbert Spencer became the idol of many Japanese intellectuals. A little later Social Darwinism, which seemed to explain the success of the Meiji leaders themselves and to justify Japan's rise as an imperialist power, became a popular theory.

The pragmatism of the Meiji leaders thus was an easy blend of Tokugawa traits and Western attitudes. It also helps explain the extraordinary moderation and flexibility of the revolutionaries who remade Japan. The wave of political assassinations of the 1860's and 1870's shows how violent Japanese can be in espousing causes, but the Meiji leaders were interested in finding formulas that worked, not in proving some dogma. They had the advantage of being completely united on what the ultimate goal was, but they were remarkably open-minded as to how it should be reached. They also had behind them the long Japanese tradition of group responsibility and decision through consensus. Though all were strong personalities, none ever sought to monopolize authority by eliminating the others. When the policies of one failed or lost support, he readily stepped aside in favor of another who might have a new approach or better represent the consensus. The result was extraordinary flexibility in policy for a government that had no formal mechanism for deciding differences of opinion, and a surprising ability to correct mistakes before they became irreparable.

Seeking New Knowledge.   The Meiji leaders clearly recognized the need for new skills and knowledge: in the "Five Articles Oath" they had stated, "Knowledge shall be sought throughout the world." One obvious way to acquire this knowledge was by sending students abroad. The shogunate and some of the domains had started doing this before the Restoration, and the new government continued the effort. No less than fifty-four students accompanied the Iwakura Mission abroad in 1871. Students returned from study in the West had important careers as political, intellectual, and economic innovators and leaders, and some, such as Yamagata, Itō, and Inoue, were among the chief architects of the new Japan.

Importing foreign experts was another way to get knowledge of the West and mastery of its technology. In the closing years of the old regime, foreign experts had been used in various industrial undertakings, and the new government greatly expanded the use of such hired talent. As we have seen, foreigners were extensively used in the development of Hokkaidō and in the bureau of mines, and by 1879 the ministry of industry employed 130 foreigners, whose salaries accounted for nearly three-fifths of the ministry's fixed expenditures.

Since the "Dutch Learning" of the late Tokugawa period had proved to be a half-century or more out-of-date, a new start in Western science and scholarship was made through the use of foreign scholars. A series of German doctors, starting in 1871, gave Japanese medicine a strong German cast. English and American scholars were more important in other sciences. Professor E. S. Morse of Harvard, who arrived in 1877, is remembered as the founder of modern zoological, anthropological, archaeological, and sociological studies, and the Japanese still feel a strong sense of debt to Ernest Fenollosa of Boston, who came as a professor of philosophy in 1878 and by his own enthusiasm helped to revive an interest in the native artistic tradition.

Foreign experts and scholars were inordinately expensive, since they required what were by Japanese standards fabulous salaries and a luxurious style of living. But perhaps just because they were so costly to the Japanese, they seem to have been more esteemed and better put to use than is often the case in developing countries today, where the costs for foreign experts have commonly been met by foreign countries or international agencies. But the great expense also made the Japanese eager to replace foreigners as soon as possible by the Japanese they had trained or students returned from abroad. This was already happening in the late 1870's, and the process was speeded by Matsukata's retrenchment policies in the 1880's. By the turn of the century, few foreign experts remained, except as language teachers. There was one exception, however. Foreign missionaries, who came at their own expense, increased in numbers and often proved valuable teachers of English and transmitters of other knowledge.

The printed word had been the chief source of knowledge of the West for the scholars of "Dutch Learning" during the Tokugawa period, and translations and books played an even greater role in the new age. The leading popularizer of knowledge about the West was Fukuzawa Yukichi (1835–1901), the most influential man in Meiji Japan outside of government service. A samurai from northern Kyūshū, he studied "Dutch Learning" in Nagasaki and Ōsaka, taught Dutch in Edo, and then switched to English when he discovered that English was the language of the foreigners flocking to Yokohama after 1859. He accompanied shogunate embassies to the United States in 1860 and Europe in 1862 and founded a school in Edo which eventually grew into Keiō University, one of Japan's two leading private universities and the source of many of its top business leaders. But

A print from the early 1870's showing the old-style "unenlightened man" in samurai garb, the "half-enlightened man" with Western-style cap, umbrella, and shoes, and the "enlightened man" in Western costume complete with a cane and dog.

his first fame came from his writings. In 1869 he published *Conditions in the West,* in which he described in simple and clear terms the political, economic, and cultural institutions of the Occident, making plain his preference for the British parliamentary form of government. This work sold 150,000 copies in its first edition. Fukuzawa followed it in the next decade with a number of others, including *The Encouragement of Learning,* which is said to have sold over 700,000 copies.

Many other private scholars shared with Fukuzawa the task of spreading Western knowledge. Fifteen intellectual leaders joined him in 1873 in founding the Meirokusha ("Sixth Year of Meiji Society"), which had a brief but influential existence, holding public lectures and publishing a magazine. The translating of Western books was perhaps the chief literary activity of the period. Samuel Smiles' *Self-Help* and Mill's *On Liberty,* appearing in 1870 and 1871, were both immensely popular. There was also a flood of translations of Western literature of all types, from *Robinson Crusoe* (1859) to Jules Verne.

Education.   The new leaders clearly saw that an organized system of education was a fundamental aspect of a modernized society and as early as 1871 created a ministry of education to develop such a system. This effort was of course aided by relatively high literacy rates and the Japanese familiarity with schools and formal education, but the various Tokugawa educational institutions did not themselves prove capable of adjusting to the new conditions. The Confucian-oriented domain schools for the samurai and the so-called "temple schools," where commoners had learned to read and write, all withered away. The only exceptions were the shogunal schools. The Confucian "University" in Edo, the medical school, and the language programs at the Institute for the Study of Barbarian Books were united in 1869 into a single government institution. The non-Western aspects of the curriculum were dropped in 1871, and in 1877 the school was renamed Tōkyō University, under which name it has remained ever since the pinnacle of the Japanese educational system.

The disappearance of most earlier schools left the government free to develop a thoroughly modernized system of education. It never had to contend with the entrenched relationship between religion and education that existed in most Western countries. It was thus able to put into practice Western concepts of a uniform, government-operated educational system more fully than was possible in much of the West itself in the nineteenth century.

The ministry of education at first adopted a highly centralized system of education along French lines. Sixteen months of schooling were made compulsory for children of both sexes. Compulsory education was extended to three years in 1880 and to six years in 1907. It was no easy matter, however, to carry out such plans because of the insufficiency of both funds and teachers. As late as 1886 only 46 per cent of the children of statutory school age were in school, but by 1905 the figure had risen to 95 per cent, and subsequently crept up still higher.

In the meantime the original centralized French system had been somewhat decentralized and remodeled partially along American lines. This was done under the influence of men like Fukuzawa, Mori Arinori (1847–1889), a Satsuma samurai, who after serving as minister to Washington, became minister of education, and Dr. David Murray of Rutgers College, who served as an adviser in the ministry from 1873 to 1879. A further liberalization of education was also fostered by the rapid development of a great number of private schools. Many were founded by missionaries, and Christian schools were particularly important in the field of secondary education for girls, which was somewhat neglected by the government. Quite a few of the missionary institutions later grew into large universities. There were also many secular private schools. Keiō, founded by Fukuzawa, was joined in 1882 by an institution set up by the former government leader Ōkuma. This grew into Waseda University, the other great private university and a prime source later for parliamentary politicians. Other private secular schools followed, some of which became in time huge even if not very distinguished universities.

*An 1877 print showing a first-grade class learning from a
vocabulary chart produced by the ministry of education in 1875.*

A shift back toward a more centralized, authoritarian educational system
came in the 1880's and reached its height in the issuance in 1890 of an
Imperial Rescript on Education. This brief document made only passing
reference to education itself but showed the revived influence of Confucian
ideology in its stress on harmony and loyalty to the throne. Its central
concept of mass indoctrination through formal education, however, was an
entirely modern emphasis. Part of the new educational policy was a desirable
return to Japanese and Chinese literature, history, and thought, to balance
the hitherto almost exclusive concern with Western subjects. Other aspects
of the new policy were an increasing emphasis on indoctrination in education, standardization of the curriculum, and increased government control
over private institutions, especially at the lower educational levels. Still
another aspect was the expansion of the government school system and the
enhancement of its prestige over the private schools. As a result, private
elementary and secondary schools shrank to relative insignificance.

Tōkyō University was reorganized into a genuine multifaculty university
in 1886 and became the principal training center for future government
officials. Until 1893 its graduates were accepted directly into government
service without examination. An inevitable result of this policy was the
domination of the higher ranks of the bureaucracy by graduates of the Law
Faculty of Tōkyō University, a tradition which still persists. Other government universities, thereafter known as Imperial Universities, were added—

Kyōto in 1897, Tōhoku (in Sendai) in 1907, Kyūshū (in Fukuoka) in 1910, Hokkaidō (in Sapporo) in 1918, and others later.

Early in the twentieth century, the new Japanese educational structure was almost complete. At the bottom were compulsory six-year coeducational elementary schools, designed to produce a literate citizenry for efficient service in the army, factories, and fields. On the level above these were three types of institutions: (1) five-year academic middle schools for boys; (2) various lower technical schools, which produced the lower levels of technical skills; and (3) girls' higher schools, which were supposed to provide all the education needed even by girls from better families. Above this level stood three-year academic higher schools for boys, inaugurated in 1896, and higher technical schools for more advanced technical skills, started in 1903. At the top of the pyramid were the three-year universities (four-year in medicine), which produced the elite leadership.

This was a beautifully logical system, more rationally conceived and uniformly carried out than in most Western countries of that period. It also worked on the whole very well. The unchallenged prestige of the government institutions, which had the lowest tuition rates, gave Japanese education a more egalitarian flavor than the schools of the English-speaking countries. An educational system that was remarkably open to all who had the desire and ability to make use of it became the chief device for selecting the leaders of the nation. As a result, a society which had only shortly before been organized along strictly hereditary feudal lines became within a generation or two less class-bound than England or many other European countries.

The system, however, had serious drawbacks too. It was so carefully tailored to fit the needs of the state, as these were envisioned by its leaders, that it did not adequately meet all the educational needs of Japanese society as it developed. Women's higher education, for example, grew up largely outside the official educational structure, and the rapid growth of private universities showed that there was a demand in Japanese society for much more higher education than that deemed adequate by the government. There was also a cramping conformity and a possibility of uniform indoctrination that were to prove extremely damaging to Japan in the long run.

The Creation of the Constitution

Early Interest in Representative Institutions. The Meiji leaders realized that their early political reforms were largely makeshift. Once they had established their unchallengeable control over the whole nation through the suppression of the Satsuma Rebellion, they turned their attention to devising some more permanent form of government. Coming from a society which had enjoyed for more than two centuries a clearly defined, fully accepted, and almost unchanging political order, they longed for an equally clear, unchanging, and unchallengeably legitimate political system. Influenced by Western ideas, they thought of it as embodying some form of representative institutions.

Their willingness to consider creating representative political bodies was a surprising departure from Japanese traditions, but it can be explained by the obvious prestige of Western institutions at the time and the assumption that, since the most advanced and powerful nations of the day had constitutions embodying representative government, there must be something in constitutions and representative institutions that produced progress and strength. They saw the specter of the French Revolution or the backwardness of Russia as the fate of regimes that were too autocratic. It was also clear to the Japanese leaders that a constitution and a parliament would greatly enhance Western respect for Japan and bring nearer the day when it would be accepted by them as an equal.

Another factor in the situation was that the government leaders were not dealing just with downtrodden peasants and politically apathetic townsmen. The whole samurai class was well educated and full of men who felt themselves rightful participants in government. Such men insistently demanded a share in the administration, and, as we have seen, the promise in the "Five Articles Oath" that "deliberative assemblies shall be widely established and all matters decided by public discussion" was probably meant as an assurance to them that they would find a place in the new political order. However, "deliberative assemblies" and "public discussion" were quite unfamiliar techniques to the Japanese at that time. The four attempts between 1868 and 1870 to create a deliberative assembly made up partly of domain representatives seemed to add nothing of value, and there was no great outcry when the effort was quietly dropped.

Interest in representative institutions revived in the autumn of 1873 when Itagaki of Tosa, after leaving the government because of the disagreement over Korean policy, founded with other Tosa leaders and Etō of Hizen a political club they subsequently named the Public Party of Patriots (Aikoku Kōtō). This was a daring step, because the word "party" had bad connotations, being associated with the bureaucratic factionalism of Chinese history. The new group, however, did not hesitate to denounce the arbitrariness of the government and call for the establishment of "a council chamber chosen by the people." Itagaki refused to become embroiled in Etō's revolt in Saga the next year but instead founded a new political group called the Risshisha, or "Society to Establish One's Moral Will," a name based on the Japanese title for Smiles' widely read book, *Self-Help*. The Risshisha aimed at the economic rehabilitation of the samurai class as well as the creation of a popular assembly. It spread widely in Tosa and early in 1875 it was renamed the Society of Patriots (Aikokusha) and began to penetrate to other areas.

It is hard to say why Itagaki among the new political leaders took this unusual turn toward democracy or why there was so ready a response to his ideas in his native Tosa. Tosa was a relatively backward, peripheral area and Itagaki a particularly soldierly samurai. One factor may have been the resentment of Tosa men at the predominant role of Satsuma and Chōshū in the new government, but of course other domains had even more to resent on this score. A more basic reason may have been that a class of "village samurai" in Tosa, together with village headmen and merchants who had been allowed to purchase samurai status, had long constituted a rural opposition to the urban administration of the domain, and their attitudes of popular opposition were easily transferred to the new government.

The government leaders were not particularly shocked by Itagaki's demands and continued to regard him as one of them. In fact, they themselves studied various proposals for a constitution and in 1875 had the emperor promise that in due time a national assembly would be formed. Itagaki was persuaded to return to the government in 1875 on the basis of an agreement that had been worked out in Ōsaka between Ōkubo and Kido to induce the latter to rejoin the government after he too had resigned in a huff the year before. The Ōsaka agreement called for a reorganization of the government. A Supreme Court was created to protect the independence of the judiciary, and a Senate was set up and given the task of preparing for a national assembly. When it finally presented the fruits of its toil in 1880, Iwakura and Itō, who were then the chief powers in the regime, shelved the draft as too closely modeled on English institutions.

Another point in the Ōsaka agreement was the calling of a conference of prefectural governors. It first met in June 1875, and at its second meeting in 1878 it decided on the establishment of elected prefectural assemblies. Although the franchise was restricted to males who paid five yen or more in taxes and the powers of the assemblies were limited to discussing tax and budgetary matters put before them by the governors, these bodies, convened in March 1879, were the first popularly elected political organs to operate successfully anywhere in the non-Western world. They were followed in 1880 by similar elected assemblies in city wards, towns and villages.

The "People's Rights" Movement.   Itagaki resigned again from the government late in 1875, ostensibly because one point in the Ōsaka agreement had not been carried out. He and his closest associates managed to avoid involvement in the Satsuma Rebellion and in 1878 renewed their efforts to create a nationwide popular movement. This time there was a tremendous response to their demand for a parliamentary form of government. One reason for the popularity of this so-called "movement for freedom and people's rights" (*jiyū minken undō*) was the dissatisfaction with current conditions among many samurai. But the most numerous and enthusiastic members of the movement actually were prosperous peasant landowners and petty entrepreneurs, probably because they, rather than the impoverished samurai, constituted the chief tax-paying group. Men of samurai origin usually remained the top leaders and intellectual guides, but peasants and businessmen provided the chief financial support and the bulk of the members of the new political associations.

Another reason for the spread of the parliamentary movement was the growing knowledge of democratic institutions among Japanese intellectuals, largely because of Fukuzawa's books and those of other writers. For example, Nakae Chōmin (1847–1901), a Tosa samurai by origin, popularized the ideas of Rousseau. Nakae also helped found in 1881 the *Tōyō Jiyū Shimbun* (*Oriental Free Press*), which became an influential organ in the movement. The first real Japanese newspaper had been started in 1870, and by 1875 there were more than a hundred. Newspapers and other periodicals were usually journals of opinion, reflecting the political views of their backers. Unemployed samurai and other political outsiders flocked into newspaper work and thus helped create in Japanese journalism a strong tendency toward political protest, which has survived to the present day.

Because of the lack of traditions of democracy and freedom of expression in Japan, the line between political agitation and opposition through rebellion was not at all clear to the people of the time. Even political assassination, the chief weapon of the "men of determination" (*shishi*) of the preceding decade, seemed legitimate to some would-be champions of "freedom and people's rights." Ōkubo, the most powerful figure in the government, was killed in May 1878 by extremists who had the curiously mixed motives of avenging Saigō's death in the Satsuma Rebellion and defending "people's rights." Itagaki attempted to control the mushrooming political movement through national conventions of the Society of Patriots. The first was held in September 1878, and at the fourth held in April 1880 the name of the organization was changed to the League for Establishing a National Assembly.

The government leaders were naturally apprehensive about the growth and occasional violence of the movement. In 1875 they adopted new press, publication, and libel laws, designed to prevent newspaper attacks on the government. A running fight resulted between journalists and officials, with the government imprisoning and fining editors, and the newspapers setting up dummy editors as a defensive tactic. In 1880 the government adopted a stringent law on public gatherings. This law required police permission for any public meeting, prohibited soldiers, policemen, teachers, and students from participating in political activities, and gave the authorities such general and vague powers that they could suppress almost any form of political agitation.

The Crisis of 1881. The government leaders were not so much opposed to the creation of some sort of parliament as determined to do this in their own way. Opinions among them were divided between those who admired British institutions and those who looked instead to the more restrictive Prussian model, and between gradualists and those who felt some step should be taken at once. To clarify the situation, all the Councilors were asked to submit their views to the emperor in writing. The responses were predominantly moderate. By this time the three most powerful leaders of the original Restoration were gone—Kido through tuberculosis in 1877, Saigō because of his revolt the same year, and Ōkubo at the hands of an assassin in 1878—and the former second line of slightly younger samurai had taken their place. Yamagata, the builder of the army, decried the popular demands for "freedom," but even he felt that some sort of national assembly should be formed by starting with the better men from the prefectural assemblies and then, through slow trial-and-error methods, creating a true national assembly. Only Kuroda, the developer of Hokkaidō, felt that all talk about an assembly was premature.

It is hardly surprising that the government leaders, already accustomed for more than a decade to guiding the destinies of the nation as they saw fit and certain that they knew best what was good for Japan, were not prepared to bow to the demands of what must have seemed to them a rabble of ill-informed agitators. What is surprising is that most of them were willing to consider forming some sort of elected body that would have at least a small share in political decisions and that one of their number, Ōkuma, proposed in March 1881 the immediate adoption of the full British parliamentary system.

Itō was thunderstruck by Ōkuma's extremism and seems to have felt that Ōkuma was trying to get ahead of him in their rivalry for leadership in the government by jumping on the "people's rights" bandwagon. In other words, he suspected Ōkuma of conniving with outsiders against his colleagues in the government. This impression was strengthened by a clamorous outburst in the press against the sale (in Matsukata's deflationary program) of the assets of Kuroda's Hokkaidō Colonization Office at a scandalous 3 per cent of investment value—a policy Ōkuma had opposed. These suspicions were probably not justified, and Ōkuma may merely have been trying to establish an extreme position for bargaining purposes with the other leaders. If so, he made a great error in tactics. Itō and his colleagues decided Ōkuma must be dropped from the government. In October they had him dismissed from office and at the same time canceled the Hokkaidō sale as a sop to the opposition. They also issued an Imperial Rescript promising a national assembly, but not before 1890.

The gradualist point of view thus won out in the crisis of 1881, and Itō emerged as the most influential man in the government. The whole top leadership also consolidated into a group exclusively from Satsuma and Chōshū.

Itagaki and other Tosa men had already withdrawn; so had Etō and other men from Hizen; and now Ōkuma of Hizen had also been forced out. Iwakura, the one truly influential court noble, died in 1883. For the next decade and a half, the leadership was in the hands of such Chōshū men as Itō, Yamagata, and Inoue and such Satsuma men as Kuroda, Matsukata, and Saigō's younger brother Tsugumichi, who had led the Taiwan expedition in 1874. There were rising complaints that the government had become a two-domain oligarchy, or a "Sat-chō clique" as it was pejoratively called.

The Party Movement.   Ōkuma, when he left the government, took with him several able young officials, including Inukai Tsuyoshi (1855–1932) and Ōzaki Yukio (1859–1954), two men of samurai origin who were to have very distinguished careers as democratic politicians. The next March, Ōkuma and his followers founded a political party, called the Constitutional Progressive Party (Rikken Kaishintō), which was oriented toward English parliamentary concepts and initially drew its chief support from urban intellectuals and businessmen. Fukuzawa and the products of his Keiō University were among its most important supporters, as was Iwasaki, head of the great Mitsubishi interests.

Meanwhile Itagaki had once again reorganized his political following under the new name of Liberty Party (Jiyūtō)—although the accepted English translation of its name has always been Liberal Party, a title more consonant with its later history. Drawing on radical French doctrines, the party proclaimed that "liberty is the natural state of man" and advocated a constitution decided upon at a national convention.

These two parties, though repeatedly disbanded, reorganized, merged, and renamed, were to remain two major political streams in Japan, and they are in fact the twin sources and the reason for the split name of the post–World War II Liberal Democratic Party. Although they were frequently able to stir up enthusiastic mass support, they had few enrolled members—at most a few thousand in the early years. Most Japanese remained too close to the feudal past to commit themselves openly by joining political parties. Both retained feudal features in their leader-follower organization and readily split into smaller leader-follower factions. While both parties supported the imperial institution as the symbol of Japan's political unity, they argued that a popularly elected parliament could better represent the emperor's will than a Satsuma-Chōshū oligarchy. Each, however, was quick to accuse the other of being a self-seeking faction merely attempting to replace the "Sat-chō clique." In particular, the Progressives would accuse the Liberals of being at the service of Mitsui interests, and the Liberals would reply by accusing the Progressives of being controlled by Mitsubishi.

The government opposed the parties by strengthening the laws on public meetings in 1882. It also got Itagaki out of the country by persuading

Mitsui to finance a trip for him to observe European governments. While he was abroad his party fell into serious difficulties. Some of its members became involved in peasant uprisings, protesting the drastic drop in prices and resultant increase in the burden of taxes caused by Matsukata's deflationary policies. The government had no trouble in suppressing the disturbances, but the Liberal Party was so disrupted and discredited by its involvement that it dissolved itself in October 1884. The faction-ridden Progressives also soon fell apart.

Another effort was made in 1887 to rally the opposition groups against the government. This time the movement was directed less toward advocacy of democratic institutions than against the government's foreign policies. In order to persuade the Western powers to relinquish extraterritoriality, Inoue, as foreign minister, had proposed a transitional period in which mixed courts of foreign and Japanese judges would try cases involving Westerners. This proposal and the planned opening of all of Japan to foreign residence were both very unpopular, and the parties seized on these issues to attack the government. Such xenophobia was frequently to characterize the stand of the parties. While advocating Western parliamentarianism, they could be as chauvinistically anti-Western on other matters as the government and, lacking political responsibility, considerably less realistic.

To counter this latest attack, the government issued on December 25, 1887, a Peace Preservation Law, which gave it the right to expel from the Tōkyō area any person felt to be "a threat to public tranquillity." In the next few days some 570 persons were removed from the capital. The revived party movement was shaken by this blow and soon collapsed completely when some of its leaders were inveigled back into the government. Ōkuma became foreign minister in February 1888 and thus replaced the Satsuma-Chōshū oligarchs as the object of popular indignation at the failure to get revision of the unequal treaties. In October 1889 he lost a leg when a fanatic threw a bomb at him.

Preparation for the Constitution.   While the parties were attempting with relatively little effect to influence political decisions, Itō and his colleagues methodically went about preparing for the promised national assembly and the writing of a constitution. Even before Ōkuma had been ousted from the government in 1881, Itō had won acceptance of several basic points, which were embodied in the final results. He was determined that, while the Constitution should not slavishly reproduce any Western system and would be adapted to Japan's special needs, it should at the same time be based on the best constitutional theory and practice of the West, so that it would stand the double test of Western judgment and Japanese use. In March 1882 he led a study mission to Europe, which visited the leading capitals but concentrated on study in Berlin and Vienna, where Itō knew he would find the theories and practices he felt were most appropriate for Japan.

Itō returned to Japan in August 1883 and the next spring was made chairman of a special commission to draft the constitution. But before setting about this task, he started creating the organs of government he felt would be needed before the risky experiment in elective institutions was inaugurated. First he created in 1884 a new peerage to populate a projected House of Peers, designed to serve as a brake on an elected House of Representatives. The new peerage, divided into the five ranks of prince, marquis, count, viscount, and baron (named after the titles used in ancient Chou China), was made up largely of the former daimyo, graded according to the size of their former domains and the latters' services in the "imperial restoration." The peerage also included the old court nobles and some of the new leaders, who kept promoting themselves until Itō and a few others ended up as princes.

Itō's most important innovation was the introduction in December 1885 of a cabinet based on the most up-to-date European models. Replacing the Council of State, in which court nobles had lingered on as official intermediaries between the emperor and the oligarchs, the cabinet was made up of the heads of the various ministries, who were mostly the chief oligarchs themselves. Thus at one stroke the leaders were consolidated into a more effective executive body. Itō himself took the post of prime minister. When he relinquished it in 1888, it went to Kuroda of Satsuma, who, following the bomb attack on Ōkuma in 1889, passed it on to Yamagata of Chōshū, just returned from a second trip to Europe. The whole system of bureaucratic appointments was also modernized, and in 1887 a civil service examination system was adopted on German models.

Itō and his colleagues saw the authority of the emperor as central to the whole system of government they were designing. After all, their own revolutionary seizure of power had been justified as an "imperial restoration," and they seem to have been to a considerable extent believers in the myth they had themselves helped create. They also probably realized that imperial prerogatives were the best bulwarks behind which the oligarchs could take refuge from the rising popular demands for a share in political power. Itō therefore did his best to enhance imperial prestige and protect the throne from popular pressures. In 1885 he revived the ancient title of Naidaijin, or inner minister, commonly translated "lord keeper of the privy seal." He also placed the imperial household ministry outside of the cabinet. In April 1888 he created a Privy Council to pass judgment in the emperor's name on the constitution being drafted, and he characteristically took the presidency of this body himself, so that he could ensure the approval of his own handiwork.

Itō Hirobumi as a young official in the finance ministry in the 1870's and with his family as a leading minister in later years.

As Itō and his colleagues gradually established what they hoped would be the permanent political pattern for modern Japan, there was a decided hardening of the official philosophy. Perhaps this was inevitable in any case, because the leaders were no longer young revolutionaries but were veteran administrators entering middle age. It was at this time that education was put under strict centralized controls, and the imitation of Western social customs was dropped. The Confucian and feudal emphasis on loyalty and obedience came back into fashion and found expression, as we have seen, in the Imperial Rescript on Education in 1890.

While Itō was setting up the chief organs of the new political order, Yamagata was pursuing a somewhat different course. He seems to have had a more literal concept of imperial rule than Itō, and as the chief architect of the army, he placed more emphasis on the armed services as a bulwark of strong executive power. He consequently devoted himself to building up the army's morale and technical competence and to developing a degree of autonomy for the armed services within the government.

In December 1878 Yamagata adopted the German general staff system and established the principle that the chief of staff in matters of military command, as opposed to financial and administrative affairs, was independent of the army minister and the civil government, acting only under the command of the emperor and with the right of direct access to the throne. To emphasize the importance of the chief of staff, Yamagata resigned as army minister and assumed this new post. In the same year Yamagata put out an "Admonition to the Military," emphasizing the old virtues of loyalty, bravery, and obedience, and in 1882 he had the emperor issue an "Imperial Precept for the Military" (sometimes called the "Rescript to Soldiers and Sailors"). The text made clear that "the supreme command" of the army and navy was in the hands of the emperor, thus strengthening the independence of the armed services from the civil organs of government.

Yamagata, as home minister between 1883 and 1888, also had a chance to build up strong executive power in other fields. He reorganized the police into a more centrally controlled and efficient force, and the Peace Preservation Law of 1887 was largely his handiwork. He also undertook a reorganization of local government into an efficient but highly centralized and authoritarian system, embodied in laws promulgated in 1888 and 1890.

The Meiji Constitution.   The actual work of drafting the constitution and its supporting legislation did not get under way until 1886. Among the chief participants, under Itō's direction, was a German, Hermann Roesler. The finished document was promulgated on February 11, 1889, the official anniversary of the supposed founding of the Japanese state in 660 B.C.

The constitution made good the promise to create a national assembly by 1890. There was to be a bicameral parliament, called in English the Diet. The House of Peers was to be made up largely of the higher ranks of the nobility, elected representatives of the lower ranks, and some imperial appointees, who turned out to be usually men of scholarly distinction. The lower house was to be chosen by an electorate limited to adult males paying

taxes of fifteen yen or more—some 450,000 persons in 1890, only about
5 per cent of the adult male population. The Diet was given a real share
in power in that the budget and all permanent laws required favorable
action by both houses. The constitution also guaranteed a whole series of
popular rights, such as freedom of religion and of "speech, publication,
public meetings, and association" and rights to property and due process of
law, although these were all hedged by phrases such as "except in cases
provided for in the law" or "within limits not prejudicial to peace and
order."

These were daring innovations in Japan, but the leaders felt that they
had adequately safeguarded imperial prerogatives, and in this way their
own power. The constitution was presented as the gift of the emperor, who
reserved the exclusive right to initiate amendments—none in fact were ever
made. It declared the emperor to be "sacred and inviolable" and the locus
of sovereignty as the descendant of a dynasty "which has reigned in an
unbroken line of descent for ages past." It made clear that the emperor
exercised all executive authority and also "the legislative power with the
consent of the Imperial Diet." It specifically stated that "the emperor has
the supreme command of the army and navy." It made the individual
ministers directly responsible to him, rather than collectively responsible as
the cabinet, which was not even mentioned in the constitution. The budget
of the imperial household remained entirely free of Diet control. The
emperor could at any time prorogue (i.e., temporarily suspend) the Diet or
dissolve the lower house, necessitating new elections. When the Diet was
not in session he could issue imperial ordinances which temporarily took
the place of laws. The oligarchs also reserved what they felt was the trump
card to prevent undue Diet control over the purse strings: if the Diet failed
to pass the new budget, the previous year's budget would remain in effect.

The constitution was a blend of many conflicting ideas, but it turned out
to be a reasonably successful balance among the various political forces of
the time. It has often been condemned in recent years for having provided
too little democracy, but this is the perspective of a later age. At the time
most Western countries themselves had limitations on the electorate and
parliamentary power, and the advice to the Japanese of most Occidentals,
including such disparate figures as President Grant and Herbert Spencer,
was to go slow on democratic experimentation. Considering the feudal
background and authoritarian experience of the men in control of the
government and the unfamiliarity of the Japanese public with democratic
ideas and institutions, the constitution defined perhaps as liberal a system
of government as could have operated successfully at the time. While disappointing to the opposition groups, it met their minimum demands, without at the same time completely alienating more conservative forces.

The Political System under the Meiji Constitution

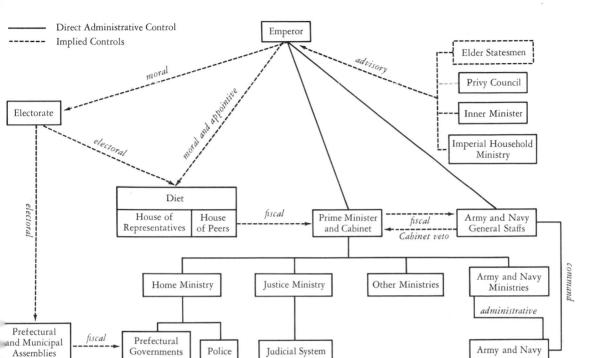

Because of this balance and the sanctity of its supposed imperial origin, the constitution was never seriously challenged from either side.

A more valid criticism could be directed against the ambiguities of the constitutional system. The pretense of broad imperial authority, when in fact the emperor remained essentially a symbol, caused no serious trouble so long as the oligarchs acted in his name. However the group of oligarchs was nowhere mentioned in the constitution, nor were provisions made for some successor body. When these men did pass from the scene, two serious problems arose. It was not clear which organs of government should exercise the imperial prerogatives. For example, who was to choose the prime minister when there were no longer oligarchs around to fill the post or appoint someone else? The almost unlimited imperial powers, moreover, could be abused by individuals or organs of government which lacked the overall jurisdiction and breadth of vision of the oligarchs. Who, for example, was to keep an independent military in line with the civil government when there was no longer an oligarchy to supervise both?

It may never be known whether Itō was blind to these problems, unconsciously assuming the continuation of people like himself in control, or purposely left the constitution ambiguous in order to make room for further evolution. In any case, the very ambiguities of the constitution probably made possible a more healthy political evolution than could have occurred under a system rigidly defined in terms of the political perceptions of the 1880's, and the failure in the long run to find successful answers to the questions Itō had left should be blamed not on him so much as on the generations that followed.

The Early Years of Constitutional Government

The First Diet Session.   The first national elections were held on July 1, 1890, and the Diet was convened in November. It soon became clear that Itō and his colleagues had made some serious miscalculations about the working of the system they had created, and the process of constitutional government started to evolve rapidly away from the picture they had in mind. For one thing, the party politicians had acquired considerable experience, both in electioneering and in parliamentary techniques, in the prefectural assemblies that had been in existence since 1879. Some had developed strong constituencies among the local electorate, which, to the consternation of the government, consistently preferred party politicians over announced supporters of the government. Of three hundred members of the first House of Representatives, 130 belonged to the newly reconstituted Liberal Party and 41 to the Progressives, while some of the independents were obviously prepared to vote with these opposition parties against the government.

The party men, wanting to establish Diet control over the cabinet, made immediate use of the one substantial power the constitution had given the Diet. They slashed the budget by about 11 per cent, concentrating on the salaries and perquisites of the bureaucratic followers of the oligarchs. Itō's trump card proved of little value. In a rapidly expanding economy, last year's budget was never enough. More control over the purse strings had been given to the Diet than had been intended, and as a consequence far more concessions had to be made to the party politicians than had been envisaged.

The oligarchs were united in feeling that the cabinet must remain "transcendent"—that is, above Diet politics. Yamagata who was among those least inclined to tolerate dictation by the Diet, was the prime minister at the time, and he did his best to override the opposition through intimidation and bribery. Eventually Itagaki and some of his Liberals agreed to restore about a quarter of the funds cut by the Diet, and the cabinet had to settle for this compromise.

Compromises of this sort were to prove the main pattern of Diet politics for the next several years. They were satisfactory neither to the Diet politicians, who hungered for official status and control over the cabinet, nor to the oligarchs, who resented this encroachment on their hitherto almost unlimited powers. The question arises as to why either side tolerated this situation. The answer for the parties is easy enough: they lacked the power to do anything else. For the oligarchs it is more difficult. Part of the answer may lie in pride of authorship in the constitution: Itō in particular desperately wanted the system to work. Another reason was the supposed imperial origin of the document, which made it difficult to flout. A still more important reason was the attitude of the Western nations: an obvious failure in this attempted "Westernization" of Japanese political institutions would have brought ridicule and further delayed the acceptance of Japan as an equal. But the most important reason probably lay in the nature of the oligarchs. They had a fairly wide spread of views, tended to operate by consensus, and were by life-long experience pragmatic men. They reacted flexibly to this new problem, presenting no monolithic stand against the Diet, which itself was divided among mutually hostile and selfishly ambitious groups. A more clear-cut confrontation between a unified popular democratic movement and a unified dictatorship would have quickly come to grief. As it was, the Japanese tendencies toward ambiguity, consensus, and compromise permitted an evolutionary development that moved with remarkable speed along the parliamentary paths blazed long before in England.

The Struggle Between the Diet and the Cabinet (1891–1898).   Yamagata resigned in disgust from the prime ministership in May 1891, and Matsukata of Satsuma succeeded him. By then the pattern of alternation in power between Chōshū and Satsuma oligarchs had become well established, and it was to continue unbroken until 1898. Matsukata attempted to carry out a strong repressive policy against the Diet, which Yamagata also had advocated. When the Diet tried to slash the budget again in November 1891, he dissolved the lower house. In the elections of February 15, 1892, the home minister, who was in charge of the police and local government, used all the powers of bribery and force he could muster to defeat opposition politicians in what was to prove the bloodiest and most corrupt election in Japanese history. But this frontal attack failed. The opposition forces again won a clear majority of 163 seats, and both houses passed resolutions condemning the government.

Matsukata was under attack from two sides. The lower house voted a cut of a third in the supplementary budget, and the army and navy ministers withdrew from the cabinet in protest against the punishment of officials who had intervened in the elections. Matsukata was forced to resign in May 1892, and Itō now took a turn at trying to deal with the Diet. He was inclined to a more flexible approach than his predecessors and early in 1892 had even suggested the formation of a government party to capture the

Diet. This starting idea, which would have ended the concept of "transcendental" cabinets, had been rejected by his colleagues, but Itō had other tricks up his sleeves.

In response to the usual attack on the budget, Itō had the emperor surrender some of his own income and order the high officials to follow suit, and through this voluntary reduction of part of the budget, he obtained enough support to pass the rest. In the Diet session of November 1893 he managed to win the cooperation of the Progressives for his foreign policies, thus dividing the opposition. But in the face of continued obstreperousness on the part of the Diet over foreign policy, he was finally forced to dissolve the lower house in January 1894 and, after March elections, again in June. The Sino-Japanese War (see pages 185–186) broke out on August 1, before the new Diet was elected, and popular enthusiasm over Japanese military successes greatly eased the conflict between the Diet and the cabinet. Reacting to a war situation in the same way as most Western parliaments have, the Diet voted all the war budgets unanimously and almost without debate.

When the Diet resumed the attack on the cabinet following the forced return to China in 1895 of one of the fruits of victory, the Kwantung (also called Liaotung) Peninsula in Manchuria, Itō took a long step away from the concept of "transcendental" cabinets. He made a deal with Itagaki and his Liberal Party, rewarding them for their support with the key post of home minister for Itagaki in April 1896 and several other official plums for his henchmen.

The coalition between Itō and the Liberals induced the Progressives, under Ōkuma, to band together with other Diet elements to form a new party, named Shimpotō, also best translated as Progressive Party. When this group started to form ties with Matsukata, Itō tried to bring both Matsukata and Ōkuma into his cabinet, but Itagaki objected. Itō then in disgust turned over the prime ministership to Matsukata in September 1896.

Matsukata, following Itō's lead, assigned Ōkuma the post of foreign minister in return for support by the Progressive Party in the Diet. This new coalition, however, fell apart when Ōkuma resigned from the cabinet in November 1897. Matsukata in pique dissolved the lower house and then resigned in January 1898. Itō returned as prime minister, but failing to get the support of either the Progressives or the Liberals, followed Matsukata's lead by dissolving the lower house and then resigning in June.

Two Unsuccessful Experiments. The confrontation between the cabinet and Diet had reached an impasse. None of the oligarchs was willing to assume the prime ministership under these conditions. Itō proposed that either he be allowed to form a government party or else the cabinet be entrusted to the two former members of their group, Ōkuma and Itagaki, who had just merged their political followings as the Kenseitō, or Constitutional Party. The oligarchs chose the less odious of the two suggestions, and Ōkuma became prime minister with Itagaki as home minister. But the parties were not ready for such heavy responsibilities. The army and navy ministers, who were always military men, held themselves disdainfully aloof from the rest of the cabinet, and the bureaucracy as a whole proved uncooperative. Moreover the old factional divisions remained strong within the new party, and Itagaki was disgruntled that only two of his henchmen were in the cabinet, as compared to four of Ōkuma's. The cabinet broke up in November after only four months in office, and the Constitutional Party redivided into its component elements, with the Liberals retaining the name of Constitutional Party and the Progressives calling themselves the Real Constitutional Party (Kenseihontō).

Yamagata then came back as prime minister and attempted to turn the political clock back. He had been in Europe when Itō had formed his coalition with the Liberals in 1896, and he heartily disapproved of this step. When Ōkuma had become prime minister, Yamagata had insisted that the army and navy ministers be appointed separately from the rest of the cabinet. But he was realistic enough to realize that he must have Diet support, and he worked out a joint legislative program with the Constitutional Party, even though he stubbornly refused its members a place in his cabinet. One result of this cooperative arrangement was the reduction in 1900 of the tax qualification for voting from fifteen yen to ten yen and the expansion of the House of Representatives to 369 members. Another result was the passage, with the aid of considerable bribery, of Yamagata's budgets and his bills for increased taxation.

Yamagata's chief efforts, however, were devoted to increasing the autonomy of the armed services and the freedom of the bureaucracy from penetration or influence by the parties. In 1899 he revised the civil service system to keep politicians out of the topmost ranks, which hitherto had been open to political appointees. In 1900 he extended the powers of the Privy Council and issued a ruling that only officers of the top two ranks on active duty could serve as army or navy ministers, thereby ensuring that the army and navy general staffs would have complete control over these two vital posts.

Yamagata, however, could not permanently hold back the currents of the time. As he devised ways to freeze the party men out of administrative posts, they wearied of their union of convenience with him. Without Diet support, of course, he could not continue effectively in office, and he resigned in October 1900.

The Seiyūkai-Supported Cabinets (1900–1912). The Constitutional Party had meanwhile approached Itō, who, finally winning the grudging approval

*Yamagata Aritomo as a
genrō, aged 78, during
World War I.*

of his colleagues for his old idea of organizing a government party, founded
in September 1900 a new party, called the Rikken Seiyūkai, or Friends of
Constitutional Government, formed out of the old Liberals in the Constitutional Party and his own supporters in the bureaucracy. Drawing from the
largest of the popular political streams and a major factional element in
the bureaucracy, the Seiyūkai enjoyed uninterrupted pluralities, and often
an outright majority, in the House of Representatives for the next two
decades.

Itō became prime minister in October 1900 with a cabinet made up
largely of genuine party men or ex-bureaucrats who had joined the party.
He had smooth sailing in the House of Representatives with the support
of the Seiyūkai, but some of his colleagues in the oligarchy remained critical
of his tactics, and the House of Peers actually voted down his tax bills.
Faced with bickering in the cabinet and weary of his fourth term as prime
minister, Itō resigned in May 1901.

Yamagata proved unwilling to re-enter the political maelstrom, and
the choice of prime minister finally went to his protégé, Katsura Tarō
(1847–1913), like him a Chōshū general. This marked the end of the
original oligarchs' titular responsibility for the government. Itō and Yamagata occupied the post of president of the Privy Council between them from
1903 until Yamagata's death in 1922, but neither they nor any other men
of their generation, with the exception of the outsider Ōkuma, ever became

prime minister again or held a cabinet post. Instead they let their slightly younger protégés take over, retaining only indirect and gradually fading control as *genrō,* or "elder statesmen," as they came to be called.

Katsura established a purely bureaucratic cabinet, in the tradition of his patron Yamagata. At first he had little difficulty with the Diet, because Itō, as party president, made the Seiyūkai support him. But Katsura ran into trouble when Ito, whose party following represented primarily the rural tax-payers, refused to support his bill for an increased land tax to pay for further naval expansion. Finally Katsura was forced to compromise, agreeing to pay for naval expansion by loans rather than increased taxes. He ran into more serious trouble late in 1903, after Itō had left the presidency of the Seiyūkai. He was forced to dissolve the Diet in December, but was saved from the usual consequences by the outbreak of the Russo-Japanese War the next February (see pages 187–188) and the enthusiastic response it produced in the Diet.

The peace terms concluding the war in September 1905, however, proved disappointing to the Japanese public. The government was accused of having snatched defeat from the jaws of victory, and there was widespread rioting. More than a thousand police and citizens were killed or wounded in Tōkyö before order was restored through martial law. Ōkuma's faction— the Real Constitutional Party—took advantage of the situation to press its attack against the government, and Katsura resigned in January 1906.

Itō had resigned the presidency of the Seiyūkai in July 1903 because of pressure from Yamagata, who found Itō's double role as party president and elder statesman too anomalous and perhaps too threatening to his own influence. Itō, however, had been replaced as party president by a man whose position was almost equally anomalous. This was Prince Saionji Kimmochi (1849–1940), a high member of the old court nobility, who had studied for ten years in France, had become a liberal newspaperman on his return to Japan, and had been forced by the court to abandon this shocking career for the bureaucracy. There he had become a protégé of Itō and had followed him into the Seiyūkai. Saionji was the obvious choice to succeed Katsura, but the oligarchs selected him ostensibly not as party president but as a noble and bureaucrat. He, however, appointed two of his party colleagues to the cabinet and naturally enjoyed full Seiyūkai support in the Diet.

With the formation of Saionji's cabinet in 1906, a fairly stable, though ambiguous, solution of the Diet problem had been reached—at least for the time being. The prime ministership was passed back and forth with relative ease between Saionji and Katsura until 1912, and neither was again forced to dissolve the Diet. The two proved able to cooperate with less open friction than had their respective patrons, Yamagata and Itō. Katsura was more flexible and conciliatory in dealing with the Diet than

Yamagata had been, and Saionji, though a more genuine supporter of parliamentary government than Itō, moved only very cautiously toward party control of the cabinet. At the same time, he was as successful as Itō in maintaining Seiyūkai support for his own cabinets and the party's co-operation with those of Katsura. The Seiyūkai politicians were at least temporarily satisfied with their share in power and access to patronage through cabinets that clearly relied on their votes for necessary legislation, and Saionji and Katsura were ready to give them this much in return for needed support in the Diet.

The Fulfillment of the Meiji Dream

Security and Imperialism. Thus by the first decade of the twentieth century, a reasonably successful, semiparliamentary form of government had been achieved. In fact, a number of small steps and a host of shifting compromises had produced a much larger beginning in democracy than most Meiji leaders would have desired, and universal education and a rapidly expanding university system were soon to carry Japan much further toward democracy. But this was scarcely the real objective of the Meiji oligarchs. Parliamentary institutions, like industrialization or universal education, were only means to an end—mere by-products of what they really sought. This was the double objective of security from the nations of the West and acceptance by them of Japan as an equal, and this they achieved with complete success, though not without creating problems for future generations.

Two key steps in the achievement of security and equality were the Japanese victories over China and Russia. These two wars proved more clearly than anything else that Japan had indeed developed the "rich country and strong military" on which security and equality seemed to depend. But they also started Japan on a course of foreign conquest and empire that was to end a half-century later in catastrophe. One naturally wonders why Japan, which was attempting to defend itself from Western imperialism, should in the process have become an imperialistic power itself.

After internal stability had been assured through the suppression of the Satsuma Rebellion in 1877, Yamagata had turned his attention abroad, arguing with increasing vehemence that the geographic line of national advantage Japan should defend lay far beyond the line of sovereignty. Such imperialist concepts might be traced to Yamagata's old teacher, Yoshida Shōin, or to the whole military mystique of the samurai class. But expansion abroad was not an important part of the Japanese tradition. There had been only two nationally organized efforts in Japanese history—the campaigns in southern Korea up until the seventh century and Hideyoshi's invasion of

Korea in the late sixteenth century. Isolation had been the usual rule for Japan.

A much more obvious source of Yamagata's line of reasoning was the example of Western imperialism. Imperialistic expansion and domination seemed an inherent part of the Western-dominated world Japan had joined. Yamagata was merely a typical military man of his day in the ideas he expressed. And Japan's foreign conquests of the next few decades received as much praise from the West as any of its other efforts at "modernization." The generally accepted ideas and practices of the time almost inevitably drew any strong military power, and particularly one in Japan's geographic position, into imperialistic adventures.

The Sino-Japanese War. Japan's opening of Korea in 1876 led to increasing embroilment with China over the peninsula. Peking adamantly insisted on its suzerainty over Korea, which Japan refused to recognize, and Korean reformers began to look to Japanese liberals like Fukuzawa for inspiration and to the Japanese government for support. When a conservative, antiforeign mob in Seoul attacked the Japanese legation in the summer of 1882, both China and Japan responded by sending troops to the aid of opposing sides. In 1884 a coup by Korean liberal elements ended with a clash between Chinese soldiers and the Japanese legation guard. To calm the situation Itō and the Chinese statesman Li Hung-chang met in Tientsin in 1885 and agreed that both countries would withdraw their troops from Korea and notify the other before sending them back.

During the next decade the Chinese intensified their efforts at modernizing their military forces, particularly the navy, while the Japanese became increasingly involved in Korea, thus setting the stage for an even more serious confrontation. When the Tonghak ("Eastern Learning"), a popular religious organization with a strongly antiforeign bias, broke out in revolt in southern Korea in 1894, China sent a small body of troops at the Korean king's request, and Japan then sent in a larger force, demanded reforms of the Korean government, and finally seized control of it and had it declare war on China. War followed between Japan and China on August 1.

The ensuing hostilities were the first real test of the efforts at military modernization both China and Japan had been making for a whole generation. Most Westerners assumed that the Chinese giant would win through sheer size, but Japan quickly proved that its modernization had been more successful. Its armies seized the whole of Korea and then invaded Manchuria. But victory was largely determined by sea power, which in the absence of railways controlled even China's access to Korea. While the Chinese fleet was larger, the Japanese was qualitatively much better. On September 17 off the mouth of the Yalu River, the Japanese, using modern British naval tactics, severely crippled the Chinese fleet, which came out like cavalry, lined abreast. The Japanese then captured the naval base of Port Arthur in South Manchuria and besieged Weihaiwei on the northern coast of Shantung, where the remainder of the Chinese fleet was bottled up. Weihaiwei fell, the fleet surrendered, and China had to sue for peace.

The terms of the Treaty of Shimonoseki, signed between Itō and Li on April 17, 1895, were relatively severe, though perhaps less so than they might have been had not a Japanese fanatic shot and wounded Li. China was obliged to cede Taiwan, the nearby Pescadores Islands, and the Kwantung Peninsula in South Manchuria; recognize Korea's independence; pay 200 million taels indemnity; open more ports; and negotiate a commercial treaty. The latter, signed in 1896, gave Japan all the privileges that the Western powers had in China and added the further privilege of carrying on "industries and manufactures," using the cheap labor in the treaty ports.

Japan's triumph, however, was soon tarnished by a blatant power play by the Western nations. Russia, which itself had ambitions in both Manchuria and Korea, was alarmed by Japan's success. It persuaded Germany and France to join in a diplomatic intervention on April 23, 1895, "advising" Japan to give up the Kwantung Peninsula. Bowing to *force majeur,* Japan complied, receiving in compensation 30 million taels of additional indemnity. There was naturally a strong reaction of indignation among the Japanese public, which became further embittered when the same three powers appropriated pieces of China for themselves in 1898, the Russians taking, under a twenty-five year lease, the Kwantung Peninsula that Japan had been forced to disgorge only three years earlier.

The Achievement of Equality.   Still, Japan's victory over China greatly impressed the West, and the British in particular, disillusioned with the incompetence of the Chinese government, began to show a decidedly more pro-Japanese attitude. Even before the war they had been enough impressed by Japan's internal order and legal reforms to agree to relinquish extraterritoriality. For years, the Japanese effort to revise the unequal treaties had been fruitless, despite increasingly explosive demands by the political parties and the public. By 1888 only one nation—Mexico—had surrendered its extraterritorial privileges. But finally Britain, in a treaty signed in London on July 16, 1894, just a few days before the outbreak of war with China, agreed to relinquish extraterritoriality as of 1899, and the United States and the other powers quickly followed. Subsequently Japan regained complete control over its own tariffs through a treaty signed with the United States on February 21, 1911.

When the fervently antiforeign Boxer uprising broke out in North China in 1900 and many foreigners were killed and the legations in Peking were threatened, Japan acted as one of the consort of "Western" powers to save the legations and safeguard foreign treaty rights. Almost half of the relief expedition of twenty thousand men which marched on Peking was made up of Japanese troops, who, in contrast to some of the Western contingents, conducted themselves in exemplary fashion.

Japan also achieved equality with the nations of the West in another more dramatic way. On July 30, 1902, the Anglo-Japanese Alliance was signed—the first military pact on equal terms between a Western and a non-Western nation. The British, seeing their long dominance of the eastern seas threatened by the rise of new naval powers, bolstered their position in East Asia by allying themselves with the only strong naval power in the area. They also forestalled by this pact any Russo-Japanese agreement to partition Northeast Asia and instead secured Japanese support for the maintenance of the treaty system in China. The Japanese, faced with growing rivalry with Russia over Korea and Manchuria, needed the alliance to ensure that, if war broke out, Russia would not be joined by other European powers, as it had been in its intervention over the Kwantung Peninsula in 1895. The wording of the alliance made clear that in such a case Britain would come to Japan's aid. The alliance also secured Britain's blessing for Japanese ambitions in Korea, recognizing that Japan was interested in that country "in a peculiar degree politically as well as commercially and industrially." Itō had favored an agreement with Russia which would give Manchuria to Russia and Korea to Japan, but Yamagata and Katsura were convinced that war with Russia was inevitable and therefore wanted the British alliance. Since they were in control of the government in 1902 their view won out.

The Russo-Japanese War.　The event that really won for Japan full status as a world power and equality with the nations of the West was its victory over Russia, the biggest, even if not one of the more advanced, of the Western powers. Russia in 1896 had obtained from Peking the right to build the Chinese Eastern Railway across Manchuria to its port of Vladivostok on the Sea of Japan, thus shortening the Trans-Siberian Railway, the rail link it had started in 1891 to construct across Siberia to the Pacific. When Russia obtained the lease of the Kwantung Peninsula in 1898, it also got the right to connect this line by a southward extension, the South Manchurian Railway, to the ports of the peninsula, Port Arthur and Dairen (Ta-lien in Chinese). These railway concessions gave Russia considerable control over Manchuria, and the Boxer crisis allowed it to overrun the whole area militarily. Its efforts to take Manchuria over completely, however, ended in diplomatic frustration, and it agreed to a phased withdrawal of its forces.

Mutual suspicion and enmity steadily mounted between Japan and Russia. In negotiations between August 1903 and February 1904, Japan won a fairly free hand in Korea but offered to recognize Russian rights only in the zones along the new railways in Manchuria. Meanwhile the Russians had been slow in withdrawing their troops and had begun transporting large reinforcements over the Trans-Siberian system, which had been completed in 1903. Japan broke off relations on February 6, 1904, started hostilities on February 8 with a night torpedo-boat attack on the Russian fleet in Port Arthur, and only two days later declared war.

In May Japanese forces crossed the Yalu River from Korea into Manchuria, while sea-borne forces seized Dairen and besieged Port Arthur. The naval base finally fell in January 1905. Meanwhile Japanese armies had been driving the Russians back in Manchuria and in March captured Mukden, the capital of the region. The Russians' last hope was their Baltic fleet. Denied by Britain the use of the Suez Canal and Britain's worldwide system of ports, the Russian fleet of forty-five ill-assorted, poorly prepared vessels, surmounted all difficulties and eventually reached East Asian waters. In its final dash to make the relative safety of Vladivostok, however, it was intercepted by the Japanese fleet on May 27 in the Straits of Tsushima and was annihilated. Both countries were exhausted by the war, and the Russians were plagued at home by revolution. They both readily accepted President Theodore Roosevelt's diplomatic initiative and met to discuss peace terms in Portsmouth, New Hampshire.

The Treaty of Portsmouth, signed on September 5, 1905, recognized Japan's "paramount interest" in Korea, restored at least in theory China's sovereignty and administration in Manchuria, and gave Japan the Russian lease on the Kwantung Peninsula and the Russian-built South Manchurian Railway as far north as Changchun. The Japanese were eager to extract an indemnity from the Russians, but the latter were adamant on this point, and eventually Japan settled for the southern half of Sakhalin instead. It was the failure to win an indemnity that the Japanese public found so disappointing.

Japan was now free of all foreign competitors in Korea. Itō took on the task of working out a new relationship between the two countries and in November secured a convention making Korea a Japanese protectorate and ending its diplomatic contact with other powers. He himself became resident general. In 1907 he extended Japanese control over the Korean government, arranged that Japanese could serve as Korean officials, and disbanded the Korean army. Widespread rioting which greeted these moves was severely repressed in 1450 armed engagements between 1908 and 1910. Meanwhile Itō, after resigning as resident general, was assassinated by a Korean patriot in October 1909 on a trip to Manchuria. In August 1910 Japan quietly annexed Korea. There was no protest from the powers, which generally approved what was judged at the time to be an inevitable step in world progress. Called Chōsen, the Japanese pronunciation of the ancient Korean name of Chosŏn, Korea was governed for Japan's strategic and economic purposes by Japanese officials under a military governor-general.

Japan thus had become not just a modern nation but a major imperialist power with important colonies in Korea and Taiwan and predominant rights in South Manchuria. It entered World War I in 1914 as Britain's ally and, although playing only a minimal military role, picked up the German colonial possessions in East Asia and the Pacific—Kiaochow Bay and the port of Tsingtao on the south coast of Shantung, which the Germans had obtained in 1898 following their intervention over the Kwantung Peninsula in 1895, and the German North Pacific Islands, which Japan was assigned at the end of the war as a Mandate under the League of Nations. Japan sat at the Versailles Peace Conference as one of the victorious Five Great Powers—the only non-Western nation to be accepted as a full equal by the West. Thus the Meiji leaders had succeeded far beyond their fondest dreams. This was already clear before Itō died in 1909. It was even clearer by the time the last members of the group passed from the scene as venerable octogenarians—Yamagata in 1922 and Matsukata in 1924.

6. Imperial Japan: Economy and Society

Japan's rise from semicolonial status under the unequal treaties to the level of a great power and ally of Britain was an unparalleled success story. For this new Japan the early decades of the twentieth century were a golden age. Having successfully met the great challenge presented by the Western powers in the nineteenth century—in fact having been the only non-Western nation to do so—why should Japan not overcome the seemingly simpler problems ahead?

Indeed, Japan in the first quarter of the twentieth century gave every promise of living up to this optimistic prospect. The nation moved ahead rapidly in all fields, continuing with amazing speed to close the technological gap between itself and the West that had so terrified the Japanese only a generation or two earlier. By 1925 Japan was a far more modernized country and much more of a world power than at the close of the Russo-Japanese War.

The next two decades saw a continuation of the same rapid technological progress, growth of power, and modernization of institutions, but meanwhile a profound change had come over the country. The brilliant successes of earlier years had somehow turned into staggering new problems. Confidence had been replaced by new fears, the old unity of purpose by inner conflict. Japan continued to rush forward, but the Japanese themselves began to wonder apprehensively where they were going. And their worries proved to be justified. Japan became involved in wars of increasing magnitude, until in 1945 its newly won empire and ancient homeland both fell in ruins in perhaps the largest single catastrophe to overwhelm any nation in modern times. Japan's unparalleled success had turned to ashes.

This second great phase in Japan's modernization is doubtless pregnant with meaning. But no one is as yet sure just what this reversal of fortune fully signifies. We have some idea of the dynamics of Japan's modernization in the nineteenth century, and the disaster that struck in the 1930's and 1940's may be clear enough, but how and why did the one so quickly turn into the other? The few who have attempted to answer the question have usually treated the disaster as if it were a direct outgrowth of the imperfections of the Meiji system, but we must remember that two generations separated the original Meiji leaders from the men who led Japan to its great defeat. One whole generation of relative stability lies between the Meiji oligarchs and the later crisis.

In transforming their society to meet the problems they faced in the nineteenth century, however, the Japanese undoubtedly did create new ones to be faced in the twentieth. A spurt in population accompanied the modernization of the economy and the introduction of modern medical science. Hence Japan, long self-sufficient and even an exporter of food in the nineteenth century, became increasingly dependent on imports of rice and raw materials. Thus the quest for economic security led to dependence on foreign markets. Similarly the quest for military security resulted in a rapid build-up of military might, which led to expansion abroad. The Japanese now found themselves embroiled in imperialistic rivalries and the difficulties of colonial rule that beset all colonial powers in the twentieth century.

Equally serious were less understood social and intellectual problems. The new economy, universal education, and many other factors were producing a vastly more complex society. Urban Japan had changed more rapidly than the countryside, and the gap in thought and attitudes was widening between the masses, who received only elementary schooling, and those who underwent the new, Western-oriented higher education. Even among the more educated, divergencies of attitude were becoming greater: professional military men, civil administrators, educators, men of letters, businessmen, and politicians were living different kinds of lives and thinking different thoughts.

There were also fresh stirrings of discontent among the lower classes. Tenancy had grown steadily in the countryside, and the new urban proletariat of factory workers, as it gradually became divorced from its peasant origins, became more vulnerable to fluctuations in the industrial economy. Living standards for the Japanese as a whole had moved steadily upward, but economic expectancies rose even faster. The unhappy conditions of life among tenant farmers and factory workers posed a major social problem.

Still another problem was leadership. The Meiji leaders had been a close-knit group, united on their goal: to achieve security and equality for Japan by using Western technology. Now professional military men, who were much more narrowly specialized than their predecessors, might argue that Japan's future lay in increased military strength in order to seize a larger empire, whereas business leaders or the politicians they helped elect might feel that such a course was both costly and dangerous and that Japan would do better to invest in industrial expansion. Such divisions of opinion are not infrequent in modern societies, and their resolution requires either strong leadership or an effective mechanism for settling disagreements—both of which Japan lacked. The Meiji oligarchs created a government which they could direct from above. They assumed the continuation of a strong and unified leadership group like themselves. The second and third generation of leaders, however, were the heirs and not the architects of the system. They were in it, not above it.

Behind the political ambiguities was a growing diversity of values. The guiding spirit of the Meiji transformation was an emperor-oriented nationalism. This had been expressed in a driving ambition to make Japan into a powerful state. But once Japan achieved power, its goals became diverse and the earlier political consensus became gravely fragmented, even though the core elements of nationalism remained strong.

Japan's political life in the late nineteenth and early twentieth centuries was partly free and partly unfree. As Japan's society became more modern, demands for greater freedom were created by new streams of Western thought, heightened social mobility, more and better education, and wider participation by the people in the political control of society. This reflected the major trend in Japanese politics through the 1920's: the step-by-step increase in the power of the Diet and in the strength of the political parties in relation to the other governmental elites. Yet during the same period the potential for greater authoritarian controls also increased. When crises arose in the early 1930's that Japan's leaders could not solve, a shift occurred in the balance of elites and Japan became a militarist state. The shift to military control demonstrated that the evils as well as the benefits of modernization could appear in non-Western as in Western nations.

The Maturing of The Economy

The base for Japan's modern industrial development was formed during the last thirty years of the nineteenth century. The first development occurred in the traditional sector of the economy. Freed from Tokugawa restrictions and given impetus by institutional innovations and reforms, Japan's traditional small industries underwent a notable expansion. The second wave of advance came in the modern sector during the late 1880's and the 1890's. But we must keep this nineteenth-century growth in proper perspective. In spite of its qualitative brilliance, it was small. In a quantitative sense Japan's "takeoff" period really began only after the Russo-Japanese War. At the end of the nineteenth century the country was still technologically backward, exporting for the most part raw or semiprocessed materials such as silk.

The rate of economic growth after 1900 was spectacular. The upsurge of the late nineteenth century continued almost without interruption for the next four decades. Between 1900 and the late 1930's the production of raw materials more than tripled, and the output of manufactured goods increased well over twelvefold. By the late 1930's the Japanese economy was relatively mature even in its heavy industries. Close to 60 per cent of the export trade, which had grown about twentyfold in the meantime, was made up of fully manufactured goods, and certain industries within the great manufacturing nations of the West had become almost hysterically afraid of Japanese competition.

Many scholars have attributed this economic growth to Japan's exploitation of its new colonial empire. The Japanese certainly wrested from their colonies what they could, and control over the agricultural products and mineral resources of Korea and Taiwan proved to be of strategic advantage. But however exploitative the empire was in human terms, it was probably more an economic drain than an asset. More was spent in the colonies than was derived from them, even if we disregard the greatly increased military outlay required for their seizure and defense.

Other scholars have stressed the role of foreign markets (of which colonial markets were but a very small part) to explain Japan's economic growth. They have argued that the inequities of landlordism and zaibatsu concentration of wealth limited domestic consumption and forced Japan to turn outward for markets. This hypothesis also is not borne out by the facts. As a source of raw materials and advanced machinery, foreign trade was necessary. But it accounted for a smaller percentage of Japan's total economic activity than was true of most European countries during the same period. Japan's economy was dominant, not satellitic. Its growth was largely self-generated.

Some of the growth was used up by an increase in the population, which came close to doubling—from 43,847,000 in 1900 to 73,100,000 in 1940. Much went into investment in the new empire and into increased military expenditures. And a high percentage was plowed back as capital investment, perhaps 15 per cent or more of net income in boom years. Yet despite these claims on Japan's total product, enough remained to effect a substantial rise in per capita consumption during the first four decades of the twentieth century. At all levels of society, standards advanced somewhat, although relative disparities between different groups also increased.

As the Japanese economy developed, it became closely integrated with the world economy. Japan lacked extensive mineral resources and so, as industrial output rose, it became necessary to import ever increasing amounts of raw materials, which could be paid for only by a corresponding expansion in exports. Most of the time these were easily obtained; but the psychological awareness of dependence became more and more intense. Moreover, while foreign trade was not the motor of Japan's economic growth, it bulked large enough to make the difference between an economy running in high or in low gear. In the 1950's and 1960's it was said that when New York sneezes, Tōkyō comes down with a cold. The beginnings of this situation were already visible in the 1920's and 1930's.

The Pattern of Growth.   A boom began after 1905 that continued until 1913. The three types of demand that contributed to this advance typify the forces that sustained Japan's growth into the 1930's. The first was continuing expansion of the traditional sector of the economy. As wages rose, consumer taste, remaining relatively constant, demanded more of traditional goods, rather than the products of new industry. The second type of demand, domestic and foreign, was for cottons, bicycles, and other products of Japan's light industries. The third type of demand was that created by government expenditures, which increased sixfold in the two decades before 1913. Most of this increase was military. Throughout the period 1887–1940 government investment in the economy, as a proportion of total investment, averaged well over 40 per cent. This created a steady market for the products of Japan's heavy industries at a time when these were not yet competitive with those of the West.

Japan's rate of government expenditure and industrial investment in the years after 1905 proved too high for it to maintain, and by 1911 it faced a serious financial crisis. This was ended by the First World War which produced a strong new impetus for economic expansion. This was the "best" war in Japan's history: its military participation was minimal, orders for munitions poured in from its allies, and there was a vast increase in demand for Japanese manufactured goods in Asian and other markets cut off from their usual European sources of supply. Between 1915 and 1920 the Japanese economy grew by leaps and bounds. The destruction of European shipping played into the hands of the Japanese merchant marine, which almost doubled in size and increased its net income about ten times. The number of factory workers almost doubled, as did the export of cotton goods. Profits were huge and, despite a sharp rise in prices, permitted a rate of capital investment in industry that was unusually high even for Japan. In addition, Japan became for the first time a creditor nation, with gold reserves of more than 2 billion yen, a sixfold increase in six years.

A spiraling inflation kept Japan's war boom going for more than a year after the armistice, but prices collapsed in March 1920. The next twelve years were economically among the least impressive of Japan's modern history. One reason was that Japanese agriculture and the domestic production of raw materials reached a plateau. This leveling off accentuated the growing gap between rural and urban income levels, and put the burden of absorbing the expanding population on the industrial sector, which had problems of its own. A second reason for the poor performance of this period was a relative decline in government expenditures. Earlier such expenditures had buffered fluctuations in the economy. During the 1920's, a time of peace and democratic tendencies, military expenses were cut without a compensatory increase in other expenditures. The result was to leave the Japanese much more exposed to the ups and downs of internal and foreign markets. A third reason was that the price structure of most countries had been more thoroughly deflated after World War I than had that of Japan. This led to an unfavorable balance of trade during the early 1920's and to the loss of gold reserves. Japan's exports were buoyed up by the prosperity of the United States during the later twenties, but were dealt a disastrous blow by the economic consequences of the Great Depression.

Other domestic factors also contributed to the checkered pattern of Japan's economic life in the twenties. The postwar depression had begun to lift in 1922, but on September 1, 1923, a great earthquake occurred in the Tōkyō area in which more than 130,000 persons died and billions of dollars' worth of property was destroyed. This set off a construction boom financed in part by foreign borrowing. After 1924 Japan temporarily went off the gold standard, letting the yen depreciate, which stimulated foreign trade. An inflationary expansion of the economy ensued; but this was checked by a bank crisis in the spring of 1927, when a number of important banks failed, and deflation once more set in. Then, after springing back briefly, the economy experienced an even greater shock in 1930. In January, Inoue Junnosuke, the orthodox-minded finance minister, unwisely put Japan back on the gold standard, just two months after the American crash and at a time when world prices had already started to drop. As a result the yen rose, exports dropped and Japan sank into a serious depression.

Despite these difficulties, the Japanese economy was not stagnant between 1920 and 1930: advances were made in technology, industry was diversified more widely, manufacturing came close to doubling in output, and the gains of World War I and of the period of inflationary expansion from 1922 to 1927 were consolidated by the elimination of unsound enterprises. But the cost in human suffering and social unrest was high. The price of rice, which had risen 174 per cent in the preceding six years, fell by more than half within a year after the 1920 deflation, recovered almost to the old high by 1925, and then sank almost to the 1914 level by 1931. The price of silk, the chief export and the most important secondary product of Japan's agriculture, fell by more than two-thirds between 1925 and 1929.

Recovery and the Rise of a War Economy.   Although the depression lasted for many years in the United States, Japan was already recovering by 1932. The major factor contributing to this recovery was an expansion of foreign trade. Japan went off the gold standard in December 1931, and the yen sank from 50 cents to 30 cents. This devaluation produced a boom in exports. Cheaper Japanese goods captured many markets in Asia and Africa that were not sealed up within European empires. A second factor responsible for Japan's rapid recovery was the return to military adventure in 1931, restoring the high level of military expenditures that had been lacking during the previous decade. Since there was slack in the economy, these two factors were complementary: trade helped build industrial strength which served the military, and military demand contributed to the recovery from depression. By 1936 industry was more diversified; technological advances had occurred in the metallurgical, machine, and chemical industries; the volume of exports abroad and to the colonies had doubled in six years; and the net national product had increased by half.

The reaction in the West to the expansion of Japanese exports was negative: tariffs were raised, restrictions were sought, and voices were lifted against "dumping" and cheap Oriental labor. When one considers that Japanese exports were only 4 per cent of world exports, and that Japanese imports from the United States and Europe were greater than exports to those areas, such fears seem hypochondriac—reflecting grave doubts in the West regarding the viability of the international economic order.

The reaction of the West provided support for those in Japan favoring expansion. Other industrial powers had either extensive colonies or vast internal resources. Japan, the Britain of Asia, was deficient in both respects. It appeared that the only way to fulfill the national destiny in the face of Western restrictions was to create an economically self-sufficient empire. Events as they unfolded after 1936, however, show that these arguments were fallacious. Despite raised tariffs abroad, Japan had successfully recovered from the depression. This recovery was based on a multilateral pattern of trade: Japan sold more than it bought in Asia and Africa, and bought more than it sold in the United States and Europe. This geographical imbalance in trade was possible because currencies could be converted.

After 1936, however, more and more of Japan's exports went to its colonies. This led to diminishing foreign credits and forced Japan to impose controls on dollar imports. Also by 1936 the Japanese economy was taut. The expansion of the early thirties had brought about full employment and few resources were idle. Hence there was little possibility of another round of growth when Japan went to war, first with China in 1937 and then with the United States and the Western Allies in 1941. Japan could increase its strategic economic potential only by imposing strict controls to reduce consumption and shift productive capacities to war industries. Dependence on foreign raw materials further limited its economic potential, thus heightening the discrepancy between Japan and the United States, which possessed vast sources of raw materials and, at the beginning of the war, was far from enjoying full employment.

The Zaibatsu System. The scarcity of capital in early Meiji Japan, the government's willingness to give financial aid and privileges to entrepreneurs who gave promise of building up the economy, and the sale in the 1880's of government industries to the few who were able to buy them enabled a relatively small group of business leaders to gain control of much of the modern sector of Japan's economy, just before industrialization started to pay off. The concerns they established in the late nineteenth century grew faster than the economy as a whole and by the 1920's controlled a large part of the nation's economic power. In the industrial upsurge of World War I, these industrialists expanded enormously, and during the economic uncertainties that followed the war they fastened their hold on the economy even more firmly. At least half of Japan's banks were eliminated during this period, leaving the financial power needed for large-scale industrial expansion concentrated in the hands of a few giant institutions.

The leading financial and industrial groups had from the start cooperated closely with the government, but now a greater equalization of roles began to take place. Businessmen were no longer dependent on the government for their capital requirements. And while continuing as an instrument of government policy, big business, by its ties within the bureaucracy and by its financial influence on the political parties, came to have a growing voice in the formation of policy. To many Japanese it appeared that the tail was beginning to wag the dog. The term zaibatsu, or "financial clique," which came into common use for these business giants, had a strongly pejorative flavor.

There has never been any clear agreement on which companies constituted the zaibatsu, but the top four are always listed, in order of their size, as Mitsui, Mitsubishi, Sumitomo, and Yasuda. In addition, no one would dispute the inclusion of other giants such as the Furukawa, Kuhara, and Kawasaki interests, as well as Aikawa's Nissan interests and other "new zaibatsu" which emerged in the 1930's by building armaments and by aiding the army to exploit Manchuria.

The greatest difference between a zaibatsu firm and a Western corporation was that the former usually spread over a variety of fields, constituting

ORGANIZATION OF THE MITSUI COMBINE
(based on specific examples among major units in the combine)

Arrows indicate percentage of stock ownership. Numbers in parentheses are paid-up capital in millions of yen (roughly 3 to the dollar).

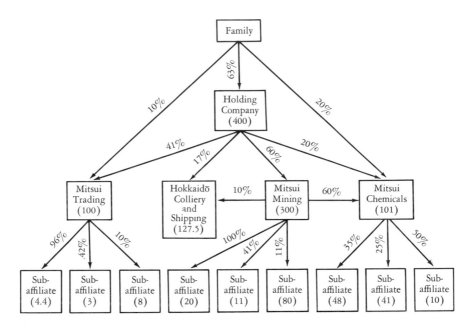

a "combine" of business enterprises, or what might be called a conglomerate today, rather than a single great company. Such a combine might spread horizontally through a variety of manufacturing or mining industries and vertically through the different stages of production of a single product. Thus one of the Mitsubishi mining companies might extract the minerals which one of the Mitsubishi manufacturing companies then fashioned into a product which a Mitsubishi trading firm marketed abroad, transporting it in ships of another Mitsubishi affiliate, and the whole process would be financed through the Mitsubishi bank.

During the 1920's and 1930's, Mitsui and Mitsubishi were probably the two largest private economic empires in the world. In 1941, the sprawling Mitsui interests consisted of a main holding company, with 70 direct corporate affiliates. The two largest, Mitsui Trading and Mitsui Mining, controlled respectively 126 and 31 other affiliates, while 108 other companies were under the control of the remaining 68 direct affiliates. At their peak the Mitsui interests probably employed about a million people in Japan proper and another million in the empire and abroad.

Mitsui was owned by the Mitsui family, which held some 90 per cent of their wealth jointly and were strictly controlled in their actions and expenditures by family laws. The family held shares directly in many of the Mitsui companies and owned a majority interest in the central holding company. This distinction between family and holding company did not exist in the more recently risen zaibatsu firms. Another difference between Mitsui and most of the others was that, while the actual business control of the Mitsui combine had long since passed into the hands of managers, the original entrepreneur or his immediate descendants might still be in control in the newer zaibatsu firms. In addition to family ownership, the internal cohesiveness and power of the zaibatsu was augmented by interlocking directorates, by the use of financial and marketing power to control affiliates in which the combine held only a minority stock interest, and by an almost feudal sense of corporate loyalty. The staff of affiliate companies regarded themselves as part of the whole organization and were loyal to it.

There has been a heated debate over the efficiency of the zaibatsu system. Today most economists agree that the system was very efficient and in its era something like it was almost inevitable. When any backward country industrializes, there is a shortage of capital, skilled labor, and technological know-how. To obtain rapid growth, these must be brought together in a concentrated form. During the second half of the nineteenth century, when free enterprise was strong and there existed no historical model of socialist development, it was natural for this to occur in private hands. The zaibatsu system afforded entrepreneurial strength to the Japanese economy: the profits from established enterprises were used by the combines as risk capital to pioneer new fields. Even the concentration of wealth in the few controlling families was probably a net economic gain—permitting the bulk of the profits to be reinvested for further expansion. There were of course tendencies toward monopoly, but the importance of foreign markets and raw materials helped to keep zaibatsu prices competitive.

It is more difficult to evaluate the social and political effects of the system. While offering a career opening to talent, the zaibatsu were bureaucratic, hierarchical, and not supportive of individualism. Whether they were more undemocratic than Japanese society in general is open to question. Some have criticized the zaibatsu concentration of wealth as an obstacle to the development of a strong middle class. Would not a wider distribution of corporate stock have been better? On the other hand, the middle management of the zaibatsu concerns (along with the professions, small businessmen, landlords, and upper levels of the bureaucracy) did constitute a recognizable middle class even during the 1920's, with homes, savings, a high concern for their children's education, and so on. Did not rapid economic growth, which the zaibatsu system promoted, do more to strengthen this class than economic concentration did to weaken it?

The relations between the zaibatsu, political parties, and the government have not been adequately studied. To what extent did zaibatsu contributions to election campaigns influence party policies? Might the parties otherwise have adopted different policies or been politically more healthy? Whatever the answers may be, there is no question that the political activities of the zaibatsu early became a target for popular criticism and helped to tarnish the concept of parliamentary government in many Japanese minds.

Although nondemocratic, the zaibatsu did not fit in very well with militarism, the other political trend then developing in Japan. Their ties to the conservative political parties led them to favor representative government as it existed during the 1920's. The higher education and foreign experience of their managers, together with an awareness of the importance of foreign trade, tended to give the zaibatsu an international outlook. Before the war it was the supporters of militarism who were the most violent critics of the zaibatsu. For example, the officer bureaucrats of the Japanese Kwantung Army in Manchuria, viewing the zaibatsu as Western, urban, liberal, and corrupt, shut them out of the early phase of Manchurian development after 1931. As Japan slipped deeper into war after 1937, the zaibatsu industries inevitably became the core of the war economy. Even then they proved difficult to control. The zaibatsu represented such aggregates of economic power that it was more expedient for the government to seek their cooperation than to force their submission. What the pattern of cooperation was has not yet been studied.

The Double Structure of the Japanese Economy.   Another distinctive feature of the Japanese economy was the tremendous number of small concerns with fewer than five workers. In 1930, for example, more than half (2,772,183) of Japan's manufacturing labor force (4,759,921) was employed in such small businesses. It is difficult to estimate their productive capacity since their tax reports grossly underestimated their actual role in the economy. It is clear that they were less efficient than the big modern factories, and that the value of their output was considerably less than their numerical strength would indicate. They cannot, however, be dismissed as merely the declining sector of traditional small industries. Relative to medium and large industry, their percentage of total production was slowly declining, yet in Tōkyō alone their number increased phenomenally from about 3000 in 1923 after the Tōkyō earthquake to almost 26,000 in 1932.

Bimodality thus marked the Japanese economy: a handful of giant combines, thousands of tiny workshops, and in between relatively few medium-sized industries. Japanese economic historians refer to this pattern as the "double structure" of the economy. In part it was a result of a split technology: zaibatsu engineers versed in Western science as contrasted with the owners of small shops rooted in the artisan tradition of Tokugawa Japan. The availability of capital was also bimodal. Zaibatsu banks catered to industries within the same combine, but small business could be started

SILK SCREENING. *Some traditional techniques survive into the modern era as artisans gradually become artists.*

with private savings or a loan from a patron. The two extremes also reflect clear differences in social organization: the zaibatsu, although paternalistic, were recognizably modern or "Western"; the workshops held to traditional Japanese small-group organization. By the late 1930's some of these distinctions had begun to blur. Universal education and ties to larger industries led to a rising level of technology in the small businesses. And changes were also taking place in social organization. In general, however, the relative differences continued into the postwar period, along with a double standard of wages.

Among the small concerns with fewer than five workers were traditional handicrafts, woven textiles, shops producing daily necessities, and repair shops, all areas of expanding demand as standards of living rose. Yet the small businesses also were integrated with the most advanced sector of the economy. Probably over half of Japan's small concerns subsisted entirely on subcontracts from zaibatsu-type industries. The time-consuming assembly of an electrical device, for example, might take place in a village shop one hundred miles from the factory.

The meaning of this double structure is controversial. Was the low efficiency of small business a drag on the economy, or did small shops perform the easy jobs, enabling the modern sector to direct all of its energies to the more complex and capital-intensive tasks of technological production and thus expand the total economy more rapidly? If the former position is taken, one can go on to see the relation between the zaibatsu and small business as exploitative: putting out simple tasks to the workers in these shops kept cheap labor cheap and maintained repressive social patterns. Had the total productive process been brought into the factory, a greater equalization of wages, more favorable conditions for labor organization, and new social patterns might have developed. In human terms, the system was obviously exploitative: working conditions in the small shops were poor.

On the other hand, the use of such shops was the cheapest way to produce, and it was this economic consideration, rather than any zaibatsu social policy, that led to the putting-out of work. Moreover, the double structure developed not because of zaibatsu planning, but in spite of zaibatsu growth. That it was not destroyed by rapid industrial growth was due to the high rate of population growth, which kept up the supply of cheap labor. In the postwar period, the same type of economic growth in the modern sector —in combination with a sharply decreased rate of population growth— pulled labor out of small industries and out of the farm villages. This situation forced small concerns to raise wages, gradually eroding the prewar double structure.

Social Change

The Japanese Family.   The family continued to be of political as well as social importance in Japan during the early decades of the twentieth century. It was seen as the building block of the unique Japanese "national polity." Its ideal virtues of harmony, solidarity, and loyalty were projected onto the Japanese state. It was the last stronghold in Japan of Confucian social practices. Even the city dweller, whose life was modern in many respects, participated in a still vital area of Japan's premodern tradition in his family life.

In the family as it existed in the late nineteenth century, lineage, not matrimony, was holy. The line extended from the ancestors to the parents to their eldest son and heir. Marriage was for the purpose of obtaining heirs for the "house." The position of the daughter-in-law was partly defined by the saying, "The womb is borrowed." If a marriage was childless the "bride" might be returned, or an heir might be adopted, or in a well-to-do family a concubine might be set up. Both the eldest son and his wife, as well as other unmarried sons and daughters, lived with the parents. The ideal family was three generations under a single roof.

Change in an institution as basic as the family proceeds very slowly. Even after World War II the pattern described above was still recognizable in most areas of rural Japan. Yet in urban Japan changes were already under way during the late nineteenth century. The expanding population that accompanied Japan's early industrialization produced a great number of second and third sons who moved to cities and formed nuclear families, centered on the husband-wife relationship rather than the line of a "house." As the economy developed, more time was spent away from the family, and for increasing numbers of wage earners the economic significance of the family as the unit of production began to disappear. The women's rights movement, the doctrine of political rights, romantic literary currents, Protestant Christianity, socialism, and other influences also contributed to the shift from lineage to the conjugal tie. All stressed the ideal of equality between the sexes. The transition to the nuclear family was not complete. Even in cities most marriages were still arranged by parents and go-betweens, although the future partners were consulted and exercised veto powers. The result was the Japanese-type conjugal family: different from the West, but also different from the traditional family system.

Rural Society.   Japanese rural society by the turn of the century was in no sense a simple peasant society. Primary education was on the point of becoming universal. Children of the well-to-do often went on to intermediate and higher education. Newspapers were read. Many Japanese had traveled as soldiers in the army. Most had relatives in the proliferating cities. New agricultural methods had been accepted. As railway lines were built, agricultural markets became nationwide. Government influence was pervasive, and rural hearts thrilled to Japanese military victories. A degree of "openness" had developed that made the village qualitatively different from the Tokugawa village. Yet it was not a modern society. In many important ways the "cake of custom" remained unbroken. Religiously, socially, politically, the practice of community solidarity that derived from the "traditional society" of Tokugawa Japan remained in force.

The unit of the local "organic" society was the hamlet—a grouping of households, from about ten to seventy in number, such as dot the Japanese countryside today. The social cohesion within such groupings had several sources. One was the ethic of harmony, the etiquette found in most face-to-face groups in Japan. Another was the rituals of hamlet shrines or temples which stressed community solidarity. Irrigation in most areas required community decisions regarding the allocation of limited water resources. And from the Tokugawa era most hamlets possessed communal pastures or wooded hills; decisions concerning these were made by a hamlet council to which each household sent one representative. This council also handled collections, aid to families in time of crises, and even plans for community recreation.

Within the hamlet one principle of organization was kinship. A lineage or related families might act as a block within the hamlet council. Another

Three generations on the farm.

more important factor was the pattern of land ownership. At the time of the Meiji Restoration about 25 to 30 per cent of the land was worked by tenants. The proportion slowly rose to 45 per cent in 1908 and was maintained at this level until after World War II (46 per cent in 1941). Most Japanese landlords were small landowners, with a few more acres than they could work themselves. Even those with larger holdings almost invariably lived on their land. And there were infinite gradations in the size and patterns of holdings. Only 20 per cent of farm families were pure tenants; 35 per cent were part owners, part tenants; and 45 per cent owned all the land they worked.

In areas where landlordism was extensive community solidarity was hierarchical. (In a fishing village, boat ownership was the equivalent of land ownership in an agricultural village.) There were always more people willing to work the land than land available to be worked. This gave the landlord the upper hand. Tenants were protected by custom, but written contracts were rare. The power of the landlords was bulwarked by ideologies such as "agrarianism," a Confucian-tinged concept stressing the virtues of obedience, loyalty, harmony, and frugality. Landlordism gave rise to serious inequities within rural society. Taxes that took about 35 per cent of the value of the crop during the early Meiji period dropped by 1902 to about 20 per cent as a result of tax cuts and creeping inflation. But rents collected from tenants remained at almost Tokugawa levels, about 50 per cent of the crop. Cities grew and prospered, but the farmers, who even in the late

1930's constituted 44 per cent of the total population, received a shrinking proportion of the national wealth. The prosperity of urban life made the hardship of the countryside, where expectations also rose with education, less tolerable than before.

After World War I tenant unions (called farmers unions) began to form, first in perfectures about Tōkyō and then in the northeast and other areas. These paralleled the rising labor unions in the cities, and for the most part were founded by city intellectuals. A major role was played during the early years by Christian socialists, but by the mid-twenties Marxists were dominant. A national organization of these unions was formed in 1922. It is possible to exaggerate the importance of these unions. Even in the peak year of 1927 they had only 365,000 members, while almost 4 million families were wholly or partially tenants. After the Manchurian Incident of 1931 the tenant movement was suppressed. Yet it is symptomatic of the new openness of rural society that ideas so at odds with tradition could have entered and been accepted at all.

Political power in rural Japan was vested in two interlocking, national hierarchies: the bureaucracy and the organizations of the party politicians. The latter began with Diet members and reached down through prefectural assemblymen to local "men of influence." Such influential local figures, often landlords or small businessmen, were brokers who could deliver blocks of votes in exchange for favors, public or personal.

Local bureaucracy began in the Home Ministry and extended downward through prefectures to cities, towns, and villages. Appointments were made from above, and the chain of authority was marked by a high degree of submissiveness and by a responsibility toward higher authority. An adjunct of the officialdom was the police, also under the Home Ministry. The political role of the Home Ministry changed with time. It was early used by the government against the parties. Then, as party men gained power in the government and as the bureaucracy was headed by party appointees, it was used by the party in power for the advancement of its candidates. At all times, but especially during the 1930's, the Home Ministry was the watchdog on guard against "dangerous thought."

The village, which usually consisted of a number of scattered hamlets, was the lowest administrative level in the bureaucratic hierarchy. Here modern bureaucracy with its records, directives, and impersonality met the hamlet society in which personal ties, the family, and collective solidarity were paramount. Village organization itself was a compromise between the two. The rules by which it operated and most of its responsibilities were imposed from above. Yet the headmen or mayors were elected; those chosen were usually men of influence in their communities, men of good family with a better than average education, men with experience in farming and farm finance. Under the mayor was an elected village council. This decided on matters of local importance, and its expression of local sentiment was expected to guide the mayor in the execution of government directives.

Urban Society.   The traditional city in Japan was freer than the country-side. Restrictive organizations did exist, such as ward associations, shrine groups, guilds, and fire-fighting groups; and in crowded areas where houses adjoined, privacy was slight and immediate neighbors were close and familiar. But personal ties could not be formed among all residents in a city district. Movement in and out of communities was frequent. And in the absence of the cooperation demanded by agriculture and communal property, the sense of community solidarity was weak.

The modern city in Japan grew out of the traditional city, following Japan's economic growth. In 1895 only 12 per cent of the 42 million Japanese lived in cities or towns of more than 10,000 persons. By the mid-1930's over 45 per cent of the 69 million Japanese lived in such urban areas, and over a quarter of the population lived in cities of more than 100,000 persons. By 1940 Tōkyō was rivaling London and New York with a population of 6,779,000, while Osaka, Kyōto, Nagoya, and the new port cities of Yokohama and Kōbe together accounted for an equal number.

Cities were the centers of Japan's modern cultural transformation. During the 1870's and 1880's material signs of the new times appeared first in Tōkyō: horse-drawn streetcars, gas lamps, meatshops selling beef, Western-style buildings, barbershops offering a nonsamurai cut, Western dress, and the new schools and colleges. Change was uneven. As late as 1901 an ordinance was issued in Tōkyō against going barefoot. Yet by this time primary school education was almost universal, and those moving in from the rural areas as well as those growing up in the cities were for the most part literate. When one considers that Japan's school-age population in-creased from 4.2 million in 1873, to 7.2 million in 1893, to 11.3 million in 1935, the magnitude of this accomplishment becomes apparent. The cities also became the centers for higher education that spread the new culture of modern Japan. Enrollments in universities and technical colleges increased from 22,910 students in 1900 to 223,477 in 1940.

By the end of World War I the changes in city life had become even more conspicuous. Standards of living had risen; workers drank beer and soft drinks; weekly magazines, movie houses, bars, restaurants, and other manifestations of popular culture had appeared. The *narikin,* the *nouveau riche* who had risen during the war, were much in evidence. This was the age of the *mobo* and *moga* (*modan boi* [modern boy] and *modan garu* [modern girl]) who strolled on the Ginza of Tōkyō or the main thorough-fares of Ōsaka, boys who wore Harold Lloyd glasses and girls who drank, smoked, and read literature. These were the years of the permanent wave,

PERCENTAGE OF SCHOOL AGE CHILDREN ATTENDING PRIMARY SCHOOLS

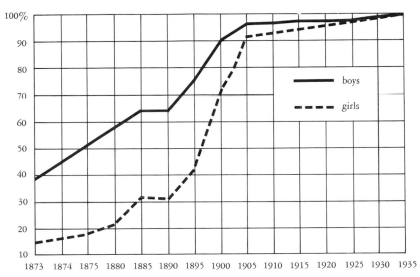

the bathing suit, the bare-legged chorus line, the dance hall and cabaret. It was a time when students not concerned with the leftist political movement became engrossed in the "three S's"—sports, screen, and sex. During the early 1930's Japan Victor and other gramophone companies suddenly expanded, selling hundreds of thousands of sad songs suggesting the transiency of life, the indistinguishability of tears and *sake,* the pleasures of jazz, liquor, and dancing, the passing of time, and the languid beauty of willows along the Ginza. Sales of records jumped from 10,483,000 in 1929 to 16,895,000 in 1931.

Although this popular culture was tame by European standards it seemed outrageous to many in Japan. Some essayists called the period culminating in 1931 and 1932 the era of *"ero, guro,* and *nansensu"* (the erotic, the grotesque, and the nonsensical). That Japan's urban culture had reached this point made the gulf between city and village seem almost unbridgeable. In 1931 and 1932 Japan was at the pit of its depression, and rural conditions were particularly bad. As a result, the cities and their mode of life were castigated by rightist spokesmen as the antipode of what was truly Japanese.

Another effect of social change in Japan was to produce wide generation gaps. In the 1930's there were many families in which three generations lived together: grandparents in their eighties, parents in their fifties, and children in their twenties. The grandparents had been born in Tokugawa Japan. The second generation had come of age just after the turn of the century when Japan's modern culture was beginning to appear. Many had come to the cities from rural areas bringing with them the social reflexes of the countryside. The third generation became adults amid the democracy, jazz, depression, and crises of the late 1920's and early 1930's. Even when three such generations were bound by close personal ties, they were in many ways three different kinds of people, far more so than in Europe or the United States where the tempo of change had been slower.

Industrial Labor.   The shift from an agricultural to an industrial economy was accompanied by a number of social ills, from which urban labor suffered more than any other group except tenants. The government was controlled from the start by men who thought in terms of national strength rather than human welfare. Even in the political parties the interests of property owners were dominant. As a result, Japan was slow to adopt social legislation to protect urban workers. Vast slums grew up in the cities, and until 1926 there were few limits on the conditions or hours of factory work. Children sometimes worked fourteen hours or more a day, and large numbers of overworked laborers suffered from tuberculosis.

Labor was abundant and cheap. In textile factories many girls worked only a few years and then returned to their rural homes. Other workers returned to the farm in time of depression. Farm families easily provided the needed industrial recruits to match industrial growth. Because of these ties the modernization of labor was slow: even in the 1930's urban labor still stood with one foot planted in the stagnant economy of the paddy field. Advances in technology also meant that the demand for labor rose less rapidly than industrial growth. Still the picture was not all black. Though unskilled labor had little bargaining power, the real wages of industrial workers increased by more than half between 1914 and 1929.

Under such conditions the labor movement remained small. By 1897 there were 400,000 workers in factories employing more than five; and by 1907, 600,000. Under the influence of the Christian and early socialist movements a few unions were formed. They soon came under police pressure, tended toward anarcho-syndicalism, and were suppressed after 1911. A second phase began during World War I under moderate Christian leadership. By the end of the war there were 1,700,000 factory workers and by 1920, 86 unions. The 1918–1920 period in particular was marked by spiraling inflation, rice riots, and labor disputes. From 1920 unionism turned toward Marxist socialism. To combat this movement the government legalized moderate unions and also passed some industrial legislation. At the same time it stepped up its pressure against the revolutionary left. The result was a plethora of small unions on the extreme left associated with the more radical of the political parties, and one or two large federations, headed by moderate socialists and containing the majority of organized labor. In the peak year of 1936, 973 unions had 420,589 members—a small

RICE RIOTS IN NAGOYA IN 1918. *The spiraling price of rice led to large-scale riots against rice merchants in many cities. Police and then army troops were called in to suppress them.*

percentage of the total industrial labor force of 6,090,116. The following year, under various pressures, the major federation switched from socialism to national socialism.

Currents of Thought

Intellectuals in Japan today are the heirs not of the early Meiji thinkers but of the generation that came to maturity just after the turn of the century. Where the Meiji thinkers were morally, socially, and even politically akin to the Restoration leaders, intellectuals after the turn of the century became increasingly alienated both from society and from the late Meiji political order.

To Western eyes, the advanced intellectuals of the early decades of the twentieth century seem almost to have bridged the cultural chasm and to be contemporary with their Western peers. Romanticism gave way to realism and then to naturalism; socialism and anarchism were issues of the day. The 1909 diary of the poet Ishikawa Takuboku reveals a life that is strikingly modern: detached introspection, reading Turgenev in bed, commuting to work on the streetcar, listening to the talk of the Kyōto University tennis team from the room next door. Even his poetic images are drawn from the modern world: "If I could...throw away this garment of obligation my body would become as light as hydrogen." Partly because he was so modern, his feeling of isolation and estrangement in the Japan of his day was profound:

Do not be loved by others, do not accept their charity, do not promise anything. Do nothing which entails asking forgiveness. Never talk to anyone about yourself. Always wear a mask. Always be ready for a fight—be able to hit the next man on the head at any time. Don't forget that when you make friends with someone you are sooner or later certain to break with him.*

The social and cultural reasons for the appearance of this sense of alienation are several. One reason was that there were more graduates than jobs, especially in the government. Another reason was that the new Western-oriented generation reacted against the neo-traditionalism of the government. But an even more basic source of alienation was the problem of Japan's cultural identity. What did it mean to be Japanese and to have abruptly borrowed so much of the culture of the modern West? Intellectuals after the turn of the century faced this problem on a much deeper level than had the previous generation. Natsume Sōseki (1867–1916), a professor at Tōkyō Imperial University (hereafter Tōkyō University) and then Japan's greatest modern novelist, wrote that Japan had only superficially mastered the teachings of the West; what would be the consequences, he asked, if Japan could complete its enlightenment in fifty years:

If, then, by our physical and mental exertions, and by ignoring the difficulties and suffering involved in our precipitous advance, we end by passing through, in merely one-half the time it took the more prosperous Westerners to reach their stage of specialization, to our stage of internally developed enlightenment, the consequences will be serious indeed. At the same time we will be able to boast of this fantastic acquisition of knowledge, the inevitable result will be nervous collapse from which we will not be able to recover.†

Before examining some of the positions taken by major Japanese thinkers, we must first ask what the Japanese tradition was at this time. For an understanding of Japan's modern history, the most important locus of tradition was the several interpretations of state philosophy that together constituted orthodoxy in Japan between 1890 and 1945.

The Orthodox Philosophies of the Japanese State.   The creation of a strong state structure had been the aim of Japan's leaders since the Meiji Restoration. Other world powers had constitutions, and the political "outs" demanded a constitution, so the Meiji Constitution was written. Though the constitution itself was based on a German model, it included certain

*Translated by Donald Keene. From *Modern Japanese Literature:* An Anthology Compiled and Edited by Donald Keene; Copyright © 1956 by Grove Press, published by Grove Press, Inc. (British publisher, Thames & Hudson).

†Kōsaka Masaaki (ed.), *Japanese Thought in the Meiji Era* (Tōkyō: Pan Pacific Press, 1958), pp. 447–448.

elements from Japanese tradition. Perhaps the key concept was the *kokutai,* the unique Japanese "national polity." This centered on the imperial house, described in the Meiji Constitution as "a single lineage for ages eternal." At the end of the lineage was the emperor, "sacred and inviolable." Also a part of the *kokutai* were the Japanese people who possessed virtues lacking in the peoples of other nations—loyalty that bound the people to the emperor, and filial piety that undergirded the family units of which the nation was composed. Integrated by such moral principles, Japanese society was viewed as a harmonious whole. During World War II a Tōkyō University economist lecturing on "Japanese capitalism" was reproved by a member of his audience who said that Japan could not be called capitalist since, harmonious and tranquil, it had never experienced the class conflict present in other industrial societies.

The essential problem for constitutional interpretation up until 1945— and thus for validation of this or that program of political action as well —was how to reconcile the real legal rights and privileges conferred by the constitution with the absolute religious authority of the emperor. Depending on whether the stress was put on Japan's Shintō tradition or on German law, and depending on which school of German law was used, the constitutional scholar would arrive at a more authoritarian position or at a position more supportive of parliamentary government.

One constitutional interpretation, which offered an explanation of Japan's imperial lineage and moral qualities, was propounded by Itō Hirobumi. Following German organic theories of the state, he saw these qualities as products of the historical evolution of the Japanese *volk.* The imperial institution had developed within the body politic as the brain had evolved within the physical body. Itō was perfectly aware that he and his colleagues made the actual decisions. His attribution of absolute authority to the emperor was in part the conscious act of a social engineer. "In Europe," he reported to the Privy Council in 1888, "religion is a common principle that penetrates and unites the hearts of the people." But does there exist in Japan a comparable basis for the national unity that a parliamentary system requires?

In our country religion is weak. There is not one that could serve as a principle of state. Buddhism today has fallen into decline. Shintō is based in the precepts of our forefathers and transmits them, yet as a religion it has little power to move men's hearts. In our country, as a common principle, there is only the Imperial House.

The most rational elements in Itō's view of the state were further developed by Minobe Tatsukichi, a professor at Tōkyō University between 1900 and 1932. Minobe accepted the core elements of *kokutai* theory. But Minobe superimposed upon this a newer German theory that described the

*Minobe Tatsukichi, professor
of law at Tōkyō Imperial
University, who saw
the emperor as an "organ"
of the government.*

state as a legal person possessing both sovereignty and the authority to rule. The emperor was the highest organ of this person with the ultimate right to carry out the executive functions of the state. The differences between this view and Itō's were slight. Yet the consequences were important. In Minobe's eyes the emperor was clearly less than the state and subordinate to its laws. This reduced the absolute character of the emperor's authority, and balanced against it the authority of other organs of the state. This interpretation weakened the sanction for autocratic rule by the bureaucracy (in the name of the emperor), opening the way for increased Diet power. It is no exaggeration to say that Minobe's theory furnished the theoretical scaffolding for the movement to establish party cabinets during the 1910's and 1920's.

Minobe's interpretation never obtained a monopoly even in academic circles. It was, however, the dominant legal interpretation of the constitution from World War I until 1935 when Minobe came under attack. It not only influenced scholars and intellectuals, but also became the prescribed subject matter in constitutional law for the higher civil service examinations, the door to the Japanese bureaucracy. The considerable rationality of the functioning of the government during those two decades was not unrelated to the rationality of this theory. Unfortunately for Japan, the bureaucrats were unwilling to have others taught what they believed themselves. Within the state system of education other less liberal views predominated.

One such view combined elements from Japanese tradition with some of the less rational elements of nineteenth-century German thought. The *kokutai* had been viewed in Confucian terms as an immanent and eternal order, and the imperial house as "coeval with Heaven and Earth." Hozumi Yatsuka, another professor at Tōkyō University (between 1888 and 1912), added the notion that Japan was a "family-state" since all Japanese were descended from a common folk ancestor, identical with the imperial ancestor. All Japan was thus a single racial and spiritual family. From the second decade of the twentieth century, passages such as the following began to appear in school texts on moral education:

Our country takes as its base the family system: the nation is but a single great family, the imperial family is our main house. We, the people, worship the unbroken imperial line with the same feeling of respect and love that a child feels toward his parents. . . . The union of loyalty and filial piety is truly the special character of our national polity.*

This conservative vision of society did not change thereafter; but revisions of textbooks during World War I did introduce complementary materials of a more liberal and international outlook.

A further development in the religious view of the *kokutai* was the union of history and Shintō myth. This amalgam also entered textbooks toward the end of the first decade of this century; one Japanese historian has called it "Japan's myth of the twentieth century." Once history is linked to myth, the emperor is sacred not simply as the embodiment of a moral order, but also as a lineal descendant of the Sun Goddess. To this theory Uesugi Shinkichi, still another Tōkyō University professor (between 1903 and 1929), appended a theory of absolute monarchy in which the emperor was identified with the body of the state. This theory opposed Minobe's during the second, third, and fourth decades of the twentieth century. Its adherents in academic circles and at the higher levels of the bureaucracy were generally less successful than their opponents, but they came into their own during the late 1930's as the ideologists of a military Japan.

In short, although the range of orthodox belief was narrow at the turn of the century, by 1914 there had developed bitterly antagonistic positions within the orthodoxy: the liberal, constitutional monarchism of Minobe versus the absolute, Shintō-tinged monarchism of Uesugi. In spite of the support the latter received from patriotic societies, military groups, rural groups, and others, it lost ground during the early 1920's to more liberal, international opinions. Yet two points should be noted. The generation that came to maturity in the 1930's had begun its education in the very years

*Ishida Takeshi, *Meiji seiji shisōshi kenkyū*, pp. 7–8.

when this "Shintō" view of Japanese tradition entered the school texts, and in the conservative nationalism of the 1930's and 1940's there can be found little that had not already developed thirty years earlier.

It is also worth noting what these strains of orthodox thought had in common. For one thing, like their Meiji predecessors, they rejected the earlier Confucian view of a changeless society. Most of the social content was stripped from the Tokugawa *kokutai,* leaving only a few fixed points —the emperor, loyalty, filial piety, and harmony. As a result, orthodox ideology was not an obstacle to many kinds of social change. Second, in keeping with earlier thought, they showed no clear distinction between nature and society. In the organic view of the state, social evolution was seen as a natural process. In the Shintō view, this world of men merges with an irrational god-world in which the transitions from myth to history, from half-human deities to half-divine humans, are imperceptible. It was this sense of a spiritual continuum between the human and the divine that permitted the attribution of divinity to the emperor until 1945. Third, in orthodox ideology there was only a weak distinction between society and self. Ethics taught self-realization through the fulfillment of one's duties to society, not through the development of a sense of independence or personal integrity. There were no grounds on which the individual could withhold loyalty to the social order: the claims of family, school, work-group, or nation always had a higher priority than those of their component members.

Perhaps because of this orthodoxy modern Japanese thinkers have shown a particularly deep concern with the problem of self. This has at times taken the form of a search for philosophic principles that will enable the individual to stand up against society. Some answers have been found in Western culture, others by transforming elements of Japanese tradition. Yet, at a time when the ultimate value of the individual was being increasingly questioned in the West itself, the search was difficult. Against the background of Japanese orthodox thought it was far easier to stress equality within the social group than independence from it.

Literature.   During the 1880's and early 1890's the novel was romantic and liberal. It paralleled the idealism of the political party movement. But with the involvement of the parties in the exchanges of power politics, the rise of alienation among intellectuals, and the influence of new currents of literary thought, Japanese writers turned away from public concerns to concentrate on the private lives of individuals. The literature they wrote was apolitical; it ignored the emperor, the army, politics, and business. It was consciously antitraditional—preoccupied with the individual and opposed to the old family system. Yet in spite of this iconoclasm, few works of literature portrayed alternatives to the old society.

The turn-of-the-century naturalist writers, for example, identified the true self with the forces of nature. Man learns what he is by liberating his natural desires, especially sex, from the constraints of an artificial society. Yet "natural man" was not so much dynamic as submissive to the internal and external demands of time, age, death, sickness, hunger, and sex. He was not a man of determined will, engaging in purposive action. Rather, great stress was put on the moods evoked by changing circumstance and on a sensitive description of the feelings of those caught up by these natural forces. The delicate, introspective, moody character of the works of the naturalists is reflected even in their titles: *Mediocrity, Dust, Mildew, Loneliness, Indulgence.**

The novelist Natsume Sōseki held that the progress of modern Japan was the result of an "external enlightenment" which had led Japan to sever its ties with tradition, to lose its "ancestral energies," and to become engrossed in "mere appearances." A true understanding of Western culture, he stressed, would lead to an independent spirit based on individually-held internal values. This standpoint led Natsume Sōseki to touch on politics. He held that individual morality was higher than state morality, and he ridiculed those who justified every action in terms of patriotism:

When the bean curd man peddles his wares he is not doing it for the state. His basic purpose is to gain the means by which to live . . . though indirectly this may benefit the state. . . . But, wouldn't it be awful if he always had to keep that in mind and eat his meals for the state, wash his face for the state, and go to the toilet for the state?

The affirmative, individualistic side of Sōseki's thought was further developed by others. Abe Jirō (1883–1959) developed a neo-Kantian ethical individualism, stressing universal principles of conscience. Popular among students, Abe emphasized the ethical nature of the self. He criticized the sensual individualism of the naturalists and the family-state ideal of the government, and he supported women's rights. The well-born, romantically individualistic writers of the White Birch School formed another such affirmative group. They extolled genius and idealism. One wrote: "Had I not known Tolstoi I might have become a politician, living from day to day without faith or a reason for existence." Contrasting the artificiality of the old society with the natural altruism of man, they attempted to define a new morality for Japan.

But predominant in modern literature were darker, pessimistic strains. In the later novels of Natsume Sōseki, the complete development of the indi-

*Howard Hibbett, "The Portrait of the Artist in Japanese Fiction," *Far Eastern Quarterly,* Vol. 14 (1955), p. 350.

Natsume Sōseki, novelist and critic, seated in the book-filled room of the Japanese scholar.

vidual led, not to freedom, but to a bleak world of fear, despair, and absolute loneliness. In *The Gate* the hero, having stolen the wife of a friend, spends the rest of his life in secluded misery with her, each suffering from the loneliness and pain of the other. At the end he attempts to find an answer in Zen Buddhism, but without success. The "gate" does not open. In *Passers-by* the protagonist is beset with even greater fears and anxieties until at the end only religion, madness, or death remains. But for Sōseki, neither religion nor madness was a live option. In *Kokoro (Mind)* the end is suicide, in *Grass by the Road* it is resignation to an answerless fate. Natsume Sōseki differs from the naturalists primarily in that suffering, in his view of life, affirms the ethical character of man—even though man's lot is hopeless.

Throughout Sōseki's writings runs the problem of what values to live by. The character Ichirō in the novel *Passers-by* reflects the crisis of the individual in a modernizing society:

He suffers because nothing he does appears to him as either an end or a means. He is perpetually uneasy and cannot relax. He cannot sleep so he gets out of bed. But when he is awake, he cannot stay still, so he begins to walk. As he walks, he finds that he has to begin running. Once he has begun running he cannot stop. To have to keep on running is bad enough, but he feels compelled to increase his speed with every step he takes. When he imagines what the end of all this will be, he is so frightened that he breaks out in a cold sweat. And the fear becomes unbearable.

Ichirō's friend, trying to assuage his anxiety, replies:

"This uneasiness of yours is no more than the uneasiness that all men experience. All you have to do is to realize that there is no need for you alone to worry so much about it. What I mean to say is that it is our fate to wander blindly through life."

Not only were my words vague in meaning but they lacked sincerity. Your brother (Ichirō) gave me one shrewd, contemptuous glance; that was all my remarks deserved. He then said:

"You know, our uneasiness comes from this thing called scientific progress. Science does not know where to stop and does not permit us to stop either. From walking to rickshaws, from rickshaws to horsedrawn cabs, from cabs to trains, from trains to automobiles, from automobiles . . . to airplanes—when will we ever be allowed to stop and rest? Where will it finally take us? It is really frightening."

"Yes, it is frightening," I said.

Your brother smiled.

"You say so, but you don't really mean it. You aren't really frightened. This fear that you say you feel, it is only of the theoretical kind. My fear is different from yours. I feel it in my heart. It is an alive, pulsating kind of fear."*

Ichirō's friend typifies the Japanese majority, who are pleased with trains, airplanes, science, their rising standard of living, and the rest of their modern life. He is representative of the student who proceeds successfully from higher school to university law school to a job in government or industry. Ichirō, however, speaks for the alienated intellectual unable to integrate, or find meaning in, the elements of his life.

Another writer hailed as the genius of his age during the 1920's was Akutagawa Ryūnosuke (the author of the short story *Rashōmon*). A disciple of Natsume Sōseki, Akutagawa continued his master's concern with the problem of what Western culture meant in Japan. Yet where Natsume Sōseki felt that "internal modernization" would come in time, Akutagawa was doubtful. In *The Faint Smiles of the Gods* Akutagawa writes from the point of view of a Portuguese priest in Japan during the late sixteenth century, struggling to sustain his faith in the power of God while beset by strange animistic forces that hinder his mission. The priest is spoken to by an old man, a god of Japan in human form:

Perhaps even God will become a native of this country. China and India changed. The West must also change. We exist in the midst of trees, in the flow of shallow water, in the wind that passes through the roses, in the evening

*From Edwin McClellan, "An Introduction to Sōseki," *Harvard Journal of Asiatic Studies,* Vol. 22 (December 1959), pp. 205–206.

light lingering on the wall of a temple. Everywhere and at all times. Watch out for us!

As a part of East Asian culture, Japan had far more to its tradition than animism. Yet after the explicit rejection of Buddhism and Confucianism during the early Meiji period, it is not strange that Akutagawa should use this symbol to contrast with the universal values of the West. Elsewhere Akutagawa likened Japan to an Olympics run by the insane. Projecting his own uncertainties onto Japan, he suggested that even Dante's hell would be better: at least it had law, fixed rules. Akutagawa's suicide in 1927 was hailed by Japanese leftist critics as the end of bourgeois literature, symbolic of the impasse reached by "middle-class culture."

It would be an exaggeration to say that religion, or its lack, was central as a literary concern in twentieth-century Japan. The dominant genre was the autobiographical novel—confessional or contemplative—in which the author appears as his own, often dissolute, hero. With this was combined a *haiku*-like description of the texture of sensual experience, often of great beauty. Yet one can say that literature reflected cultural anxieties that were widespread among intellectuals. These were not unrelated to the fact that Japan had jettisoned most of its own philosophic tradition without finding anything to replace it more substantial than emperor-centered nationalism.

Philosophy. The philosophical history of Japan in modern times is incredibly complex. Virtually every school of thought in Europe or America, not to mention schools of Buddhist philosophy and the like, has been represented in one form or another. Yet the strongest current of Western philosophical thought in Japan, beginning in the late nineteenth century and gaining ground in the twentieth, was German. A song sung by higher school students in the late Meiji period began:

> *Dekanshō (Descartes, Kant, and Schopenhauer)*
> *Dekanshō*
> *Half the year we live with them,*
> *The other half we sleep.*

By the 1920's the most popular Western philosophy was German idealism, the most popular philosopher, Hegel. That this type of thought should have found acceptance is related to the earlier interest in German state philosophy. In part, too, there was an affinity between intellectual life in twentieth-century Japan and the anguish of German metaphysics. As student types in Japan, the "literary youth" and the Werther-like "philosophic youth" replaced the "political youth" of the late nineteenth century. Within this broad current of thought, the most original synthesis with Japanese tradition was that of Nishida Kitarō.

Nishida was born in 1870, only three years after Natsume Sōseki. His graduation from the philosophy department of Tōkyō University in 1894 was followed by a period of hardship. He taught in high schools and junior colleges, receiving little recognition. He began the practice of Zen Buddhism, but his diary tells of years of frustration. Although he meditated, he found it difficult to concentrate, his body ached, he daydreamed about traveling abroad or becoming famous, and his mind remained clouded. Not until 1905 does the entry appear: "Zen is music, Zen is art, Zen is action; beyond this there is nothing that need be sought to give peace of mind." From this time Nishida's task was "to provide a philosophic foundation" for "the vision of the shapeless shape, the voice of the voiceless reality" which was the "basis of oriental culture."*

To accomplish this task Nishida drew on a wide range of Western philosophers such as Hegel, James, and Bergson, all of whom were concerned with the philosophic expression of religious experience. Nishida's first concern was to find universal categories for the "moment of true existence" he had found in Zen. In his first work, *A Study of the Good*, published in 1911 after he had become an assistant professor at Kyōto University, he termed this "pure experience," experience before the differentiation of knower and known. Nishida's second concern was to relate this insight to the universe of existence. Nishida's third concern was to apply the Buddhist "logic of nothingness" to define the position of Japanese culture in relation to world culture.

The meaning of Nishida's philosophy for prewar Japan was ambiguous. On the one hand, it appears to be a philosophy with no social implications, since once the self is unified in "pure experience," all conflicts are resolved and further action is unnecessary. Nishida stressed the importance of harmony, community, and other values found in orthodox thought, and some of his followers became scholarly propagandists for the Greater East Asia Co-Prosperity Sphere during World War II. They argued that the contradictions inherent in modern culture could be transcended only by a return to the unique spirituality of Japan. On the other hand, Nishida himself spoke up in 1938 and 1939 to criticize those who attacked science and free inquiry in the name of patriotism. He stressed that Japanese culture, though unique, was meaningful only as a part of a universal, world culture composed of unique particulars. Likewise, his emphasis on the Japanese state was in a context of a world society of nations. Cast in the concepts of Western philosophy, his experience of religious individuality took on implications lacking in traditional Zen.

Christianity in Modern Japan. During the Meiji era Christianity entered Japan as a part of Western culture, and gradually spread in both the cities

*Ueyama Shumpei, "Nishida Kitarō," in *Nihon no shisōka II*.

and the countryside. Then during the 1890's, as the new nationalism took hold, Christianity declined in rural areas and became concentrated among the urban middle class and among intellectuals. The percentage of Christians remained small and even in the early 1970's constituted only one-half of 1 per cent of the population.

Christianity was clearly incompatible with the dominant intellectual tendencies during Japan's century of modernization. For one thing, Christianity was seen as unscientific, as unsuited to the temper of a secular age. For another, Christianity did not fit in well with the values of orthodox Japanese thought. When an early samurai convert, Ebina Danjō, "took God as his feudal lord," he described the change within himself from world-immanent loyalties to a transcendental loyalty as "Copernican." The transcendental negation of the family-state ideal is reflected in the words of Niishima Jō, the founder of Dōshisha University: "God, not my parents, created me." Another Christian, Uchimura Kanzō, opposed Japan's actions in the 1905 war against Russia on the grounds of Christian pacifism, while also opposing the missionary churches of his day.

Thus a corollary of the observation that Christianity was incompatible with orthodox thought is that, when it was accepted, it could effect at times a radical change. Christians initiated many social welfare projects, an area in which the Meiji government had little interest. They were concerned with women's higher education, opened orphanages, aided outcast communities, worked with the poor in the slums, helped rehabilitate prostitutes, and were active in women's rights movements. They were politically active in the early phase of the labor and socialist movements, and many worked for democracy in government.

Yoshino Sakuzō (1878–1933), for example, became a Christian while in higher school. While at Tōkyō University he helped edit a Christian journal and associated with Christian socialists. In 1916, when a professor of law at Tōkyō University, he wrote "The Essence of Constitutional Government," a manifesto for parliamentary reform. Working within the framework of Minobe's constitutional interpretation, he advocated universal suffrage, reform of the House of Peers, the subordination of the army to the cabinet, and so on. His second concern was social democracy; he favored a gradual evolution toward socialism by parliamentary means.

One Japanese historian has written that while "Europeans and Americans find it difficult to understand" the degree to which Marxism has entered the consciousness of the Japanese intellectual, "Japanese intellectuals have not understood the extent of the attraction held by the word 'liberal' in the historical life of Europe and America."* Why did Yoshino maintain his liberal position? Why did he not only support social equality,

*Tsurumi Shunsuke, in *Gendai Nihon no shisō*, p. 55.

Yoshino Sakuzō, political liberal and professor at Tōkyō Imperial University.

but also stress the value of the individual? The answer seems to be that these commitments derived from his Christian belief and his German idealistic philosophy. German philosophy provided him with an abstract humanistic ideal. Christianity made this concrete and gave it life. "To realize democracy thoroughly, humanism must function as a living concept," he wrote. Yoshino found this in the Christian belief that "sees all men as the children of God, and recognizes in all men a spark of divinity." Or more briefly: "Christian belief, as it asserts itself in every aspect of society is democracy."*

Marxism in Japan.   Socialism as a theory entered Japan in the last decade of the nineteenth century. In 1901 a Social Democratic party was formed —mainly by Christian socialists—and banned the same day. In the next ten years Marxist socialism and anarcho-syndicalism also became known. The entire movement, however, was suppressed after 1911 when a plot to assassinate the emperor was discovered.

A second wave of socialist thought arose in the years after World War I: the age of liberalism and internationalism. The economy had leaped ahead during the war, the number of workers and students increased, and the Rice Riots of 1918 turned the thoughts of many toward the new social problems within Japan. Also influential were the Russian Revolution and new cur-

*Takeda Kiyoko, "Yoshino Sakuzō," in *Nihon no shisōka II.*

rents of European socialism. By the mid-twenties liberalism, syndicalism, and anarchism had largely been replaced by Marxism.

The government reaction to socialism was to suppress the revolutionary left while, tacitly at least, recognizing the parliamentary left. This policy in large measure shaped the course of the movement. The largest political parties and their associated unions were moderate. They were usually Marxist in doctrines, even if led by Christian socialists, but they accepted parliamentary means. This was the force that by 1937 had won 10 per cent of the vote at the polls. Inevitably the moderate socialists were also most vulnerable to the appeal of nationalism.

On the revolutionary left were a great number of student "social science study groups," splinter parties, and radical unions. These were usually small in size, and were reorganized so frequently that it is almost impossible to treat them by name. Police pressure on the Japanese Communist Party, founded in 1922, was so great that there were often more leading Communists in jail than out. In the revolutionary left a key role was played by the universities. After each purge a new generation of graduates would revitalize the leftist parties. Even after 1933 when the parties and unions of the extreme left had been almost completely suppressed, university study groups continued to read and produce Marxist writings. The re-emergence of Marxism after World War II was largely due to this prewar generation of academicians.

A clear sign of the intellectual vitality of Marxism was its strength in literature. From 1927 till 1932 the proletarian school dominated Japanese letters until writers of other persuasions protested at the "tyranny of the left." The proletarian school believed that the purpose of literature was social enlightenment. It portrayed the aimless, frivolous character of bourgeois existence. It described the heroism of the worker. It attacked the effeteness of Japanese tradition, as in the following poem:

> *Don't sing*
> *Don't sing of scarlet blossoms or the wings of dragonflies*
> *Don't sing of murmuring breezes or the scent of a woman's hair*
> *All of the weak, delicate things*
> *All the false, lying things*
> *All the languid things, omit.*
> *Reject every elegance*
> *And sing what is wholly true,*
> *Filling the stomach,*
> *Flooding the breast at the moment of desperation,*
> *Songs which rebound when beaten*
> *Songs which scoop up courage from the pit of shame*
> *These songs*
> *Sing in a powerful rhythm with swelling throats!*

These songs
Hammer into the hearts of all who pass you by! *

Why did Marxism spread as it did? What did it mean in Japan? What were its limits? One reason it spread, certainly, was that the twenties were more open and tolerant than any other decade in prewar Japan and at the same time the least impressive decade in terms of economic growth. Some Japanese scholars have suggested that Marxism grew because of its resonance with Japanese tradition: would Japan evolve, they asked, from a premodern (collective) society to a postmodern (socialist) society without ever developing a modern (individualistic) society? And did not Marxism appeal to the moral sense of many Japanese, offering an opportunity to sacrifice self for the "good of the people" as they had been taught to sacrifice "for the good of state"? Others have pointed out that Marxism in Japan was opposed to both tradition and nationalism. It taught that family, state, and the economy were exploitative, and demanded heroic action against them. Some have even compared it to Christianity, saying that the spiritual function of both was to reject the imperial cosmology. Certainly the appeal of Marxism in Japan was different from that in most other Asian countries. In the latter the spread of Marxism depended on Lenin's theory of imperialism and on the idea of industrialization through socialism. But in Japan, itself an imperialist power, it was Marx's analysis of the ills within capitalist society that was central.

Finally, the fact that Japan was a fairly modern state made the objective situation in which revolutionary Marxists found themselves discouragingly different from the situation in other Asian countries. The intellectual vitality of Marxist groups in the universities had little impact on the larger society. Nonstudent organizations had little staying power in the face of strong governmental and business bureaucracies. The centralized police system was highly efficient: it blanketed Japan far more thoroughly than any Western police system. Nor were there any "ungoverned" mountain redoubts in Japan in which revolutionaries could group their forces beyond the reach of government authority.

---

7. Imperial Japan: Democracy and Militarism

The Growth of Parliamentary Influence

The Political Elites.   Government in Japan between 1890 and 1945 was constitutional, but it was not mainly parliamentary. The constitution gave different powers to different bodies. These bodies may be termed the elites of the system.

One pair of elites was the army and navy. They had two kinds of power in the structure of government. First, the chiefs of staff of the services were directly under the emperor and not responsible to the cabinet. This was their "right of autonomous command." At certain critical moments it was hard to define where this right ended and foreign policy began. Second, the services had leverage over cabinets, for, by withdrawing their ministers they could cause a cabinet to collapse and by withholding a minister they could prevent the formation of a new one. On the other hand, the cabinet and Diet could exert pressure on the services through the service ministers and by control of military appropriations.

Another elite was the civil bureaucracy, the "officials of the emperor." Its power derived not from the constitution but from its responsibility in carrying out the executive function. Within the bureaucracy the top men in the central ministries were of particular importance. Graduated in most cases from the Law School of Tōkyō University, they were the cream of the educational cream who had passed the difficult examination for a career in state service. Their ability was great and their social status high. Designed to be a neutral body, they were conservative by inclination, though some sectors of the bureaucracy became politicized as time went on. They influenced government by such means as drafting the legislation presented in the Diet, access to the cabinet ministers, administration of laws, and the holding of high policy-making positions by their more influential members after retirement from the regular bureaucracy.

Another elite consisted of various persons or groups close to the emperor. The emperor had the right to name the prime minister, but someone else always did it for him. At first it was the oligarchs, an entirely extra-legal body. After 1922, the year in which Yamagata died, it was Saionji or a group of ex-prime ministers. The right to name a prime minister was extremely important, since the person named could form a cabinet, call an election, and usually win it. Other influential officials near the emperor were the Inner Minister, Imperial Household Minister, and the members of the Privy Council. The latter had the constitutional authority to ratify treaties; its real power was that it was composed of influential men, ex-officials and ex-ministers.

Still another influential group, if not a constitutional elite, was the zaibatsu combines. These were politically powerful because elections cost money, particularly as the size of the electorate increased. Between 1915 and 1924 campaign expenditures rose from about 5 to 22 million yen. During the same period cases of bribery and election offenses doubled. Campaign contributions meant influence on legislation—when such influence seemed necessary. The question is sometimes asked: did the zaibatsu run the Diet? The answer seems to be that the functions of state and economic enterprises were largely separate. Their goals—state power and growth—were largely compatible. The compatibility of goals made cooperation easy. Not till the social criticism of the 1920's and the depression years of the early 1930's did the question arise of whether the interests of the two were in fact the same.

Another elite was the Diet which had an appointed House of Peers and an elected House of Representatives. The former body of nobility and eminent men was intended as a conservative check on the lower house. It performed this function well and there is little else to say of it. The House of Representatives was powerful because only the Diet could pass permanent laws and any increase in the budget required its approval. The latter prerogative made the lower house more powerful than Itō had intended, because he had not realized that increased budgets would always be needed. From 1890 on the big question in Japanese government was how to control the lower house. No good answer was found, so the parties which dominated the lower house gradually won out in competition with the other elites and moved toward the control of the cabinet, the central stage of government.

The Workings of Government by Compromise.   But the elites did not merely compete. They also cooperated. The constitution gave different but real powers to the various elites. In order for the work of government to be done the elites had to work together. Looking closely, we see that each elite was not self-contained and united. Rather, within each elite there existed rival cliques: coteries competing within the Peers, bureaucratic factions within the ministries, a Chōshū clique versus non-Chōshū officers within the army, a Satsuma clique versus opposing cliques in the navy, parties within the Diet, Mitsui versus Mitsubishi among the zaibatsu, and Itō and Saionji versus Yamagata and Katsura among the oligarchs. Therefore coalitions of cliques that cut across the different elites emerged to rule in Japan.

The ties joining a faction of one elite with a party or faction of another were personal and sometimes antedated the formation of the Diet. For example, Hoshi Tōru, a politician in the party that became the Seiyūkai, was a friend of Mutsu Munemitsu. Mutsu was a protégé of Itō. This led to Itō's leadership of Hoshi's party after 1900. Itō in turn was a friend of Inoue Kaoru who had close ties to the Mitsui house. This led the Mitsui to become the angel of the early Seiyūkai. A comparable inter-elite coalition was also put together—drawing on the aid of the Mitsubishi zaibatsu—about the second major party formed in 1913.

Up until 1905 cooperation among the elites was obtained by oligarchic control at the top. It is only a slight exaggeration to think of the oligarchs as puppeteers at a constitutional Punch and Judy show. Yamagata in particular was powerful. Men loyal to him ran the army, staffed the higher bureaucracy—especially the Home Ministry which in turn controlled local government and the police—and also sat in the House of Peers and Privy Council. Pulling the right strings, Yamagata and the other oligarchs (or *genrō* as they are called in their later years) coordinated the work of the various elites. Even with these resources the Yamagata "machine" proved unable to control the lower house in the period 1890–1900. Consequently Itō in 1900 coopted the Liberal Party and formed the Seiyūkai. Using its connections with power, the Seiyūkai became the majority party. But until 1905 it depended on its oligarchic connection and was largely manipulated from above like the other elites.

The year 1905 was a turning point. In the economy there began a boom that marked the start of sustained economic growth in Japan's modern sector. The victory over Russia expanded Japan's colonial empire and made it the pre-eminent power in East Asia. The war also marked the awakening of a nationalism far stronger than that of the preceding decades, and was a turning point in politics. Itō had proved a failure as a party leader. He could not dominate the party as he wished and could not stand the deals, petty machinations, and abuse that he met in dealing with the party rank and file (he was once pissed on during a party caucus). Saionji had succeeded him but was no more successful. While Saionji served twice as

Unlike the earlier Meiji leaders, Hara was a man of compromise who built his power amid competing elites, factions, and coalitions.

prime minister between 1905 and 1912, he actually conducted himself more as a *genrō* than as a party president after 1905, while Hara Kei became the real party leader.

Hara, born in 1856, was of a different generation from the Meiji leaders. He was also from an area in northeastern Japan that played no role in the Restoration. As an "outsider," his career was accordingly different: at twenty-three he became a newspaper reporter, then a profession close to politics; he entered the Foreign Office at twenty-six and advanced steadily until fifteen years later he became ambassador to Korea. He then went on to become the editor of one of Japan's great daily papers, a bank official, the president of a company, and a member of the Diet. He also helped Itō to found the Seiyūkai in 1900. Patient, intelligent, hard-working, and paternalistic, Hara was the most able politician in the Japan of his day. The national ends for which he worked were enunciated in a later program: "the perfection of national defense, the expansion of education, the encouragement of industry, and the expansion of communications." Hara's goals, perhaps, were not too different from those of Yamagata during his later years. Yet he felt that they should be achieved by a government led by the political parties, not the oligarchy. From 1905 Hara worked sedulously to build the power of the Seiyūkai. The inner history of Japanese government during much of the next sixteen years was the struggle of Hara's machine against that of Yamagata.

One means Hara used to build power was to create a vertical party organization. For a Diet member to win an election required support by politicians in the prefectural assembly and local support by influential men. In some regions there were personal political organizations like the "iron constituency" in Okayama Prefecture which sent a member of the Inukai family to the Diet in every election from 1890. From this region 76 per cent of the votes went to Inukai or to candidates designated by him in the decade after 1890, 47 per cent of the votes after 1932 when the son inherited the "fief" from the father, and 35 per cent, still enough to win a Diet seat, in the years immediately after World War II.

But such constituencies were exceptional. In most areas the local bosses would swing their blocks of votes from one party to another to get patronage from the party in power. A block of votes was an expression of local solidarity: a higher percentage of rural voters turned out for elections than city voters. In rural Japan there was a feeling against wasting votes; a vote counted if it joined other votes to elect a candidate who would get schools, roads, dams, bridges, or tax relief for the area concerned. Hara's tactic was to win these blocks of swing votes by pork barrel politics. He served as Home Minister three times and used the resources of his ministry to favor those districts that supported the Seiyūkai. Communities that aligned themselves with the Seiyūkai got schools and roads, and those that did not were overlooked. Railways, nationalized in 1906, were another area of patronage. The military wanted to change Japan's railways over to the same broad-gauge lines used on the continent. Hara defeated this plan in order that available funds could be spent in laying down new narrow-gauge track into Seiyūkai constituencies.

A second means used by Hara to extend party power was to politicize the bureaucracy. The heights of the bureaucracy were still manned by men appointed by the oligarchs in pre-examination days. The civil service examination system and the regulations governing the bureaucracy had been drawn up by Yamagata to make sure that the next generation of officials would also stay free from party influence. In practice "neutrality" meant loyalty to superiors who were loyal to the oligarchy—who in turn saw themselves as standing above the ruck of partisan interests and concerned only for the good of all Japan. In Hara's eyes the bureaucracy and particularly the influential Home Ministry was the heart of the Yamagata machine.

Hara in time gained the right of some patronage appointments in the bureaucracy. More significant, however, was his success in winning over regular civil service bureaucrats to the party cause. The bureaucracy grew from 29,000 in 1890 to 72,000 in 1908. By 1905 new men from the examination system were starting to replace oligarchal appointees at the top of the system. When Hara became Home Minister in 1906 he established a working relation with some of these new men, appointing them to strategic positions in the police and in the offices controlling public

PRIME MINISTERS 1898–1921

Yamagata	November 1898–October 1900
Itō	October 1900–June 1901
Katsura	June 1901–January 1906
Saionji	January 1906–July 1908
Katsura	July 1908–August 1911
Saionji	August 1911–December 1911
Katsura	December 1912–February 1913
Yamamoto	February 1913–April 1914
Ōkuma	April 1914–October 1916
Terauchi	October 1916–September 1918
Hara	September 1918–November 1921

works, railway construction, and local affairs. These were the men who implemented the pork barrel policy described earlier. Hara also made changes at the prefectural level, firing "unpopular" governors who would not carry out his policies and appointing in their place "effective" men more in tune with his ideas. By the second decade of the twentieth century there were many civil service officials who stood to gain high office under cabinets associated with the Seiyūkai and lose their positions when the Seiyūkai was out of power. That is to say, portions of the bureaucracy had been penetrated by the parties.

A third means of extending party power was to penetrate the other elites. This proved more difficult. As the oligarchy weakened, some younger Peers became more independent of it and some new Peers appointed through party influence became aligned with a party. In the 1920's Hara's party thus succeeded in establishing a working alliance with the largest faction in the Peers. But this was of short duration. At certain times the cabinet also succeeded in bringing pressure to bear on the Privy Council, but it too was in the main successful in resisting party influence. With the military the parties were even less successful. Thus the advance to power of the parties continued to depend heavily on compromises with the other elites.

The Taishō Political Crisis of 1912–1913.   The years between 1905 and 1912 were on the surface like those from 1900 to 1905. Katsura and Saionji alternated as prime ministers as had their mentors Yamagata and Itō in an earlier period.

For both Katsura and Saionji, support in the Diet was provided by the Seiyūkai. It was furnished, of course, for a price. This arrangement broke down in the winter of 1912–1913 in what Japanese historians call the Taishō Political Crisis, named after the reign name chosen for the new emperor who had ascended the throne in the summer of 1912. The Crisis is worth examining in some detail since it exemplifies some of the forces in Japanese government at this time.

Saionji became prime minister for the second time in the summer of 1911. In line with the demands of the Seiyūkai and in response to Japan's needs, he was determined to enforce a policy of retrenchment. But the army and navy pressed for increased appropriations. After months of negotiations the demands of the services were refused. The army minister, therefore, after conferring with Yamagata, sent his resignation to the emperor without previously informing Saionji. With this, Saionji's cabinet fell.

The oligarchs, faced with finding a new man, first asked Saionji to form another cabinet. He refused. Yamagata wanted General Terauchi, but the others refused, feeling that an army man would not be accepted by the parties. The oligarch and financial authority Matsukata was asked, but he too refused, as did another one of Yamagata's favorites. Admiral Yamamoto Gombei of Satsuma also turned down the post, saying in effect that the Chōshū army clique should clean up its own mess. Finally, as a last resort, Katsura was asked to form his third cabinet and he accepted.

Katsura was a Chōshū man and an ex-general. He had risen in the army at a time when it was led by men with great breadth of vision (unlike the narrower, professional officers of the thirties). At the turn of the century he shared Yamagata's view that cabinets should be "transcendent," above party control. But by 1912 he was used to cooperating with the Seiyūkai and was ready to form a party of his own. He saw himself not as a soldier but as a statesman, and he accepted the post of prime minister with the intention of continuing the retrenchment policy of his predecessor. Nor was he simply a pawn of Yamagata. In 1911 he had recommended Saionji as his successor in direct opposition to Yamagata and he had been reported to the old man as having said, "When I come back [from a trip to Europe] I will push into retirement such people as Yamagata."

In the eyes of the public and parties, however, Katsura had arranged for the army to overthrow Saionji's cabinet in order to get the post for himself. He was viewed as a Chōshū general attempting to perpetuate oligarchic rule. The first problem facing Katsura was the navy's demand for battleships. It too threatened to withhold a minister if its demands were not met. Countering this, Katsura had an imperial rescript issued directing the navy to furnish a minister. Newspapers and the political parties interpreted this not as opposition to the services, but as an undemocratic and high-handed action in making use of the emperor's supreme authority.

The opposition parties, some businessmen, some intellectuals, and a few professional men had formed in 1912 a League for the Protection of the Constitution. It called for a "Taishō Restoration": just as the early years of the Meiji emperor had witnessed sweeping reforms toward a modern

Katsura began as a Chōshū general, but the demands of the age forced him to attempt to become a party politician.

Japan, so the reign of the Taishō emperor must open with similar changes toward a democratic Japan. The League staged massive protest rallies against Katsura's use of the imperial rescript. Orators at meetings in the main cities of Japan shouted, "Destroy the Satchō leaders and off with Katsura's head." Newspapers supported the movement and local Seiyūkai politicians joined in. For a time the ex-bureaucratic leadership of the Seiyūkai remained neutral, but, since Katsura was moving to form his own political party, they felt released from their earlier pledge to support his cabinet and joined in the opposition movement. Katsura's party lacked a majority in the Diet. His ministry was so unpopular that he had little hope of winning at the polls. The Diet was often surrounded by jeering crowds. Perceiving that the situation was hopeless, Katsura resigned and died later in the year, a broken man.

A new cabinet was formed by Admiral Yamamoto, who had earlier refused the post. It marked a temporary return to the pattern of pre-Crisis days—of government by a cabinet of moderate ex-bureaucrats with the support of the Seiyūkai in the Diet. Most of the ministers joined the Seiyūkai when they entered the Yamamoto cabinet. Much legislation favorable to the parties was passed by this cabinet. It continued the earlier policy of retrenchment, cutting the budget by more than 13 per cent and reducing the bureaucracy by more than ten thousand persons. It was at this time that some party men were first appointed to influential posts in the bureaucracy. The Yamamoto cabinet also opened the posts of army and navy minister, heretofore limited to active-service generals and admirals subject to the discipline of the services, to retired general-rank and flag-rank officers. None were ever appointed, but the fact that they could be deterred the services from further attempts to overthrow cabinets.

Domestic Politics during World War I.   A by-product of the Crisis was the formation in 1913 of Japan's second major political party, the Dōshikai (which through mergers became the Kenseikai in 1916 and the Minseitō in 1927). After almost thirteen years of Seiyūkai monopolization of power and patronage, the other groups in the Diet were hungry. Thus when Katsura set about to form a second party that could effectively compete for a partnership role in government (like that of the Seiyūkai), many members of the lower house of the Diet flocked to join. The oligarchs were also unhappy with the burgeoning strength of the Seiyūkai and its almost effortless resumption of power during the Yamamoto cabinet. They saw in the Dōshikai a potential counterweight. When a scandal caused the Yamamoto cabinet to collapse in 1914, Ōkuma—who had founded the distant predecessor of the Dōshikai in 1881—was asked to form a new cabinet. Ōkuma naturally relied on the Dōshikai for support in the Diet and appointed the president of the party, Katō Kōmei, to be foreign minister in his cabinet.

Ōkuma dissolved the Diet and called an election in March 1915. This election saw the first of the modern political campaigns in Japan. Ōkuma and his ministers spoke at rallies throughout the country. A speech by Ōkuma on "The Power of Public Opinion in Constitutional Politics" was recorded and played from gramophones on platforms all over Japan. On election morning telegrams were sent in Ōkuma's name to voters in critical districts. At the same time the Dōshikai showed that it too could use effectively those techniques that the Seiyūkai had developed earlier: it mobilized the police and local officials to aid Dōshikai candidates and it promised patronage to districts in which it hoped to gather the swing vote. The Dōshikai won an absolute majority in the Diet. This victory was the only break in Seiyūkai control of the Diet from the time of its formation in 1900 to 1924.

Once the election was won and the Seiyūkai put down, the interests of the oligarchs and the Dōshikai diverged. The oligarchs found it no easier to deal with the Dōshikai than the Seiyūkai. In control of the Diet, both parties acted much the same, pushing for increased party power in the government. Yamagata was angered especially by the actions of Foreign Minister Katō. It earlier had been the custom to circulate secret diplomatic documents to the oligarchs. Katō put an end to this. Instead, when requested by the oligarchs, he sent officials to explain matters. Katō sent the ultimatum to Germany that brought Japan into World War I on the side of the Allies without informing Yamagata beforehand. He was called on the carpet for this and promised to behave in the future. But in 1915 when he imposed the Twenty-One Demands on China, he again failed to consult the oligarchs. Yamagata's reaction was that Katō was worse than Hara. A deep rift developed between the two men, and as long as Yamagata lived he saw to it that Katō was not asked to form a cabinet. These were lean years for Katō's Kenseikai, as the Dōshikai had been renamed in 1916.

In the meantime, Hara had become aware in the election of 1915 that all of the gains of the Seiyūkai could be washed away if the opposition party came to power. He therefore set about to mend his fences, approaching those who had the ear of Yamagata and eventually meeting with Yamagata himself. As a result when the Ōkuma cabinet fell in 1916 and General Terauchi, a protégé of Yamagata, was appointed as the new prime minister, it was Hara to whom he turned for support in the Diet. But Hara kept a distance between himself and the "bureaucratic" prime minister: he gave his support on issues favorable to the party cause and withheld it when he pleased. The Seiyūkai re-established its position as the largest party in the election of 1917. When the cabinet fell in the aftermath of the rice riots of 1918, the process that had begun in 1905 reached its logical conclusion: Hara was appointed prime minister.

Hara's three-year ministry between 1918 and 1921 achieved many of the ends for which he long had been striving. He abolished the subprefectural district offices, thus reducing bureaucratic control over towns and villages and increasing the autonomy of municipal governments which were normally under party influence. He established small electoral districts (one-seat districts like those of the United States) in place of multiseat districts which left room for representation by minority political groups. This gave the advantage in elections to the major parties. He continued his pork barrel policy, building schools and undertaking an 800-million-yen railroad expansion program. He obtained some openings for political appointees in the colonial bureaucracy. He enfranchised the rural small landowners—the Seiyūkai was especially strong in rural Japan—by reducing the tax qualification from ten to three yen. (Members of the more urban-based Kenseikai saw this not as a democratic advance but as "the perpetuation of class despotism" in the Diet.)

What Hara did not do was to change the structure of government. To attempt more than minor modifications would have produced conflicts with the other elites and would have rocked the foundations of the "Hara machine." In Hara's eyes structural changes were not necessary. It was better to manipulate the other elites and attain party goals by compromise. As Hara's biographer puts it, "Prime Minister Hara in 1918 was still Home Minister Hara," both in his goals and his tactics. Another thing that Hara did not do was to advance social legislation; he was economically conservative and opposed to the rising social movement.

Taishō Democracy

Hara's assassination in 1921 by an ultranationalist brought a sudden tragic end to his brilliant career, but the years after his death saw continued steps in the direction of constitutional government. These new developments, though of course reflecting economic, social, and intellectual changes within Japan, were also responsive to new influences from the West where liberal tendencies were in the ascendant during the twenties. This period is rather loosely called the time of "Taishō Democracy" after the reign period that extended from 1912 to 1926.

The Diplomacy of Empire.   Japan's foreign policy from the Taiwan Expedition of 1874 to the annexation of Korea in 1910 had been consistent. Actions were carried out by a government unified under the oligarchs for the sake of commonly held objectives. The objectives were security, autonomy, and big-power status. Security was obtained by industrial and military development. Autonomy was regained in the mid-nineties when the unequal treaties were revised. Big-power credentials came with the victories over China and Russia in 1895 and 1905, which gave Japan an empire. The empire was bulwarked by bilateral agreements with other imperialist powers. The Anglo-Japanese Alliance of 1902, renewed in 1905 and 1911, was a key agreement. Between 1907 and 1916 Japan also entered into four pacts with Tsarist Russia which protected Japan's special position in Korea and Manchuria. The United States, too, acknowledged Japan's empire; Taft and Katsura in 1905 gave mutual assurances regarding the Philippines and Korea, and the Lansing-Ishii Agreement of 1917 recognized that "territorial propinquity" gave Japan special interests in China. Expansion against other Asian peoples was rationalized within Japan by the doctrines of Social Darwinism, by notions of the superiority of Japan's unique national polity, and by the idea of a Japanese national mission to bring progress and modernity to its backward neighbors.

A second brief period in the history of Japanese imperialism was from World War I to 1922. During the first half of this period the European powers were involved in the business of war, leaving a power vacuum in East Asia. Japan took advantage of this. As an ally of Britain, Japan declared war on Germany and took over the German position in Shantung. The following year, 1915, Japan issued the so-called Twenty-One Demands to China—an attempt to strengthen the position it had won in Manchuria as a result of the Russo-Japanese War and to make new advances in China. The first fourteen demands asked for Chinese confirmation of the newly gained Japanese position in Shantung, economic concessions in Manchuria and Mongolia, and so on. The last group of demands, successfully resisted by the Chinese, were for extensive rights within China proper, including the

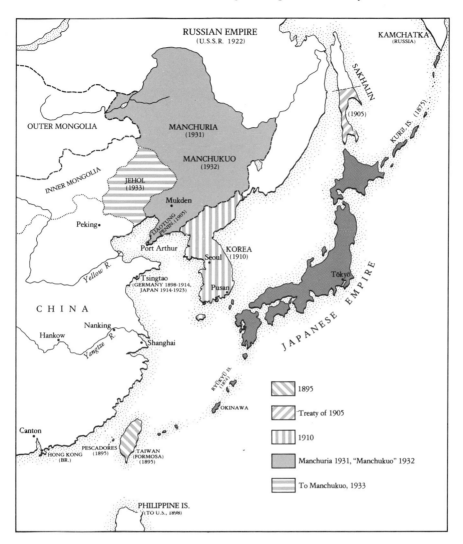

GROWTH OF JAPAN'S EMPIRE

appointment of Japanese advisers within the Chinese government. A third attempt to fish in troubled waters came in 1918 when Japan at the behest of the Allies sent troops to eastern Siberia to join an Allied intervention. Once the government had committed troops, the army took advantage of its "autonomy of command" and sent in many times the number of troops originally agreed on and kept them there long after the other Allies had withdrawn. This action was enormously expensive and enormously unpopular within Japan. It contributed to the declining prestige of the military, and the troops were finally withdrawn in 1922 with nothing to show for their efforts.

In the meantime international relations were entering a new postwar phase. Parallel to the victory of the democracies in World War I was the rise of the Wilsonian "new diplomacy" that emphasized self-determination and the sovereign rights of each people. The thrust of the new diplomacy was to shift from wartime armaments to a peacetime system of limited disarmament, and from a prewar system of bilateral treaties to a postwar system of multilateral treaties. The system was embodied in three treaties reached at the Washington Conference between November 1921 and February 1922. The "Four Power Pact" among Japan, Britain, the United States, and France replaced binational security arrangements with a weaker collective agreement for mutual consultation in case of threats to insular possessions. The "Five Power Pact" established a military equilibrium in the Pacific, stipulating that Britain and the United States would not build fortifications east of Singapore or west of Hawaii, and that the ratio of capital ships between Japan's one-ocean fleet and the two-ocean fleets of Britain and the United States would be 3-5-5. France and Italy, the other two of the "five powers," agreed to a 1.75 ratio. The intention of this agreement was to make Japan secure in its own waters, but unable to wage war against either the United States or Britain. The "Nine Power Treaty" dealt with China. On the one hand it recognized unequal-treaty rights in China and tacitly recognized Japan's position in Manchuria. On the other hand it confirmed the "sovereignty, the independence, and the territorial and administrative integrity of China." In effect it was a statement of principles intended, first, to prevent the powers from taking advantage of Chinese disunity to further dismember China, and second, to apply when a goverment worthy of the name should emerge in China.

The Washington Conference system was, thus, not opposed to the colonial status quo. One could say, even, that it protected a stable colonial order in the hands of the victors in World War I. It was understood, however, that there was to be no new aggression, no new grabbing of colonies, that would upset this diplomatic order.

In keeping with this pattern of big-power relationships, Japan changed over to a foreign policy of internationalism, sometimes called "Shidehara diplomacy" after Shidehara Kijūrō, foreign minister in 1924–1927, and 1929–1931. Indeed, internationalism characterized all of Japan's foreign relations during the 1920's. It was supported by the parliamentary coalition in the Diet, the bureaucrats, and the businessmen, who were international in culture and whose ascendancy paralleled Japan's close ties with the United States, England, and France, the democratic victors in World War I. It was associated in the public mind with the rise to power of the parliamentary coalition.

The New Liberalism.   The postwar internationalist climate affected Japan internally too. When Itō went to Europe in the 1880's in search of a consti-

A rally in 1919 at Ueno Park in support of universal manhood suffrage.

tution, he found German principles most to his liking. In 1918, however, the democracies were strong and victorious. The popular Japanese image of the war was that of the *Punch* stereotypes: the bearded Kaiser of German militarism fighting the beautiful goddess of liberty, who represented the Allied cause. The influence of this democratic current was felt as early as 1916–1917 when school texts were revised to include (alongside the religious view of the emperor) an emphasis on internationalism. Needless to say, this was oriented toward the West; few in Japan at this time were intellectually concerned with the nationalistic stirring in neighboring China, not to speak of changes in the rest of the non-Western world.

Liberal intellectual currents within Japan, always sensitive to Western opinion, blossomed at this time. Yoshino Sakuzō (1878–1933), a professor at Tōkyō University, presented in various magazine articles his plans for the reorganization of government structure so as to subordinate the various elites to a party cabinet. The spirit of the age was reflected in the romantic individualism of the novelist Mushakōji Saneatsu, who wrote that "only a country without authorities is livable" and hoped that at last Goethes and Emersons would be born in Japan.

A Japanese writer has described a universal suffrage rally he attended as a youth in 1919. It was held under the auspices of the Yūaikai, the labor union which had risen after 1912 under the moderate leadership of the Christian, Suzuki Bunji. The three hundred who went to meet the speaker, the veteran Diet member Ozaki Yukio, sang a song written by the pioneer Christian social worker Kagawa Toyohiko as they marched through the streets of Kyōto: "Realizing that labor is a sacred vocation, let our spirits bravely advance, aiming at a distant ideal. . . ." The lecture hall was packed, and the crowds that were turned away broke windows and doors in order to hear Ozaki's oration. The manifesto passed that day amidst tumultuous applause pointed out "the misery of the proletariat and their oppression by the propertied classes," and, while "pledging loyalty to the sacred Emperor," demanded universal suffrage as a means of "extirpating the injustices of the [present] socio-economic system."

Here in microcosm we see a temporary union of labor, an incipient leftist political movement, the Christian social movement, liberal party politicians, journalists, and scholars that characterizes the brief span between 1917 and 1920. The same ideological variety can be found in various student societies established at this time in Tōkyō. A magazine put out by one carried pictures of Lincoln, Rousseau, Kropotkin, Marx, Lenin, and Rosa Luxemburg. A writer described the intellectual content of the era as a melange of different ingredients "swallowed whole without sufficient chewing," and his own position in his student years as a "leftist, emperor-oriented faith in democracy." Born of wartime prosperity and ideological ferment the "social movement," as it was called, was buoyed by the participation of intellectuals. Appealing to new democratic symbols and influenced by egalitarian doctrines, they campaigned for universal suffrage, social legislation, and women's rights. Workers' and tenants' organizations mushroomed overnight. A variety of leftist political groups were also formed. As early as 1918, Hara said that radical thought was the most serious problem he had to deal with. The movement was strong, in part, because it was diffuse enough to draw support from every group that opposed some aspect of state orthodoxy.

The political parties were also affected by this change in the spirit of the times. The Kenseikai, continuously out of power after 1916, not only played the role of an opposition party, but was somewhat changed in character by the "social movement." The election of 1917 appears to have been a turning point in this respect. The Kenseikai lost the election of 1917 to the Seiyūkai, but it won in certain urban districts that had previously gone to the Seiyūkai, and many of its successful candidates were a new type of men—journalists, professors, or lawyers—more liberal than the party leadership. Many of these men joined in the universal suffrage movement in 1917 and 1918 in alliance with the social movement. In the Seiyūkai, too, new men appeared who recognized that they would have to represent new interests if they were to win sufficient votes. Such tendencies were accelerated by the factional wrangling that broke out within the Seiyūkai after the death of Hara in 1921. Hara's successor as party president and prime minister was unsuccessful at maintaining unity within the party. His ministry was followed between 1922 and 1924 by three nonparty cabinets of varied character. As a consequence, some of the more liberal factions of the Seiyūkai allied themselves with the Kenseikai and in 1923 launched the Second Movement for the Protection of the Constitution.

If this movement had had support from the new white-collar class and from the students' and workers' groups that were appearing at this time in urban Japan, and if the alliance of liberal Diet members and the social movement that characterized the universal suffrage movement had continued, then the history of the next two decades might have been different. As it was, however, by the early months of 1920 the principal components in the social movement had abandoned the idea of political action within the framework of the constitution. The main reason for this was the 1920 defeat of the universal suffrage movement. But they also were angered by the antilabor, antiunion stance of Hara's Home Ministry. Labor groups were hurt by the recession of 1920. And more generally, these new idealistic groups were disillusioned by the realism with which the parties had compromised their way to power. As a result, labor unions, political groups, and student organizations turned left to anarcho-syndicalism and direct action, and then to Marxism, and, except for a few journalists, the Second Movement for the Protection of the Constitution lacked the support of intellectuals. Even the liberal Yoshino Sakuzō was cool toward it, pinning his hopes for the future democratization of Japan on labor groups. Rallies were held in the major cities of Japan, but the turnout was not enthusiastic.

The lack of support did not mean that the parties were weakened at the polls; the coalition of parties that supported the Second Movement for the Protection of the Constitution won the election of 1924 handily. This caused the resignation of the cabinet, and a new party cabinet under Katō Kōmei as prime minister was formed. Yet the alienation of "progressive intellectuals" from the two main parties meant that social elements which in other advanced countries defended parliaments from attacks by the right were in Japan critics of the parliamentary state. The significance of this situation was not to become clear until the early 1930's.

The Era of Party Governments. The high-water mark of party government in prewar Japan was the cabinet of Katō Kōmei in 1924–1926. It inaugurated an eight-year period in which the post of prime minister went to the president of one or the other of the two major parties. It was not party government in the British sense, since the president of the majority party in the Diet did not automatically have the right to form a cabinet. At times the post was given to the head of the minority party, who then went out and got his majority in an election. But government was by party leaders, and majority support in the Diet was recognized as necessary for rule.

PRIME MINISTERS 1924–1932

Seiyūkai	*Kenseikai-Minseitō*
	1924–1926 Katō Kōmei
	1926–1927 Wakatsuki
1927–1929 Tanaka	
	1929–1930 Hamaguchi
	1931 Wakatsuki
1931–1932 Inukai	

Katō Kōmei has been aptly described as the very model of a modern Meiji bureaucrat. Born in 1860, he got his start (like his successors in the Minseitō, Wakatsuki and Hamaguchi) as a graduate of Tōkyō University. He entered Mitsubishi at twenty-one, married the boss's daughter, spent some time in England, entered the Foreign Ministry (unlike Wakatsuki and Hamaguchi, who rose in the Ministry of Finance), and at the age of forty became foreign minister. Like Hara he was a man of parts, becoming in rapid succession a Diet member, the president of a large newspaper, several times foreign minister, ambassador to England, and from 1914 on served as president of the Dōshikai and its successor the Kenseikai (after 1916). His last cabinet office prior to 1924 was that of foreign minister in Ōkuma's cabinet at the time of the Twenty-One Demands to China. As a man Katō was blunt, cold, haughty: a purist respected if not popular. He has been called an "enlightened conservative," a term that might be applied to his government as well. An Anglophile, he both understood and staunchly supported party government on the British model.

The accomplishments of the Katō cabinet were considerable, although each seems to have had a darker side. One major achievement was the passage of a universal manhood suffrage bill in 1925. With this the electorate increased from 3 to more than 12 million. When one considers that the national electoral system had begun only in 1890, this marked an amazingly rapid advance. Coupled with this was the re-establishment of the middle-sized election district which has continued ever since. Yet earlier in 1925 Katō agreed to pass a strengthened antisubversive measure, the so-called Peace Preservation Law, which prohibited the formation of groups that advocated a change in the Japanese "national polity" or the abolition of private property. Penalties up to ten years in prison were provided for membership in such a group; these terms were made even more harsh in 1928 for use against the Japanese Communist Party. The conjunction of this law with the suffrage act indicated a willingness to recognize the political potential of every man, as well as a conservative desire to limit the range of political alternatives to which he would be exposed. Also involved in the bargaining for this bill was the restoration of diplomatic relations

GROWTH OF THE JAPANESE ELECTORATE

The Criteria of Eligibility	Election Year	Size of Electorate	Total Population
1889: male subjects 25 and over, paying 15 yen or more in taxes	1890	453,474	40,072,000
1900: male subjects 25 and over, paying 10 yen or more in taxes	1902	983,193	45,227,000
1919: male subjects 25 or over, paying 3 yen or more in taxes	1920	3,069,787	55,963,000
1925: all male subjects 25 and over	1928	12,409,078	63,863,000
1947: all citizens 20 and over	1949	42,105,300	78,100,000

with the Soviet Union (eight years before a similar action by the United States).

A second accomplishment of the Katō ministry was a program of social legislation favorable to labor. Article 17 of the Public Peace Law, which had been used against unions, was abolished. A National Health Insurance Law and a Labor Disputes Mediation Law were enacted, and the Factory Law enacted in the late Meiji period was revised. These, together with the suffrage bill, in effect, legalized union support for the nonrevolutionary socialist movement that was rising at this time. Against the revolutionary left, that is, those who advocated the overthrow of the emperor, the Katō cabinet was draconian; but toward those who were willing to work within the Japanese constitutional framework, Katō was permissive.

A third reform dealt with the Peers. This body, heavy with the post-1885 nobility, was a thorn in the side of party government, often blocking bills passed by the lower house. Katō originially had wanted to change the constitution so as to curtail the functions of the Peers. This proved impossible, but he was able to change the Peers' composition, limiting the number of members from the nobility and increasing the number of imperial appointees, who were usually men of legal, academic, or other achievement.

The ascendancy of the parties, the rise of democratic currents in the cities, and the foreign policy of internationalism led to a decline in the prestige of the services. Army officers took to wearing civilian clothes when off duty. Four divisions were cut out of the army in 1924 as part of a broader retrenchment program that cut the civil bureaucracy by twenty thousand men. Military expenses, which were 42 per cent of the budget in

1922, were pared to 29 per cent in 1925 and 28 per cent in 1927. Yet the army was by no means out of the picture altogether. This was the period during which it was mechanized. Military training was introduced into middle and higher schools, and local training units were set up for youths who did not continue their education. Many officers of the eliminated four divisions became instructors under this program. At the height of party power in December 1925 the moderate army minister, General Ugaki, could write in his diary:

More than 200,000 troops in active service, more than 3,000,000 in the veterans organization, 500,000 or 600,000 middle and higher school students, and more than 800,000 trainees in local units: all of these will be controlled by the army, and their power will work as the central force aiding the Emperor in war and peace alike. The right of autonomous command over the Emperor's army is, in a time of emergency, not limited to the command of troops, but contains the authority to control the people.

The Troubled Years of Party Government 1927–1932.   Katō Kōmei died in 1926 and was succeeded by Wakatsuki of the same party. Shidehara continued as foreign minister and there was little break with the policies of Katō. The Seiyūkai, however, returned to power -in 1927, its fortunes revived by General Tanaka Giichi, who had become its president in 1925. Tanaka was born in Chōshū in 1863. Entering the army, he rose to become army minister in the Hara cabinet in 1918. His association with party politicians was so close that some generals distrusted him, feeling that his ambition might work against the interest of the army. Tanaka was neither a military oligarch nor a real party politician, but he was broader in outlook and more astute than the narrowly professional generals of the late 1930's who were to follow.

As prime minister, Tanaka spoke of a "positive foreign policy," of strengthening Japan's position in Manchuria, and of taking a tougher attitude toward the Chinese. In fact, Japan's relations with China remained by and large the same as under Shidehara, but Tanaka's bellicose tones provoked an anti-Japanese reaction in China. This boomeranged on the Tanaka cabinet when in 1928 officers of the Japanese Kwantung Army in Manchuria assassinated Chang Tso-lin, Japan's client warlord in the area, in the hope that his son would be less nationalistic and more compliant to Japanese suggestions. Tanaka tried to cover up the incident, even telling the young Shōwa emperor, who had succeeded his father in 1926, that the army was not responsible. When the truth came out, the emperor called Tanaka a liar. This led to his resignation.

The return of the Minseitō to power in 1929 (the cabinets of Hamaguchi and Wakatsuki with Shidehara as foreign minister in both) was a return to a government more committed to party rule. One of the major accomplishments of Hamaguchi's cabinet was Japan's participation in the London Naval Conference of 1930, which saw the Washington Conference formula of 5-5-3 for capital ships extended to heavy cruisers, and a 10-10-7 formula applied to light cruisers. Basing his policy on friendship with the United States and Britain and on a determination to avoid an arms race, Hamaguchi used moderate admirals to override majority opinion in the navy. The Naval General Staff declared that he had infringed on its right of supreme command. The Privy Council, the Peers, and the Seiyūkai attacked the concessions made at London. The Seiyūkai was unaware that criticism of the Minseitō at this critical juncture had the effect of weakening party power in general. Hamaguchi successfully stood up to this barrage of criticism until November 1930 when he was shot by a rightist "patriot."

In addition to the furor over the cruiser ratio, the political mud-slinging at times, as in the elections of 1928 and 1930, was such that it almost seemed as if the two major parties themselves were intent on hastening the downfall of party government. The Minseitō called the government of the Seiyūkai between 1927 and 1929 a "Mitsui cabinet," since the bank crisis of 1927 had been settled on terms highly favorable to the Mitsui. In reply, in 1930 the Seiyūkai called the government of Hamaguchi a "Mitsubishi cabinet." Whether the Japanese politicians of this period were in fact more venal than those in the West can be questioned. But the very size of the zaibatsu made the sources of their campaign donations more obvious, and infractions of the highly restrictive election laws were legion. Furthermore, there was probably a higher level of ethical expectation regarding government morality (deriving from the same Confucian assumptions that lay behind Yamagata's belief that government should be above parties and other private interest groups). Corruption, magnified by suffering due to the depression and by slashing attacks from both the left and the right, thus attracted much attention, and faith in party government weakened even during the era in which the parties' gains seemed irreversible.

Reviewing the history of the 1924–1932 period, we note first that it occurred within the constitutional structure of multiple elites. The power balance shifted in favor of the lower house, society became more open, mass media became more influential, the economy became more diversified, and yet no breakthrough to a new political structure occurred. Even the enactment of universal suffrage did not disrupt the usual workings of the system. The intermediate institutions—prefectural organizations, veterans' associations, shrine and temple associations, business groups, the police and lower bureaucracy, and the system of education—that served as the transmission belt between town or village and nation remained firm. The newly enfranchised were accommodated within the existing political scheme.

Universal suffrage did affect the socialist movement. It gave new strength to moderate unions and political organizations. Even many organizations that were Marxist in ideology adopted parliamentary tactics after 1925. Their rosy hopes for gains at the polls were dashed by the elections of 1928, 1930, and 1932, when, to their chagrin, the newly enfranchised gave most of their votes to the two old parties. To some extent it was the inability of the moderate left to attract voters that fed the revolutionary fringe. The weak showing at the polls underlines the point that the significance of prewar socialism was more intellectual than numerical.

The inability of the two main parties to change the political structure may have stemmed from the conservative character of the leaders, who usually entered the parties only after serving long apprenticeships in other more conservative elites. But it is also possible to say that the parties were as liberal as they could have been, if they were to cooperate effectively with the other elites and avoid a possibly violent reaction from the right. The two parties were alike in most respects, at least when they were in power. The choice between them was rarely such as to inspire a voter with democratic fervor. But their essential similarity was the precondition for the gains that were made; the slight difference between them at any one time—such as the Kenseikai stress on universal suffrage before 1924—defined the next goal for legislative advance. Had the Kenseikai been conspicuously more advanced than its opposition, the government might have formed a stable alliance with the Seiyūkai, permanently excluding the Kenseikai from power.

Comparative history is still in its infancy, but a contrast between Japan and pre-Weimar Germany with its comparable government of plural elites offers a relief from the perspective that comes from interpreting Japanese government in terms of the Anglo-American democracies. Both Japan and Germany were late developers and both had semifeudal survivals, such as the power of the family head and the prestige of the military. Both had imperial consitutions, Prussian in inspiration, that limited the powers of the legislature. Both were run by academic, elitist bureaucracies, and the armed services in both were directly under the monarchy. One significant difference between them was that Japan's society was much more homogeneous: there were no politically significant religious splits, no strong regional loyalties, no Junker class with its own party, and no powerful socialist party with widespread political support. The pace of evolutionary change was so even that both major parties represented, by and large, the same social groups—rural landlords, "men of influence" in the rural political structure, and urban industrial interests. A comparison with the underdeveloped parliamentary state of Germany before World War I also suggests a higher evaluation of Japan's gains under the Meiji constitution—especially when one considers that Japan not only had to build its parliamentary organization, but also to implant the very vocabulary necessary for its articulation.

The Rise of Militarism

Had Japan not been subject to new outside influences after 1929 it might have continued its earlier pattern of slow gains in a parliamentary direction within the framework of the constitution. It is possible, even, that the principle of automatically selecting the head of the majority party in the Diet as prime minister might have been established. But this trend came to an end. There was no reversion to the pre-1913 pattern of oligarchic control; nor were there revolutionary changes in the post-1890 structure of government. Rather, what happened was a small shift in the balance between the elites, the advantage passing from the parties to the military. This small shift produced an enormous change in political climate and policy, setting Japan upon the course that led to disaster in World War II. The three most important outside influences were: the world depression that began in the United States in 1929, the march north of the Kuomintang troops together with the emergence of a strong Chinese nationalism that threatened Japan's position in Manchuria, and the rise to power of Hitler and Mussolini in Germany and Italy.

The Depression. In Japan the domestic depression of 1926 led to the bank crisis of 1927 in which a number of weak banks were wiped out. These developments took place against the economic backdrop of the relatively weak showing of the Japanese economy during the 1920's. These minor crises were followed by a major catastrophe when the world depression hit Japan early in 1930.

Objective indices show that the value of Japanese exports dropped 50 per cent from 1929 to 1931. Workers' real incomes dropped, from an index of 100 in 1926, to 81 in 1930, to 69 in 1931. Unemployment rose to about 3 million, with much of the burden falling on farm families. Rural Japan bore the brunt of the depression suffering; for example, between September 1929 and September 1930 the price of silk cocoons fell 65 per cent. In 1930 the "bumper crop famine" occurred. On October 2 a crop 12 per cent greater than that of the previous years was predicted; by the following day the price per unit (five bushels) of rice had fallen to sixteen yen, although the cost of production was seventeen yen. By October 10 the price had fallen to about ten yen. In 1931 the evil of too much was followed by the greater evil of too little. An unprecedented crop failure occurred in northeastern Japan and Hokkaidō. Images of the depression in Japan were formed by this event: children begging for food outside the dining-cars of trains, starving peasants stripping off the tender inner bark of pine trees or digging for the roots of wild plants, the agents for city brothels bargaining with farmers who had nothing left to sell but their daughters. Between 1926 and 1931, rural cash incomes fell from an index of 100 to 33, and

A hamlet discussion during the depression year of 1934 in Aomori.
Topic is how to survive without selling daughters.

by 1934 were back only to 44. Because of lower prices, the peasants' real income, never high, was down about one-third. The condition of tenants and poorer farmers, at near-subsistence levels even in good times, was far worse.

The blame for the depression fell on the parties. This was because party leaders, in the public mind, were intimately associated with the zaibatsu, the bureaucracy, the landlords, and the urban white-collar class. All the groups of this "parliamentary coalition," with the possible exception of the landlords, had a common vision of economic growth by participation in the international, economic order that paralleled the comity of democratic nations. This was the 1920 outgrowth of the Meiji vision of limited democracy and paternalistic capitalism at home working in cooperation with the great powers abroad. The depression called into question the validity of the international economic order; this in turn cast doubts on the worth of the comity of democratic nations and Japan's parliamentary government. At the same time the emergence of the Fascists in Italy and the Nazis in Germany contributed to the rise of antidemocratic forces in Japan. It seemed particularly significant to many that Germany, the most admired of Western states and the constitutional model for Japan, had turned its back on democracy and was looking to authoritarian and militarist policies as the wave of the future.

These developments revived the unsolved question of the Meiji constitution: Who would rule in Japan? Who best represented the will of the emperor and the interests of the people? Was it the party politicians, the lackeys of the zaibatsu who worked cheek by jowl with the self-satisfied higher bureaucracy, under whose government the farmers had suffered so much? Or was the imperial army, which had preserved untarnished its honor and sense of duty, best fitted to rule? Some in the army, at least, saw the question in these terms. Those who advocated a greater role for the army at home asked further whether Japan could afford to depend on the world economy in view of rising tariff barriers, protests against cheap Japanese goods, and the problem of finding adequate raw materials and markets. They argued that military expansion abroad could create an autonomous empire within which Japan could insulate itself from the vagaries of the world economy—a controlled imperial economy within which the livelihood of farmer and worker would be guaranteed.

Party government acted effectively, if late, to counter the depression. Inukai Tsuyoshi became prime minister of a Seiyūkai cabinet in December 1931 and took Japan off the gold standard. This led to the boom in exports that made Japan the first nation to recover. By 1936 domestic consumption was up 20 per cent. Some of this was taken up by a 7 per cent rise in population to 70 million, but a rise greater than 10 per cent in real incomes occurred for the nation as a whole. This was not evenly distributed. The salaried classes benefited the most. But unemployment dropped, and the real wages of workers rose from an index figure of 155 for 1925–1929 to 174 for 1930–1934, and then declined to 166 for 1935–1939 as moderate inflation set in. Rural incomes also recovered somewhat, but, since new debts made even heavier the earlier burden of taxes and rents, few gains were made. Economic recovery, however, came too late to benefit the parties.

The Army in Politics: The Manchurian Incident.   Ever since the decline of the oligarchy, the army had had the capacity for independent action. This was guaranteed by the position of the General Staff directly under the emperor. The use of this autonomy was not new in 1931. The army had used its powers to prolong the Siberian Expedition in the early 1920's, and to fight for military appropriations at other times. Examples also can be found of independent actions by field-grade officers that, when successful, tended to commit the army as a whole to some policy that it might not otherwise have chosen. In general, however, a decline in the army relative to the other elites, combined with moderate leadership by a transitional generation of generals willing to cooperate with the parties, had kept the army in line until the late twenties.

The attachment of the army and of Japan as a whole to Manchuria was of long standing. In popular sentiment Manchuria was viewed as a recompense for the 100,000 Japanese lives lost in the Russo-Japanese War. Army planners saw Manchuria as a buffer against Russian power in the north.

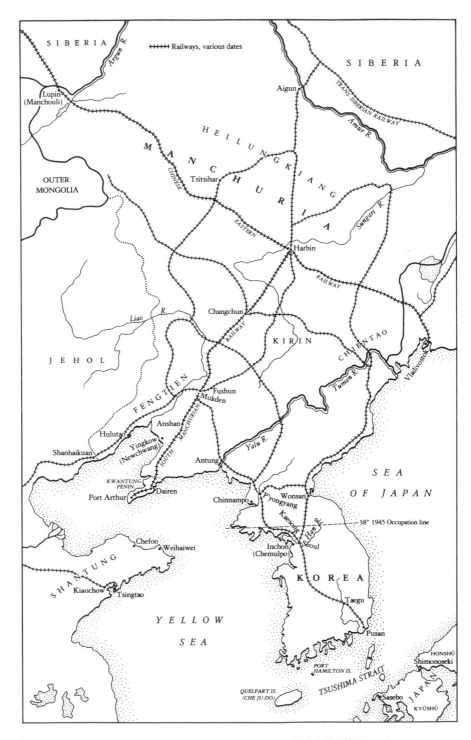

INTERNATIONAL RIVALRY IN KOREA AND MANCHURIA

Military considerations were strengthened after 1918 by a policy of containment of Communism. Of foreign investment in Manchuria, 75 per cent was Japanese; particularly important was the South Manchurian Railway Company. There were a million Japanese subjects in Manchuria, mostly Korean, and 40 per cent of Japan's China trade was with this area. Arguments in favor of the expansion of this economic position had been powerfully bolstered by the depression.

In spite of these various interests, Japan did not have a policy of reducing Manchuria to a colony. It was content to maintain a façade of Chinese sovereignty under a semipuppet warlord, a balance possible because of Chinese disunity. By the late 1920's, however, this balance had been upset by the unification of China by the Nationalists in 1926–1928 and the rise of Chinese nationalism, which increasingly challenged the Japanese position in Manchuria. Faced with this new situation, no important group in Japan considered withdrawing. Japan's party leaders, such as Wakatsuki and Shidehara, argued for peaceful diplomacy and international trade, but the status quo was crumbling. Action was necesssary if Japan's position in Manchuria was to be maintained. Even many in the parties recognized this, and all groups in the army favored some kind of action. In August 1931, Minami, the most powerful of the moderate generals, drew up a plan. While predicated on cooperation with the Foreign Office, it aimed at the formation of a "fundamental policy for Manchuria" to obtain practical results by the spring of 1932. A second group, the army's China experts, under General Tatekawa, favored direct action by the army, as did many field-grade officers both in Tōkyō and in the Japanese military in Manchuria (known as the Kwantung Army).

The Mukden incident that led to the Japanese takeover in Manchuria has often been described as a coup carried out by junior officers without the knowledge of their superiors. This is not true. The architects of the plot were indeed only field-grade officers, Colonel Itagaki and Lieutenant-Colonel Ishiwara of the Kwantung Army, but late in August 1931, Ishiwara told General Tatekawa of the General Staff and others of his plan to provoke an incident that would lead to a Japanese takeover of Manchuria. No one objected. He also told General Honjō, the commanding general of the Kwantung Army, who is said to have replied that he would take "immediate action" in case of a crisis. When the chief of staff of the Kwantung Army heard of the plot, he asked the army in Tōkyō to send someone to inform the Kwantung Army of Tōkyō's policy. Tatekawa was sent, but before leaving dispatched a cable to alert the plotters. Tatekawa arrived in Manchuria on the evening of September 18 and went straight to a geisha house, his message undelivered. On the same night a bomb exploded on the tracks of the Japanese railway north of Mukden. Colonel Itagaki ordered a full-scale attack against the Chinese troops in Mukden, and General Honjō, hearing of the crisis, called out the whole Kwantung Army. Once action had begun, no one in the army was willing to consider a return to the earlier situation.

The effects on the government of the army's aggression were disastrous. On the day after the fighting began the Wakatsuki cabinet decided on a policy of "nonexpansion of hostilities." But on September 21 the army advanced into areas beyond the South Manchurian Railway zone. On September 24 the Japanese government announced that "the action of the Japanese army was taken in self-defense and hence unavoidable," but that "the army was already returning to the railway zone." Actually the army continued to advance and the Japanese government was unable to control it. By early 1932 the conquest of all Manchuria had been completed. In March 1932 Manchuria was proclaimed an independent state under the last Ch'ing ruler (P'u-yi). The Lytton Commission of the League of Nations visited Manchuria in the spring of 1932 and condemned Japan as an aggressor. The report was adopted by the League of Nations, from which Japan withdrew in protest the following year. By this time the Japanese armies had already moved west from Manchuria to occupy about five thousand square miles of the Inner Mongolian province of Jehol.

The Wakatsuki cabinet was unable to take effective action because it was split. Several ministers supported the action of the Kwantung Army; most disapproved silently; only two were openly critical. Divided, the cabinet vacillated for several months and finally resigned in December. The next cabinet was formed by Inukai, the last party prime minister in prewar Japan. Inukai's Seiyūkai was also disunited. One faction favored military expansion. The majority, including the prime minister, accepted the conquest of Manchuria but opposed further army expansion into China. Long a fighter for party rule, Inukai was particularly enraged by the army's usurpation of the decision-making functions of the cabinet. He therefore attempted to negotiate directly with the Chinese. According to his son, Inukai also sought, unsuccessfully, to obtain an imperial rescript to restrain the army in Manchuria. But such moves were without effect, and Inukai was assassinated by ultranationalists on May 15, 1932.

At this point the parties became the victims of the methods which they had used so successfully for four decades. They had risen to power by manipulating other elites and by compromise. In 1932 compromise could lead only to a weakening of party power. The parties needed strong leaders who could dig in their heels and fight. But none was forthcoming. Had Saionji been a stronger person, had he spoken resolutely against the army in the name of the emperor, the "parliamentary coalition" might have rallied. The rationale of the army's defiance of the cabinet was the fiction that the army acted on the direct orders of the emperor. But Saionji saw as his first duty the protection of the emperor from involvement in political controversy; this took precedence over his weaker concern for parliamentary government.

The year 1932 was the pit of the depression and the peak of agitation by the revolutionary right. Stirred by the conquest of Manchuria, by the fighting between Japanese and Chinese forces that had broken out in Shanghai in January and February, and by the "patriotic assassinations" of establishment figures, many hoped that an army general would be chosen prime minister. In this situation the best that Saionji could do was to appoint as prime minister Saitō Makoto (1858–1936), a moderate admiral, in the hope of reconciling the services and moderate elements within the parties. Wakatsuki, the president of the Minseitō, was too liberal to be acceptable to the services. The new president of the Seiyūkai was an expansionist who might have encouraged the army in its continental policy. As military men, both Saitō (prime minister May 1932–July 1934) and his successor Admiral Okada (prime minister July 1934–March 1936) were not unacceptable to the army in spite of their moderate character. Saitō's cabinet of "national unity" was made up of ex-bureaucrats and politicians appointed from both parties. Split into factions and jealous of each other, the parties were willing to accept their reduction to a ministerial role in government. The parties continued a vigorous criticism of the military from the floor of the Diet, but in general the four years of the Saitō and Okada cabinets saw a steady drift away from the policies of the 1920's.

The Rise and Fall of the Revolutionary Right, 1931–1936. Until the mid-1920's there had been few civilian patriotic societies, but then they began to proliferate, and they became extremely numerous during the 1930's and 1940's. Charts drawn by Japanese scholars to show their lineages and interrelationships look like computer wiring diagrams. Most groups were small. Ideologically, all were committed to the emperor, the "national polity," and to the Japanese virtues of harmony and duty. Most opposed internationalism and favored Japanese expansion and pan-Asianism. Some advocated direct action against the "traitors at the side of the emperor."

A second component in the revolutionary rightist movement of the 1930's consisted of certain groups of young army and navy officers. Educated in army schools after leaving middle school, officers were more traditional in outlook than most other segments of society. They were sympathetic to the postdepression plight of rural Japan from which most service recruits were obtained. Some were therefore susceptible to the traditional idea of morally pure direct action to overthrow the corrupt government of party politicians. Mixed in with these feelings were animosities against the monopolization of army control by Chōshū generals or against the domination of the army bureaucracy by graduates of the elite War College.

In 1931 military and civilian ultranationalist groups joined in two plots to overthrow the government and establish a "national defense state" under an army-led cabinet. Both plots fizzled. Early in 1932 the civilian League of Blood assassinated a party politician and then a Mitsui executive. On May 15, 1932, a group of junior officers in the army and navy, acting in concert with a rural patriotic group, murdered Prime Minister Inukai and attacked the Seiyūkai headquarters, the Bank of Japan, various official residences, and the Tōkyō Police Headquarters. In 1934 a lieutenant-colonel killed one of the triumvirate of top generals, who belonged to an opposing clique. The last and greatest coup by the revolutionary right was the rebellion of the First Division on February 26, 1936. Young officers led fourteen hundred troops into the streets of Tōkyō. They attacked government offices, killed cabinet ministers and members of the Imperial Household Ministry. For three days the center of the city was in a state of seige, with soldiers occupying the Diet, the Army Ministry, the General Staff Headquarters, and other government centers. At first some army generals wanted to placate the rebels. But the high officials around the throne had the emperor stand firm, and the other elites—including the navy—joined in opposition to the rebellion. On the 29th the insurgents were branded as rebels and put down by soldiers brought in from outside commands.

The rebellion was followed by purges of generals who had been involved in clique politics within the army. It was at this time that power came into the hands of officers, including General Tōjō, who were later to lead Japan into World War II. The leaders of the rebellion were quickly tried and executed, and the powers of the military police to root out those who advocated "direct action" were augmented. The re-establishment of discipline within the army did not mean that the army as an elite had become depoliticized. If anything its voice in Japan became greater: the threat of renewed violence if the army were not given its way became a potent argument in political councils and a determining factor in foreign policy.

A second consequence of the period of terror was the suppression, first of the left and then of liberals. Under attack by the right, many in the government, including some party politicians, intensified their persecution of the left to demonstrate their own patriotism. The lack of a tradition of civil rights for minority groups proved fatal. The revolutionary left, openly heretical in its attacks on the emperor, was the first to go. In 1932, fifteen hundred socialists, Communists, and union organizers were arrested and as many again in 1933. Many were sent to prison, a few were killed. From 1933 liberal professors came under fire. Some lost their jobs. In 1935 Minobe was attacked in the Diet for having suggested that the emperor was an organ of the state; he was dismissed from all his posts and his works were banned. From this time, what had been orthodox constitutional theory became heresy, and the religious interpretation of the state became official.

Cross-Currents, 1936–1937. The period after the February Rebellion of 1936 and before the beginning of the China war in the summer of the following year was politically confused. In it two cross-currents appeared: a stronger voice for the army in a government thinking of war, and a resurgence of the political parties in opposition to the army-dominated government.

The Okada cabinet resigned after the rebellion, and a new cabinet was formed by Hirota Kōki, the former foreign minister, a career diplomat and an advocate of a stronger foreign policy. The army interfered from the start, vetoing as cabinet ministers a leading Foreign Office official, Yoshida Shigeru (prime minister 1946–1947, 1948–1954), and several others on the grounds that they were too liberal. In the end, only four party men were able to enter the cabinet. The policies carried out by this cabinet, and that of General Hayashi which followed it, form a logical bridge between the conservatism of the years 1934–1936 and the intensified militarism after the onset of the China war.

One act of the Hirota cabinet was the passage of more stringent laws for the control of dangerous thoughts. Another was the passage of a greatly augmented budget for military expenditures. This provided the funds for army modernization that the military had long been advocating. In foreign policy the cabinet aligned its policies with those of the army, calling for the neutralization of five northern Chinese provinces. It also stressed, for the first time, Japan's concern with the regions to the south of China. And in December 1936 Japan signed the Anti-Comintern Pact with Germany.

The Hirota cabinet also re-established the ruling that only generals and admirals on active duty might be appointed as service ministers. One purpose of this was to prevent the generals ousted after the 1936 rebellion from re-entering politics by the side door. The result, however, was to make cabinets clearly dependent on the good will of the military services, as they had been before 1913. This became obvious early in 1937 when General Ugaki was asked to form a cabinet. Because of his close ties with the political parties, his association with cliquism in the army, and his responsibility for the 1924 reduction of four divisions, the army refused to furnish an army minister. As a retired general Ugaki was unable to become his own army minister and was forced to withdraw. In his place, General Hayashi Senjūrō, who faithfully followed the army line, became prime minister. The character of the four short months of his cabinet is summed up in the slogans it used: "Respect the gods and honor the emperor," and "The union of government and religion."

The second cross-current during this period was the revival of the parties and their opposition to the army. In the election of February 1936 (one week before the rebellion), the Seiyūkai, with its more nationalistic "positive" foreign policy, entered with 301 incumbent Diet seats to the Minseitō's

PRIME MINISTERS 1932–1945

Moderate Admirals	Saitō	May 1932–July 1934
	Okada	July 1934–March 1936
Growing Militarism	Hirota	March 1936–February 1937
	Hayashi	February 1937–June 1937
China War	Konoe	June 1937–January 1939
	Hiranuma	January 1939–August 1939
Diplomatic Pause	Abe	August 1939–January 1940
	Yonai	January 1940–July 1940
Axis Pact	Konoe	July 1940–July 1941
	Konoe	July 1941–October 1941
World War II	Tōjō	October 1941–July 1944
Ending the War	Koiso	July 1944–April 1945
	Suzuki	April 1945–August 1945

146. Yet the Minseitō, using slogans such as "What shall it be, parliamentary government or fascism?" won a notable victory at the polls, coming out of the election with 205 seats to the Seiyūkai's 174. Such a result was not simply habitual voting by a lethargic populace. Rather, it shows a positive awareness of the problems of the day.

Increasingly ignored by the bureaucratic-military cabinets, the parties gradually came to oppose the government. In January 1937 a Seiyūkai Diet member made an impassioned speech attacking the army's interference in government. The army minister replied; a bitter debate followed; the Diet member recommended that the army minister commit hara-kiri; the army minister wanted to dissolve the Diet. The navy minister and others refused, and therefore the Hirota cabinet resigned. The Hayashi cabinet, which lasted only four months, was also brought down by the parties. Like Yamagata at the turn of the century, Hayashi felt that cabinets should be above the factional strife which the parties represented. He demanded that those who entered his cabinet renounce their party ties. To attain the unity he desired, he dissolved the Diet shortly after getting the budget passed and threw the support of the government behind the Shōwa-kai, a pro-militarist party. Apparently his idea was to realize in Japan the "one country, one party" formula of the Nazis. Yet in the election of April 1937 the Shōwa-kai won only 19 seats out of a total of 466 and Hayashi was forced to resign. It had been made plain, as in the late Meiji period, that government parties could not win an election.

The 1937 election reveals the extent to which, in spite of the drift to the right in the balance of governmental elites, the Japanese people had maintained a moderate, antimilitary position. Devotion to the emperor and

Japan did not automatically lead them to favor the more extreme forms of nationalism in politics. The bulk of the people, as in the elections of 1930, 1932, and 1936, stayed with the two major parties, which, although severely factionalized, made a common front against the Hayashi government. These parties received over 7 million votes and won 354 seats in the Diet. Pro-government parties won only 40 or so seats. By and large, the voting pattern of the 1930's represents not a break with that of the 1920's but a continuation. This also can be seen in the gradual growth of moderate socialism, which won 8 Diet seats in 1928, 5 seats in 1930 and 1932, 18 in 1936, and 37 in 1937 (receiving over 900,000 votes). Since the Social Mass Party (formed in 1932) was plagued by a national-socialist fringe on one side and antiparliamentary Marxism on the other, it cannot simply be described as a democratic force. Yet it was led by moderates such as the Christians Abe Isoo and Katayama Tetsu (prime minister 1947–1948), and its slogan, "Anticommunism, antifascism, anticapitalism," had a genuinely democratic appeal. Votes for this party were concentrated in the cities and represented elements that would emerge in much stronger force in postwar Japan.

To resolve the conflict between the parties and the government, and to promote a "Shōwa restoration" of national unity, Prince Konoe Fumimaro was asked to form the next cabinet. Konoe had ties with the army, the political parties, and the Japanese financial world. A civilian, a descendant of the ancient court aristocracy, a protégé of Saionji, a skillful and popular writer, a man who in his youth had gone to Kyōto University expressly to study with the philosopher Nishida and the Marxist economist Kawakami Hajime, Konoe had some appeal for every group. His appointment was greeted enthusiastically in all quarters. Certainly the parties expected from him a greater liberality than had existed under Hayashi. Yet, whatever potential he might have had in peacetime, in the course of the war that broke out a month after the formation of his cabinet, he proved too weak to resist the demands of the military and belligerent civilians whose hold on the government became stronger and stronger.

Japan at War

The China War. In 1937 all Japanese army planning was predicated on the assumption that the Soviet Union was Japan's only serious enemy in East Asia. By 1935 Russia had more troops in its Far Eastern Provinces (about 240,000) than Japan had in Manchuria (160,000), as well as more planes and greater mechanized strength. At the Seventh Comintern Congress of 1935 it was proclaimed that the fascist states of Germany and Japan were the enemies of the Soviet Union. In March 1936 the Soviet Union concluded a mutual defense pact with Outer Mongolia, and it obviously benefited from the united-front policy which brought the Kuomintang and

Chinese Communists together after 1936. To match the military strength of the Soviet Union in East Asia, the Japanese army in the summer of 1937 drew up a "Five-Year Plan for the Production of War Material." To fulfill this required time and peace; the last thing Japan needed was a full-scale war with China.

Indeed, apart from Manchuria, Japan's strategic concern in China was limited to the formation of buffer zones in North China to protect Manchuria from surprise attack during a possible war with Russia. These limited objectives in the main had been achieved by the end of 1935, although Japan still wanted the Nationalist government to recognize formally the special importance of the North China provinces to the security of Japan's continental empire. A few among the army's China experts and some radical officers in the Kwantung Army in Manchuria argued that the Nanking Government should be crushed before it had time to enter into an alliance with the Soviet Union and menace Manchuria from the south. But such a tactical emphasis represented a minority opinion within the overall strategy directed against the Soviet Union. Nevertheless, when on July 7, 1937, a local, unplanned clash took place between Chinese and Japanese troops in the Peking area, it quickly spread into a general war.

One reason for the spread of war was a Sino-Japanese difference in moral assumptions. Japan saw its position in China as based on national destiny, economic need, and history. Most Japanese felt their actions since 1931 were necessary to protect legitimate imperial interests. They judged events in terms of a status quo that was being disturbed by Chinese nationalism. China, on the other hand, saw its entire modern history as one of continuous aggression by foreign powers. Japan's encroachments were the most recent and outrageous. Rising Chinese nationalism could tolerate these no longer. A second reason was a crisis of mobilization: generals on both sides sent in troops so they would not be forced to negotiate from weakness, and once troops were on the ground they were committed to battle to improve their positional strength. A third reason was that within the Japanese government the question of what policy should be made became entangled with the question of who should make it. As military men and jingoistic bureaucrats won out in power struggles, policy became more aggressive. Several times armistices were reached by armies in the field only to be overturned by decisions made in Tōkyō.

As the fighting increased so did sentiment in favor of a knockout blow against Nationalist China. The General Staff argued that if the Chinese capital of Nanking fell, the Chinese government would give in to Japanese demands. Nanking was captured in December, and the willingness of army commanders to see this former center of anti-Japanese agitation punished led to days of wanton slaughter. The Nationalist leader Chiang Kai-shek, however, held out, so in January 1938 it was decided to launch an all-out offensive in China in order to set up a new central government favorable to the Japanese. By October 1938 Hankow and Canton had been captured. The threat of the Soviet Union in the north led Japan to limit its involvement in China to the control of railroads and major cities. On November 3 Konoe announced the establishment of Japan's New Order in East Asia. For a while, Japan hoped that Chiang Kai-shek would give up and head a government under Japanese control. When this hope proved futile Japan turned to Chiang's rival Wang Ching-wei who, reviving the pro-Japanese writings of Sun Yat-sen, the founder of the Nationalist movement, became the head of a puppet government at Nanking in March 1940.

The Background of the Pacific War. In the China War the army was central, but in the events leading to the Pacific War the navy was perhaps the more important service. The 1930 London Disarmament Conference had galvanized opinion within the navy. In the years that followed, those who had been opposed to the Treaty became dominant and used their power 1) to purge many of those in the navy who had supported the Treaty, 2) to push a program of weapons development (new submarines, airplanes, ships, and torpedoes) that would strengthen the navy without infringing on the 5-5-3 capital ships ratio, and 3) to force Japan to withdraw from the international disarmament system by presenting a demand for complete naval parity that of course proved unacceptable to the other powers at the Second London Conference in 1935. Free from the Treaty, Japan began in 1937 a larger program of naval construction. This was carried on secretly so as not to alarm the United States and Britain. As a result, by 1940 the Japanese navy was strong. Its leaders felt that, though it was not a many-ocean fleet, it was more than the equal of any other power in its own waters of the western Pacific.

Following Japan's withdrawal from the disarmament system, which like its earlier withdrawal from the League of Nations weakened its ties to the United States and Britain, Japan moved closer to rapprochement with Germany and Italy. This proved to be a diplomatic blunder, for the problem of Germany was uppermost in the minds of American and British leaders, and only when the problem of Japan become connected with the problem of Germany did United States–Japanese relations begin to worsen decisively. Events in China alone would not have produced the same result.

It is not surprising that militarist Japan eventually became allied with Nazi Germany and Fascist Italy, the only two states in the West that were dissatisfied with the international disarmament system and not critical of Japan's aggression in China. Japan had been culturally close to Germany since the late Meiji period, and there were many who admired the accomplishments of the Nazis. Japan's "New Order in East Asia" almost sounded like a translation from the German. Moreover, the 1936 Anti-Comintern

Pact expressed a common animus against the Soviet Union that prefigured later, more compelling ties. In addition, among the great powers, Japan, Germany, and Italy, were have-not nations, covetous of the riches in the empires of the Western democracies. Still, even given the above factors, there was no straight line linking the Japanese situation in 1937 to the 1941 attack on Pearl Harbor.

Japan's concerns were Asian, not European. From the end of 1938, Japan's main problem was how to settle the mess in China. Each new cabinet proclaimed its intention to extricate Japan from China. Obviously this was to happen on terms favorable to Japan. Much of Japan's diplomatic and military strategy during the late 1930's was directed toward bringing about a situation in which the Chinese government would give in to Japan. A second problem was relations with the Soviet Union. The Soviet potential for action in Asia was in inverse proportion to its involvement in Europe. The threat to Russia in Europe was Germany. This made relations with Germany extremely important to Japan. A third problem was the American Pacific fleet. The Japanese navy viewed this as its most dangerous potential enemy, hence the navy was disposed not to antagonize the United States, if this could be accomplished without weakening the navy. A fourth concern was Southeast Asia, rich in the raw materials needed by Japan for the formation of an autarkic economy. Here Japan was faced by the colonies of France, Holland, and Britain.

Throughout the early part of 1939 Japan sought to strengthen its position against the Soviet Union and to bring pressure to bear on the Chinese government by establishing an alliance either with Germany and Italy or with Britain. Most of the army and many civilian bureaucrats, including Hiranuma (prime minister January–August 1939), leaned toward Germany. But Germany was not willing to ally itself with Japan against Russia alone and insisted that Japan commit itself against Britain and the United States as well. The Foreign and Naval Ministries resisted an alliance based on these terms.

Pro-German groups in Japan were gaining ground when in August 1939 Germany signed a nonaggression pact with the Soviet Union and turned to war on the West. The reaction of the Japanese was that the Germans had made fools of them. Hiranuma said on resigning as prime minister: "Japan's foreign policy is in a state of having been practically betrayed." Japan had wanted an alliance as protection against Russia. Concern with this had mounted during 1938 as Russia extended aid to China, and during the summer months from May to September 1939, even as Germany was concluding the pact, Japanese troops were battling several Russian divisions in a large-scale battle near Nomonhan on the Mongolian-Manchurian border. An armistice was signed in September, but victory had gone to the more highly mechanized Soviet forces. Now Germany had freed the Soviet Union to take an even stronger stance in Asia and had gone to war with Britain.

This brought about a reorientation of Japanese policy. Hiranuma was succeeded as prime minister first by General Abe and then by Admiral Yonai, the latter noted for his pro-British and pro-American leanings. During this period (August 1939–July 1940) German diplomatic advances were repelled by the Japanese, and many leaders attempted to improve relations with the United States and Britain. China remained the stumbling block. The United States Secretary of State, Cordell Hull, was not willing to countenance aggression by abandoning China; hence negotiations in this direction came to nothing. Some have argued that this was a critical moment: had the United States been more flexible, it might have reached an agreement with Japan that would have precluded the later Japanese pact with Germany and Italy. Yet even if the Japanese Foreign Ministry had concluded an agreement with Britain, France, and the United States, the agreement subsequently might have been undone by the Japanese military services.

By late spring of 1940 the situation was changing again. Japan was amazed by the German victories in Europe. The fall of Britain appeared at hand. Again voices were raised in favor of an alliance with Germany. In July the army withdrew its minister, overthrowing the Yonai cabinet. The second Konoe cabinet that replaced it was the most militant yet formed. General Tōjō came in as the representative of the army. Hoshino, a former economic planner in Manchuria, entered as minister without portfolio and head of the Planning Board. And Matsuoka, blunt, erratic, contradictory, and American-educated but wildly pro-German, became foreign minister.

This government signed a Tripartite Pact with Germany and Italy in September 1940. The Pact provided that the signatories would go to war against any nation attacking one of their number—excepting those already at war at the time the Pact was signed. Japan hoped to get four things from this Pact: 1) It wanted better relations with the Soviet Union. Germany, ostensibly on good terms with Russia, offered to act as a go-between. The negotiations took time, but in April 1941 Japan got a neutrality pact with the U.S.S.R. 2) Japan wanted assurances that the colonies in Asia of the colonial powers that Germany was defeating in Europe would enter its New Order. 3) Japan wanted to end the war in China. It felt that China would collapse if materiel and moral support from outside were cut off. It hoped that a Eurasia divided into spheres among Germany, Russia, and Japan would bring about this end. 4) Japan felt that this pact would isolate the United States more than ever, and therefore make it less likely to intervene in China or elsewhere.

*Party celebrating the signing of the Tripartite Pact. General Tōjō
(in knee boots) watches while Foreign Minister Matsuoka (facing
left in the right foreground) proposes a toast, calling the
document a "pact for peace."*

United States policy in East Asia in the years between 1931 and Pearl
Harbor espoused the principles of the Open Door, China's territorial integrity, and nonaggression, but avoided supporting these principles by military action. In part the United States was incapable of action: its army was
small and its navy was divided between two oceans. Confronted by Japanese
aggression, the United States could only disapprove. Public indignation at
Japanese actions in China slowly rose. The bombing of Chinese cities—
with bombs made from American scrap, and planes using fuel bought from
American companies—was viewed with horror. But, on the whole, the
American people were firmly behind the government policy of noninvolve-
ment. The election campaign of 1940 saw each candidate outpeacing the
other. When Japan began to move southward in spite of American warn-
ings, the most the United States could do was to invoke economic sanctions.
When the Germans overran France, Japanese army observers were sent to
Tongking in northern Indo-China in June 1940, and in September army
units followed. In response the United States adopted a licensing system
to limit exports of aviation gasoline, steel, and scrap iron to Japan. Until
this time the United States had been preoccupied with Europe. It had only
a secondary concern with East Asia and wished to avoid any Asian entangle-
ment that would weaken its power in the Atlantic. But when the Tripartite

Pact was signed in September 1940 the European crisis merged with the Far Eastern crisis. The slowly rising public opinion against Japan merged with the greater antipathy already felt toward Germany. Consequently, far from isolating the United States as Japan had intended, the Tripartite Pact made the United States more anti-Japanese than before.

The months between the signing of the pact in September 1940 and mid-1941 were in Japan a time of preparation for a further move to the south. Japan wanted to cut off the Chinese government from southern supply routes and to obtain strategic resources. It was felt in Japan, especially in naval circles, that a total embargo might be put into effect by the United States at any moment and that therefore a self-sufficient empire, including the oil-rich Dutch East Indies, was a military necessity. Some favored a move south even at the risk of war. Many, however, were hesitant about moving against Dutch and British colonies while Britain still stood. They did not want war with the United States, which through Lend-Lease and joint military planning, was increasingly involved on the British side.

In June 1941 Japan again found itself betrayed by Germany. Instead of finishing off Britain, and thus facilitating a Japanese move to the south, Germany attacked Russia, giving its ally Japan little advance notice. The German attack put Japan in the humiliating position of having just concluded a neutrality pact with the Soviet Union through the good offices of Germany, while Germany was preparing to invade that country. Germany then compounded the insult by asking Japan to attack the Soviet Union in the east. This occasioned a fierce debate in the army between those who favored war with Russia and those who wanted to move to the south. At an Imperial Conference on July 2, 1941, it was decided to fight Russia if the German armies proved victorious in the west. By September the German armies had been stopped short of Moscow. Japan therefore decided to honor its neutrality pact with Russia and ignore the German request. Instead, with its northern flank in Manchuria now safe from a Soviet attack because of German pressure in Europe, Japan decided to proceed south even at the risk of war with Britain and the United States, unless the United States through last minute negotiations could be persuaded to accept Japan's objectives in China.

Preparation for southward expansion, however, ruined what little chance for success the negotiations might have had. Japanese troops entered southern Indo-China in July 1941, and the United States reacted by placing a total embargo on all exports to Japan. This cut Japanese oil imports to 10 per cent of their previous volume and produced the "crisis of the dwindling stockpile." The Navy General Staff, not averse to war, said that Japan's oil reserves would last only two years. If no action were taken by October, any later action would become impossible and Japan would be forced to retreat step by step until all its gains were lost. This concept was embodied in "an outline plan for carrying out the national policy of the empire" submitted to a meeting of the Liaison Council on September 3, 1941. Faced with the either-or logic of this plan, Japan's leaders decided to go to war with the United States if an agreement regarding oil was not reached by early October. Two days later at a briefing for an Imperial Conference, the emperor said, "This would seem to give precedence to war." Konoe replied that such was not the case; war would come only if diplomacy failed. The naval chief of staff, when asked what a war would mean, compared Japan to a patient critically ill, an operation, though extremely dangerous, might save his life. At the Imperial Conference held the next day that approved this fateful decision, the emperor read a poem by the Meiji emperor:

> *Since all are brothers in the world,*
> *Why is there such constant turmoil?*

What did Japan have in mind when considering the possibility of war? During World War II some fantastic reports of Japanese aims were circulated in the United States: that Japan expected to dictate the terms of peace from the White House or to reduce the United States to the original Thirteen Colonies. This was nonsense. No person in a position of responsibility in Japan held such views. The strategy was to carve out an area within which economic self-sufficiency would be possible and to defend it until the United States tired of war. This was to be achieved by sinking America's Pacific fleet—a stroke in which Japan succeeded, missing only the aircraft carriers. The Japanese plan assumed the victory of Germany in Europe, the defeat of England, and the collapse of the Chinese government, all of which seemed probable in late 1941. It further assumed that, with these conditions fulfilled, Japan could fight the United States on a one-to-one basis in East Asia. It bet the land-based airpower, shorter supply lines, and supposed greater will power of Japan against the greater productivity of America. Beyond war were vague schemes for the division of the world into spheres (Japanese, German, Russian, and American) and the transformation of international relations into intersphere relations.

Yet, though the decision had been taken to go to war if oil were not obtained through negotiations, most Japanese leaders still felt that diplomacy would win out. Japanese efforts to this end began seriously in July 1941 and continued frantically even after the September decision and the formation of the Tōjō cabinet in October. (Of course, the negotiations for peace were accompanied by the move into Indo-China mentioned earlier and by preparations for the Pacific war—Pearl Harbor was rehearsed for months in advance at Kagoshima Bay in southern Kyūshū.)

In July 1941 the second Konoe cabinet was dissolved and the third Konoe cabinet formed in order to get rid of the pro-German foreign minister,

Matsuoka. Concessions were planned. The reasoning of Japan's leaders was that the United States had little effective power in the western Pacific. If Japan pledged minor withdrawals, then the United States ought to be willing to rescind its embargo on oil. War would be averted, and the long-term political outcome in East Asia would depend on the result of the war in Europe. Konoe pressed for a meeting with Roosevelt. He apparently was willing to stipulate that Japan would not go to war with the United States under the provisions of the Axis Pact even if American actions involved it in a war with Germany. More than this the "peace party" in Japan could not offer. Had negotiations been successful, it is conjectural whether the Japanese military services would have accepted this much. The army was clearly not willing to give up its conquests in China, or even to return to the status quo ante of 1937. The navy was aware that the United States' ship-building program, launched by Roosevelt in 1940, would gradually diminish Japan's naval superiority in the western Pacific. Perhaps Japanese military planning had progressed so far that these negotiations were little more than window-dressing—however seriously they were intended by civilian leaders.

In contrast to Konoe's realism, the reasoning of Secretary of State Cordell Hull, the dominant voice in shaping American Far Eastern policy, was sternly moral. Japan was an aggressor. Any compromise would sanction aggression. The United States should not negotiate unless Japan underwent a change of heart. The last chance to put off the war came in November when Japan offered as a temporary *modus vivendi* to turn the clock back to June 1941: withdrawal of Japanese troops from southern Indo-China in return for oil and a United States "hands off" policy toward China. Roosevelt was interested, but Hull blocked acceptance. He feared that any sudden change in American policy would endanger the network of relations that had been established between the United States and Britain, Holland, Australia, and China. He countered by submitting to the Japanese a ten-point program requiring the withdrawal of all Japanese armed forces from Indo-China and China. Behind this uncompromising stand was a calmness and a sense of the ampleness of time that ultimately rested on the belief that Japan would not dare to attack the United States, and that, if it did, it could be quickly and easily defeated.

The Japanese took Hull's program as the rejection of further negotiations. Possessed by the vision of an East Asia dominated by Japan and trapped in a timetable of their own making, they attacked Pearl Harbor on December 7, 1941.

The Nature of Japanese Militarism.   Modern society has both democratic and totalitarian potentials. Industrialization, universal education, the nationalism that enables a government to tap the political energies of the masses, communications and transport, and even modern weapons can be used to create new freedoms or to suppress human rights. Both Nazi Germany and the Soviet Union of Stalin exemplified the totalitarian potential of modern, or modernizing, societies. Postwar Japanese historians, viewing their own history in terms of world experience, have been almost unanimous in terming the changes of the thirties as the growth of fascism in Japan. There were indeed many points of similarity.

Both Japan and Germany moved away from parliamentary government. In both countries a narrow-minded nationalism and the use of terror by a revolutionary right contributed to the rise of authoritarianism. Both limited the freedoms of speech, press, and assembly; and in both, liberals and leftists who attempted to speak out against aggression or oppressive legislation were persecuted. Both were expansionist, aggressive states. Thus, at a high level of abstraction it is possible to combine these features of Japan and Germany with their common historical character as late modernizers and construct a "fascist model" of political change. Yet the differences between Japan and Germany seem as important as the similarities.

First, their governmental structures were basically dissimilar. Germany had undergone the Weimar change; its government was completely parliamentary and power was in the hands of the dominant coalition of parties in the Reichstag. To gain power the Nazis had to obtain a plurality of the votes in a national election. Japanese government in the 1930's was still at the "pre-Weimar" stage. As in Germany before World War I, the Diet was only one of several elites. A shift could occur in the character of the government without a shift in the balance of party power in the Diet. Victory at the polls was not a prerequisite for the rise of authoritarian government.

Second, not only was Japanese government in the 1930's more like that in Germany before World War I, but its society was also considerably less "modern" than that of Hitler's Germany. In Germany there was an almost point-to-point correlation between economic change and political polarization. After the runaway inflation of 1922–1923 both the Nazis and the Communists rose from very small beginnings to become major parties in the elections of 1924—at the expense of the centrist parties. The economic stabilization achieved by 1928 caused both parties to decline sharply at the polls. Then, in the wake of the world depression both spurted ahead in the early thirties and the numerically superior Nazis maneuvered themselves into power. Of this pattern one can say that the direct relation between the individual's awareness of his predicament and his reaction to politics at the national level was pathological, not normal. It reflected the breakdown of intermediate institutions—business, welfare, judiciary, police—that ordinarily buffered the relation between the individual and the state. The Weimar framework was used to carry out what amounted to direct plebiscites between two extreme, antiparliamentary programs.

In contrast, the traditional (post-1890) social structure was relatively firm in Japan. The two major parties were both centrist, and they were never seriously challenged by an extremist mass party. They continued to get the bulk of the votes, and often the votes went to the more parliamentary of the two. The revolutionary extremist groups that came to prominence in 1931–1936 had little influence on the support given to the Seiyūkai and the Minseitō at the polls. And these two parties totally defeated the government-supported parties in the 1936 and 1937 elections. The only other tendency visible in the elections of the 1930's was the slow secular trend in favor of semiliberal socialist parties. Behind the stability in Japanese voting was the fact that intermediate institutions—as in the 1920's—were in good condition. They "contained" the misery of the poorer peasants and workers in the worst years of the depression. The Japanese middle class, such as it was, was also in better shape than its German equivalent. War and inflation wiped out the savings of the middle class in Germany; when the depression came there was nothing for it to fall back on. The Japanese middle class did very well during the war and the 1920's without encountering any serious inflation. The depression hurt small and medium-sized businesses, but bank savings and salaries were worth more than ever. Many remember the early thirties as the "best" period in prewar Japan.

Third, because the government structures and societies were different, the process by which the "antiparliamentary forces" rose was also very different. The Nazis rose as a mass party with a revolutionary program. Taking over the government, the Nazi party remade it in its own image, step by step establishing authoritarian controls. Having created a totalitarian regime, it then made war. Without exaggerating its efficiency, there is no denying its dynamism. But in Japan the antiparliamentary forces were not a dynamic, purposive, united group. It is hard even to characterize those who in the 1930's gradually replaced the party leaders in the cabinets, except to say that they were ex-bureaucrats and ex-military men, former members of the Peers and former members of the Privy Council. Those men did not plot to seize power. Rather, they were appointed in the hope that they would be more effective than the parties in controlling the army. The times were not propitious for the parties, so nonparty prime ministers and then more and more nonparty ministers were appointed. Behind this "drift" within the establishment were the disputes, maneuvers, and compromises among the multiple elites of government. Communications were often poor and actions uncoordinated. One Japanese scholar has described Japan's path to war as a gradual nervous breakdown within the system. The most dynamic groups

Ceremonial send-off given by schoolmates for a student entering the army.

were the military services, which tended to confuse military strategy with national policy. Military services tend to be politically strong in early modernizing states and weak in fully modern states. Japan was not fully modern. Within a relatively modern state structure, the power of the Japanese army and navy stemmed from the fact that legally they had never been fully subordinated to civil control. By the summer of 1937 Japan was less parliamentary than in 1931, but was not yet totalitarian in the Nazi sense.

The first turning point came when Japan blundered into war with China. The second turning point was Pearl Harbor. War led to wartime controls. A Liaison Council was formed to coordinate policy making between the cabinet and services. A Planning Board was established to direct wartime economic expansion and administer economic controls over resources, labor, trade, prices, wages, and public services. The economy became laced and overlaced with regulations, moving largely in response to government direction. Finally an Imperial Rule Assistance Association—patterned after the Nazi "one country, one party" model—was set up for spiritual mobilization and all of Japan's major political parties were brought within it as well as unions, veterans organizations, and many others. Such control made Japan into something more of a totalitarian state by 1941. Moreover, official controls were reinforced by community and family pressures far greater than those in the West. These demanded "right thoughts" as well as "right actions," and led to the ethical climate in which university students could be recruited as suicide pilots in the last desperate years of the war. But Japan in this period is better labeled militarist than fascist. The basic state apparatus was not new or revolutionary, but merely the old "establishment," now dominated by the military elite, overlaid by controls, and swept up in a spiritual nationalism. When the war ended, opinion shifted and the controls were removed, and until the reforms of the Occupation took hold, the basic state structure was much the same as it had been earlier.

Finally, the spiritual difference between Nazi Germany and militarist Japan was immense. In Germany Teutonic myths were used as a vehicle for values that would sanction aggression, but the myths were never presented as literal truth. The problem of reconciling myth with science did not arise. The break with the past was with the moral position of Christianity, liberalism, and socialism. The enormity of the break necessitated concentration camps for those who opposed Nazi power. In Japan it was not necessary to disinter archaic myths. They were still alive in the traditional sector of Japan's cultural double-structure and could be used to justify Japanese expansion.

Moreover, along with myths, there was a rational dimension to the Japanese position in the 1930's. Certainly the colonial powers of the West were hypocritical in condemning Japan's takeover of Manchuria. In the depression world of rising tariff barriers and preferential markets, arguments for economic autarky were reasonable, even if the means taken to obtain it were not. As a result, most Japanese could make the transition from the liberal orthodoxy of the 1920's to the wartime orthodoxy of the late 1930's with little sense of a moral break. Many persons were sent to prison, but concentration camps were unnecessary. And after the war, although antimilitarism (the total rejection of the policies of the former leadership) was strong, there was little sense of individual guilt—except in the attitudes of intellectuals toward the countries overrun in Asia.

26. The New Japan

World War II in East Asia

At times, history seems to follow a yin-yang dialectic: any action pushed to an extreme results in an opposite reaction. The objectives of the Japanese leaders who began World War II in East Asia were to maintain Japan's position in Manchuria, gain a new empire, preserve the conservative "national polity," and oppose communism in Asia. Instead, the result of the war was the total loss of Japan's colonial empire, the destruction of the old polity, and the rise of Communist China.

One of the stated objectives of the Japanese during the war was the liberation of Asian colonies from the yoke of European imperialism. "Asia for the Asians," said Japanese spokesmen, proclaiming their own Monroe Doctrine for the continent. The "liberated" countries found Japan's New Order to be harsher than the former colonial rule. Still, changes occurred during the Japanese occupations that made the reestablishment of the colonies after the war impossible. In the long run, this may have been the most significant consequence of the Pacific War.

Pearl Harbor and Japan's Blitzkrieg in East Asia. On the morning of December 7, 1941, a Japanese surprise attack by carrier-based planes sank seven U.S. battleships and many lesser vessels and destroyed more than half of the American aircraft at Pearl Harbor and the other American bases in Hawaii. This was a brilliant tactical victory for Japan. Yet public opinion in the United States, so long divided by isolationism, immediately became unified. Further Japanese expansion in Southeast Asia would have left the American people divided and uncertain, but the attack on Pearl Harbor shocked them into an all-out war effort.

The shock became even greater when Americans realized that the losses at Pearl Harbor were related more to their unpreparedness of mind than to lack of materiel. U.S. Ambassador Joseph C. Grew had warned from Tokyo that Japan might attack with dramatic suddenness, as in previous wars. And Washington, on the basis of decoded Japanese secret messages, had been expecting an attack somewhere for weeks. At Pearl Harbor, enemy submarines had been sighted and depth charges dropped, and the approaching planes had actually been detected by radar well before the attack. Yet on that Sunday morning the American forces were not awake to the danger.

The Pearl Harbor disaster would have been even greater had not three aircraft carriers of the Pacific Fleet been at sea, thus remaining unharmed, and had the sunken battleships not been close to obsolescence. But a second disaster followed immediately afterward in the Philippines, where United States bases were undermanned, poorly armed, and inadequately linked by communications. When news of the outbreak of war reached these islands, U.S. bombers and fighters took to the air, but then landed for lunch and refueling and Japanese air attacks caught them on the ground lined up wing to wing. The commander in the Philippines was General Douglas MacArthur. A third disaster occurred on the following day, when the British battleship *Prince of Wales* and the battlecruiser *Repulse,* lacking air cover, were sunk off Malaya by carrier-based Japanese planes.

These disasters pulled the cork from the Southeast Asian bottle. The Japanese launched amphibious drives through the Philippines, Borneo, and the Celebes, and through Malaya and Sumatra to Java. Japanese troops advanced through "impenetrable" jungles to take Singapore, at the tip of the Malayan peninsula, from the rear. Its only defenses facing the sea, the great naval base fell in February 1942. Japan expanded overland from Indochina to Thailand to Burma. Victory followed upon victory. The Philippines were conquered by April, and by the end of May Japanese troops in northern Burma had closed the Burma road, cutting off most supplies to China. In the Pacific, too, Japan went on the offensive, taking the western Aleutian Islands of Kiska and Attu in the Bering Sea, and moving into the Solomon, Ellice and Gilbert island chains in the central Pacific, and into northern New Guinea. By the summer of 1942, Japan possessed a vast oceanic and continental empire stretching four thousand miles south from Sakhalin almost to Australia, and six thousand miles from Burma east to the Gilberts.

Japan's Attempt to Consolidate Its Conquests.   In the second phase of the war, from mid-1942 to mid-1944, Japan tried to develop its empire and exploit it economically, while the Allies assailed its periphery.

The area overrun by Japan was culturally diverse. Burma, Cambodia, and Thailand were Theravada Buddhist in culture. Vietnam had a mixture of Mahayana Buddhism and Confucianism. The peoples of Malaya and most of the Dutch East Indies were Muslim, and those of the Philippines had an American-Spanish Catholic culture with an admixture of indigenous elements. The peoples of each area spoke different languages and had different ethnic origins and different national histories. With the exception of Vietnam, Japan's new conquests were not a part of the East Asian culture zone. For this reason and also because of wartime pressures, only a weaker and severely modified form of the "Japanese colonial pattern" that had developed in Taiwan, Korea, and Manchuria could be applied in these areas.

Within these limitations, the Japanese attempted to supplant the long-established Western colonial governments, and to meet the need for raw materials and markets that had emerged from the depression and political developments of the thirties and had inspired the whole push southward. Japan sought to accomplish both goals simultaneously by creating a Greater East Asia Co-Prosperity Sphere, an autarkic economic community, mutually beneficial to Japan and the countries it had conquered. To deal with the national governments within the sphere—and to keep the Foreign Ministry from meddling in the affairs of the army—a Greater East Asia Ministry was established in Tokyo in November 1942. Staffed by civilians, this ministry was responsible for a variety of cultural exchange programs and for foreign relations within the new empire. But the real power in the conquered areas was held by military administration teams responsible, through the local army commanders, to the Army General Staff in Tokyo.

As in Taiwan and Korea, the Japanese occupiers attempted to implant a new cultural and moral order—their particular blend of the East Asian tradition and the Japanese pattern of modernity. Their occupation policies embodied the ambivalence toward the West so strong in wartime Japan itself: a utilization of Western technology and cultural forms that made Japan the most advanced and Westernized Asian nation, together with an attack on Western materialism, communism, and liberal, individualistic values. In founding its New Order, Japan tried to revitalize traditional forms of social authority by strengthening the power of the family head, subordinating women to male authority, and stressing filial piety, loyalty, and group responsibility. Japan also supported the local religious traditions as conservative forces promoting order. Just as Confucianism and

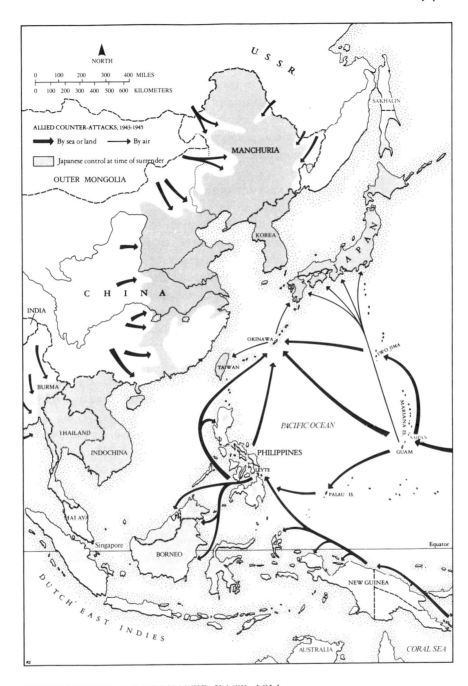

WORLD WAR II IN GREATER EAST ASIA

the "Kingly Way" had been promoted in Manchukuo and North China, so the Japanese encouraged Buddhism in Thailand and Burma, Islam in Malaya and the Dutch East Indies, and Catholicism in the Philippines. They invited religious and cultural leaders and local dignitaries to visit Japan, and sent teachers to each area to make Japanese the second language and the medium for intrasphere communication. Under the wartime conditions in the occupied areas, refusing to learn the Japanese language became a form of passive resistance.

Although the occupations went smoothly enough during 1942 and 1943 while the Allies were still unable to mount a counteroffensive, in the end Japan's New Order was unsuccessful. In Southeast Asia, Japan had neither the time nor the resources to carry out programs of mass education, to develop communications and transportation, to achieve striking advances in agricultural productivity, and to integrate the diverse area into its own economy, as it had done in Taiwan and Korea. But even if there had been time, Japan was no substitute for the world economy: it could neither absorb all of Southeast Asia's tropical exports, nor could its strained wartime economy supply the needed industrial products. In the last years of the war as Japanese shipping dwindled, it was unable even to transport the raw materials the occupied countries produced. These areas were thrown back onto stagnant, subsistence economies subject to maldistribution, shortages, and inflation, all of which resulted in severe hardships to the local populations.

In the occupied countries the response to the Japanese conquests took the form of nationalism. Prior to World War II, nationalism had been rising in all of the colonial states of Asia, yet nowhere had it been strong enough to oust the colonial power. Billing themselves as the champions of Asia against Western imperialism, the Japanese occupiers attempted to encourage and use nationalism to obtain local cooperation. Thus, in one area Japan called its takeover a "liberation," in another it granted "independence" to a native government, and in a third it set up a native government where none had existed before. In the early years this policy worked well, but as the local economies deteriorated and it became clear that the Allies would win the war, the nationalist movements turned against Japan. Again, there was no uniform pattern to this response. Thailand, for example, which had been independent before the war, was given new territories by the Japanese and kept considerable autonomy during the war. A "Free Thai" movement arose in the last years of the war but there was little fighting; Japanese troops remained well-disciplined in Thailand, and no anti-Japanese feelings persisted after the war. In the Philippines, in contrast, independence had been promised by the United States, and pro-American sentiment was widespread; a strong anti-

Japanese resistance movement arose, and it was harshly suppressed. In addition, during the fighting to recapture the Philippines, Japanese military discipline broke down and many atrocities were committed. This left a residue of embitterment against Japan that shaped Philippine attitudes in the postwar era.

In most of the occupied countries, there was continuity between wartime nationalist leaders and postwar leaders. In Indonesia, for example, the Dutch had ruled through minorities. After the war, the government of the Muslim majority established by the Japanese was successful in winning independence from the Dutch. In Indochina, contradictions in the Japanese attitude toward nationalism were particularly sharp. On the one hand the Japanese army, short of military administrators, ruled Indochina through the Vichy French officials and tried to suppress the nationalist movement. (The Viet Minh policy was to avoid clashes with Japanese troops.) On the other hand, Japanese generals in Saigon denounced European imperialism, younger Japanese officers were openly contemptuous of the French, and early in 1945, after the fall of the Vichy government in France, the Japanese arrested the French officials and proclaimed Vietnamese independence. Then, when the war ended, the Japanese acquiesced in Ho Chi Minh's establishment of the "Democratic Republic of Vietnam," which led to the anticolonial movement of the postwar period.

The Allied Drive on Japan. If World War I was the first "industrial war" in history—the first in which raw materials were processed into armaments and hastily mobilized civilians were processed into soldiers, with both then shipped to front lines and expended in massive quantities—then World War II was the first "industrial-*scientific* war." It was a war of attrition, in which Japanese forces were ground down by a steadily growing American industrial-military power. Already stretched taut by the war with China, the Japanese economy could not match the American capacity for rapid expansion. It was also a war of science and technology. At the start, Japan probably had an edge with its superior Zero fighter planes and long-distance torpedoes—that contrasted sharply with the less maneuverable fighters and ineffective torpedoes used by the United States during the first twenty-one months of the war. But America then pulled ahead, developing new planes, radar, homing torpedoes, proximity fuses, new medicines, and eventually the atomic bomb.

The Allied counterattack in the Pacific was slowed by two factors: the Anglo-American decision to defeat Germany first and the start-up time to convert the U.S. economy to war production. The first major engagement in the Pacific War was the Battle of the Coral Sea, fought northeast of Australia in May 1942. A month later, a large Japanese armada approached Midway Island, the westernmost island in the Hawaiian chain, hoping to annihilate the U.S. Pacific Fleet. But U.S. cryptoanalysts broke the Japanese naval codes and American planes sank the four aircraft carriers of the superior Japanese fleet. Having lost its striking force, Japan was henceforth on the defensive. But it managed to hang onto its new empire for two more years.

In the final phase of the war, two great amphibious island-hopping offensives brought Allied troops to the doorstep of Japan. In one of the most destructive and costly campaigns of the war, one Allied offensive began in the south and swept up from the Solomons to New Guinea and on to the Philippines. By June 1945, the Philippines were in Allied hands. Earlier, MacArthur had pledged to return to the Philippines, and he did, but some military historians challenge the necessity of this southern offensive. The other Allied offensive pushed straight across the central Pacific from the Gilberts to the Marshalls and Carolines, and then took a thousand-mile jump to the Marianas and Iwo Jima. Saipan and Tinian in the Marianas brought Japan within U.S. bomber range. Iwo Jima became a haven for disabled U.S. planes returning from Japan. In April 1945, the two offensives converged on Okinawa, which fell in June. The offensives combined carrier-based air superiority, naval barrages, perfected amphibious techniques, landing crafts, and men. Considering the size of these small islands, the losses were staggering. At Okinawa more than 85 percent of the defenders were killed and there were 49,100 Allied casualties, about a fifth at sea, where massed attacks by Japanese suicide planes called *kamikaze* ("the divine wind") sank 34 ships and damaged 368 others.

One critical factor in the Pacific War was the Allied success in isolating Japan from its empire by destroying its merchant marine, navy, and naval air power. At the start of the war, Japan had a merchant marine of 6 million tons. Conquest and new construction brought this to a total of more than 10 million tons. By the end of the war, all but 1.8 million tons, mostly small wooden ships plying coastal waters, had been sunk. Shells from surface ships accounted for 10 percent of the Japanese losses, bombs from aircraft for 30 percent, and torpedoes from submarines for almost 60 percent. Submariners made up 2 percent of the United States naval personnel but sank thirteen hundred Japanese vessels.

As Japan became less able to transport men, equipment, food supplies, and raw materials, its economy began to weaken and its empire to wither on the vine. Bypassed by the Allied offensives, China, Burma, Malaya, Thailand, Indochina, the Dutch East Indies, and the remaining Japanese bases on Pacific islands became irrelevant to the course of the war. Chinese and Russian offensives at the end of the war affected the postwar situation, but contributed little to the defeat of Japan.

A second factor was the destruction by bombing of Japan's industries and urban housing. Begun during the second half of 1944, the raids mounted in intensity and in the months preceding surrender culminated in saturation bombings by thousand-plane flights. Terrible destruction was wrought on the dense populations and wooden houses of Japan's cities. In one raid in March 1945, Allied planes dropped incendiary bombs in parallel swathes across Tokyo, unleashing a firestorm in which more than 100,000 people died. In all, 668,000 civilians were killed and 2.3 million homes destroyed. By the last days of the war, railroads were breaking down, coal production was falling, oil was almost gone, aircraft production was dropping, nonmilitary industrial production was nil, and the average civilian was consuming fewer than fifteen hundred calories a day. The horror of war had become a part of the daily life of millions of Japanese. Japan was beaten, yet would not acknowledge defeat.

The Politics of War and Defeat.   At the outset of war, General Tōjō Hideki was both prime minister and his own army minister. Wearing two hats, he could oversee both civil and military affairs. He donned a third hat in February 1944, becoming chief of the General Staff to coordinate administrative and command functions within the army. In a general election in April 1942, the government-sponsored Imperial Rule Assistance Association secured the election of a pro-Tōjō Diet, which assured him of support in that quarter as well. Controlling the top posts and this broad base, he continued in power until July 1944.

Yet, as noted in the preceding chapter, Tōjō was no Hitler. He was the first among the many generals and admirals who led the military services. The military services were the most powerful elites of wartime Japan. But the Meiji constitution remained in force and the other nonmilitary elites continued to function. Above Tōjō was the emperor, and around the emperor were the senior statesmen—the inner minister, the president of the Privy Council, and the various former prime ministers such as Konoe, Yonai, and Hiranuma—who maintained extensive contacts with officials of the numerous wartime ministries.

From the start, Japan planned to negotiate a peace when the United States grew tired of fighting. Its leaders envisioned a military standoff in the mid-Pacific. When the tide turned in 1944, the men around the emperor favored negotiation: make peace before all is lost and before army radicals impose a system of "imperial communism." But in Japan's wartime atmosphere, and after years of spiritual mobilization, even these highly placed men met in secret and could not speak out, fearing assassination by army fanatics. The fall of Saipan and the start of bombing raids on Japan provoked a crisis: the senior statesmen joined with cabinet ministers to oust Tōjō. In his place they appointed General Koiso Kuniaki as prime minister (July 1944–April 1945) and the moderate Admiral Yonai Mitsumasa (former prime minister, January–July 1940) as deputy prime minister and naval minister. Koiso's cabinet was toppled in turn by the April invasion of Okinawa. The senior statesmen selected as his successor an old but prestigious admiral, Suzuki Kantarō, former head of the Privy Council. Suzuki appointed as his foreign minister Tōgō Shigenori, a diplomat who favored an early peace. Yet even the new foreign minister could not accede to the Allied demand for an unconditional surrender that left unclear the emperor's fate. In public all reaffirmed Japan's intention to fight to the end.

At Yalta, in February 1945, the Soviet Union had pledged to enter the war against Japan within three months of Germany's surrender, which came in May. At Potsdam, in July, the Allies told Japan to choose between an "order of peace, security, and justice" if it would surrender and "utter destruction" if it refused to capitulate. The official Japanese response was a decision "to press forward resolutely to carry the war to a successful conclusion." Faced with the high casualties expected in an autumn invasion of Japan, U.S. President Harry S Truman decided to use the atomic bombs that had been developed too late to use against Germany. Hiroshima was obliterated on August 6. Russia, which had been moving troops from Europe to Asia since the German surrender, declared war on Japan on August 8 and invaded Manchuria. The following day a second atomic bomb destroyed Nagasaki.

Even after these catastrophes, the Japanese military remained adamant, unmoved by those in the cabinet and Supreme Council who favored surrender. Therefore, an Imperial conference was called, at which the emperor broke the deadlock with the decision to surrender. All insisted, however, that the prerogatives of the emperor as "sovereign ruler" must not be prejudiced. The Allied reply was that he would be under Allied control and his fate would be determined by the Japanese people. On the morning of August 14, a second imperial conference was called. Opinion split three to three: the two chiefs of staff and the army minister were in favor of continuing the war, and Navy Minister Yonai, Prime Minister Suzuki, and Foreign Minister Tōgō wanted to end it. The emperor gave his support to the group favoring unconditional surrender, saying that "the unendurable must be endured." It was a final commentary on the tenacity of the emperor-centered political orthodoxy that had emerged in Japan after 1890 that although Japan was smashed and beaten, only the emperor could sanction a surrender that put the emperor system in jeopardy.

The American Occupation and the Yoshida Ministries, 1945–1954

The first postwar decade set the pattern for Japan's future. The first segment of the decade was the American Occupation, which lasted only seven years. The Occupation succeeded because it built on earlier trends, yet also broke with the prewar system in revolutionary ways. It made changes that would not have occurred had Japan not been subject to a foreign power. The second and partially overlapping segment of the decade was the era of Yoshida Shigeru's prime ministries. Yoshida began as the reluctant implementer of Occupation reforms. Then, after being out of office for a year and a half, he returned to establish the policies—in some respects at odds with those of the United States—that with minor evolutionary changes would continue for decades afterwards.

The Setting of the Occupation.   In September 1945, Japan showed an openness to change unusual in history. Whole cities had been gutted by fires and bombings, factories had been damaged or destroyed, railroads were disrupted, and the people were hungry and ill-clothed. When the emperor's surrender speech was broadcast, the civilian populace had been girding for a final "battle of Japan." The surrender shattered the sense of national mission, leaving the Japanese psychically benumbed and without direction. Most Japanese were relieved that the war was over but apprehensive at what might follow.

The Japanese expected a cruel and harsh occupation but found a benevolent one. They feared a vindictive rule but found a constructive one. Under these conditions, the sense of duty that had enabled them to bear the sacrifices of war turned to positive, and at times even enthusiastic, cooperation with the new authorities. The rejection of wartime policies and the shift toward democracy were reinforced by the discovery that, contrary to what the Japanese people had believed during the war, their nation was reviled in all the countries that had been a part of its Co-Prosperity Sphere. Some Japanese writers, comparing this time marked by Japan's receptivity to change to the years after Perry, have labeled it the "second opening" of Japan.

It was of great significance that the Occupation was American. In 1945 Japan had both democratic and totalitarian potentials. On the one hand was the post-1890 parliamentary tradition; on the other, the prewar factors that had stifled this tradition and the wartime structure of economic controls and national mobilization. Had Japan been occupied by the Soviet Union, Japanese capabilities for national planning and collective endeavor would doubtless have made it a model Communist state. Occupied by the United States, however, it revived the parliamentary institutions of its modern tradition to move in the direction of a more open society. The basic American assumption was that a democratic Japan would be less likely to disturb the world's peace again. It was also in America's strategic interest to remake Japan in its own image—strengthening its representative system of government and making its capitalist economy more competitive—and thus building up America's own side in the cold war with the Soviet Union that after the war spread rapidly from Europe to East Asia. Like the Soviet Union's establishment of a totalitarian Communist state in North Korea, the democratization of Japan contributed to the polarization of the postwar world.

The Structure of the Occupation.   In theory, the Occupation was international, with a thirteen-nation Far Eastern Commission in Washington and a four-power Allied Council for Japan in Tokyo. General Douglas MacArthur was given the title of Supreme Commander for the Allied Powers (SCAP) and the whole Occupation administration under him also came to be known as SCAP. In fact, the Occupation was carried out almost entirely by MacArthur, his staff, and the American and some British troops under his command. MacArthur was in many ways the ideal man for the post. He viewed himself as a man of destiny acting on the stage of history. Self-confident and speaking in broad historical themes, he inspired the Japanese during the hard early postwar years, giving them hope for a better future. He was also ideal from the point of view of American politics: as a conservative Republican under a Democratic administration, he could carry out the most radical reforms without arousing criticism at home.

Unlike Germany, Japan was not governed directly by foreign troops. The army of occupation ruled through the Japanese administrative structure. The General Headquarters of SCAP under MacArthur was in Tokyo, and it contained various staff sections roughly parallel to the ministries of the Japanese government. In the prefectures were "military government" teams, which acted as an inspectorate to ascertain that reforms enacted into law were carried out. Liaison between the SCAP sections in which policy was formulated and the Japanese government was undertaken by the Central Liaison Office, staffed chiefly by Foreign Ministry personnel. After 1948, the liaison arrangement was eliminated in favor of direct contact with government ministries.

Some criticized the pattern of SCAP rule, saying that the same bureaucracy that had formerly followed the dictates of the Japanese military now followed the American military, and pointing out that this was

The Japanese emperor visits General MacArthur. In his 1946 New Year's rescript Emperor Hirohito reaffirmed the Meiji Charter Oath, including the "elimination of misguided practices of the past" and "love of mankind," and referred to "the false conception that the emperor is divine." MacArthur commented that the emperor "squarely takes his stand for the future along liberal lines. His action reflects the irresistible influence of a sound idea."

poor preparation for democracy. In the early years there was an uneasy tension between the supposed power of a democratized Diet and the actual power of SCAP. Yet in practice, after the initial reforms, SCAP gradually turned over the reins of government to the Japanese.

Occupation policies were based on a devil theory of history: that Japan's leaders since the early 1930s had been engaged in a giant conspiracy to wage aggressive war. This view was clearly brought out in the Tokyo war crimes trials. The leaders had attained their ends because Japanese society was "feudal," its values militaristic, its huge financial combines "merchants of death," and its political system reactionary. So faulted was Japan's character that only the most radical action could reform it. This theory of conspiracy was partly false and partly exaggerated, but it was responsible for the thoroughness of the early reforms. American conservatives became radical, and joining with liberal New Dealers, enacted reforms that would have been impossible otherwise. The Occupation's enthusiasm for the job of democratizing Japan often outran its grasp of the situation, but it was dedicated and largely successful.

Demilitarization and Reform. The Occupation began with the liquidation of the apparatus of Japanese militarism. The empire was dismembered and all Japanese abroad, soldiers and civilians alike, were returned to Japan. The military services were demobilized; paramilitary and ultranationalist organizations were dissolved. Shinto was disestablished. Armaments industries were dismantled. The Home Ministry was abolished. The police were decentralized, their powers curtailed, and their authority to regulate speech and "thought" revoked. Political prisoners were released from jail.

The Occupation next acted to remove the old leadership. Twenty-five of the top leaders were brought to trial for having begun the war. Seven of these, including General Tōjō, were hanged in December 1948. Most of the others were given long prison sentences. In retrospect, it is clear that Japanese militarism was not of the same genus as Nazism (it ran no Dachaus) and that the application of the principles of the Nuremberg trials at Tokyo was winner's justice. The Occupation also purged—in the sense of barring from office—about 200,000 former politicians, military officers, and businessmen. This brought to the fore a younger generation of Japanese, better able to adjust to the reforms of the Occupation.

The most significant reform was the enactment of the 1947 constitution. The Meiji constitution had begun:

Having, by virtue of the glories of Our Ancestors, ascended the Throne of a lineal succession unbroken for ages eternal; desiring to promote the welfare of, and to give development to the moral and intellectual faculties of Our beloved subjects . . . We hereby promulgate . . . a fundamental law of the State, to exhibit the principles, by which We are to be guided in Our conduct, and to point out to what Our descendants and Our subjects and their descendants are forever to conform.

The new constitution began:

We, the Japanese people, acting through our duly elected representatives in the National Diet, determined that we shall secure for ourselves and our posterity the fruits of peaceful cooperation with all nations and the blessings of liberty throughout this land, and resolved that never again shall we be visited with the horrors of war through the action of government, do proclaim that sovereign power resides with the people and do firmly establish this Constitution.

The 1947 constitution transformed Japan's political life, making Japan into a truly parliamentary state. Some of the major changes were:

1. Some prewar elites (the military services, the Privy Council, etc.) were abolished and others were strictly subordinated to the cabinet.
2. The cabinet, on the British model, became a "committee" of the majority party or coalition in the Diet.
3. Both houses of the Diet became fully elective, and the franchise was extended to all men and women aged twenty or over. The 466 (later increased to 491, and then to 511) members of the more powerful House of Representatives were chosen from 124 electoral districts, which usually had 3 to 5 seats each, allowing a certain degree of pro-

portional representation. The 250 members of the House of Councilors were to be chosen from prefectures (150) and from the nation at large (100).

4. The judiciary was made independent, and the Supreme Court was given the power to pass on the constitutionality of Diet legislation.

5. Governors of prefectures, as was already the case of mayors of municipalities, were made elective, and local government was given increased powers.

6. Human rights were guaranteed. Among these were the classic Western rights of assembly, a free press, and life, liberty, and the pursuit of happiness, but also included were newer rights such as "the right to maintain the minimum standards of wholesome and cultural living," "academic freedom," and the right of workers to bargain collectively.

The position of the emperor was also changed. Formerly sacred as well as sovereign, he was stripped of all "powers related to government" to become "the symbol of the state and of the unity of the people, deriving his position from the will of the people with whom resides sovereign power." The change in the actual role of the emperor was small, because, except for the surrender decision, he had not been a decision maker. But the change in theory was immense. That the emperor was not thrown out altogether eased the transition to the postwar world. Yet the effect of his changed position, going far beyond the political restructuring demanded by Yoshino Sakuzō in the 1920s, was to weaken myth and secularize the state. This was a decisive break with Japan's long Shinto tradition and the form it had taken in the Meiji constitution. The minority of conservatives who lamented the change usually cared less for the imperial institution itself than for the moral order associated with it. They sensed in the emperor a special kind of power by which the Humpty Dumpty of tradition might be put back together again. Those who subsequently fought to preserve the new constitution saw their struggle as directed against the total prewar syndrome of emperor, state, family system, and the obligations associated with each.

That Japan was ready for the new constitution became clear in the subsequent decades of parliamentary government. Yet the difficulty of effecting this reform clearly illustrates the nature of the Occupation as a revolution from outside. SCAP informed the prime minister of the importance of constitutional change in September 1945. The cabinet produced a draft constitution little different from that of Meiji. Thereupon, the Government Section of SCAP prepared its own draft for use as a "guide." A slightly modified version of this draft was then adopted, ostensibly in accordance with "the freely expressed will of the Japanese people," as an amendment to the Meiji constitution. One Japanese journalist wrote that some passages in the new constitution "by Japanese literary standards, sound quaintly and exotically American." His comment, like all references to the Occupation's direction of government reforms, was censored by SCAP.

Another achievement of the Occupation was land reform. It required the cooperation of SCAP and reformist-minded Japanese officials. All land owned by absentee landlords and all land held by others above ten acres per family was bought by the government and sold to former tenants on extremely easy credit terms. This left a maximum holding of seven and a half acres farmed by the owner himself and two and a half acres more to rent out. Since the land was paid for at preinflationary prices, this was tantamount to expropriation. The percentage of land worked by tenants dropped from 46 to 10 per cent, and rents were limited to modest levels. Because farmers prospered in hungry postwar Japan, debts were quickly paid off, and there emerged a countryside of small, independent, relatively prosperous, and politically conservative farmers.

In the modern sector of the economy, the target of the reformers was the *zaibatsu*. The first wave of reforms dissolved eighty-three *zaibatsu* holding companies, froze the assets of *zaibatsu* families, and then wiped out their fortunes with a capital levy. This broke the giant combines into their component subcombines, companies, and banks. To prevent their reestablishment, SCAP instituted antimonopoly laws and new inheritance and income taxes. In December 1947, SCAP planned the further deconcentration of twelve hundred companies, but this was abandoned as Occupation policy swung from reform to recovery.

Critics have argued that these reforms meant little and that the post-Occupation Japanese government ignored the antitrust laws. It is true that former *zaibatsu* companies tended to reestablish relations with the banks of their former combines. Depending heavily on these banking resources, and benefiting also from centralized marketing facilities and other business advantages, loose coalitions of industries emerged, each centering on a bank and a marketing company, and in some cases they readopted the old names—Mitsui group, Mitsubishi group, and so on. But there were differences too. The new coalitions were less hierarchical and much less closely knit than before the war, and their degree of control was very much reduced, permitting competing banks to be used. Some companies did not reestablish connections at all. And many important new companies emerged outside the *zaibatsu* tradition.

Along with "*zaibatsu*-busting," the Occupation helped labor unions. Workers were given the right to organize, bargain, and strike. New laws bettered the conditions of employees. Within this changed climate, men who had been active in the prewar labor movement again began to organize workers; by 1949, 6.5 million had joined unions and the number rose steadily for some years thereafter. More of the total labor force was unionized than in the United States, and only a little less than in England.

The vigor of labor's response at first delighted Occupation reformers. Their enthusiasm waned, however, when, instead of becoming an American-type labor movement, it became, like prewar Japanese unionism, political and Marxist. As the Occupation emphasis shifted toward economic recovery, SCAP took the position that further wage gains must await increases in production. In 1949, earlier labor laws were revised and a more restrictive Taft-Hartley type of legislation was passed. In 1950, Communist leaders were driven from the unions in the so-called Red Purge. These measures, however, had little immediate effect on the continuing vitality of the movement.

The surge of the labor movement within the new framework underlines a larger thesis that applies to the Occupation as a whole: though the Occupation was a revolution from outside, the response of the Japanese people, desiring more freedom and democracy, made the reforms successful. Without this, the changes would not have endured, and the swing away from the reforms after 1952 would have been far greater.

By the end of 1947, the Occupation had achieved its primary goals. The continued presence of foreign troops in Japan's cities, of censorship, and of SCAP direction of government could only provoke a negative reaction. The United States wanted to get out, but the Soviet Union, demanding a veto, blocked a peace treaty, so the Occupation drifted on for another five years. There were two policy shifts during these later years. One in 1948 was from reforms to an emphasis on economic recovery. The awful poverty of the early postwar years was no basis for a stable parliamentary democracy. A second shift occurred in June 1950, when North Korea invaded South Korea. The American concern turned from the Occupation to the war in Korea, and decision-making in Japan passed almost wholly into Japanese hands. When Japan finally regained its independence in 1952, the transition was almost imperceptible to the average citizen. A last object lesson of the power of civilian government in a democracy was given to the Japanese in April 1951, when President Truman fired General MacArthur for his disagreement over the conduct of the war in Korea.

The Yoshida Years. A 1984 public opinion poll asked, Who is the greatest Japanese figure of the twentieth century? The hands-down winner was Yoshida Shigeru (1878–1967).

Yoshida had an entire career in prewar Japan; his personal history almost spanned Japan's modern century. He was born a year after the Satsuma rebellion of 1877. One of fourteen children of a Tosa domain loyalist, he was adopted nine days after birth into the house of a wealthy

Yoshida Shigeru in 1954.

Yokohama trader, where he was raised as a "young master." He went to a Confucian school, to the elite Peers School, and then to the Law School of Tokyo Imperial University. After graduating, he entered the Foreign Ministry. His career, one biographer notes, coincided with the rise of imperial Japan, and his consciousness was that of the great empire of Japan. He was only moderately successful as a diplomat, for he belonged to the Anglo-American clique, not the mainstream German clique. On domestic social issues, he was deeply conservative, but he took the British empire as the model for Japan and advocated close ties between Japan, Great Britain, and the United States. From this standpoint, and with an independence of character rare among Japanese bureaucrats, he criticized Japan's twenty-one demands on China during World War I and the military during the early thirties, turning down the Washington embassy in 1932 as a protest against Japan's seizure of Manchuria. In 1936, he capped his career as ambassador to England. He spoke out against the Anti-Comintern Pact with Germany and Italy. He retired in 1939 at the age of sixty-one.

In the final year of World War II, Yoshida became a member of a conservative group centering on former Prime Minister Konoe Fumimaro. The group wanted to negotiate a peace to forestall the rise of "imperial communism" as conditions in Japan worsened. Nothing came of their plan, but Yoshida had the good fortune to be arrested by the military police and jailed for two months. This opened the way for his role in the Occupation era, first as foreign minister in the two early postwar cabinets, and then as president of the Liberal Party and prime minister after the sudden purge of Hatoyama Ichirō in April 1946. Yoshida was unenthusiastic about the Occupation reforms, but calling himself the "loyal servant of the emperor," he did his duty and carried them out.

Politics in the immediate postwar period was confused. Many ran for office as independents, and of those who were elected to the lower house in 1946, 81 per cent were new faces. By the 1947 election, however, politics had shaken down. The two great prewar conservative parties reemerged, as did the socialists, all with new names.

TABLE 26.1

	1937 Election			1947 Election
Minseitō	36% of vote	→	Democratic Party	25% of vote
Seiyūkai	35% of vote	→	Liberal Party	27% of vote
Social Mass Party	9% of vote	→	J. Socialist Party	26% of vote

The voting pattern was basically an extension of prewar trends; it was almost as if a decade of militarism and war had not intervened. The Socialists had five per cent of the vote in 1936 and 10 per cent in 1937; by 1947 the labor and white-collar votes were larger, so the Socialists' gains were substantial. Otherwise, the two conservative parties contended for power as they had in the prewar era. Their sense of rivalry was so strong that in 1947 the Democrats even joined with the Socialists for a short period to shut the Liberals out of power. But the coalition government did not work. The Liberals returned to power in 1948, won an absolute majority of lower house seats in 1949, and stayed in power until December 1954. Backed by both a popular mandate and the Occupation, Yoshida's style of governance was so autocratic that admirers and detractors alike called him "one man Yoshida." Yoshida saw himself as the builder of a new Japan that would preserve the values of the old—like the Meiji oligarchs whom he admired above all other figures in Japanese history.

Conditions in Japan in 1947 and 1948 were bleak. The empire was gone, the devastation of war was still in evidence, the population was swollen with discharged servicemen and Japanese returned from the colonies, and foreign trade was nil. Production in 1947 was only 37 per cent of the prewar level. Predictions about Japan's future were uniformly pessimistic. Yoshida's policy—sometimes called the Yoshida doctrine—was to give primacy to economic growth.

American aid, much of it in the form of foodstuffs, began in 1947. From 1948 on, SCAP emphasized recovery. Inflation hindered exports, so in 1949 SCAP forced Japan to adopt a politically unpopular austerity program. The first boom in manufacturing came during the Korean War, spurred by $4 billion worth of American military procurement orders. Yoshida called the war "a gift from the gods." By 1955, Japan's productivity had regained prewar levels.

Yoshida's singular emphasis on economic growth had a political context. In 1946, Yoshida had remarked to an associate that "history provides examples of winning by diplomacy after losing in war." The danger Japan faced in the postwar world, according to Yoshida, was that it might be drawn into the American-Soviet cold war and waste its substance on military spending. If that danger could be avoided, Japan might win. In short, though Yoshida was a hard-line conservative on domestic social and political issues—probusiness, antiunion, and strongly anti-Communist, his international policy was passive and sought to avoid military commitments.

John Foster Dulles, the special emissary of the U.S. Secretary of State, made the first of many visits to Japan in June 1950, which coincided with the outbreak of the Korean War. As the price for a peace treaty and the restoration of sovereignty, he demanded that Japan rearm. Yoshida refused. He cited Article 9 of the new constitution, in which "the Japanese people forever renounce war as a sovereign right of the nation," and will never maintain "land, sea, and air forces" or "other war potential." Yoshida pointed out Japan's economic weakness and persuaded MacArthur to back his position. There is evidence that he even encouraged the opposition Socialists to mount antirearmament demonstrations while Dulles was in Japan. Dulles was taken aback by this tough old man, and in the end gave more than he got, settling for only minimal concessions. On September 8, 1951, the United States and forty-seven other nations signed a treaty with Japan by which Japan regained its independence on April 28, 1952. The Soviet Union and China boycotted the proceedings.

On the day the peace treaty was signed, Japan also signed a Mutual Security Treaty with the United States. It provided what Yoshida wanted most: a long-term guarantee of Japan's security by the United States—later referred to as Japan's "nuclear umbrella." All subsequent Japanese defense planning occurred within the framework of this treaty. In return, Yoshida made two concessions to Dulles: United States bases in Japan and the establishment of a small Japanese military force—called the National Police Reserve in 1950 and renamed the National Safety Force in 1952 and the Self Defense Forces in 1954. The cost of this force was held thereafter at about 1 per cent of GNP, so little that foreign critics later accused Japan of enjoying a "free ride." Japan, it might be noted, made no guarantee regarding the security of the United States. Its new military forces could not be used outside Japan or its waters. The treaty was very much one between unequals. Of course, in 1950 Japan was in no condition to offer more. Given the strength of antimilitary sentiment in Japan, even the concessions it made seemed large. And as United Nations troops fought to repel the North Korean invasion of South Korea, Japan and its American bases became critical as a staging ground and workshop for the United Nations forces.

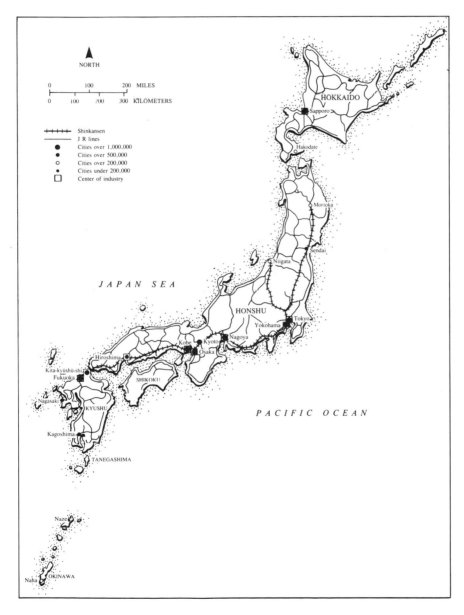

MODERN JAPAN

Social and Political Change in an Era of High Growth

The early postwar period ended when Yoshida's last ministry fell, in December 1954. There followed almost two decades of double-digit economic growth that transformed Japan. In 1955 Japan had recovered from the devastation of war but was still only marginally ahead of other Asian nations; by the mid-seventies Japan had attained a level of affluence comparable to that of Europe. Japan entered this era with a village society still in place; it emerged in the seventies a predominantly urban nation. It entered with a tiny educated elite and poorly educated masses; by the seventies it had undergone a cultural transformation, becoming a nation of high school and university graduates. The era opened with a bitter confrontation between the conservative and socialist parties; by the early seventies the kind of consensus needed for parliamentary politics had begun to take shape.

The Growth Economy.   Between the early 1950s and the early 1970's, the Japanese economy averaged an 11 per cent yearly growth. As with compound interest, the results were astonishing: gross national product rose by a factor of 20, while per capita product rose by a factor of 16.

TABLE 26.2

Twenty Years of Economic Growth

	GNP (in billions of dollars)	Per Capita GNP (in dollars)
1955	$ 24	$ 268
1960	43	461
1965	88	898
1970	203	1939
1975	484	4320

By 1975 Japan's economy was the third largest in the world, surpassed only by that of the United States and the Soviet Union, both continental nations with vast territories and resources. One economist argued that this was "the most extraordinary success story in all economic history"; others called it a "miracle." But it is better seen as a consequence of favorable conditions and a national policy that single-mindedly focused on development. An often heard slogan was "growth at any cost."

Some factors that contributed to postwar growth had been important in prewar times as well. Workers were diligent, literate, and technically skilled. A German industrialist visiting Japan in the late sixties commented—to the delight of his Japanese counterparts—that Japanese workers work the way German workers used to work. Japanese saved four or five times as much from their paychecks as did Americans. A bank advertisement on a Tokyo billboard in 1970 showed a smiling family—a mother, father, and a single child (a son). The caption read: "Happiness is a bank account with a million yen (about $3000)."

Some factors were new. A technological gap had opened between Japan and the United States during World War II, and the U.S. was willing to share its science and technology. Japan had the scientists and engineers needed to utilize this backlog, and they often improved on the technology they imported. Bringing in the most recent equipment, Japan leapfrogged ahead, and its industries became the most efficient in the world. One lesson that all but the most advanced countries can learn from Japan's experience is that it is cheaper to buy or license new technology than to develop it yourself. By the mid-seventies the backlog had all but disappeared.

Low military spending, a consequence of the Yoshida doctrine, was a key contributor to Japan's economic advance. Consider the following 1974 defense budgets (the countries are listed in order of economic size):

United States	$66.3 billion
Soviet Union	$61.9 billion
Japan	$ 1.9 billion
West Germany	$ 7.8 billion
France	$ 5.8 billion

Japan spent far less than the others. Its one per cent cap on military expenditures meant that its rising revenues could be put to productive purposes. The manufacturers of other nations, burdened by taxes for defense spending, had to compete with one hand tied behind their backs. Until the seventies, few countries knew enough about Japan to think of profiting from its example.

Even agricultural productivity increased. Japan's original agricultural revolution (1868–1920) was contemporary with its industrialization. The import of foodstuffs from the colonies during the 1920's led to a leveling off of domestic productivity. After 1945, fresh advances were made using more chemical fertilizers, new insecticides, light farm machinery, and new seed strains. Japan became self-sufficient in rice and increased its production of fruits and meat. Per unit of land, Japanese agriculture was the most efficient in the world. But in terms of output per farmer, it was one of the least efficient. The prices of domestically produced foodstuffs, usually several times the world level, were maintained by a system of subsidies and tariffs. The decision to maintain these was political, not economic.

Another vital contributor to growth was trade. Exports grew apace:

1955	$ 2.01 billion
1965	$ 8.45 billion
1975	$55.75 billion

It cannot simply be said that foreign trade was the motor of economic growth. Goods for the Japanese masses were produced by new giants, such as Matsushita, Toshiba, and Sony. The domestic market was critical in creating the economies of scale that made Japan so formidable a competitor abroad. As a per cent of GNP, Japan's exports were less than those of England, France, or West Germany. Still, trade was necessary to a Japan poorly endowed with raw materials. About three-fourths of Japan's imports in 1975 were raw materials, such as oil, ores, coking coal, steel scrap, rubber, cotton, wool, and lumber.

Japan's most important single trading partner was the United States, which in 1975 took more than 22 per cent of its exports. The openness of the American market was vital to Japan. Since more than half of United States sales to Japan were of raw materials or agricultural products and virtually all Japanese sales to the United States were of finished goods, a few American critics argued that the United States had become an economic colony of Japan. Japanese turned this argument around, saying that Japan had become a factory producing goods for the benefit of the United States, with its rich natural resources and more efficient agriculture. On the whole, criticism was muted, since American imports from and exports to Japan were balanced. Japan's second most important customers were the non-Communist nations of East, Southeast, and South Asia, which took 20 per cent of Japan's exports. This trade was balanced overall, but, country by country, those with raw materials sold more than they bought, while others coveted Japanese automobiles and machinery but had few products to sell in return. This occasioned political protests and a gradual increase in Japanese foreign aid. Europe provided fewer than 8 per cent of Japanese imports and took 14.4 per cent of Japanese exports. It feared Japanese competition and matched Japan in protectionist policies. Trade with China and the Soviet Union rose gradually during these two decades. In 1975, exports to Communist states were 8.4 per cent of the total.

During the fifties and sixties, the manufacturing process itself was characterized by a high degree of teamwork between labor and management. This was facilitated, to be sure, by steadily rising wages. Despite an ideology of class struggle that colored union pronouncements and led to the display of red flags in May Day parades, and despite labor's hard bargaining in the annual "spring offensives," there were few crippling strikes in

Japanese plants. Unions were organized on the basis of companies, not trades. Most workers in large companies enjoyed the security of lifetime employment and showed a high degree of company loyalty.

A final factor was the combination of free enterprise and government guidance that businessmen from other countries labeled "Japan, Inc." Several points may be noted. First, the Bank of Japan backed commercial banks in providing capital for investment—on the assumption that future profits would suffice to pay off debts. Whereas in the average American company two-thirds of the capital requirements were met by stock and one-third by debt, in Japan the percentages were reversed. This "overextended" banking credit effectively refinanced industry during these decades of rapid growth.

Next, the government was more deeply involved in planning than any other nonsocialist state and guided the economy with greater skill than any socialist state. The Finance Ministry and the Ministry of International Trade and Industry (commonly called MITI in English), coordinating their efforts through the Economic Planning Agency, cooperated in charting Japan's future expansion. They targeted growth industries, set production goals, and estimated foreign markets. And they rewarded growth with high depreciation allowances, cheap loans, subsidies, and light taxes. Some businesses benefited as well from research carried out in government laboratories that was then turned over to companies for commercial development.

A third aspect of in "Japan, Inc." was the protection the government afforded growth industries. The government permitted foreign competition mainly in areas where foreign companies could not compete or where Japanese production was not planned. It protected infant industries, particularly in new technologies, by successive walls of tariffs, quotas, currency controls, foreign investment controls, and bureaucratic red tape. And it welcomed only that foreign investment that brought in new technology, and then only as a minority interest. Between the late sixties and the early seventies, as Japan grew to superpower proportions, the justification for this protectionism disappeared. To maintain its access to other markets, Japan was forced to "liberalize," opening its own markets to the imports of other nations. However, by this time, few of the manufactured products of other countries were able to compete with Japanese goods.

Lastly, despite the government's large role in the economy, and despite the bureaucrats' continued claim to credit for Japan's progress, Japan was not a socialist country and competition among companies was fierce. Most decisions were made within companies, and each company rested on its own financial bottom. Throughout the economy, businessmen chafed at government regulations and government decisions were frequently wrong. The Japanese automobile industry was developed against the advice of MITI, which felt it inappropriate for a small, crowded country like Japan.

TABLE 26.3

Production of Cars

Year	Vehicles, in thousands
1953	8
1960	165
1970	3,178
1979	6,176

Still, Japanese businessmen took for granted a favorable and supportive business climate such as did not exist in most other countries.

By the early seventies, even the casual visitor to Japan was assaulted by evidence of well-being—television antennas sprouting from tile roofs, new office buildings with air-conditioning and automatic doors, men wearing dark blue suits and women stylishly dressed, the bustle of the city, and the whirring of farm equipment in the countryside. The trains were the best in the world—fast, clean, and punctual. The old trunk road between Tokyo and Osaka—the once scenic Tōkaidō familiar in the West through Hiroshige's woodblock prints—had become an almost unbroken industrial belt, through which ran the "bullet trains" that were the envy of other nations.

A sampling of Japanese exports in 1975 reveals the fecundity of its manufacturers. Japan built more than half of the world's ships that year. It bought iron ore and coking coal from the United States and sold steel in return. By then, the giant Mitsui and Mitsubishi combines could build chemical factories, hydroelectric plants, or harbors anywhere in the world. The Japanese ability to move rapidly from a new technique to a finished product to a marketing effort was remarkable. Motorcycles from Honda and Suzuki and cars from Honda, Toyota, Nissan, and other makers were sold throughout the world. Sony, Matsushita (Panasonic), Fujitsu, and NEC were known for their electronic products—from microchips to electron microscopes—as Nikon and Minolta were for cameras. In fact, in 1970 a paralysis of will among German camera manufacturers resulting from Japanese competition was called the "Japan complex." Before the war the words *made in Japan* had connoted cheap ten-cent-store goods, but increasingly they came to suggest a high-quality product.

Japan's nationwide network of 125-mile-per-hour bullet trains is almost complete. Every fifteen minutes one leaves Tokyo for Osaka. Developed by the state, the transportation network was divided into privately owned companies in 1988.

Society. One significant change in postwar Japan, and one that distinguished Japan from China and most other nations in Asia, was the decline in the growth rate of its population. Between the Meiji Restoration and the end of World War II, Japan's population more than doubled because use of modern hygiene had reduced the death rate. The immediate postwar years saw a baby boom, and between 1970 and 1975, when those born during the boom began having babies themselves, a second ripple occurred. But after 1950 the overall rate of increase headed downward:

1945	72 million
1955	89 million
1965	98 million
1975	112 million

One explanation for the stabilization of population credits the government, which in 1948 and 1949 passed "eugenics protection" laws. These laws legalized abortions, which during the fifties at times exceeded live births. The government set up family planning clinics, and factories established family planning groups. Picture posters in post offices contrasted small families with well-fed, happy children with large families burdened by thin, poorly clothed, cheerless children. Public opinion polls in the early seventies revealed that younger couples favored family planning more than older ones.

A second explanation for the reduction in births contends that government policies worked only because Japanese customs and social institu-

Left: Toyota plant near Tōkyō. Flowers were brought from a
worker's garden. Right: Girls on Sony assembly line.

tions were evolving along the course taken by other advanced nations.
Medical facilities had improved, more education meant later marriages
and fewer children, and the educated were more willing to accept a two-
child ideal. Also, the young were postponing marriage to avoid living
with in-laws or simply to prolong the independence and pleasures of the
single life. A newspaper cartoon showed Japanese office girls discussing
their vacations in Hawaii and Europe, while young men, who in the
interests of their careers took few vacations and saved their earnings,
listened enviously. Few women in Japan during the seventies were critical
of the implicit assumption that women would not have careers like men.

A third explanation for the change is that the Japanese had begun
to perceive their self-interest differently. In prewar Japan, children left
school early, often to work for the family enterprise or farm, and sons
supported their aged parents. Children were a valuable commodity, and
having many was the best insurance. During the 1950's and 1960's, however, Japan reached the stage of development where children became
increasingly expensive and contributed little in economic terms. They
went to school for many years, then to work for a company, and then,
as a 1975 census confirmed, married and established separate households.
Unless there was a special need, they did not regularly aid their parents,
who in old age came increasingly to depend on savings and retirement
benefits. Two children met the parents' human needs; more made savings
difficult.

A second major trend in postwar Japan was the redistribution of population. The combination of a rapidly expanding economy and a slowly growing population produced a labor shortage. First men and then women were drawn willy-nilly from agriculture and small and medium-sized industry into the new large industries of the cities. During the 1960's, this flow of workers to better jobs began to erode the "double structure" characteristic of the prewar economy. Small and medium-sized businesses were forced to raise wages to compete for labor with firms in the modern sector that offered higher wages, greater security, and extra fringe benefits.

During the early postwar era, changes in the village were not apparent on the surface. The tiled- or thatched-roofed houses, the green, terraced fields, and the ubiquitous shrines and temples had an air of timelessness. But by the 1960's, even the physical setting had begun to change. Factories were built in rural areas to take advantage of cheaper labor costs. New concrete buildings appeared—schoolhouses, warehouses, and sales outlets for automobiles and tractors. Roads were improved; trucks and farm machinery appeared in the most remote villages; small hills were bulldozed to provide sites for new construction; houses were roofed in blue or yellow or brown tile, and sheds sported sheets of bright blue or green plastic. In the new countryside, temples and shrines often looked like intruders from another age.

Beneath the surface, changes were even more profound. Far more than before the war, farming became commercialized, with considerable amounts of capital involved. Farming became an enterprise for profit, not subsistence: if pigs were in oversupply, farmers slaughtered them and raised chickens, and the same attitude extended to agricultural crops. The number of farm families in 1960 was 6 million, almost the same as during the early Meiji period. Then the number began to decline: to 5.67 million in 1965, and then to 4.95 in 1975. Even those Japanese who remained on the farm usually commuted to jobs in nearby cities, while those in remote areas found jobs in small towns, replacing others who had migrated to cities. As as result, nonagricultural employment furnished an ever higher percentage of "farm" family income: 47 per cent of the 1960 average income of $1,143, 66 per cent of the 1975 income of $11,086, and ever higher percentages thereafter. Often, women, with the help of grandparents or older children, performed the bulk of the farm work.

Village society also changed drastically. Until about 1955, the rural community remained tightly knit and many activities—economic, social, political, and religious—were communal. But then the hamlet dweller began to look outward. Administrative amalgamation consolidated villages into "cities," where the decisions governing hamlet life were made. Tele-

SCENES OF TOKYO: *at the end of World War II (above), and in the 1970's after recovery.*

Commuter crowds at rush hour in the Tokyo subway.

vision sets in every household brought in world news and the gamut of Japanese and American programs (with Japanese expertly dubbed in). Farm boys went to high school and then off to jobs in the cities, and farm girls resisted becoming farmers' wives. With the heads of families and other able-bodied men leaving the countryside during the working day, the fabric of traditional society began to wear thin, and hamlet solidarity to crumble. Men with land and an outside job had little interest in spending their weekends on communal activities, and in regions near cities, villages were close to collapse. Only in the exceptional village were old patterns of human relations renewed in more egalitarian forms, centering on farmers' cooperatives, perhaps, or some village project.

The new Japan was basically urban. In 1972, one of every nine Japanese lived in Tokyo, and one out of four lived in the Tokyo-Osaka industrial belt. Tokyo was to Japan what Paris was to France: the center of government, finance, business, industry, and the arts and letters. Tokyo was also the center of a huge net of feeder electric railways, whose terminals intersected with a constantly growing web of subway lines. At such intersections there developed, in addition to the old downtown of the Ginza, eight or nine newer "downtowns," each with magnificent department stores, shopping areas, business offices, banks, movie houses, coffee shops, restaurants, bars, and nightclubs. So crowded were the commuter trains that during the late fifties and early sixties, students were hired as "pushers" and "pullers" to pack and unpack the passengers of the overstuffed cars.

In the heart of the city were areas of private homes and increasing numbers of new luxury condominiums, known in Japanese as "mansions" and sporting such names as "Versailles Heights." Surrounding the inner city were older, middle-class residential areas that expanded outward to envelop what in prewar times had been farm villages. And still further out along the rail lines were *danchi,* planned residential developments. Some of these were composed of model houses, prefabricated but available in great variety. Other danchi consisted of drab rows of multi-story concrete buildings containing tiny crowded apartments often set down incongruously in the middle of rice fields in areas under cultivation since the dawn of Japanese history.

In this urban society, the twin revolutions of the Occupation and fast economic growth had sweeping social consequences. The status of women rose. As most girls went to high school and many to college, the legal rights of women increasingly became accepted. The ideal of the conjugal family advanced (newspapers occasionally received letters complaining of brides who were cruel to their mothers-in-law). In the new climate of religious freedom, popular religious sects proliferated. Social relations between boys and girls became freer, and the pursuit of happiness—or of pleasure—in coffee houses, movie theaters, and pinball parlors, at symphonies, and on ski slopes, beaches, and camping grounds became more acceptable, especially for the young. These changes can be seen as quantitative advances along lines laid down in prewar Japan, yet the changes were not simply linear. Rather, they created a new social configuration, a new way of life. The older generation recognized this by saying that the *apure (après la guerre)* generation was entirely different from their own—more relaxed, franker, less polite, and more egoistical. The older observers regretted the change, viewing juvenile delinquency and other urban phenomena as signs of moral decay, and they criticized the postwar system of education. Yet, by the 1970's, the old themselves were accepting and participating in a way of life that had not been foreseen at the end of World War II.

During the postwar decades of frenetic growth, so much of Japan's economic surplus was plowed back into new plant and equipment that little remained for social programs. Welfare for the sick and old was minimal. Education was underfinanced, and sewage disposal was antique. But from the seventies onward, government budgets for such items, particularly welfare expenditures, gradually increased. The opposition parties were never able to make these issues their own.

Housing was another serious problem by the sixties. A French visitor said that the Japanese lived in rabbit hutches—an unfair if not totally untrue comment that the Japanese have neither forgotten nor forgiven. But the government left housing to the private sector: to individuals, companies, and developers. As salaries rose and bank loans became available during the early seventies, a substantial upgrading and expansion of the housing stock began.

By the mid-1960's perhaps the greatest internal ill was pollution. It was as if half the population of the United States and a third of its industry had been crammed into the single state of California. The blossoming of Japan's automobile culture—in congested cities with inadequate roads and parking—also contributed to the pollution problem. The skies of Tokyo were often gray, the sun was dimmed to a pale moonlike orb, and Tokyo Bay was sludgy with the voided effluents of industry. Traffic policemen, though rotated every two hours, suffered from lead poisoning. The Japanese began to recognize the problem in about 1970. Magazines and newspapers were filled with articles asking, "Where are we going?" and "What are we doing to ourselves?" Some editorial writers felt that the government's extreme probusiness stance would prevent it from tackling the problem head on. But just as the opposition parties began to take up the issue, the government enacted tough new legislation against pollution, preempting their response. There is a site in Tokyo called "the bridge from which Mount Fuji can be seen" (Fujimibashi). During the 1960's, the name was inappropriate, but by the late 1970's on a clear day Mount Fuji was again visible.

Considering the rapid pace of change in Japanese society, one would expect deep psychic dislocations and considerable social unrest. These disturbances were not entirely absent, but the high degree of social integration was remarkable. Japan appeared to be free of many ills that plagued other advanced societies. Drugs were never a serious problem in Japanese society. Gun laws were severe and strictly enforced: hunting rifles were tightly controlled and civilians were not permitted to own handguns. Japan had no conscription system, no soldiers abroad, and no involvement in foreign wars. Vestigial prejudices did exist against the former outcast community of the Tokugawa period whose social assimilation, even in the postwar era, was incomplete, and there were strong prejudices against the 600,000 Korean residents in Japan. But these groups were both law-abiding and so small a part of the total population that bias against them did not seem a major social problem in the eyes of most Japanese.

Japan also lacked a "culture of poverty." Even the poor and the marginal subscribed to the ethic of enduring, forbearing, and making do. Thus, even lower-class districts seemed somehow middle class in character.

Crime rates in Japan were among the lowest in the world, and walking the streets at night was safe in all Japanese cities. The incidence of divorce was one of the lowest among advanced countries. Suicide had been a national literary tradition in both Tokugawa and modern times, yet in 1974, rates were lower than those of twenty years earlier, and lower than those in Austria, West Germany, Switzerland, and several other European nations. Even the life span was up—men gained eight years, living to an average age of 72, and women nine, living to an average age of 77. Well aware of the problems in other advanced societies, Japanese became increasingly satisfied with the accomplishments of their own.

One development promoting social integration during this era of sweeping changes was the spread of the so-called new religions. A few dated back to the Tokugawa; others were more recent. Some drew on Shinto or Buddhism; others, more eclectic, drew on both and on Christianity as well. The most successful of these groups in postwar Japan was the Value Creating Society (Sōka Gakkai). This sect's membership rose from a few thousand families in the early 1950's to 4.3 million families in 1964, leveling off after that. (The Japanese Communist Party paid the Society the supreme compliment of studying its organizational techniques.) About one of every twelve Japanese was a member. The down-to-earth appeal of the sect attracted urban Japanese who felt uprooted, who missed the traditional community, or who did not share in Japan's new prosperity. First spreading among shopkeepers, taxi drivers, coal miners, and unskilled labor, the Sōka Gakkai then began to attract members from other groups as well, and its success among younger Japanese was notable. Members asked potential converts, "Why are you living? Are you satisfied with your life?" In response to the problems of the atomization of postwar society and the alienation of the individual, the group gave a traditional answer: that only the Nichiren Sect of Buddhism and faith in the Lotus Sutra could bring salvation to the individual, the nation, and the world. Teaching faith healing and mutual assistance, the sect brought its members together in warm, tightly knit, supportive local associations. Although Buddhist, in its early years the Society placed a heavy emphasis on profit in this world as a sign of the efficacy of belief. By the early seventies, however, profit had become less important.

Because the Sōka Gakkai used paramilitary terminology to describe its hierarchy, emphasized traditional cultural content, and had a predilection for parades, pageants, and mass convocations, some saw the sect as a dangerous reaction against modernity. Another view, more sympathetic, stressed the degree to which the Sōka Gakkai imbued immigrants from the countryside or the city poor with a sense of community and belonging, similar to what others obtained from the social group within factories, companies, or government offices.

For the majority of Japanese, however, life centered on family, home, job, and possessions. Before the war, families mainly sought traditional goods, but modern husbands and wives wanted new products. The "three sacred treasures"—in ancient Japan the mirror, the jewels, and the sword —became, in the late 1950's, the television, the refrigerator, and the washing machine. In the early 1960's, a new set of consumer "treasures" was designated the "three Cs": the car, the color television, and the "room cooler." And by the late 1960's, there were the "three Vs": the villa, the vacation, and the visit to a foreign country. By the early seventies, as the novelty of well-being wore off, such terms lapsed, but the orientation toward a more affluent life style became even stronger. The media described the privatistic attitude toward home and possessions as "my-home-ism" and "my-car-ism." In a 1969 poll, for example, more than fourteen thousand married couples were asked, "What have you to live for?" Almost 83 per cent of the women and more than 57 per cent of the men replied "home and children." The rest of the men, and a much higher percentage among those with a university education, gave first place to their work. In a sense "my-job-ism" was an orientation of such long standing that it was not necessary to coin a phrase to describe it. Opinion polls showed a shift from traditional loyalty to the company toward the desire for personal gratification in work. Identification with the company, however, was still strong.

Education also transformed postwar society. Prewar education had been dichotomous: the masses received a primary or middle school education, while a tiny elite—3 per cent—attended university. Without a doubt, the gap between the two groups weakened prewar parliamentary democracy. During the late forties, the Occupation carried out basic reforms, which the Japanese accepted because they met a felt need, and the impact of these reforms came in the decades that followed.

In the least important reform, since it merely accelerated a trend already well underway, middle school was made compulsory in 1947. The number of middle school students increased from 2.4 to 4.3 million, and thereafter reflected the size of that age group in the population. In the following year the old higher schools were replaced by American-style high schools and the number of high school students shot up from 380,000 to 1.2 million, and then further increased to 2.6 million in 1955 and 4.3 in 1975.

The dramatic growth of universities was also initiated by Occupation reforms. At the end of the war, there were 84,000 university students, a small increase over the 70,000 of 1936. The number jumped to half a million in 1955 and 1.73 million in 1975. (These figures do not include two-year women's colleges.) In all, the number of students going on to some form of higher education was in the middle 30 per cent range, higher than in most European countries. By 1975 the prewar educational gap between the elite and the masses had disappeared, and almost 90 per cent of the Japanese populace—high school and university graduates —defined themselves as middle class.

Bare figures and administrative reforms, however, tell only part of the story. Japanese families believed in getting ahead and believed that education was the way to do it. Parents sacrificed to give their children every advantage, and children, on the whole, cooperated or at least put up with their parents' exertions. Private kindergartens became immensely popular, both as daycare centers for working mothers and as "headstart" programs for anxious parents. A few such preschools even tested the very young applicants before admitting them. Parents of middle and high school students hired university students to tutor their children or sent them after regular school hours (longer and for more days than in American schools) to special private tutoring schools. One result has been that Japanese high schoolers consistently outscore those of Western nations on international mathematics tests, the only tests for which comparisons are possible.

This grueling regimen had a single goal: the university entrance examination. This examination alone—not recommendations, extracurricular activities, or high school grades—determined university admissions. Those who failed usually entered private cram schools, where they were drilled in the exam subjects and given mock entrance examinations on a regular basis. These cram schools in turn had their own entrance examinations, for they lived off of the success of their students. The tuition at the best of these schools was many times that of Tokyo University. Their students, existing in a limbo of uncertain prospects, were called *rōnin* (masterless samurai).

Intellectual Currents. In the process of prewar modernization, Japan destroyed much of its tradition in order to build a strong nation. A few traditional concepts, however, were enshrined at the core of the new nationalism in order to preserve symbolically what was being destroyed in fact. Mesmerized by the emperor ideology as a "teaching . . . infallible for all ages and true in all places," the Japanese marched into the modern world. The most important ideological change in postwar Japan was the destruction of this emperor-state orthodoxy.

The national consciousness of the Japanese as a distinctive people and culture *(kokuminshugi)* was not lost. The Japanese sense of "we-ness" versus "they-ness" remained stronger than in any other modernized country. A Japanese victory in sports or the conquest of a Himalayan peak was hailed enthusiastically by the whole nation. The

*"I'm in, I'm in! I've passed
the examination and been
admitted to Tokyo
University."*

admission of Japan to the United Nations brought a sense of national fulfillment. A steel company in Kyushu mounted a poster on the inner wall of a rolling mill: "In quantity and quality let us lead the world." But nationalism in the sense of devotion to the state *(kokkashugi)* came under a dark cloud. The Japanese flag was rarely flown in the first two decades after the war. Actions could no longer be justified "for the sake of the nation." Or if a sanction was sought, it was "for the sake of a new Japan," international in outlook and democratic in practice. And militarism or anything pertaining to war was viewed by intellectuals and by most of the people as anathema.

The rejection of the old orthodoxy left many in a state of aimlessness. One reaction was a vogue of existentialism and existentialist literature with roots in Japan's prewar tradition of German philosophy. The existentialist novel *The Stranger* by Albert Camus became a best seller. Many intellectuals felt that this novel depicted their predicament and sense of estrangement as accurately as did the writings of Japanese authors. The brilliant writer Dazai Osamu, indulging in women, alcohol, and drugs, continued the "negative identity" of Akutagawa that had become all the more palatable as the result of a meaningless war and a crushing defeat. The "hero" of Dazai's *The Setting Sun* speaks: "It is painful for the plant which is myself to live in the atmosphere and the light of this world. Somewhere an element is lacking which would permit me to continue." Dazai died in a double suicide in 1948.

In another reaction to aimlessness and uncertainty in postwar intellectual circles, Marxism was revived. It became particularly strong in universities, but also influenced unions and the parties of the left. Some scholars who had repudiated Marxism during the 1930's picked it up again after Japan's defeat. To many students, this system seemed the antithesis of militarism, offering a worldwide and historical schema in terms of which they could interpret the upheavals of modern Japan. Conditions at Japanese universities facilitated the spread of Marxism. In the postwar years the campuses were physically depressing; the food was bad; most students were poor; classes were large; contact with instructors was minimal, and learning was often rote memorization. Entering students, however high their status in their home communities, often found themselves at loose ends, and felt let down as the tremendous pressures they had experienced through high school ended.

Even under these conditions, the majority of students were apolitical or only mildly leftist in their politics. But a minority joined activist groups that soon took over the student self-government organizations established by the Occupation. Known by the name of their national federation, the Zengakuren, these students held periodic protest meetings, rallies, and demonstrations. They filled their university grounds with political posters. And when the national political situation enabled them to mobilize wider student support, they demonstrated outside the universities as well. Such demonstrations reached a high pitch in the early fifties and again in 1960.

After 1960, the student movement splintered into factions, with the mainstream faction subordinate to the Japanese Communist Party. The student group followed the party policy of building organizational strength while abstaining from violent actions that would surely invite repression. Within the spectrum of Marxist student groups, this group appeared almost conservative. To the left of the mainstream faction were a variety of extremist and anti-Communist Party groups that became violent during the late sixties, occupying university buildings, demonstrating at airports, tossing fire bombs in subways, and clashing with the police. These groups were Marxist in their political criticism of the government but they were also anarchic and existentialist. They sought to achieve self-realization through open opposition to the status quo. Members derided their professors as purveyors of "dead learning" and compared their own lives in the tightly ordered Japanese society to ball-point pens: at any time they could look at the transparent barrel and tell how much ink was left.

As the bleakness of the immediate postwar era passed, Japan returned to more normal patterns of life and thought. In keeping with its intense and varied intellectual life, Japan became one of the leading book publishing nations in the world, with its literature marked by an ample variety. The Japanese also read more newspapers per person than any other people in the world (a single subscription covers both the morning and evening paper). Proletarian literature revived and continued as one small stream of literary activity; an antiwar literature, describing the brutality of army life and the horror of Hiroshima, arose to form another. Popular literature abounded with tales of samurai and contemporary stories with sad-happy endings. Science fiction and detective stories, called "novels of deduction," came to be widely read. Younger writers were generally sympathetic to the left, yet not so blindly sympathetic as to take contemporary Russian or Chinese novels as models. They built, in the form and content of their work, directly on Japan's prewar syncretism of the European and the traditional. Serious novels continued to explore the prewar themes of family, sex, loneliness, death, man's inability to communicate, mental aberrations, an aesthetic view of life, and the dissolute lives of novelists themselves.

The postwar years were marked by great creativity in the arts. Tanizaki Junichirō's *The Makioka Sisters,* banned during the war, was published in 1948. Kawabata Yasunari wrote *The Sound of the Mountain* and *A Thousand Cranes,* and was awarded the Nobel prize for literature in 1968; he committed suicide in 1972. Mishima Yukio and Ōe Kenzaburō, younger writers of stature, emerged as well. Architects such as Tange Kenzō and sculptors such as Nagare Masayuki and Noguchi Isamu attained world repute. The films of Kurosawa Akira, Ozu Yasujirō, and Naruse Mikio were shown in art theaters around the world. In painting, along with the works of such modernists as Okada Kenzō, there were the sensuous Buddhist figures of the Munkata Shikō woodblock prints and the black ink paintings of modern calligraphers who turned Chinese ideographs into forms of abstract art.

With the sixties, two new tendencies began to appear in Japanese intellectual life. One was a thaw in Japanese Marxism. The revelation of Stalin's crimes, followed by the Sino-Soviet split, produced schisms in the leftist movement. One writer who repudiated his Marxism in 1964 suggested that these revelations had the effect in Japanese intellectual circles that the 1936 Russian purge trials had had on the European intelligentsia. Some magazines that had been Marxist in orientation began to accept other types of writing as well. Marxist scholars at universities became more eclectic. Marxism remained an influential intellectual current in Japan in a way that was true only of Italy or France in Western Europe. Even Japanese businessmen often unconsciously used categories derived from it. But as a total system of thought it slowly began to lose ground, its insights enveloped in other, newer ideas.

A second trend of the middle sixties was the reemergence of national self-confidence. The Japanese came to realize how successful their economic growth had been and took pride in it. They were also gratified by the plaudits they received from abroad for their staging of the 1964 Tokyo Olympics and the 1970 Osaka Exposition. The latter, in which space technology bordering on science fiction was a handsdown winner over traditional themes, reflected the same optimism about a technological future that was invariably revealed in public opinion polls. And from the late 1960's, books and movies began to appear about the heroism of the Japanese forces in World War II.

However, this new nationalism, like that of other modern states, was diffuse. It involved no significant revival of emperor ideology, and individualism—seen as egotism in much prewar thought—continued to be a conscious goal among students and Japanese youth. Students wanted jobs that would permit self-expression. The old lineal family ideal continued to decline, and no one viewed the state any longer as an aggregate of families. And, as Japan's Shinto past became less and less meaningful, the myth of the emperor continued to decline. The emperor was a popular figure, but he had lost his awe. In a 1970 poll, 81 per cent favored keeping the emperor as a symbol, 9 per cent (26 per cent of those age sixteen to twenty) felt Japan would be better off without an emperor, and only 8 per cent (18 per cent of those sixty or over) wanted to increase the emperor's authority.

In retrospect, the most significant changes in Japanese culture after 1945 were its openness and receptivity to new influences from the West and the strong reemergence of the universalistic tendencies of Japan's own modern tradition. After having been shut off from new Western intellectual influences since the start of the China War in 1937, Japan quickly made up for lost time. Particularly influential were new intellectual currents from the United States. American texts became widely used in medicine, law, the sciences, and engineering; economics faculties translated books on business management. American anthropology, psychology, and sociology entered to mix with Marx, Weber, and English social science. Perhaps only in the arts and letters did the European influence continue dominant, but here too Japan was open to English and American influences. These multiple influences were not doctrinally coherent. Yet on the whole, combining with liberal ideas that existed in the penumbra of the prewar orthodoxy, they reinforced the democratic pluralism that marked Japanese intellectual life.

Some thinkers in Japan most committed to parliamentary democracy felt keenly the lack of a doctrinally coherent, democratic consensus rooted in Japan's history. They lamented the shallowness of Japanese liberalism— in contrast to that of Western nations, which, having experienced a Renaissance, Reformation, and Enlightenment, were able to fashion their own democratic institutions. They argued that the postwar changes were even more of an "external enlightenment" than those so designated by Natsume Sōseki at the turn of the century. Some critics pointed to the dramatic suicide of the right-wing novelist Mishima Yukio in 1970 as a sign of a crisis of meaning in Japanese culture. Mishima's last work was titled *The Sea of Fertility*. The name was taken from a "sea" on the moon and conveyed Mishima's view of contemporary Japanese culture as sterile, cut off from its own tradition. Other Japanese, however, argued that important elements of Japanese tradition were still alive. They cited as evidence both arts and institutions that were modern, yet different from those of the modern West. Some argued further that the Japanese tradition had been successfully fused with elements of the Western tradition, and that since the values and experiences that had shaped the West were implicit in modern Japanese culture, those elements would gradually unfold in the society.

Politics.   A new phase of politics began in October 1955, when the left- and right-wing Socialists, divided since 1951, joined to form a single socialist party. In the face of a united opposition, the two conservative parties could not afford to remain apart, so they merged a month later, forming the Liberal Democratic Party (LDP). Journalists heralded these unions as the start of a two-party system in Japan, although one in which the conservatives held the preponderance of Diet seats. For both sides, these arrangements were sensible. The Japanese Socialist Party (JSP), with 29 per cent of the popular vote, made itself into a more effective opposition. The Liberals and Democrats were almost indistinguishable in the policies they espoused. Each was too small to govern alone—in the February 1955 election they received, respectively, 26.6 and 36.6 per cent of the votes—but together they commanded an easy majority of Diet seats. The LDP was the party in power during the entire 1955–1976 period.

In many parts of the world, single-party government is the sign of a dictatorship. This was not true of Japan. The cabinet was a "committee" of the largest party in the Diet. The elections in which Diet members were chosen were open, fair, and had few irregularities. All parties, from the Communists on the left to little fringe groups on the right, were legal. Electoral campaigns were vigorous, noisy, and unmarred by violence. Newspapers of every stripe competed for circulation, and the human rights guaranteed by the constitution were upheld by law. It was the freely expressed will of the majority of the Japanese people that the LDP govern.

Single-party rule clearly had some drawbacks in Japan. As in other democracies, electoral campaigns depended on private funding given in expectation of some return. Since there was no alternation of parties in power, a permanent funding arrangement developed by which the Federation of Economic Organization dunned companies for funds and distributed them to the LDP factions. A permanent policy-formation arrangement also developed between the parties and the bureaucracy—some political scientists asked which was in the saddle and which was the horse. Even though it got the votes to stay in power by increasing the well-being of the Japanese people, this "establishment" of business, bureaucracy, and a single party in power was not what the Occupation had in mind when it attempted to democratize Japan. Another drawback was that the opposition parties, continuously separated from the responsibility of governing, tended to become irresponsible and found it hard to recruit talent. But single-party rule also gave Japan some advantages, the greatest being continuity of policies. This was important for foreign relations and even more so for the industrial policies that defined what the Yoshida doctrine meant in practice. Businesses could plan for the long-term, knowing exactly what to expect of government.

Another basic change within the Diet in the two decades following 1955 was a shift away from confrontation toward consultation and consensus. Parliamentary democracy did not fare well during the first five years. Both parties were led by prewar or wartime politicians. The Socialist leaders, Marxists and moderates, had been persecuted and sometimes jailed for their political beliefs. The LDP was led by those who had done the persecuting. The last Yoshida cabinet had ended in December 1954. He was replaced by Hatoyama Ichirō (1954–1956), who as education minister in the early thirties had purged liberals from the faculty of Kyoto University. The other important prime minister was Kishi Nobusuke (1957–1960), a minister in the 1941 Tōjō cabinet that had declared war on the United States. The two parties confronted each other in the Diet. The Socialists lacked the votes to defeat LDP bills, so they physically blocked the voting process. Fights broke out on the floor of the Diet and the police were often called in. The LDP used "snap votes," votes called unexpectedly and without the usual parliamentary debate, to counter the planned obstructions of the Socialists. The Socialists denounced this tactic as "the tyranny of the majority."

Policy issues contributed to the fray and fury of Diet politics. Both Hatoyama and Kishi had been purged by the Occupation. Hatoyama came to power on an anti-Yoshida platform. Both he and Kishi attempted to turn back the clock on some Occupation reforms. The police had been recentralized in 1954. They further extended the powers of the police to cope with riots and matters of internal security. In 1956 they empowered the Ministry of Education to appoint education boards—previously elective—and then strengthened the ministry's control over school textbooks. This led to recurrent controversies over the treatment in history texts of the emperor and Japanese aggression in China during the 1930's. They gave the Local Autonomy Office—a pale ghost of the prewar Home Ministry —greater powers to oversee local government, and in 1960 they made it a cabinet ministry. They continued to expand Japan's armed forces within the 1 per cent limit. The government argued, despite the clear constitutional prohibition in Article Nine, that "defensive forces" did not constitute a war potential. A conservative Supreme Court was unwilling to declare the actions of the government unconstitutional. Finally, the conservatives wanted to revise the constitution. They were unhappy that the emperor was only a "symbol" and that Japan had renounced the sovereign right to maintain military forces. They appointed a commission to recommend revisions, but nothing came of it since they lacked the two-thirds vote in the Diet needed for an amendment.

In retrospect, the bark of the Hatoyama and Kishi ministries was worse than their bite. What these ministries achieved were very small revisions of massive reforms. But given the historical context, it was not surprising that the Socialists saw Hatoyama and Kishi as bogeymen and their legislation as the first steps back toward the repressive, prewar system. Without the determined opposition of the Socialists, the revisions would have been greater.

Confrontation politics reached a climax in the spring and summer of 1960 over the revision of the Security Treaty with the United States. The changes proposed were uniformly favorable to Japan: the new treaty dropped as unnecessary a provision allowing the government to use American troops "to put down large-scale internal riots," and it required, as the earlier treaty had not, prior consultation before the United States could use military bases in Japan for actions elsewhere in Asia. But the Socialists wanted to abolish the treaty altogether. Any treaty, they argued, might lead to Japanese involvement in an American war in Asia. The tensions of the previous five years came to a head over this issue, and were exacerbated by Soviet-American ill feelings, criticisms of the revisions in Japanese papers, the unpopularity of Prime Minister Kishi— seen by the public as a narrow bureaucrat, by political cartoonists as a monkey, and by the Socialists as "war criminal Kishi"—and the LDP ratification of the treaty at a special night session of the Diet without the usual "democratic debate."

Massive demonstrations broke out in Japan's main cities in opposition to the ratification. In Tokyo, more than 100,000 people took to the streets. Among the demonstrators, many of whom had never before participated in demonstrations, were unionists, housewives, professors, an unusually large number of students, and members of cultural, professional, and women's organizations. Most of the marches through Tokyo's boulevards were peaceful, though some radical students clashed with the police. The conservatives saw the demonstrations as a species of mass hysteria, while the Socialists hailed them as the dawn of a revolutionary consciousness that would inaugurate a new age in Japanese politics.

Once the treaty was ratified, Kishi resigned, the demonstrations ended, and a more peaceful era began in which both parties were for a time more moderate. Both saw a new generation of leaders emerge—men who cared less than their predecessors for the battles of the past and were less antagonistic toward each other. Within the LDP, younger politicians who had been recruited by Yoshida and were identified as members of his faction came to the fore and stressed the primacy of economic issues. Ikeda Hayato (1899–1965), a former finance minister, became prime minister in 1960 and proclaimed a policy to double the income of the Japanese in ten years. The goal, in fact, was achieved in less than seven. In a pleasing contrast to the arrogance of his predecessors, Ikeda adopted a "low posture" toward the opposition parties. He consulted with leaders of the opposition before introducing government bills in the Diet, and took heed of their advice, at least to the extent of making token changes.

After Ikeda, confrontation again flared up during the late sixties. The Socialist party fell into the hands of its left wing, and "high-posture" Satō Eisaku (prime minister from 1964 to 1972) became president of the LDP. But after Satō the trend toward consensus reemerged stronger than ever. The LDP would routinely confer with the opposition parties before introducing cabinet bills and make small, often cosmetic changes in the bills to placate the other parties. By the late seventies, the number of cabinet bills to which no party offered opposition had risen from 43 to 68 per cent. In contrast to the atmosphere of the fifties, then, a new mutual trust had emerged among the parties in the Diet. The opposition parties no longer saw the LDP as right-wing traditionalists seeking

*Students demonstrating in 1960 against the Security Treaty, Prime
Minister Kishi, United States spy flights over the Soviet Union,
and a proposed visit of President Eisenhower to Japan.*

to restore the values and politics of the prewar era, and the LDP no
longer saw the opposition as radical visionaries who would disrupt the
social order and impede Japan's economic advance. Significant differences between the parties remained, but the differences no longer posed
a threat to the very workings of parliamentary government.

Two other trends were important during these decades: a decline in
the LDP popular vote and the fragmentation of the opposition into a
handful of parties that competed with each other as well as with the LDP.
The decline reflected a growing support for the antiestablishment parties.
The fragmentation of the previously united opposition, however, strengthened the LDP. One trend offset the other, enabling the LDP to retain
more than half the Diet seats while receiving less than half of the vote.

The decline in the LDP's popular vote went from 63 per cent in the
1955 election to less than 50 per cent in 1967, to 42 per cent in 1976. The
decline, at the rate of about 1 per cent a year, can be thought of as a
sociological erosion. That is to say, the very success of the conservative
government in transforming the economy had the effect of diminishing
the segments of the population that voted conservative and increasing
those that voted for the opposition. The 1972 election polls showed that

over 70 per cent of farmers and fishermen voted for the LDP, as did a majority of the self-employed and shopkeepers. But these groups were an ever smaller component of the total population. On the other hand, the rapidly expanding numbers of office workers, production workers, and people in sales and services gave only a quarter or less of their votes to the conservatives. Between the early fifties and early seventies, labor unions had doubled their membership and all but about 12 per cent of their votes went to the socialists or other opposition parties.

The fragmentation of the opposition began in 1960, when the Democratic Socialist Party (DSP) split off from the Japanese Socialist Party (JSP) over the issue of the Security Treaty. The socialists were the heirs of the partly Marxist, partly Christian or moderate prewar tradition. The socialist left wing was revolutionary in theory if not in practice. They usually spoke of China and the Soviet Union as the camp of peace, they talked of a class party, and they argued about whether Japan's greatest enemy was American imperialism or Japanese monopoly capitalism. The right-wing Socialists, in contrast, were reformers and supporters of parliamentary government. Like British labor, they criticized the conservatives in the name of egalitarianism and welfare programs. The two wings of the Socialists were paralleled by two great labor federations. On the left was the largest and most powerful federation, Sōhyō, representing government employees and white-collar workers as well as factory labor. To the right of Sōhyō, taking a bread-and-butter approach to unionism was Zenrō (later Dōmei) and other smaller federations.

Socialist candidates with support from several federations tended to do well at the polls; those without union support did poorly. So dependent were the Socialists on the unions for campaign funds that they were called a one-pressure-group party. The 1960 split involved policy issues and personal cliques, but in general those moderates whose backing came from the smaller Zenrō formed the DSP, while those moderates and leftists supported by the larger Sōhyō stayed within the JSP.

In the years that followed, the DSP remained a stable but small splinter party. By 1976, when it received about 6 percent of the votes and Diet seats, it had become a centrist party advocating stronger welfare policies. The JSP had a more checkered history, marked by constant struggles between its left and right wings. In the early sixties, the JSP advocated a moderate program of "structural reform." This concept, borrowed from the Italian Communists, aimed at a socialist future that would combine Japan's no-war constitution, Britain's democracy, the Soviet Union's welfare system, and the United States' standard of living.

In the mid-sixties, however, the left won control and pushed a more radical line. In the eyes of some, the JSP, which praised the Great

Cultural Revolution occurring in China, seemed to stand somewhat to the left of the Japanese Communist Party. This stance lost the party votes: support dropped from 29 per cent of the popular vote in 1963, to 28 per cent in 1965, to 21 per cent in 1969. Still, as Japan became more prosperous, even the party's left wing gradually became more moderate, and in 1976, with 21 per cent of the popular vote and 123 Diet seats (24 per cent), the JSP remained the largest opposition party.

The Japanese Communist Party (JCP) emerged as a legal party after World War II. By 1949, its representatives occupied thirty-five seats in the Diet. In 1950, after the outbreak of the Korean War, the JCP dropped the slogan of "a lovable Communist party" and came to favor violent demonstrations. As a result, the party nearly dropped out of sight in electoral politics until the late sixties. In 1963, the JCP broke with the Soviet Union over the issue of a nuclear test ban treaty, and from that point until 1966 it leaned toward China. It took an even clearer stand against the Soviet Union in 1966 by advocating the return to Japan of the four islands north of Hokkaido that the Soviet Union had seized at the end of World War II. Overall, the JCP tried to represent itself as both patriotic and Marxist—for example, JCP campaign posters sometimes showed the candidate with Mount Fuji in the background. In the election of 1976, JCP candidates won 10 per cent of the popular vote and seventeen Diet seats.

Another opposition party, the Komeito, emerged in 1964. It resisted being defined in religious terms, but essentially it was the political wing of the Sōka Gakkai. *Kōmeitō* has been translated as "Clean Government Party." Its appeal was moral: end corruption, stop inflation, improve living conditions, and work for international peace. Since many members of the "parent" Sōka Gakkai were recruited from the urban poor, the party competed for votes with the JCP. It began by entering local and upper-house elections, but in 1967 started to enter candidates for elections to the more powerful lower house. By 1976, the Kōmeitō had 11 per cent of the popular vote and fifty-five seats in the lower house of the Diet and was viewed as a possible swing party in some future coalition government.

With the opposition vote dispersed among these several parties, the LDP was able to stay in power. Also helping the LDP was its over-representation in some conservative rural districts where redistricting had not caught up with population losses. Still, by the early seventies the party was experiencing difficulties. As the conservative margin in the Diet narrowed, the LDP lost control of some Diet committees. Developments in 1975 and 1976 added to the LDP predicament. In 1975, five young Diet members broke with the LDP and formed a new party, the New Liberal Club, in protest against the continued domination of the party by elderly politicians, and in the election of 1976 this splinter group gained seventeen seats. At any other time such a defection would not have mattered (and therefore would not have occurred), but in the 1976 election the LDP fell seven seats short of a Diet majority. The LDP just barely managed to stay in power without including members of the New Liberal Club in the cabinet, and only succeeded because the needed number of independents joined the LDP after the election. But its lease on power, everyone agreed, was running out. Political scientists proclaimed the arrival of an "age of parity," and newspapers and magazines speculated about what would come next. Would the LDP be forced to enter a coalition with a moderate opposition party? Or would moderate LDP factions break away from their party and join with a moderate opposition party to form a new party? And how would such changes affect the policies Japan had followed for thirty years?

International Relations.   For Japan, as for most other countries in the world, from the fifties to the seventies, foreign relations developed within the overarching nuclear balance between the United States and the Soviet Union. In 1964, China became a nuclear power and entered the balance in a very minor way, as had England and France in Europe.

Throughout this era and beyond, the central principle of Japan's foreign policy was to maintain close ties to the United States. The United States sponsored Japan's reentry into international political and economic organizations—the United Nations, the International Monetary Fund, the World Bank, and so on. The United States was far and away Japan's largest single market, and the source for most of its technology. And the Security Treaty with the United States provided for Japan's defense.

Of course, Japan's own Self-Defense Forces also grew during these decades, and by 1970 they numbered a quarter of a million troops and one thousand jet planes. Critics pointed out that the Self-Defense Forces were the fastest growing military in the world. Defenders replied that they cost less than one percent of GNP and were, relatively, the smallest in the world. By the early seventies, questions were arising in Japan regarding adequacy of its own defenses and the trustworthiness of the United States. A few Diet members openly discussed nuclear weapons, breaking a taboo that in earlier years would have cost them their seats. But a 1970 "white paper" (an official statement of government policy) on defense reiterated what had been the consistent government policy: "Japan is a great power economically, but it will not become a great power militarily. Rather it will become a new kind of state with social welfare and world peace as its goals."

Despite the growth of Japan's conventional military forces, there was little coordination between them and the American military until 1978. But with the defeat of the United States in Vietnam, Japan feared a general American withdrawal from Asia, so it began more actively to coordinate the efforts of the two forces with respect to logistics, strategic planning, and military intelligence. Still, Japan remained completely unwilling to consider the use of its military forces outside Japan. The Yoshida doctrine, which stressed Japan's economic development and dependence for security on the United States, continued paramount.

The very closeness of Japan's ties to the United States caused problems. Japanese conservatives criticized the increasing openness and freedom in their society as "Americanization." American military bases in Japan were a frequent source of irritation; the lengthening of an airfield almost inevitably provoked a political demonstration. Another sensitive issue in Japan was American atom bomb testing in the Pacific. Because American bombs had leveled Hiroshima and Nagasaki, because America was Japan's ally, and because the Japanese left was highly vocal, American bomb tests were more heavily criticized than those of the Soviet Union or China.

Yet another problem lay in the continued American possession of Okinawa and its use as a military base. Conservatives saw this as an affront to Japanese sovereignty. The parties of the political left saw the Okinawa base as an advance on Japanese territory and a symbol of an aggressive American military policy in Asia. The Okinawans themselves, who had been second-class citizens in Japan before the war, became quite nationalistic and in protest against American control of the island elected a Communist as mayor of Naha. The issue abated in November 1969 when the United States promised to return the island to Japan, and control reverted to the Japanese in May 1972.

Besides the maintaining of close U.S. ties, a second guiding principle of Japan's foreign policy was support for stable, open markets and world peace. Japan imported most raw materials and paid for them by exporting manufactured goods. Even small signs of foreign protectionism were viewed with alarm in Japan, and even small wars disrupted its worldwide trade.

Japan's view of itself as a peace state was buttressed by its geopolitical position. Even if militarism had not been so thoroughly discredited by Japan's defeat in World War II, there was no scope for it in the postwar world. Of Japan's neighbors, the Soviet Union and China had nuclear weapons, North Korea and (North) Vietnam were Chinese or Soviet client-states, and South Korea and Taiwan were American client-states.

Had Japan rearmed more substantially, the only use for its increased military power would have been to provide more of its own defense and, possibly, to aid the United States in defending South Korea and Taiwan. These countries, however, had no desire for military ties with Japan, and China, in any case, would not have countenanced such ties with Taiwan. In short, remilitarization would have incurred substantial costs with few benefits.

The benefits to Japan of a peaceful trading order can be seen in its developing relations with Southeast Asia. In the late forties and early fifties, Japan had no relations with the countries of its former Greater East Asia Co-Prosperity Sphere and the question of reparations for war damages was pending. Beginning about 1950, there developed a balance in Asia between the continental Communist powers (China, North Korea, and, shortly afterward, North Vietnam) and an arc of peripheral, non-Communist states from Thailand to South Korea backed by the United States. In the mid-fifties, Japan reached reparations agreements and re-established diplomatic and trading relations with the rim nations, and reparations were followed by aid, credits, and loans. Japan also started investing heavily in these countries, sometimes building factories but more often securing sources of such raw materials as oil, ore, or timber.

By the mid-sixties, Japan had become the leading economic power in the area. Neon signs in Bangkok advertised Japanese products; the streets of Saigon were filled with Japanese motorscooters. A reporter observed at the time that the United States was at war in Vietnam to protect Japanese markets. By the early seventies, some countries in Southeast Asia that did not export raw materials had such an unfavorable balance of trade with Japan that anti-Japanese sentiment—analogous to the anti-Americanism the United States had long experienced in Latin America—had begun to rise. Some Japanese commentators wondered why these countries loved our products but not our people. Partly in response to such sentiments, Japanese foreign aid began to increase.

If there was a third guiding principle of Japan's foreign policy, it was that diplomacy should follow economic self-interest. For example, Japan needed oil. In 1941 it had gone to war when its supply was cut off, and by 1976, the 1941 yearly supply of oil would have fueled Japan for only three days. About 80 per cent of Japan's oil supply came from the Middle East. This dictated a foreign policy that leaned toward the Arab states and away from Israel. And when oil states fought among themselves, Japan took great pains to maintain an evenhanded neutrality, combined with measures to increase imports from safer areas, such as Venezuela, Indonesia, Canada, and the United States. Another case in point was South Africa, a good trading partner, which sold Japan raw materials and bought its finished goods. Whatever views Japan had of South Africa's internal politics, they did not interfere with trade. Japan would move to restrict its trade with South Africa only much later, when it perceived that the trade might damage its relationship with the United States.

Of all the countries in the arc of peripheral states, Japan's nearest neighbor was South Korea. The two countries were important to each other. Had there been no Japan, Korea would not have been viable as a non-Communist state; were there no South Korea, Japan would have felt uncomfortably exposed to the continental Communist powers. Yet for a long time Japan found it difficult to establish ties with South Korea. The Korean memory of Japan's colonial rule was still fresh, and the South Koreans feared domination by Japan's more powerful economy. They demanded higher reparations than the Japanese were willing to pay, they barred the more efficient Japanese fishing boats from their waters, and they resented the willingness of the Japanese government to let Japan's 600,000 Koreans choose for themselves which Korea they would acknowledge. The political left in Japan also opposed the establishment of relations with South Korea, on the grounds that it would deepen the rift between North and South Korea and harden Japan's anti-Communist stance. By 1965, these difficulties were overcome sufficiently to permit the normalization of relations with South Korea, which led to Japanese aid, loans, investments, and increased trade, contributing to a spurt of economic growth in South Korea. In the decades that followed, despite several incidents that marred the relationship, attitudes improved on both sides. The Japanese, who had tended to look down on their former colonial subjects, began to admire Korean economic achievements. (The majority of foreign visitors to the 1988 Seoul Olympics would be Japanese.) The Koreans, for their part, grew more self-confident, and there emerged a new generation of Korean leaders who had no personal experience of a colonial past.

Japan's attitudes toward Taiwan and China were also complex. At American insistence, Japan had recognized the Nationalists on Taiwan in 1952. Taiwan was an important trading partner of Japan, usually more important than mainland China, and Japanese investments in Taiwan were considerable. Using these investments as a lever, the Nationalist government repeatedly put pressure on Japan not to recognize the government in Peking or to give it economic credits. A minority of conservative party leaders in Japan felt that a Taiwan ruled by Peking might strategically endanger Japan, and advocated stronger ties with Taiwan. Relations between the two countries were also helped by the fact that anti-Japanese feelings were weaker among the Taiwanese population of Taiwan than in any other part of East Asia. Yet Japan very carefully avoided the kind of political commitments that would interfere with a future improvement of relations with China.

In the years soon after the Communist revolution, Japan's image of China was not unfavorable. Many in the universities felt that China would forge ahead of Japan. But after the failure of the Great Leap Forward and the political turmoil of the Cultural Revolution, Japan's image of China became negative. Even on the political left, all but the most extreme groups dismissed China as a possible model for Japan. Nevertheless, China and the Chinese continued to hold a special fascination for the Japanese—as the fount of inspiration for Japan's traditional culture, a people of the same race, a potential source of raw materials, a potential trading partner, an experimental society run by revolutionary leaders, and a nuclear power lying just across the China Sea. In general, the Japanese were eager for better economic and political relations with China. Even those in the government wanted to regularize relations with China, but not at the risk of damaging other, more important economic and political relations.

The opportunity for regularization came with the announcement in July 1971 that U.S. President Richard M. Nixon would visit China in 1972. Polls taken later in the year showed that a majority of Japanese welcomed this move. All parties in Japan had held, at least privately, that America's China policy had been unrealistic. Yet the suddenness of the American announcement disconcerted the Japanese government. Why had its closest ally made a major change in its Asian policy without forewarning Japan? (The announcement was known in Japan as the "Nixon shock.") What was the meaning of the fact that this change occurred just as the United States was withdrawing from Vietnam and reducing its military presence in the rest of Asia? Did statements about a new U.S. policy based on relationships among the five world powers (Europe, the Soviet Union, Japan, China, and the United States) prefigure a turn to neoisolationism? How would this change affect the fortunes of the perimeter nations of Asia, and how would subsequent changes in these countries affect Japan? In the eyes of some, not only had Japan been slighted, but the basic assumptions on which its foreign policy rested had been called into question. The United States, after the fact, moved quickly to assuage the consternation of the Japanese. President Nixon invited Prime Minister Satō to the San Clemente White House before going to Peking. At their meeting, he stated that no agreement would be reached with China that would prejudice America's relation to Japan.

In August 1972, Tanaka Kakuei, the new Japanese prime minister (July 1972–November 1974) met with Nixon in Hawaii. A month later he met with Chinese Premier Chou En-lai (Zhou Enlai) in Peking (Beijing), establishing diplomatic relations with the People's Republic and recognizing it as the sole legal government of China. The accord stated, "Although the social systems of China and Japan are different, the two countries should and can establish peaceful and friendly relations." (Journalists in Tokyo, aware that Japan's recognition of Peking went far beyond the American initiative in China, and conveniently forgetting the Hawaii talks in their desire to stress Japan's new independence of action, labeled the event the "Tanaka shock.") This accord was given substance with an exchange of ambassadors, an airlines agreement in April 1974, a maritime agreement in November of the same year, and a fisheries agreement in August 1975.

These steps led finally to the signing of a peace treaty between Japan and China in 1978. Such a treaty had been delayed for years by the Chinese demand for a clause directed against Soviet "hegemony" in Asia. Japan, desiring an even-handed diplomacy with both Communist giants, had refused to include the clause. Diplomatic recognition and the new peace treaty opened the way for trade, which tripled from $1.1 billion in 1972 to $3.8 billion in 1975 and continued to expand thereafter. Trade between the two countries in 1975 was 3.3 per cent of Japan's total trade and 25 per cent of China's. Japan's exports to China were always higher than its imports from China. China was attracted by Japanese technology but had little to offer in return and it was reluctant to be simply a supplier of oil and other raw materials.

The recognition of China necessarily led to a rupture in Japan's diplomatic relations with Taiwan. Taiwan denounced the Japanese action, calling it one of the three worst mistakes in the history of Japanese diplomacy—the other two being the 1937 Sino-Japanese War and the attack on Pearl Harbor. In fact, however, economic and cultural ties continued much as before. Japanese–Taiwanese trade increased from $1.6 billion in 1972 to $2.6 billion in 1975, and continued to grow thereafter, and Japanese investment in Taiwan continued to expand. In July 1975, a Japanese airline (a front company for JAL) reopened service to Taiwan, which had been broken off in 1972. In effect, however embittered the Kuomintang leadership on Taiwan had been by the Japanese recognition of Peking, it could not afford to end its ties with Japan. And however unsatisfactory Peking found Japan's economic two-China policy, it had no choice but to go along with it.

Japan's relations with the other great power in East Asia, the Soviet Union, had been "normalized" in 1956, but a full peace treaty had not been achieved. A background factor was that the Soviet Union was not a popular country in Japan, in public opinion polls, often topping the list of countries Japan disliked. The antipathy stemmed from past events: the Russo-Japanese War of 1904–1905, the surprise Soviet attack on Japanese troops in Manchuria a week before the end of World War II, the suffering of captured Japanese soldiers in Siberian prison camps, and the Soviet occupation of the southern Kuriles, the island chain stretching northeast from Hokkaido to the Kamchatka Peninsula. Japan had renounced its claim to the Kuriles in the 1951 peace treaty (in which the Soviet Union did not participate). Yet it claimed the two southernmost Kuriles and two other small islands by right of discovery and insisted that they be returned. The four islands were of little importance except symbolically, but they are physically close to Japan (the southernmost one can be seen from Hokkaido). The Soviet Union maintained that the status of the islands was settled, but the Japanese raised the matter at every opportunity.

Still, the Japanese were careful not to let themselves be used by China against the Soviet Union. Soviet and Japanese foreign ministers met from time to time to talk of Japanese participation in the development of Siberia, though nothing came of the talks. Given the gargantuan dimensions of the Japanese and Soviet economies, their economic ties remained small.

A New Epoch

The seventies, and especially the late seventies, saw the emergence of an era in Japan with a new and different character. Economic growth slowed down, and balanced trade gave way to huge export surpluses, which made Japan the world's premier financial power. Consumerism and the habits of affluence appeared in the society. A burst of political conservatism reversed the twenty-year decline of the LDP's popular vote and ended the "age of parity." But beyond these specific changes, in the late seventies Japan finally achieved its Meiji goal, more than a century old, of catching up with the West.

Catching up had implications for every aspect of domestic and foreign policy and vastly increased Japan's visibility in the world. Whether in bookstores in France and Germany, in the newspapers in Australia and Canada, or in writings by Third World scholars, the output of articles and books on Japan doubled and then doubled again. Government leaders and intellectuals in every country asked whether they could not learn valuable lessons by studying the Japanese experience. Not all reactions to Japan's new prominence were favorable, however. Japan's goods were feared as well as coveted. Many felt unable to compete with Japan and, faced with massive trade deficits, advocated some form of protectionism.

Within Japan this spate of attention, both favorable and unfavorable, sparked a debate extending from the narrow economic issues to those of defense and foreign policy. In the eyes of some Japanese political thinkers, the Yoshida doctrine had been designed for catching up but had little to say about what to do next.

Slower Growth for an Economic Superpower.   After 1972, as the gap between Japan and other advanced nations closed, the 11 per cent growth rate of the previous two decades declined to 4 per cent or slightly less. This was still at the high end of growth rates among advanced nations, but the slowdown, though long predicted, came as a surprise to most Japanese.

Some of the favorable factors that had helped Japan earlier continued: high-quality labor, the propensity to save, low defense costs, open world markets, and so on. But other advantages were lost. In 1953, Western Electric had licensed solid state transistor technology to a Japanese company for a one-time payment of $25,000. By the seventies, the backlog of cheap foreign technology that Japan had been drawing on since the end of the Pacific War had almost run out. Having caught up with the West meant that Japan would have to use its own laboratories for basic research and product development, driving up manufacturing costs. Similarly, the postwar economy had been geared to cheap oil, and the formation of OPEC and the oil price shocks of 1972 and 1979 hit Japan hard. Japan recovered quickly—it had been energy-frugal before the shocks and became more so—but even so production costs rose.

Another earlier advantage had been the combination of cheap labor and high productivity. By the seventies, this advantage had passed to South Korea, Taiwan, Hong Kong, and Singapore. Labor was no longer cheap, and slower growth meant a rising proportion of more expensive older workers. Government costs also rose. As noted earlier, until the early seventies Japan was badly polluted and had an extremely low level of welfare, but then in one powerful surge it enacted the toughest anti-pollution laws in the world and set up an extensive welfare system. During the eighties, Japanese journals frequently debated whether Japan would be able to pay welfare costs for its aging population after the turn of the century.

The slowdown in growth must be kept in perspective: by the seventies, Japan's economy was so large that even increments of 4 per cent led to substantial gains. In Table 26.4, compare Japan's 1985 gross national product with those of other nations in East Asia and elsewhere.

It is also useful to compare Japan's "island economy" with the economies of the world's two continental superpowers. In 1985, Japan's GNP of $1,329 billion trailed the GNPs of the United States ($3,988 billion)

TABLE 26.4

A Comparison of Gross National Products

Country	GNP (in billions of dollars)		
China	$ 354		
Taiwan	60		
South Korea	86		
North Korea	20		
Hong Kong	23		
Singapore	16		
Philippines	33		
Thailand	37		
India	190		
Pakistan	28		
Australia	153		
Brazil	214		
Argentina	63		
Venezuela	45		
Total	$1,322	Japan	1,329

and the Soviet Union ($2,063 billion). But then the previously under-valued yen began to rise, eventually almost doubling. In 1988, some economists predicted the yen would rise further; others more cautiously suggested it would fluctuate within its current range. If we use an exchange rate of 130 yen to a dollar, the estimated 1988 GNP of 363 trillion yen was the equivalent of $2,792 billion. That is to say, the Japanese economy may have become larger than that of the Soviet Union. It was still smaller than that of the United States, but considering that Japan's population was only half that of the United States, this estimate puts its per capita GNP several thousand dollars higher than the equivalent American figure.

Of course, per capita GNP does not equate with standard of living. More of Japan's GNP was plowed back into future growth, partly through higher savings. Food prices were much higher in Japan, because of tariffs to protect domestic agriculture. Land prices were astronomical compared with those in the United States; Japan's total land surface—about the same as Montana—was valued at two or three times the land surface of the fifty American states. Tokyo alone was "worth" more than California. Accordingly, housing was more costly and less spacious. In comparing standards of living, should one argue that cramped living quarters detract from the Japanese standard of living, or instead say

Robots and workers constructing cars in Japan. Using a technology originally licensed from the United States, Japanese productivity has forged ahead.

that the Japanese have culturally adjusted to smaller spaces and therefore see no such devaluation? And how does one balance off the long hours Japanese workers spend in commuting against the higher urban crime rates in the United States?

Japan's international trade also changed in the eighties. In the seventies, Japan had bought as much from abroad as it sold abroad. At the start of the eighties, however, that balance was lost. Both consumers around the world and those within Japan wanted more of Japan's high-quality products. Therefore, between 1980 and 1985 Japanese imports declined from $141 billion to $130 billion and Japanese exports soared from $130 billion to $176 billion. The surge in exports was mainly in automobiles, cameras, electronic equipment, and other high-value-added manufactures. The United States was especially hard hit as its trade deficit with Japan rose from $0.3 billion in 1975 to $7 billion in 1980 to $40 billion in 1985. This deficit sparked a debate over trade between the two countries.

Japanese spokesmen argued that Japan was playing fair and that the United States should put its house in order. The huge American federal deficit, half financed by Japanese purchases of U.S. government bonds, could be eliminated, they said, if Americans worked harder and saved more —like the Japanese. There should be more investment in new plants and equipment, they advised, and corporate managers should pay themselves less and be more concerned with the long-term health of their companies. Furthermore, Japanese economists pointed out, proportionally speaking the American trade deficit with Japan was lower than U.S. deficits with Taiwan, South Korea, Mexico, or Canada.

Within the United States the reactions were diverse. Some economists and politicians upheld open markets and free trade, arguing that a cheaper dollar would suffice to trim imports and stimulate exports. Others maintained that Japan was not playing fair: American farm products were shut out of the Japanese market by a wall of tariffs, and American high technology was excluded by a variety of nontariff barriers. America shouldered the heaviest defense burden among free world nations, almost 7 per cent of its GNP, while the figures were 5 per cent for the United Kingdom, 4 per cent for France, 3 per cent for West Germany, and 1 per cent for Japan. The Security Treaty, they argued, gave Japan a free ride.

Still other American observers saw the attractiveness of Japanese products as the crux of the problem. Consumers, they suggested, had voted with their pocketbooks. If America was to compete, it would have to make better products. During the mid-eighties, members of Congress and scholars alike talked of "industrial policy," and during the late eighties, U.S. presidential candidates advanced agendas to increase American competitiveness—or to protect American markets. A final argument sometimes voiced in the United States was that the Japanese ought to amend their lifestyle and become less formidable competitors: they must stop working half a day on Saturday, take more vacations, spend more of their incomes, retire earlier (45 per cent of Japanese workers work past the age of sixty-five compared with 17 per cent of Americans), and in general enjoy life more. These recommendations sound like wishful thinking, but in fact all were issues being discussed by the Japanese themselves.

One immediate consequence of the gap between exports and imports was a huge dollar surplus in Japanese accounts. Japan became the world's leading creditor, and the United States the biggest debtor. In 1988 the Dai Ichi Kangyō Bank was the largest bank in the world, and the nine other largest banks were all Japanese as well. The Japanese presence loomed over world financial markets. Japanese banks, insurance companies, and individuals bought not only United States government bonds, but office buildings in New York and Los Angeles, farmland in the Midwest, electronics companies, and real estate in Hawaii. In the late eighties the American reaction was still muted, but editorialists noted

with irony that Japan made loans to the United States, while the United
States made loans to Latin America.

Society in the New Age. One trend of the eighties was the continued
moderation of the rate of population growth. By the late eighties there
were 122 million Japanese. One projection held that the population would
peak in the year 2115 and then ever so slowly decline. In terms of the
ratio between population and usable land, Japan was the most densely
peopled country in the world. Life in Japan would be easier if its population were smaller. But in comparison with countries whose population
growth was wildly out of control, Japan's demography was stable and
no threat to its future.

During the previous era of high growth, the Japanese life span had
advanced to a European level. By the late eighties, the Japanese were
living longer than any other people in the world; women had gained four
years for an average longevity of 81, and men's average lifespan had gone
up three years to 75. But living longer had its costs. Financial planning
for retirement—called the "silver years" in Japan—became a standard
feature of magazines otherwise devoted to stock market profits, high
rates of interest, information on company bonuses, and the quest for
jobs paying ten million yen ($75,000) a year. Women's magazines
discussed how to cope with the shock of having a resident husband—
after decades of married life in which he left home early in the morning
and returned late at night. More retirement homes and hospitals were
built and geriatric wards were expanded. Tokyo districts built civic centers with sports, social, and educational facilities, used frequently by
retirees as well as other district residents. Because the age distribution in
Japan was skewed by World War II and the postwar baby boom, the
new longevity also portended a serious future problem: by the turn of the
century, Japan would have a higher percentage of nonworking old
people than would any other country.

Education was a third area in which the gains of the sixties and seventies extended into the eighties. High school enrollments inched up from
4.3 million in 1975 to 5.4 million in 1987. By the late eighties, though
not compulsory, 96 per cent of middle school graduates went on to high
school. Post-secondary enrollments also increased: in 1987, 1.9 million
students were enrolled at four-year universities, 438,000 at two-year colleges, and 50,000 at higher technical schools. A spate of new universities
was established to meet the demand. As earlier, the gate to higher education remained narrow. In 1986 2.9 million students took the entrance
examinations, but only 436,000 were accepted. Twice as many students

*Tokyo's Shinjuku Gyoen
National Garden.*

took the examinations as graduated from high school—more than half
were putting themselves through the "examination hell" for a second,
third, or fourth time.

During the eighties Japanese education was the most pyramidal in the
world, with Tokyo University attracting the brightest students, followed
by Kyoto, Hitotsubashi, and others. The system was like a machine that
sorts half-dollars, quarters, dimes, nickels, and pennies. Many Japanese
were satisfied with the system, arguing that the kind of talent that excels
at examinations is also the kind that can run a high-tech economy. The
Japanese tended to dismiss American criticisms of educational testing as
racial politics or sentimentalism. But some Japanese leaders pointed out
the shortcomings of education in Japan, saying that it must become more
international to meet the needs of Japan as a world economic power,
and arguing for a greater emphasis on creativity to produce mavericks of
the sort who founded computer software companies in the United States.

In the pattern of marriage, too, postwar changes reached into the
eighties. In the early postwar period, most marriages were still arranged
by go-betweens with the approval of the parents. This gave way in the
sixties and seventies to "love marriages," in which the partners made
their own arrangements, although sometimes asking an office superior or

Movies, television dramas, and pop culture rank with airplanes as successful U.S. exports to Japan.

teacher to serve as an honorary go-between. During this time most young couples lived apart from their parents, and by the eighties almost four out of five marriages were of this new type. The old-fashioned "arranged marriage" became a fall-back device for those who had failed earlier to find partners on their own by their late twenties. Courtships in such marriages were short, since the idea was to make up for lost time, and even these relationships had some features, such as dating, of the dominant pattern.

The love marriage reflected the social patterns of a new generation that had no memory of poverty or hardship. Apart from the hours spent on study, the lives of the young people centered on easy socializing with schoolmates, and later, with workmates. This generation grew up with television and VCRs. They ate McDonald's hamburgers, Kentucky Fried Chicken, and the products of the Japanese fast food chains. They listened to Michael Jackson and Madonna as well as to the stars of Japanese rock and roll. The older generation sometimes criticized them as "a new human species." But apart from taking affluence for granted and enjoying its benefits, the new generation was in fact closer to the old than either imagined.

Conservative Politics. One clear political trend in the transition from the seventies to the eighties was a growing conservatism. Catching up with the West occasioned a groundswell of pride in Japan's achievements. Discussions of national character, long a favorite topic in magazines and journals, became decidedly upbeat. A 1953 public opinion poll had asked, "Do you think Japanese are superior or inferior to Westerners?" Only 20 per cent said superior. But in a 1983 poll, the figure rose to 53 per cent. In electoral politics the new mood of national self-confidence benefited the Liberal Democratic Party.

The benefit took the form of a reversal of the twenty-year decline in the party's popular vote. The nadir in the fortunes of the ruling LDP was the 1976 election, when the party garnered only 43 per cent of the vote. It was in that figure that political scientists saw the dawning of an age of parity in which the LDP would lose its grip on the Diet. Contrary to their dire predictions, however, a reversal of the trend began in 1979, and by the 1986 election the LDP popular vote had risen to 49.4 per cent, giving it a comfortable majority of 300 (of 512) seats in the Diet. The specter of parity had vanished, and the LDP, the conservative heir of the two major prewar political parties, looked as if it would remain in power.

The reversal in the voting pattern was not due to the end of the "sociological erosion" described earlier, but rather to a shift in votes to the LDP by groups that had voted for opposition parties out of inertia despite their participation in Japan's new prosperity. The white- and elite blue-collar classes, who used to vote socialist, for example, gave half of their votes to the LDP in the 1986 election. It was education that made the difference. By the eighties, those with a postwar education predominated in the electorate. The longer years of the new style education did not necessarily make Japanese voters more conservative but did make them more flexible, and the rise in the conservative vote was their response to affluence. A weakening of labor unions was also a factor.

TABLE 26.5
Union Membership as a Percentage
of Total Labor Force

Year	Percentage
1950	46.2
1960	31.6
1970	35.0
1980	30.8
1985	28.9

After the war, with SCAP encouragement, Japanese labor attained an almost European level of organization, but then declined. By the mid-eighties it was closer to the level of union membership in the United States—about 20 per cent of the work force. The loss of union membership was a body blow to the socialist parties.

The conservatism of the eighties also affected local politics. During the sixties and seventies, residents' movements—a local response to instances of pollution, the location of nuclear power plants, and so forth—were a part of antiestablishment politics in Japan. In the eighties these movements all but came to a halt. Similarly, until the mid-seventies the LDP hegemony in national politics was often counterbalanced by Socialist or Communist control of city and prefectural governments. From the late seventies the LDP began to win back control in local elections.

Even the elite universities, which had been seedbeds for radicalism during the early postwar decades, were influenced by the conservative tide. In 1977 incoming freshmen at Tokyo University were asked which political party they favored. Twenty-three per cent favored the Liberal Democratic Party, but an equal number favored the Communist Party. However, a year later the response was 45 per cent for the conservatives and only 3 per cent for the Communists. Such an abrupt shift is hard to believe but other evidences also point to the late seventies as a political watershed in student attitudes. By the late eighties Japanese campuses were congested with automobiles. Students were well dressed, some read fashion magazines, and many had studied or traveled abroad. A student from the fifties, revisiting his old university, felt like a Urashima Tarō (a Japanese Rip Van Winkle) returning home after a sojourn in the timeless palace of the sea god.

Policies for the Twenty-First Century. A second political development of the eighties was a debate within the conservative camp over how to position Japan to meet the challenges of the twenty-first century. This debate was sparked by a new awareness that Japan could no longer look to foreign models and that henceforth it would have to define its own future goals and sail on uncharted seas.

On economic policy, most conservative leaders saw eye to eye. One agreed-upon step was to make government smaller but more effective. The number of public officials was to be reduced by 5 per cent between 1987 and 1992. Taxes were reformed, and government industries and public corporations were privatized. The Japanese National Railways, public since 1906, was broken up into six private concerns, and the Nippon Telegraph and Telephone Company and Japan Air Lines were also made private. These measures were taken not simply because the private sector was more efficient but because the government had other, more important tasks to perform and could not afford the distraction that the management of these enterprises entailed.

Some conservative academicians saw the job of the government as guiding Japan to a new stage of civilization. In the nineteenth century, England had been the technological and financial leader of the world; the United States then succeeded to that position, and now the baton was about to pass to Japan. These theorists called this new stage in world history the "information society." By this they meant a society based on electronics and communications and marked by computers in every household, national data bases, and communication networks so extensive that regional technopolises would rise to rival Tokyo. In the early eighties, the Ministry of Finance established thirty-nine teams of bureaucrats, businessmen, and scholars to draw up guidelines for various areas. Government bodies drew up plans to make education more flexible, creative, and international, and to develop information-technology faculties and new research institutes. Most of these initiatives, which built on developments of the seventies, were associated with the prime ministry (1982–1987) of Nakasone Yasuhiro.

The tantalizing vision of a new kind of society not deriving from the United States or Europe caught the imagination of LDP leaders and sparked a number of interesting innovations. But behind the catchy notion of an information society, and beyond the planning, guidance, and support given by government ministries, was a deep and broad determination on the part of Japanese industrial leaders to maintain Japan's momentum and become the front-runner in every field of high technology. Japan must advance from world dominance in memory chips to the same in logic chips. It must move from peripheral equipment to computers, and especially supercomputers. Already the world leader in materials technology, it must further strengthen its position, using, for example, its preeminent position in ceramics technology to become the leader in superconductivity. During the mid-eighties, building on its drug, chemical, and fermentation industries, Japan began to make large investments in biotechnology. It also moved to stake out a position in aircraft, concluding an agreement with Boeing in 1986 for joint development of a new generation of commercial airliners.

The large measure of consensus that existed within Japan on the question of the country's economic future was less marked on questions of defense and foreign policy. The LDP mainstream continued resolutely to uphold a minimalist defense and a passive foreign policy that, while giving ever larger amounts of foreign aid, would avoid disputes and foreign entanglements. One former bureaucrat compared today's world to the highly stratified society of Tokugawa Japan, and suggested that the United States and Soviet Union were samurai, Japan was a merchant *(chōnin)*, and Third World countries were like peasants. He suggested

*Children in a Tokyo kinder-
garten study how to operate
personal computers in a
traveling computer school
bus sponsored by the Japan
Science Foundation.*

that each class of nations had a role to play and urged Japan to continue as a *chōnin*, putting aside higher political principles and cultivating the merchants' "information gathering and planning ability."* The LDP mainstream also wished to preserve the advantage of low defense spending. Every white paper on defense reiterated a policy of cooperation with the United States within the framework of the Security Treaty. Some political scientists contended that Japan would be able to continue this policy both because of American ambivalence on the question of Japanese rearmament and because Japan was too important in American strategic thinking not to be defended. One politician put it cynically: "If we continue to bet on the Anglo-Saxons, we should be safe for at least twenty years."

---

*Kenneth B. Pyle, "The Future of Japanese Nationalism," p. 32. A textbook by its nature draws on so many secondary works that they cannot be listed book by book. But we would like to acknowledge a special debt to Professor Pyle for the brief quotations that appear on the next three pages. Also see Pyle (ed.), *The Trade Crisis: How Japan Will Respond* (Society for Japanese Studies, University of Washington, 1987).

Prime Minister Nakasone's rule coincided with Japan's emergence as a world power. His foreign and economic policies were based on a close partnership with the United States. Here U.S. President Ronald Reagan greets Nakasone at a White House meeting in April 1987.

Others within the conservative camp noted that the Security Treaty dated back to an era when Japan had a weak economy and no military forces. In this arrangement, the United States held a nuclear umbrella over Japan, which contributed little in return. Japan could not even use its naval power abroad to protect its own vital interests, such as the shipping lanes for oil. It was, in short, an arrangement between unequals. Some in the LDP, who may be called the "new realists," argued that the Security Treaty, even after several revisions, was not appropriate to Japan's new stature. They urged the building of a stronger military and the adoption of a positive foreign policy. One described Japan as an economic giant but a political dwarf. When a mainstream minister praised Japan as something new in world history, a "peace state" that while economically advanced has no comparable military power, a new realist countered, saying that Japan was, rather, an international eccentric that relied on American nuclear defense yet refused to permit American nuclear arms to pass through its waters. Another new realist argued that the liberal and free-trading world order maintained by the United States was vital to Japan, and that Japan should contribute more to its upkeep. Behind such an argument, of course, was a keen awareness of trade frictions and a fear of rising protectionism within the United States.

Still another new realist argued that Japan shared philosophical principles with the West, and that, as a part of the Western camp, it must bear more responsibility. Prime Minister Nakasone was a leading figure among the new realists. He stressed the gravity of the Soviet threat to Japan. Speaking in the United States, he advanced the view that Japan should become a "huge aircraft carrier" serving the mutual strategic purposes of both countries. In Japan, however, the prime minister's speeches were more moderate. And though he obtained the passage of a defense budget that broke through the one per cent limit, the overage was only one four-thousandth of one per cent. As of 1988, the LDP mainstream was still in charge.

A third segment of opinion that emerged during the eighties was a "new right." This group had little representation in the Diet, but was interesting in several respects. First, it freely expressed opinions that had been taboo or rarely heard earlier. Second, it made the LDP new realists, once seen as hawks, appear almost moderate by comparison. Third, it was composed mainly of journalists and academics who wrote for leading magazines and newspapers. It was socially more respectable and ideologically more modern than the ultrarightist, proemperor fringe groups of the earlier postwar decades. Finally, while it would exaggerate the importance of the new right to say that it engaged in a dialogue with the LDP mainstream and the new realists, it can be said that it wrote in dialectical opposition to them, and that LDP Diet members, in turn, were aware of the new rightist critique.

The new right began its case by pointing out that internationally the United States had been weakened by its defeat in Vietnam, and that internally its society had been weakened by industrial inefficiencies, a declining work ethic, crime, drugs, the spread of AIDS, high divorce rates, illegitimate births, unchecked immigration, and minority problems. During the sixties, Japanese publicists had spoken of the "English disease" to describe the ailments of England's economy. After Vietnam, some editorialists began to talk of the "American disease." One critic waxed lyrical in the Asahi newspaper: "Watching the United States suddenly losing its magnificence is like watching a former lover's beauty wither away. It makes me want to cover my eyes." Some drew the conclusion that Japan could no longer depend on the United States for defense.

The new right was no less critical of what Japan had become under the Yoshida doctrine, calling it "abnormal," "effeminate," "a Peter Pan state." Favoring the development of nuclear weapons, a former Marxist, who had swung over to the new right, said that putting political pressure on Japan was "like twisting the arm of a baby." In his book, *Japan! Be a State, Go Nuclear*, he asked why Japan, "while splendidly possessing the

*When Japanese politicians win an election, they paint in the eye of a
doll representing Bodhidaruma, the legendary founder of the Zen
sect. Here Noboru Takeshita, elected prime minister in November
1987, performs this celebratory ritual.*

qualities to be a super power . . . was behaving like a physically handicapped person right in plain view of the world?" Some thinkers of the
new right asserted the need for a completely independent defense strategy.
Others felt that Japan, as an equal partner after rearming, could safely
cooperate with the United States for their mutual security.

In the late eighties, what these new voices would mean for the future
of Japanese politics was unclear. Some political commentators likened the
new right to prewar ultranationalism and warned of its danger. The
new right, they pointed out, appeals to the deep Japanese sense of national
pride in a way that the pacifism—or passivism—of the Yoshida doctrine
did not. Other writers, sympathetic to the new ideas, countered that these
ideas were not ultranationalistic at all but merely expressed the kind of
everyday patriotic sentiment that would be taken for granted in the United
States, France, Britain, and the Soviet Union. More than forty years have
passed since 1945. Is it not time, they asked, for Japan to become a normal
nation-state?

Still other commentators downplay the significance of the new right. There had always been gadflies on the left, they pointed out. Now there were some on the right as well. The new right was merely one small and not especially coherent voice in the polyphony of Japanese political opinion. The opposition parties of the Old Left were better organized, better financed, and enjoyed a broader base of support. And more importantly, the policies of the LDP mainstream would endure because they reflected the feelings of the increasingly educated Japanese electorate: a pride in Japan's culture and industrial might, a desire for better housing and more leisure, and a disinterest in flag-waving, whether old- or new-fashioned.

Conclusions about Japan are not difficult to reach. Economic and educational statistics, census returns, and the results of public opinion polls are sufficiently numerous that even foreigners may know more about certain aspects of Japan than the leaders of other Asian nations know about their own countries. Like other parliamentary states, Japan since the end of World War II has been a goldfish bowl open to scrutiny by all.

Yet that very openness may deceive. In this overwhelming amount of data, which aspects are fundamental and which indices pivotal? Unlike neighboring states where early industrialization is only now transforming traditional agricultural societies, Japanese society is complex. The blurring of class lines, the ideological diversity, the release from the constraints of tradition, the range of choices open to individuals in society, and the vigor of the modern culture make appreciations possible from differing, and even conflicting, points of view. Since many of these same characteristics are found in Europe and the United States, Westerners find Japan more intelligible than the rest of Asia. Still, there is a danger in finding Japan too easily intelligible, too Western. For just as the modern West continues to be inspired by its Judeo-Christian-Greek tradition, so the influence of Japan's recent non-Western past continues within its modern life. These cultural roots invite questions whose answers are not to be found in the study of the West. As the only fully modern non-Western nation, Japan may be an archetype with which developing non-Western nations may fruitfully be compared. The study of this archetype is underway.

Illustration Acknowledgments

Chapter 1 p. 6, (top) Courtesy Museum of Fine Arts, Boston, Edward S. Morse Memorial Fund, (bottom left) Asian Art Museum of San Francisco, The Avery Brundage Collection 605204, (bottom right) Tōkyō National Museum; p. 11, (top) Norman F. Carver, Jr., Kalamazoo, Michigan, (bottom) Editoriale Fotografico; p. 22, (both) Asuka-en, Nara; p. 36, Kozan-ji, Kyoto.

Chapter 2 p. 41, Metropolitan Museum of Art, Rogers Fund, 1904; p. 48, Imperial Palace; p. 52, Tōkyō National Museum; p. 54, Asuka-en, Nara; p. 55, Kyoto National Museum; p. 66, *Japanese Architecture and Gardens,* Kokusai Bunka Shinkokai; p. 68, Tōkyō National Museum; p. 69, Consulate General of Japan; p. 70, *Japanese Architecture and Gardens,* Kokusai Bunka Shinkokai; p. 71, Consulate General of Japan.

Chapter 3 p. 76, Japan National Tourist Organization; p. 85, *Illustrations of Famous Places in Edo;* p. 96, *Illustrations of Famous Places in Edo;* p. 102, Nagami Tokutarō, *Nagasaki no bijutsu shi;* p. 108, *Collection of Illustrations for the Cultivation of Ethics;* p. 109, Okumura Masanobu, Interior View of the Nakamura-za Theatre in Edo, 1740, Gift of Miss Katherine S. Buckingham to the Clarence Buckingham Collection, 1925. © 1988 The Art Institute of Chicago. All Rights Reserved; p. 111, Courtesy Museum of Fine Arts, Boston.

Chapter 4 p. 120, (left) Carl Boehringer Collection, Exhibition circulated by the Smithsonian, (right) Honolulu Academy of Arts, 1960; p. 125, Time Life Picture Agency; p. 133, *Utsusareta bakumatsu,* vol. 3, Asoka Shobō Book Co.; p. 135, (both) *Kensei hiroku,* Yamanda Shoin Publishing Co.

Chapter 5 p. 156, *Meiji bunka zenshū, zasshi-hen,* vol. 18; p. 163, Kanagaki Robun, *Seiyō dōchū hizakurige;* p 165, *Meiji bunka zenshū, kyōiku-hen,* vol. 10; p. 174, (bottom) Library of Congress; p. 182, International Society for Educational Information, Inc., Tōkyō.

Chapter 6 p. 201, Rene Burri, Magnum Photos; p. 204, Carl Mydans, *Life* Magazine, © Time Inc., p. 209, Tokugawa-Reimeikai Foundation; p. 212, *Nihon hyakunen no kiroku,* Kodansha Publishers; p. 216, Kodansha Publishers; p. 221, International Society for Educational Information, Inc. Tōkyō.

Chapter 7   p. 227, *Kensei Hiroku,* Yamada Shoin Publishing Co.; p. 231, Radio Times Hulton Picture Library; p. 237, *Nihon hyakunen no kiroku,* vol. 2, *Sekai to Nihon,* Kodansha Publishers; p. 246, *Nihon hyakunen no kiroku,* Kodansha Publishers; p. 260, Kyodo Photo Service, Tōkyō; p. 266, *Nihon hyakunen no kiroku,* Kodansha Publishers.

Chapter 8   p. 279, Wide World Photos; pp. 284 and 293, UPI; p. 294, (left) Scheler/Black Star, (right) Eiji Miyazawa/Black Star; p. 296, (top and bottom) *Japan of Today;* p. 297, Wide World Photos; p. 303, Thomas P. Rohlen, *Japan's High Schools;* p. 311, Hamaya/Magnum Photos; p. 323, Wide World Photos; p. 326, Japan National Tourist Organization; pp. 327 and 331, Bettmann Newsphotos; p. 332, White House Photo; p. 334, Wide World Photos.

Index

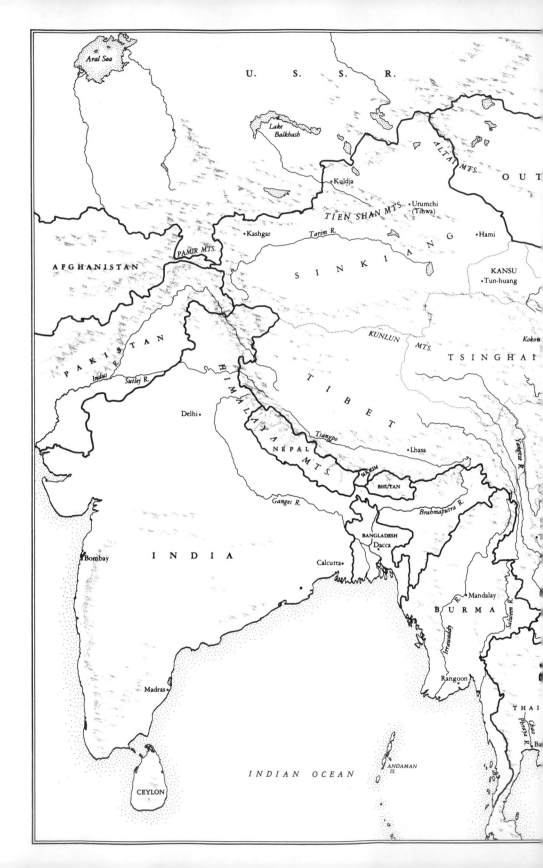

Lake Baikal

Khabarovsk

SAKHALIN

MARITIME PROV.

HEILUNGKIANG

Ulan Bator
(Urga)

Harbin

HOKKAIDO

KURIL IS.

MONGOLIA

KIRIN
Ch'ang-ch'un
(Hsinching)

Sapporo

Amur R.

INNER MONGOLIA

Mukden

SEA OF
JAPAN

Vladivostok

LIAONING

NORTH
KOREA

Ta-t'ung

Peking

Shanhaikuan

Yalu R.

P'yǒngyang

Sendai

HONSHŪ

Ta-lien
(Dairen)

Seoul

Tōkyō

HOPEI

Tientsin

SOUTH
KOREA

Kyōto

Nagoya

SHANSI

SHANTUNG

YELLOW SEA

Pusan

Ōsaka

JAPAN

SHENSI

Loyang

Kaifeng

Yellow R.

SHIKOKU

Sian

HONAN

KIANGSU

MTS.

Han R.

Nanking

Shanghai

Nagasaki

KYŪSHŪ

Yangtze R.

HUPEI

Wu-han
(Hankow)

ANHWEI

Soochow

EAST CHINA
SEA

Hangchow

Ningpo

Changsha

HUNAN

KIANGSI

CHEKIANG

PACIFIC

CHOW

Foochow

RYŪKYŪ ISLANDS

OCEAN

FUKIEN

KWANGSI

KWANGTUNG

Taipei

TAIWAN

Hsi (West) R.

Canton

HAINAN

ᴸᴸᴸᴸ Great Wall

Modern Grand Canal

Huê

Provincial boundaries in
China proper

SOUTH CHINA SEA

PHILIPPINE

Manila

SOUTH
VIETNAM

ISLANDS

Sanderson

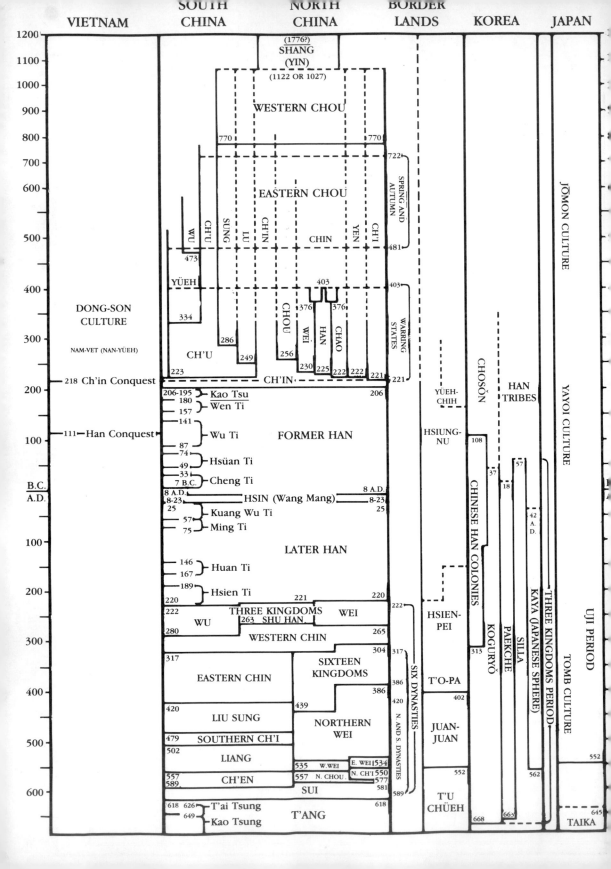

A chronological chart comparing the historical periods and dynasties of Vietnam, South China, North China, Border Lands, Korea, and Japan from 1200 B.C. to 649 A.D.

VIETNAM	SOUTH CHINA	NORTH CHINA	BORDER LANDS	KOREA	JAPAN

Time scale (left axis): 1200, 1100, 1000, 900, 800, 700, 600, 500, 400, 300, 200 (B.C.), B.C./A.D., 100, 200, 300, 400, 500, 600

NORTH CHINA:
- SHANG (YIN) (1776?)
- (1122 OR 1027)
- WESTERN CHOU
- EASTERN CHOU — 770
- SPRING AND AUTUMN — 722, 481
- WARRING STATES — 403
- States: SUNG, LU, CH'IN, CHIN, YEN, CH'I
- WU, CH'U — 473
- YÜEH — 334
- CHOU, WEI (376), HAN, CHAO (376), 403
- 256, 230, 225, 222, 222, 221
- CH'IN — 221

SOUTH CHINA:
- CH'U — 286, 249, 223
- CH'IN — 218 Ch'in Conquest
- 206 Kao Tsu (206–195), 180 Wen Ti (157)
- FORMER HAN — 141 Wu Ti (87), 74 Hsüan Ti (49), 33 Cheng Ti (7 B.C.)
- HSIN (Wang Mang) 8–23 A.D. (8 A.D., 25)
- 25 Kuang Wu Ti, 57 Ming Ti (75)
- LATER HAN — 146 Huan Ti (167), 189 Hsien Ti, 220
- THREE KINGDOMS: WU (222), SHU HAN (263), WEI (221, 220)
- WESTERN CHIN — 265, 280
- EASTERN CHIN — 317
- SIXTEEN KINGDOMS — 304, 386
- LIU SUNG — 420, 439
- NORTHERN WEI — 386
- SOUTHERN CH'I — 479
- LIANG — 502
- W. WEI 535, E. WEI 534
- CH'EN — 557, 589
- N. CHOU 557, N. CH'I 550, 577
- SUI — 581, 618
- T'AI TSUNG (618, 626), 649 Kao Tsung
- T'ANG

VIETNAM:
- DONG-SON CULTURE
- NAM-VET (NAN-YÜEH)
- 218 Ch'in Conquest
- 111 Han Conquest

BORDER LANDS:
- YÜEH-CHIH
- HSIUNG-NU
- HSIEN-PEI — 222
- T'O-PA — 317, 386
- SIX DYNASTIES (N. AND S. DYNASTIES) — 420
- JUAN-JUAN — 402, 552
- T'U CHÜEH — 589

KOREA:
- CHOSŎN — 108
- CHINESE HAN COLONIES — 37, 18
- KOGURYŎ — 313
- PAEKCHE
- SILLA — 57
- KAYA (JAPANESE SPHERE) — 42 A.D., 562
- 668, 662

JAPAN:
- JŌMON CULTURE
- YAYOI CULTURE
- HAN TRIBES
- THREE KINGDOMS PERIOD
- UJI PERIOD
- TOMB CULTURE — 552
- TAIKA — 645

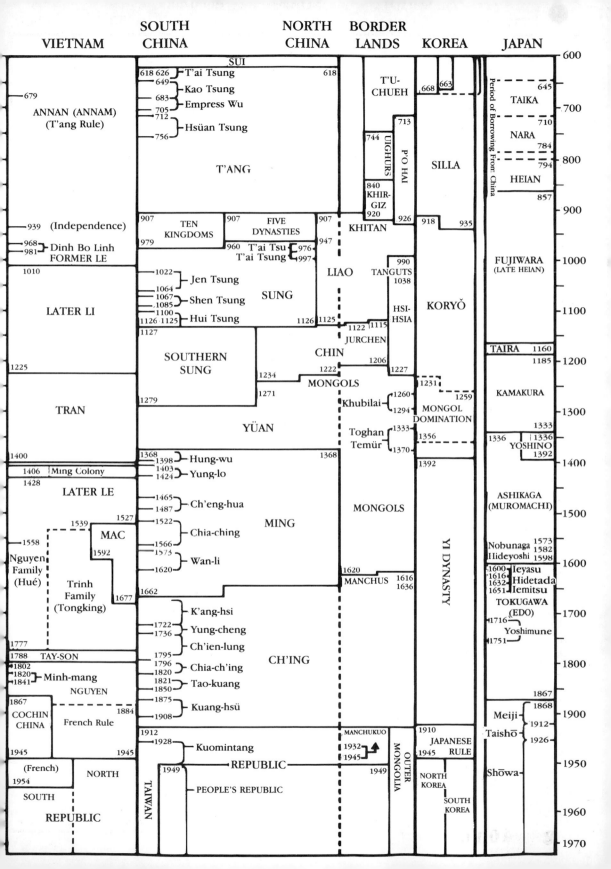